英美小说欣赏导论

Understanding British and American Fiction

师彦灵 编著

图书在版编目(CIP)数据

英美小说欣赏导论/师彦灵编著. —北京：北京大学出版社，2011.2
ISBN 978-7-301-18476-9

I. 英… II. 师… III. ①英语—文学批评—高等学校—教材 ②小说—文学欣赏—英国 ③小说—文学欣赏—美国 IV. ①H319.4：I

中国版本图书馆CIP数据核字(2011)第012005号

书　　　名：	英美小说欣赏导论
著作责任者：	师彦灵　编著
责 任 编 辑：	黄瑞明
标 准 书 号：	ISBN 978-7-301-18476-9/I·2311
出 版 发 行：	北京大学出版社
地　　　址：	北京市海淀区成府路205号　100871
网　　　址：	http://www.pup.cn
电　　　话：	邮购部 010-62752015　发行部 010-62750672
	编辑部 010-62759634　出版部 010-62754962
电 子 邮 箱：	编辑部 pupwaiwen@pup.cn　总编室 zpup@pup.cn
印　刷　者：	北京虎彩文化传播有限公司
经　销　者：	新华书店
	650毫米×980毫米　16开本　17.25印张　334千字
	2011年2月第1版　2024年1月第6次印刷
定　　　价：	59.00元

未经许可，不得以任何方式复制或抄袭本书之部分或全部内容。
版权所有，侵权必究　举报电话：010-62752024
电子邮箱：fd@pup.cn

前言

英美小说是英美文学的重要组成部分。自18世纪以丹尼尔·笛福的《鲁滨逊漂流记》(1719)为代表的现代意义上的英语小说产生以来,英语小说在关注问题的视角、表现方式、叙事技巧等方面一直发生着变化。与此同时,人们对小说的认识也在不断发生变化,同一部小说,不同时期的人们对它的认识和评价有时是完全不同的,因为社会不断发展,文化环境不断变化,文学批评方法不断丰富。《英美小说欣赏导论》以英美小说文本为基础,比较系统地论述了英美小说的基本理论和批评方法,以培养和提升读者对英语小说原著自身特质的认识水平,提高运用不同批评理论、方法欣赏英语小说的思维和感悟能力,使英文小说阅读过程既是语言接受能力的提升过程,也是读者获得心灵愉悦的过程,更是心灵得到启迪、思维得到拓展、世界观得到充实和完善的过程,从而使英文原著小说的阅读既愉快又富有成效。

《英美小说欣赏导论》分两部分,共14章,选取小说文本14篇,其中短篇11篇、中篇1篇(节选自《黑暗的中心》)、长篇2部(节选自《哈克贝利·芬历险记》和《大卫·科波菲尔》)。之所以这样选择,主要考虑到短篇小说篇幅短小,故事完整,读者容易把握;节选的中篇和长篇可帮助读者认识其形式、结构、表达方式等与短篇小说的异同,对英语小说的形式、结构和表达方式有一个相对完整的认识。

第一部分"小说要素"包括七章,即情节、背景、人物、视角、主题、风格、象征,其中每章包括五个部分,即:小说要素、作者小传、小说文本(Text)、小说赏析(Understanding the Text)和扩展阅读(Further Reading)。"小说要素"主要以经典文本为例,论述各小说要素的定义、特征和功能;"作者小传"简要介绍所选小说的作者;"小说文本"以脚注的方式对所选文本相关背景知识、人名、地名、语言难点予以注解;"小说赏析"对该章所涉及的小说要素进行分析和阐释,如第七章之"小说要素——象征"中,只对所选文本《白象似的群山》中的象征手法及其相关问题进行分析和解读;"扩展阅读"为读者提供进一步学习、研究所需的书目和论文。

第二部分"批评理论和方法"包括七章:历史传记批评、形式主义批评、心理分析批评、神话批评、性别研究、读者反映批评、文化研究,其中每章包括五个部分,即:批评理论和方法、作者小传、小说文本(Text)、小说赏析(Understanding the Text)和扩展阅读(Further Reading)。"批评理论和方法"论述不同批评理论和方法的概念、特征、主要论点、代表人物及其主要观点等;"作者小传"简要介绍所选小说的作者;"小说文本"以脚注的方式对所选文本相关的背景知识、人名、地名和语言难点予以注解;"小说赏析"运用该章所涉及的批评理论和方法对所选文本进行具体分析和阐释;"扩展阅读(Further Reading)"为读者提供进一步学习和研究相关批评理论和作品所需的书目和论文。

《英美小说欣赏导论》重点突出以下几个方面:

第一,在"小说要素"和"批评方法"阐述方面,不求全面,但求论点明确、简明扼要。

第二,在小说文本的选择方面,强调所选作家身份、题材、写作风格的多样性,所选作品的代表性、经典性、趣味性。所选美国小说包括:"美国文学之父"华盛顿·欧文的浪漫主义短篇经典《瑞普·凡·温克尔》;被称为"第一位真正的美国作家"的美国现实主义作家马克·吐温的《哈克贝利·芬历险记》;以描写19世纪末美国中西部开拓者顽强创业精神而著称,并对同性恋予以特别关注的薇拉·

凯瑟的《保罗案》；以美国南方家族小说闻名的威廉·福克纳的《献给艾米莉的玫瑰》；受罗马天主教文化思想影响颇深的弗兰纳里·奥康纳的《好人难寻》；生长于克里奥尔文化中的凯特·肖邦的《一小时的故事》；以"冰山"写作风格著称的欧内斯特·海明威的《白象似的群山》；以幽默见长的林·拉德纳的《理发》；被誉为"纽约郊区的契诃夫"的约翰·契弗的《团聚》等。所选英国小说包括：现实主义作家查尔斯·狄更斯的《大卫·科波菲尔》；现代主义作家凯瑟琳·曼斯菲尔德的《莳萝泡菜》；擅长意识流叙事的弗吉尼亚·伍尔夫的《墙上的斑点》；擅长揭示人类性心理现象的 D.H. 劳伦斯的《木马赢家》；以及出生于波兰、以航海小说闻名的约瑟夫·康拉德的《黑暗的中心》等。通过不同文化身份的作家的不同风格、题材的经典作品来阐述小说相关要素以及各种批评理论和方法，读者可在有限的时空中感受英美小说之博大深广、丰富多彩。

第三，"小说赏析"部分不是对小说文本的全面分析，而是对所选小说文本中的某一小说要素进行具体分析，解读某一批评方法在文本中的具体运用，给读者提供一个比较完整的解读样式，帮助读者建立对小说要素和批评方法的感性认识，从而在分析和阐释其他文本时能够熟练运用。

第四，所选文本为英文原著，脚注为汉语，对小说文本中的背景知识、历史人物、地名、语言难点进行解释和说明，以帮助读者扫清语言、文化背景知识方面的障碍，能够流畅地阅读。语言力求简明易懂，力避专业术语的生硬堆砌。

本书的各章相对独立，但又彼此联系。读者在使用本书时既可按照本书的编排次序进行系统阅读和学习，也可灵活、选择性地使用部分内容。因此，它既可为英语文学研究者、爱好者的小说理论指导性读物，亦可为英语专业本科生、研究生"英美小说理论和欣赏"课程教材，或大学英语"英语文学选修课"、"通识选修课"教材。作为教材使用时，教师应针对不同的学生群体，侧重点要有所不同。

英语专业高年级的学生经过二至三年的专业学习，对英语语言的理解和英文原著的感悟能力相对较高，以本书作为"英美小说理论和欣赏"课程教材，主要是让他们了解小说欣赏所需的理论和方法，并运用相对比较专业的视角和方法对英文小说进行分析和理解，为将来从事英美文学研究打好基础，做好准备。教师可以根据本书的编排次序进行讲授，在引导学生细读文本的基础上，帮助学生逐步熟悉和掌握各种文学批评理论，形成自己的认识和见解，能够独立撰写论文。

英语专业文学硕士研究生在经过大学四年的专业学习之后，多读过一些经典英语小说，对英语小说的基本要素和各种批评方法有了一些基本认识。由于英语专业文学硕士研究生的培养目标是培养具有英语文学研究专业技能的研究人员或教师，文学批评理论和文学批评实践是教师授课时的两个主要关注面。本书尽管在深度和广度上不足以完全实现以上目标，但它的系统性和完整性则是不可忽视的，有助于英语专业文学硕士研究生尽快地全面掌握英语小说基本要素和批评方法。教师可以此书为基本教材，在讲授过程中对现有文本分析和批评方法进行补充、深入和拓展，这样，补充拓展的新内容更容易为学生理解和接受。

"英美小说欣赏"作为大学英语或通识选修课，其目的是培养非英语专业学生对英语语言和文学的初步认识和欣赏能力，激发他们的英语阅读兴趣，深化他们对世界文学的认识，从而以不同的视角看待生活、看待世界。因此，快乐阅读是必须的，教师在使用本书时，一定要注意不可使这门课成为学生的负担，教师应建议学生在阅读小说文本时不要过多地查生词，而是在阅读过程中体会英语小说的语言、结构和风格魅力，形成初步的阅读感受和认识，与同学们一起分享、感受小说阅读的快乐，在不知不觉中提高语言感知和小说欣赏能力。

本书编写过程中，参考了以下资料：X. J. Kennedy 的 *Literature: An Introduction to Fiction, Poetry, and Drama*, Michael Meyer 的 *The Bedford Introduction to Literature: Reading, Thinking,*

Writing (8th Edition), R.S. Gwynn 的 *Literature: A Pocket Anthology*, Robert Scholes 和 Rosemary Sullivan 合编的 *Elements of Fiction: An Anthology*, 以及 Nina Baym 等编著的 *The Norton Anthology of American Literature* (3rd Edition)。在此，向相关的作者、编者及出版社表示衷心的感谢！

  本书的编写还参考了一些网络资源，由于过于琐碎，除直接引用文献之外，不一一注明，在此向所有相关人士表示真诚的谢意！

  北京大学出版社的李颖女士、黄瑞明女士为本书的顺利出版付出了辛勤的劳动，在此深表谢意！

  由于编著者水平有限，书中难免有错误和不足之处，敬请广大读者批评指正。

师彦灵
兰州大学

Contents

Introduction 1
Part One　Elements of Fiction 3
Chapter One　Plot 4
　Paul's Case 6

Chapter Two　Setting 25
　A Rose for Emily 27

Chapter Three　Character 38
　A Good Man Is Hard to Find 40

Chapter Four　Point of View 56
　Reunion 58

Chapter Five　Theme 64
　A Dill Pickle 66

Chapter Six　Style and Tone 75
　The Rocking-Horse Winner 78

Chapter Seven　Symbolism 93
　Hills like White Elephants 95

Part Two　Critical Approaches 102
Chapter Eight　Historical and Biographical Approaches 104
　Adventures of Huckleberry Finn 106

Chapter Nine　The Formalist Approach 130
　The Mark on the Wall 133

Chapter Ten　The Psychoanalytic Approach 142
　David Copperfield 145

Chapter Eleven　The Mythological Approach 171
　The Story of an Hour 174

Chapter Twelve　Gender Studies 179
　Rip Van Winkle 183

Chapter Thirteen　Reader-response Criticism 200
　Haircut 202

Chapter Fourteen　Cultural Studies 214
　Heart of Darkness 218

Works Cited 267

目　　录

引言	1
第一部分　小说的要素	3
第一章　情节	4
保罗案	6
第二章　背景	25
献给艾米丽的玫瑰	27
第三章　人物	36
好人难寻	38
第四章　视角	56
团聚	58
第五章　主题	64
莳萝泡菜	66
第六章　风格	75
木马赢家	78
第七章　象征	93
白象似的群山	95
第二部分　批评方法	102
第八章　历史传记批评	104
哈克贝利·芬历险记	106
第九章　形式主义批评	130
墙上的斑点	133
第十章　心理分析批评	142
大卫·科伯菲尔	145
第十一章　神话批评	171
一小时的故事	174
第十二章　性别研究	179
瑞普·凡·温克尔	183
第十三章　读者反映批评	200
理发	202
第十四章　文化研究	214
黑暗的中心	218
引用文献	267

Introduction

"Fiction," derived from the Latin *fictio, fingo, fictum* which means "to create," is a general term for stories of imagined or invented events. It usually refers to narratives that are written in prose such as short stories, novellas, and novels.

Fiction interests us because of its "imitation" of life. Fiction is at once like and unlike life. This is what we mean when we call it an "imitation." We recognize aspects of ourselves and our situations in the more ordered perspectives of fiction. While we are reading fiction, it seems that it is speaking to us directly. We can be moved to laugh, cry, tremble, dream, ponder, shriek, or rage by simply turning a page. Thus, fiction helps us interpret our own experiences, understand life, and nourish our emotional lives.

In addition to appealing to our emotions and helping us understand life, fiction broadens our perspectives on the world. Our knowledge of the Western cultures that make up part of our world is superficial as well as limited. British and American fiction allows us to move beyond the boundaries of our own lives and culture while it introduces us to people different from ourselves, places remote from our neighborhoods, times other than our own, and beliefs, values, and customs that in some ways resemble our own but in others seem foreign and strange. Thus, we are more aware of prejudices, uncertainties, value judgments, and emotions of the people in the Western cultures.

The study of fiction is also practical. British and American fiction is mostly created by people with first-rate intelligence and rich life experiences, who prefer to experiment the proper literary techniques rather than translate automatically their understanding, sense, and deep thinking of the world, the life, and even the supernature into their works. While we try to go beneath the surface to reveal the underlying structures and meanings, we are engaged in the kinds of problem solving important in a variety of fields, from philosophy to science and technology, and enlightened by their insights into the world and human mysteries. Reading British and American fiction encourages a suppleness of mind that is helpful in any discipline or work.

To discover the insights that fiction reveals requires careful reading and sensitivity. One of the purposes of this book, which is based on two premises: that reading literature is pleasurable and that reading and understanding a work sensitively by thinking, talking, or writing about it increases the pleasure of the experience of it, is to cultivate the analytic skills and abilities necessary for reading well.

Understanding the elements of fiction, such as setting, point of view, symbol, theme, tone, irony, and so on, is a prerequisite to an informed appreciation of literature. Although different writers produce their works in quite different ways, these basic elements of fiction can be found in almost every literary work of fiction. It is these elements that work together to create a particular kind of effect, emotion, or insight which distinguishes this work from any other. Therefore, understanding how these elements work

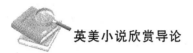

together to produce an overall effect enhances and sharpens our perceptions.

The critical approaches are indispensible to our satisfying reading of fiction. Each of these approaches raises its own questions and issues while seeking particular kinds of evidence to support itself. An awareness of the assumptions and methods that each approach informs us can help us make a better sense of a literary work of fiction, and therefore enhance our critical thinking.

The subsequent chapters will cover the elements of fiction and the major critical-interpretive approaches to fiction. The elements of fiction introduced here include plot, setting, character, point of view, theme, style and tone, and symbolism; and the critical approaches interpreted here contain the autobiographical and historical approaches, which have long been practiced, the Formalist Approach, the Psychoanalytic Approach, the Mythological Approach, and Gender Studies, Reader-Response Criticism and Cultural Studies which recently catch the readers' attention. These elements and critical approaches, along with comments on selected works, will help us achieve an easier, richer, and more satisfying reading of the literary work of fiction.

This book may be read from cover to cover as a continuous unit, of course, but it has been organized for both flexibility and adaptability. However you read it, everything that follows in this book is intended to help readers toward an enriched and pleasurable experience of fiction.

Part One
Elements of Fiction

A fiction writer uses character, setting, plot, point of view, theme, tone, and various kinds of symbolism to create artistic effect in fiction. These aspects of fiction are generally known as the elements of fiction. Once a reader is aware that all stories have elements of character, setting, plot, theme, point of view, tone, and symbolism, he can be encouraged to ask himself to identify the characteristics of each for a story. An understanding of these elements will enhance the reader's appreciation and perceptions of any piece of fiction. The more familiar he becomes with the different kinds of elements the better he will become at understanding and analyzing stories. For example, a reader who has knowledge of elements of fiction is more inclined to identify the symbolisms in Kate Chopin's "The Story of an Hour"—"patches of blue sky", "chair", "spring", "open window", and "heart trouble" — and their contributions to the theme of this story—the yearning for freedom of women in the late 1800s who were oppressed and repressed like Mrs. Mallard.

While the list of the elements encourages the reader to divide a story into parts, in the story itself these elements work together to create a whole. A reader can perceive the story's unique effect in his first reading of a piece of fiction because he reads for the first time without applying these divisions. However, the reader must analyze each of these elements of a piece of fiction if he wants to have an insight of how the unique effect is produced. "A Rose for Emily" is considered to be a readable, fascinating and insightful story. Its unique effect is produced by William Faulkner's successfully employing the setting, plot, narrator, and symbolism. The setting creates the mysterious atmosphere while it makes the story believable by locating the story in Jefferson, a small town of the south of America in the post—Civil War years in which Miss Emily and the townspeople take actions; the plot which is not narrated in the linear fashion builds suspense for the reader as the plot unfolds bit by bit; the fascinating narrator, "we," who speaks sometimes for the men of Jefferson, sometimes for the women, and often for both, and spans three generations of Jeffersonians, including the generation of Miss Emily's father, Miss Emily's generation, and the "newer generation," made up of the children of Miss Emily's contemporaries, makes the reader easy to see how the first two generations' treatment of Miss Emily may have led to her downfall; and the watch Miss Emily carries in a pocket within her clothing symbolizes Emily's attempts to control the passage of the years and the consequences of such an ultimately futile effort. All these elements blend to create a story which all the time involves the reader in detecting the mystery of both the story and Miss Emily like a detective and having an insight of what the author intends us to know: privileges, constraining rather than liberating our true selves, can sometimes be a prison.

Chapter One
Plot

Plot holds the first important position in a work of fiction. We are attracted into the writer's fictional world by the plot. Like many terms used in literary discussion, **plot** is loaded with several meanings. Sometimes it refers simply to the events in a story. In this book, plot means the author's artistic or dramatic arrangement of events in a story. The same material can be arranged in different order.

A writer might decide to tell of the events in the **chronological order**, beginning with what happens first, then second, and so on, until the last event is related. A writer also might begin his story at the end, and then tell what led up to it. William Faulkner's "A Rose for Emily" begins with the funeral of the title character and then goes back in time to narrate events that happened in the past. In this way it gives the reader a surprise which would not have been produced if it is arranged in the chronological order.

Sometimes a writer chooses to begin a story in the **middle** of things (the Latin term for this common plot device is *in medias res*), first presenting some exciting or important moment, then filling in what happened earlier. John Updike's "A & P" begins with the narrator, a teenager working at a checkout counter in a supermarket, by telling us: "In walks these three girls in nothing but bathing suits." Then right away we are brought into the middle of a situation that will ultimately create the conflict in the story.

Another device writers often use is the **flashback**. It tells us about events that happened before the opening scene of a work. **Foreshadowing** is also a device useful for writers to provide hints of events to come in. Its effective use prevents a story from looking contrived. This way some descriptive, explanatory or transitional phrases can compress an action which could have taken many years into a second or leap over uneventful periods. The opening sentence of the second paragraph of John Cheever's "Reunion" ("We went out of the station and up a side street to a restaurant.") compresses into a second or two an action that in reality would have lasted at least several minutes.

When we read a story, our emotional involvement in the plot is increased or relaxed with the **dramatic structure** of a story. The first part of the dramatic structure is the **exposition** that sets the scene, introduces the main characters, relates what happened before the story opens, and provides any other background information that we need in order to understand and care about the events to follow. It usually describes the stable situation of a story. In "Reunion" Charles tells us that his parents got divorced when he was three years old and he has not seen his father since then. And his letter to his father makes his "reunion" with his father come true.

The appearance of "trouble" constitutes the second part of a plot, the **complication**, which shakes up the stable situation and begins the rising action of the story. Complication in a story may be either external or internal, or a combination of the two. In "Reunion" the complication is a combination of the father's confrontations with waiters (the external complication) and Charlie's growing sense of pity and revulsion (the internal complication). And it is heightened by the conflict between Charlie and his father who obviously have different personalities: he escapes his father at the end.

The body of a story, called the **rising action**, contains action and dialogue which build to moments of crisis. The central moment of crisis is the **climax**, or moment of greatest tension. At this moment, the tension is momentarily resolved and the outcome is to be decided.

The final part of a plot is **denouement** or **resolution**, which quickly follows the climax and returns the characters to another stable situation. A story may end with a closed denouement or an open denouement. A closed denouement states everything explicitly and explains all unanswered questions the reader might have; an open denouement leaves us with a few questions at the end, which invites us to speculate.

Although a highly dramatic story may tend to assume such a clearly recognizable structure, many contemporary writers avoid it, considering it too contrived and arbitrary. And the presence of these elements does not necessarily indicate inferior literature.

Whatever the plot arrangement, you should be aware of how the writer's conscious ordering of events affects your responses to the action.

Willa Cather (1873—1947)

Willa Cather was born in rural Virginia but moved to the Nebraska farmlands in childhood. There she grew up among the immigrants from Europe, who were establishing their homesteads on the Great Plains. After her graduation from the University of Nebraska she lived in Pittsburgh for some years as a drama critic and a brief period as a high school English teacher, and then moved to New York, because her first collection of short stories *Troll Garden* (1905) brought her to the attention of S.S. McClure, owner of *McClure's Magazine*, whose managing editor she ultimately became. Her novels about Nebraska inspired by Sara Orne Jewett, *O Pioneers!* (1913) and *My Antonia* (1917), were very successful and she devoted the rest of her life to writing fiction. In her later years Cather wrote *One of Ours* (1922), for which she won the Pulitzer Prize, her modernist book *A Lost Lady* (1923), and some of her greatest novels during this period, such as *The Professor's House* (1925), *My Mortal Enemy* (1926), and *Death Comes for the Archbishop* (1927). These novels of hers focused on the destruction of provincial life and the death of the pioneering tradition, and had the darker tones.

"Paul's Case," one of the stories that helped Cather get the position with *McClure's Magazine*, was first published in *McClure's Magazine* in 1905. It marks the beginning of Cather's artistic maturity.

Paul's Case[1]

I

It was Paul's afternoon to appear before the faculty of the Pittsburgh High School to account for his various misdemeanors[2]. He had been suspended a week ago, and his father had called at the principal's office and confessed his perplexity about his son. Paul entered the faculty room suave and smiling. His clothes were a trifle outgrown and the tan velvet on the collar of his open overcoat was frayed and worn; but, for all that, there was something of the dandy about him, and he wore an opal pin in his neatly knotted black four-in-hand[3], and a red carnation in his buttonhole. This latter adornment the faculty somehow felt was not properly significant of the contrite spirit befitting a boy under the ban of suspension[4].

Paul was tall for his age and very thin, with high, cramped shoulders and a narrow chest. His eyes were remarkable for a certain hysterical brilliancy, and he continually used them in a conscious, theatrical sort of way, peculiarly offensive in a boy. The pupils were abnormally large, as though he were addicted to belladonna[5], but there was a glassy glitter about them which that drug does not produce.

When questioned by the Principal[6] as to why he was there, Paul stated, politely enough, that he wanted to come back to school. This was a lie, but Paul was quite accustomed to lying; found it, indeed, indispensible for overcoming friction. His teachers were asked to state their respective charges against him, which they did with such a rancor and aggrievedness[7] as evinced that this was not a usual case. Disorder and impertinence[8] were among the offences named, yet each of his instructors felt that it was scarcely possible to put into words the real cause of the trouble, which lay in a sort of hysterically defiant manner of the boy's; in the contempt which they all knew he felt for them, and which he seemingly made not the least effort to conceal[9]. Once, when he had been making a synopsis of a paragraph at the blackboard, his English teacher had stepped to his side and attempted to guide his hand. Paul had started back with a shudder, and thrust his hands violently behind him. The astonished woman could scarcely have been more hurt and embarrassed had he struck at her[10]. The insult was so

---

1. 该小说的副标题为：A Study in Temperament。
2. account for his various misdemeanors：对他之前的种种恶行作个解释
3. four-in-hand：打活结的领带
4. not properly significant of the contrite spirit befitting a boy under the ban of suspension：没能恰当地表达出一名因受到停学处分的学生理应表现出的忏悔心态
5. belladonna：(植)颠茄，莨菪(一种有毒植物)，颠茄制剂
6. Principal：校长
7. they did with such a rancor and aggrievedness：老师们在讲述他所作所为的时候都表现出对他的极大的怨恨和不满
8. impertinence：无礼
9. he seemingly made not the least effort to conceal：他似乎丝毫不想掩饰
10. struck at her：向她打去

involuntary and definitely personal as to be unforgettable. In one way and another he had made all his teachers, men and women alike, conscious of the same feeling of physical aversion[1]. In one class he habitually sat with his hand shading his eyes; in another he always looked out of the window during the recitation; in another he made a running[2] commentary on the lecture, with humorous intention.

His teachers felt this afternoon that his whole attitude was symbolized by his shrug and his flippantly red carnation flower, and they fell upon him without mercy[3], his English teacher leading the pack[4]. He stood through it smiling, his pale lips parted over his white teeth. (His lips were continually twitching, and he had a habit of raising his eyebrows that was contemptuous and irritating to the last degree.) Older boys than Paul had broken down and shed tears under that baptism of fire[5], but his set smile did not once desert him, and his only sign of discomfort was the nervous trembling of the fingers that toyed with the buttons of his overcoat, and an occasional jerking of the other hand that held his hat. Paul was always smiling, always glancing about him, seeming to feel that people might be watching him and trying to detect something. This conscious expression, since it was as far as possible from boyish mirthfulness, was usually attributed to insolence or "smartness."[6]

As the inquisition proceeded, one of his instructors repeated an impertinent remark of the boy's, and the Principal asked him whether he thought that a courteous speech to have made a woman. Paul shrugged his shoulders slightly and his eyebrows twitched.

"I don't know," he replied. "I didn't mean to be polite or impolite, either. I guess it's a sort of way I have of saying things regardless."

The Principal, who was a sympathetic man, asked him whether he didn't think that a way it would be well to get rid of. Paul grinned and said he guessed so. When he was told that he could go, he bowed gracefully and went out. His bow was but a repetition of the scandalous red carnation[7].

His teachers were in despair, and his drawing master voiced the feeling of them all when he declared there was something about the boy which none of them understood. He added: "I don't really believe that smile of his comes altogether from insolence; there's something sort of haunted about it. The boy is not strong, for one thing. I happen to know that he was born in Colorado[8], only a few months before his mother died out there of a long illness. There is something wrong about the fellow."

The drawing master had come to realize that, in looking at Paul, one saw only his white teeth and the forced animation of his eyes. One warm afternoon the boy had gone to sleep at his drawing-board, and his master had noted with amazement what a white, blue-veined face it was; drawn and wrinkled like an old man's[9] about the eyes, the lips twitching even in his sleep, and stiff with a nervous tension that drew them back from his teeth.

---

1. aversion: 反感
2. running: 连续不断的，不停的
3. fell upon him without mercy: 他们毫不留情地向他发起了攻击
4. the pack: 文章中指所有在场的老师
5. baptism of fire: 炮火的洗礼，士兵初临战场的考验。文章中指老师的严厉批评和指责。
6. attributed to insolence or "smartness": 归因于傲慢或"机敏"
7. a repetition of the scandalous red carnation: 与之前纽扣孔佩带的红色康乃馨持有相同的效果
8. Colorado: 科罗拉多州，位于美国西部
9. drawn and wrinkled like an old man's: 像一位历经沧桑的老人一样形容憔悴，眼角已出现皱纹

His teachers left the building dissatisfied and unhappy; humiliated to have felt so vindictive toward a mere boy, to have uttered this feeling in cutting terms[1], and to have set each other on, as it were, in the gruesome game of intemperate reproach[2]. Some of them remembered having seen a miserable street cat set at bay[3] by a ring of tormentors.

As for Paul, he ran down the hill whistling the Soldiers' Chorus[4] from *Faust*[5], looking wildly behind him, now and then, to see whether some of his teachers were not there to writhe under his light-heartedness. As it was now late in the afternoon, and Paul was on duty that evening as usher in Carnegie Hall, he decided that he would not go home to supper. When he reached the concert hall the doors were not yet open and, as it was chilly outside, he decided to go up into the picture gallery—always deserted at this hour—where there were some of Raffaelli's gay studies[6] of Paris streets and an airy blue Venetian scene[7] or two that always exhilarated him. He was delighted to find no one in the gallery but the old guard, who sat in one corner, a newspaper on his knee, a black patch over one eye and the other closed. Paul possessed himself of the place[8] and walked confidently up and down, whistling under his breath. After a while he sat down before a blue Rico and lost himself. When he bethought him to look at his watch, it was after seven o'clock, and he rose with a start and ran downstairs, making a face at Augustus[9], peering out from the cast-room, and an evil gesture at the Venus of Milo[10] as he passed her on the stairway.

When Paul reached the ushers' dressing-room at about half-past seven that evening, half a dozen boys were there already, and Paul began, excitedly, to tumble into his uniform[11]. It was one of the few that at all approached fitting, and he thought it very becoming—though he knew that the tight, straight coat accentuated his narrow chest, about which he was exceedingly sensitive. He was always considerably excited while he dressed, twanging all over to the tuning of the strings and the preliminary flourishes of the horns in the music-room; but tonight he seemed quite beside himself[12], and he teased and plagued the boys until, telling him that he was crazy, they put him down on the floor and sat on him.

Somewhat calmed by his suppression, Paul dashed out to the front of the house to seat the early comers. He was a model usher; gracious and smiling, he ran up and down the aisles; nothing was too much trouble for him; he carried messages and brought programmes as though it were his greatest pleasure in life, and all the people in his section thought him a charming boy, feeling that he remembered and admired them. As the house filled, he grew more and more vivacious and animated,

---

1. cutting terms：尖酸刻薄的言语
2. intemperate reproach：肆无忌惮的责备
3. set at bay：被逼到绝路
4. Soldiers' Chorus：《士兵大合唱》，《浮士德》中的主题曲。
5. Faust：文章中指《浮士德交响曲》，是受歌德的诗剧《浮士德》启发而作。作者李斯特 (Franz Liszt, 1811—1886) 为匈牙利钢琴家、指挥家、作曲家
6. Raffaelli's gay studies：拉法埃利关于同性恋的研究
7. an airy blue Venetian scene：一个既轻松而又让人忧郁的威尼斯场景
8. possessed himself of the place：把自己当作这个地方的主人
9. Augustus：奥古斯都，罗马帝国的开国君主，统治罗马长达 43 年
10. Venus of Milo：断臂维纳斯，一尊希腊神话中代表爱与美的女神维纳斯的大理石雕塑
11. to tumble into his uniform：匆忙穿好制服
12. he seemed quite beside himself：他似乎完全不在状态

and the color came to his cheeks and lips. It was very much as though this were a great reception and Paul were the host. Just as the musicians came out to take their places, his English teacher arrived with checks for the seats which a prominent manufacturer had taken for the season. She betrayed some embarrassment when she handed Paul the tickets, and a *hauteur*[1] which subsequently made her feel very foolish. Paul was startled for a moment, and had the feeling of wanting to put her out[2]; what business had she here among all these fine people and gay colors? He looked her over and decided that she was not appropriately dressed and must be a fool to sit downstairs in such togs. The tickets had probably been sent her out of kindness, he reflected as he put down a seat for her, and she had about as much right to sit there as he had.

When the symphony began, Paul sank into one of the rear seats with a long sigh of relief, and lost himself as he had done before the Rico. It was not that symphonies, as such, meant anything in particular to Paul, but the first sigh of the instruments seemed to free some hilarious and potent spirit within him; something that struggled there like the Genius in the bottle found by the Arab fisherman. He felt a sudden zest of life; the lights danced before his eyes and the concert hall blazed into unimaginable splendor. When the soprano soloist came on, Paul forgot even the nastiness of his teacher's being there and gave himself up to the peculiar stimulus such personages always had for him. The soloist chanced to be a German woman, by no means in her first youth, and the mother of many children; but she wore an elaborate gown and a tiara, and above all, she had that indefinable air of achievement, that world-shine upon her, which, in Paul's eyes, made her a veritable queen of Romance.

After a concert was over Paul was always irritable and wretched until he got to sleep, and tonight he was even more than usually restless. He had the feeling of not being able to let down, of its being impossible to give up this delicious excitement which was the only thing that could be called living at all. During the last number he withdrew and, after hastily changing his clothes in the dressing-room, slipped out to the side door where the soprano's carriage stood. Here he began pacing rapidly up and down the walk, waiting to see her come out.

Over yonder the Schenley, in its vacant stretch, loomed big and square through the fine rain, the windows of its twelve stories glowing like those of a lighted cardboard house under a Christmas tree. All the actors and singers of the better class stayed there when they were in the city, and a number of the big manufacturers of the place lived there in the winter. Paul had often hung about the hotel, watching the people go in and out, longing to enter and leave school-masters and dull care behind him forever.

At last the singer came out, accompanied by the conductor, who helped her into her carriage and closed the door with a cordial *auf wiedersehen*[3], which set Paul to wondering whether she were not an old sweetheart of his. Paul followed the carriage over to the hotel, walking so rapidly as not to be far from the entrance when the singer alighted and disappeared behind the swinging glass doors that were opened by a negro in a tall hat and a long coat. In the moment that the door was ajar, it seemed to Paul that he too entered. He seemed to feel himself go after her up the steps, into the warm, lighted building,

---

1. *hauteur*:(法语)傲慢,自大
2. put her out:让她退场
3. *auf wiedersehen*:(德语)再见

into an exotic, a tropical world of shiny, glistening surfaces and basking ease. He reflected upon the mysterious dishes that were brought into the dining-room, the green bottles in buckets of ice, as he had seen them in the supper party pictures of the Sunday World supplement. A quick gust of wind brought the rain down with sudden vehemence, and Paul was startled to find that he was still outside in the slush of the gravel driveway; that his boots were letting in the water, and his scanty overcoat was clinging wet about him; that the lights in front of the concert hall were out, and that the rain was driving in sheets between him and the orange glow of the windows above him. There it was, what he wanted-tangibly before him, like the fairy world of a Christmas pantomime, but mocking spirits stood guard at the doors, and, as the rain beat in his face, Paul wondered whether he were destined always to shiver in the black night outside, looking up at it.

He turned and walked reluctantly toward the car tracks. The end had to come sometime; his father in his night-clothes at the top of the stairs, explanations that did not explain, hastily improvised fictions that were forever tripping him up, his upstairs room and its horrible yellow wall-paper, the creaking bureau with the greasy plush collar box and over his painted wooden bed the pictures of George Washington and John Calvin[1], and the framed motto[2], "Feed my Lambs," which had been worked in red worsted by his mother.

Half an hour later, Paul alighted from his car and went slowly down one of the side streets off the main thoroughfare. It was a highly respectable street, where all the houses were exactly alike, and where business men of moderate means begot and reared large families of children, all of whom went to Sabbath-school[3] and learned the shorter catechism, and were interested in arithmetic; all of whom were as exactly alike as their homes, and of a piece with the monotony in which they lived. Paul never went up Cordelia Street without a shudder of loathing. His home was next to the house of the Cumberland minister. He approached it tonight with the nerveless sense of defeat, the hopeless feeling of sinking back forever into ugliness and commonness that he always had when he came home. The moment he turned into Cordelia Street he felt the waters close above his head. After each of these orgies of living, he experienced all the physical depression which follows a debauch; the loathing of respectable beds, of common food, of a house penetrated by kitchen odors; a shuddering repulsion for the flavorless, colorless mass of everyday existence; a morbid desire for cool things and soft lights and fresh flowers.

The nearer he approached the house, the more absolutely unequal Paul felt to the sight of it all; his ugly sleeping chamber, the cold bath-room, with the grimy zinc tub, the cracked mirror, the dripping spigots, his father at the top of the stairs, his hairy legs sticking out from his night-shirt, his feet thrust into carpet slippers. He was so much later than usual that there would certainly be inquiries and reproaches. Paul stopped short before the door. He felt that he could not be accosted by his father tonight, that he could not toss again on that miserable bed. He would not go in. He would tell his father that he had no car fare, and it was raining so hard he had gone home with one of the boys and stayed all night.

---

1. John Calvin:约翰·加尔文(1509—1564),法国基督教新教加尔文宗的创始人
2. the framed motto:装裱起来的格言
3. Sabbath-school:主日学校,基督教教会为了向儿童灌输宗教思想,在星期天开办的儿童班

Meanwhile, he was wet and cold. He went around to the back of the house and tried one of the basement windows, found it open, raised it cautiously, and scrambled down the cellar wall to the floor. There he stood, holding his breath, terrified by the noise he had made, but the floor above him was silent, and there was no creak on the stairs. He found a soap box, and carried it over to the soft ring of light that streamed from the furnace door, and sat down. He was horribly afraid of rats, so he did not try to sleep, but sat looking distrustfully at the dark, still terrified least he might have awakened his father. In such reactions, after one of the experiences which made days and nights out of the dreary blanks of the calendar, when his senses were deadened, Paul's head was always singularly clear. Suppose his father had heard him getting in at the window, and come down and shot him for a burglar? Then, again, suppose his father had come down, pistol in hand, and he had cried out in time to save himself, and his father had been horrified to think how nearly he had killed him? Then, again, suppose a day should come when his father would remember that night, and wish there had been no warning cry to stay his hand[1]? With this last supposition Paul entertained himself until daybreak.

The following Sunday was fine; the sodden November chill was broken by the last flash of autumnal summer. In the morning Paul had to go to church and Sabbath-school, as always. On seasonable Sunday afternoons the burghers of Cordelia Street always sat out on their front "stoops," and talked to their neighbors on the next stoop, or called to those across the street in neighborly fashion. The men usually sat on gay cushions placed upon the steps that led down to the sidewalk, while the women, in their Sunday "waists[2]," sat in rockers on the cramped porches, pretending to be greatly at their ease. The children played in the streets; there were so many of them that the place resembled the recreation grounds of a kindergarten. The men on the steps-all in their shirt sleeves, their vests unbuttoned-sat with their legs well apart, their stomachs comfortably protruding, and talked of the prices of things, or told anecdotes of the sagacity of their various chiefs and overlords. They occasionally looked over the multitude of squabbling children, listened affectionately to their high-pitched, nasal voices, smiling to see their own proclivities reproduced in their offspring, and interspersed their legends of the iron kings with remarks about their sons' progress at school, their grades in arithmetic, and the amounts they had saved in their toy banks.

On this last Sunday of November, Paul sat all the afternoon on the lowest step of his "stoop," staring into the street, while his sisters, in their rockers, were talking to the minister's daughters next door about how many shirt-waists they had made in the last week, and how many waffles some one had eaten at the last church supper. When the weather was warm, and his father was in a particularly jovial frame of mind, the girls made lemonade, which was always brought out in a red glass pitcher, ornamented with forget-me-nots in blue enamel. This the girls thought very fine, and the neighbors always joked about the suspicious color of the pitcher.

Today Paul's father sat on the top step, talking to a young man who shifted a restless baby from knee to knee. He happened to be the young man who was daily held up to Paul as a model, and after whom it was his father's dearest hope that he would pattern. This young man was of a ruddy complexion,

---

1. stay one's hand：使……住手
2. waists：束身衣

with a compressed, red mouth, and faded, near-sighted eyes, over which he wore thick spectacles, with gold bows that curved about his ears. He was clerk to one of the magnates of a great steel corporation, and was looked upon in Cordelia Street as a young man with a future. There was a story that, some five years ago—he was now barely twenty-six—he had been a trifle dissipated, but in order to curb his appetites and save the loss of time and strength that a sowing of wild oats might have entailed, he had taken his chief's advice, oft reiterated to his employees, and at twenty-one had married the first woman whom he could persuade to share his fortunes. She happened to be an angular schoolmistress, much older than he, who also wore thick glasses, and who had now borne him four children, all near-sighted, like herself.

The young man was relating how his chief, now cruising in the Mediterranean[1], kept in touch with all the details of the business, arranging his office hours on his yacht just as though he were at home, and "knocking off work enough to keep two stenographers busy." His father told, in turn, the plan his corporation was considering, of putting in an electric railway plant at Cairo[2]. Paul snapped his teeth; he had an awful apprehension that they might spoil it all before he got there. Yet he rather liked to hear these legends of the iron kings, that were told and retold on Sundays and holidays; these stories of palaces in Venice[3], yachts on the Mediterranean, and high play at Monte Carlo[4] appealed to his fancy, and he was interested in the triumphs of these cash boys who had become famous, though he had no mind for the cash boy stage.

After supper was over, and he had helped to dry the dishes, Paul nervously asked his father whether he could go to George's to get some help in his geometry, and still more nervously asked for car fare. This latter request he had to repeat, as his father, on principle, did not like to hear requests for money, whether much or little. He asked Paul whether he could not go to some boy who lived nearer, and told him that he ought not to leave his school work until Sunday; but he gave him the dime. He was not a poor man, but he had a worthy ambition to come up in the world[5]. His only reason for allowing Paul to usher was, that he thought a boy ought to be earning a little.

Paul bounded upstairs, scrubbed the greasy odor of the dish-water from his hands with the ill-smelling soap he hated, and then shook over his fingers a few drops of violet water from the bottle he kept hidden in his drawer. He left the house with his geometry conspicuously under his arm, and the moment he got out of Cordelia Street and boarded a downtown car, he shook off the lethargy of two deadening days, and began to live again.

The leading juvenile of the permanent stock company which played at one of the downtown theatres was an acquaintance of Paul's, and the boy had been invited to drop in at the Sunday-night rehearsals whenever he could. For more than a year Paul had spent every available moment loitering about Charley Edwards's dressing-room. He had won a place among Edwards's following, not only because the young actor, who could not afford to employ a dresser, often found the boy very useful, but because he recognized in Paul something akin to what Churchmen term "vocation."

---

1. Mediterranean：地中海，位于欧、亚、非三大洲之间
2. Cairo：开罗，埃及首都
3. Venice：威尼斯，意大利港市
4. Monte Carlo：蒙特卡洛，位于摩纳哥
5. a worthy ambition to come up in the world：飞黄腾达的崇高志向

Chapter One Plot

It was at the theatre and at Carnegie Hall that Paul really lived; the rest was but a sleep and a forgetting. This was Paul's fairy tale, and it had for him all the allurement of a secret love. The moment he inhaled the gassy, painty, dusty odor behind the scenes, he breathed like a prisoner set free, and felt within him the possibility of doing or saying splendid, brilliant, poetic things. The moment the cracked orchestra beat out the overture from *Martha*, or jerked at the serenade from *Rigoletto*[1], all stupid and ugly things slid from him, and his senses were deliciously, yet delicately fired.

Perhaps it was because, in Paul's world, the natural nearly always wore the guise of ugliness, that a certain element of artificiality seemed to him necessary in beauty. Perhaps it was because his experience of life elsewhere was so full of Sabbath-school picnics, petty economies, wholesome advice as to how to succeed in life, and the unescapable odors of cooking, that he found this existence so alluring, these smartly clad men and women so attractive, that he was so moved by these starry apple orchards that bloomed perennially under the limelight.

It would be difficult to put it strongly enough how convincingly the stage entrance of that theatre was for Paul the actual portal of Romance. Certainly none of the company ever suspected it, least of all Charley Edwards. It was very like the old stories that used to float about London of fabulously rich Jews, who had subterranean halls there; with palms, and fountains, and soft lamps, and richly appareled women who never saw the disenchanting light of London day. So, in the midst of that smoke-palled[2] city, enamored of figures and grimy toil, Paul had his secret temple, his wishing carpet, his bit of blue-and-white Mediterranean shore bathed in perpetual sunshine.

Several of Paul's teachers had a theory that his imagination had been perverted by garish fiction, but the truth was that he scarcely ever read at all. The books at home were not such as would either tempt or corrupt a youthful mind, and as for reading the novels that some of his friends urged upon him-well, he got what he wanted much more quickly from music; any sort of music, from an orchestra to a barrel organ. He needed only the spark, the indescribable thrill that made his imagination master of his senses, and he could make plots and pictures enough of his own. It was equally true that he was not stage struck-not, at any rate, in the usual acceptation of that expression. He had no desire to become an actor, any more than he had to become a musician. He felt no necessity to do any of these things; what he wanted was to see, to be in the atmosphere, float on the wave of it, to be carried out, blue league after blue league, away from everything.

After a night behind the scenes, Paul found the school room more than ever repulsive; the bare floors and naked walls; the prosy men who never wore frock coat[3], or violets in their button-holes; the women with their dull gowns, shrill voices, and pitiful seriousness about prepositions that govern the dative. He could not bear to have the other pupils think, for a moment, that he took these people seriously; he must convey to them that he considered it all trivial, and was there only by way of a jest, anyway. He had autographed pictures of all the members of the stock company which he showed his

---

1. *Rigoletto*:《弄臣》。这是由朱塞佩·威尔第 (Giuseppe Fortunino Francesco Verdi, 1813—1901) 作曲的著名四幕歌剧。该剧的意大利语剧本由范切斯科·皮尔亚基根据法国文豪维克多·雨果所作的法语戏剧《国王的弄臣》改编而成，是现在各大歌剧院的标准保留剧目之一。
2. smoke-palled: 烟层厚厚的
3. frock coat: 双排扣长礼服

classmates, telling them the most incredible stories of his familiarity with these people, of his acquaintance with the soloists who came to Carnegie Hall, his suppers with them and the flowers he sent them. When these stories lost their effect, and his audience grew listless, he became desperate and would bid all the boys good-bye, announcing that he was going to travel for a while; going to Naples[1], to Venice, to Egypt. Then, next Monday, he would slip back, conscious, and nervously smiling; his sister was ill, and he should have to defer his voyage until spring.

Matters went steadily worse with Paul at school. In the itch to let his instructors know how heartily he despised them and their homilies[2], and how thoroughly he was appreciated elsewhere, he mentioned once or twice that he had no time to fool with theorems; adding—with a twitch of the eyebrows and a touch of that nervous bravado which so perplexed them—that he was helping the people down at the stock company; they were old friends of his.

The upshot of the matter was that the Principal went to Paul's father, and Paul was taken out of school and put to work. The manager at Carnegie Hall was told to get another usher in his stead, the doorkeeper at the theatre was warned not to admit him to the house, and Charley Edwards remorsefully promised the boy's father not to see him again.

The members of the stock company were vastly amused when some of Paul's stories reached them—especially the women. They were hard-working women, most of them supporting indigent husbands or brothers, and they laughed rather bitterly at having stirred the boy to such fervid and florid inventions. They agreed with the faculty and with his father that Paul's was a bad case.

II

The east-bound train was plowing through a January snowstorm; the dull dawn was beginning to show gray, when the engine whistled a mile out of Newark[3]. Paul started up from the seat where he had lain curled in uneasy slumber, rubbed the breath-misted window glass with his hand, and peered out. The snow was whirling in curling eddies above the white bottom lands[4], and the drifts lay already deep in the fields and along the fences, while here and there the long dead grass and dried weed stalks protruded black above it. Lights shone from the scattered houses, and a gang of laborers who stood beside the track waved their lanterns.

Paul had slept very little, and he felt grimy and uncomfortable. He had made the all-night journey in a day coach, partly because he was ashamed, dressed as he was, to go into a Pullman[5], and partly because he was afraid of being seen there by some Pittsburgh[6] business man, who might have noticed him in Denny & Carson's office. When the whistle awoke him, he clutched quickly at his breast pocket, glancing

---

1. Naples：那不勒斯，意大利西南部港市
2. homily：(宗)(指讲解《圣经》的)布道，(冗长乏味的)说教
3. Newark：纽瓦克，美国新泽西州港市
4. bottom land：水泛地，河滩地
5. Pullman：卧车，普式火车。19世纪美国发明家 George M. Pullman 设计的豪华型列车车厢，常用为特等客车。
6. Pittsburgh：匹兹堡，美国宾西法尼亚州西南部城市，美国的钢铁工业中心

about him with an uncertain smile. But the little, clay-bespattered¹ Italians were still sleeping, the slatternly women across the aisle were in open-mouthed oblivion², and even the crumby, crying babies were for the nonce³ stilled. Paul settled back to struggle with his impatience as best he could.

When he arrived at the Jersey City station, Paul hurried through his breakfast, manifestly ill at ease and keeping a sharp eye about him. After he reached the Twenty-third Street station, he consulted a cabman, and had himself driven to a men's furnishing establishment that was just opening for the day. He spent upward of⁴ two hours there, buying with endless reconsidering and great care. His new street suit he put on in the fitting-room; the frock-coat and dress clothes he had bundled into the cab with his linen. Then he drove to a hatter's and a shoe house. His next errand was at Tiffany's⁵, where he selected his silver and a new scarf-pin. He would not wait to have his silver marked, he said. Lastly, he stopped at a trunk shop on Broadway, and had his purchases packed into various traveling bags.

It was a little after one o'clock when he drove up to the Waldorf⁶, and after settling with the cabman, went into the office. He registered from Washington; said his mother and father had been abroad, and that he had come down to await the arrival of their steamer. He told his story plausibly and had no trouble, since he volunteered to pay for them in advance, in engaging his rooms, a sleeping-room, sitting-room and bath.

Not once, but a hundred times, Paul had planned this entry into New York. He had gone over every detail of it with Charley Edwards, and in his scrap book at home there were pages of description about New York hotels, cut from the Sunday papers. When he was shown to his sitting-room on the eighth floor, he saw at a glance that everything was as it should be; there was but one detail in his mental picture that the place did not realize, so he rang for the bell-boy and sent him down for flowers. He moved about nervously until the boy returned, putting away his new linen and fingering it delightedly as he did so. When the flowers came, he put them hastily into water, and then tumbled into a hot bath. Presently he came out of his white bath-room, resplendent in his new silk underwear, and playing with the tassels of his red robe. The snow was whirling so fiercely outside his windows that he could scarcely see across the street but within the air was deliciously soft and fragrant. He put the violets and jonquils on the taboret beside the couch, and threw himself down, with a long sigh, covering himself with a Roman blanket. He was thoroughly tired; he had been in such haste, had stood up to such a strain, covered so much ground in the last twenty-four hours, that he wanted to think how it had all come about. Lulled by the sound of the wind, the warm air, and the cool fragrance of the flowers, he sank into deep, drowsy retrospection.

It had been wonderfully simple; when they had shut him out of the theatre and concert hall, when they had taken away his bone, the whole thing was virtually determined. The rest was a mere matter of opportunity. The only thing that at all surprised him was his own courage— for he realized well enough

---

1. clay-bespattered: 溅满泥土的
2. in open-mouthed oblivion: 张着大嘴, 半睡半醒
3. for the nonce: 〈口〉目前, 暂且
4. upward of: 超过, 多于
5. Tiffany's: 蒂凡尼, 世界著名的珠宝品牌
6. the Waldorf: 宾馆名称, 位于纽约曼哈顿中心

that he had always been tormented by fear, a sort of apprehensive dread that, of late years, as the meshes of the lies he had told closed about him, had been pulling the muscles of his body tighter and tighter. Until now, he could not remember the time when he had not been dreading something. Even when he was a little boy, it was always there—behind him, or before, or on either side. There had always been the shadowed corner, the dark place into which he dared not look, but from which something seemed always to be watching him—and Paul had done things that were not pretty to watch, he knew.

But now he had a curious sense of relief, as though he had at last thrown down the gauntlet to the thing in the corner.

Yet it was but a day since he had been sulking in the traces[1]; but yesterday afternoon that he had been sent to the bank with Denny & Carson's deposits as usual—but this time he was instructed to leave the book to be balanced[2]. There were above two thousand dollars in checks, and nearly a thousand in the bank notes which he had taken from the book and quietly transferred to his pocket. At the bank he had made out a new deposit slip[3]. His nerves had been steady enough to permit of his returning to the office, where he had finished his work and asked for a full day's holiday tomorrow, Saturday, giving a perfectly reasonable pretext. The bank-book, he knew, would not be returned before Monday or Tuesday, and his father would be out of town for the next week. From the time he slipped the bank-notes into his pocket until he boarded the night train for New York, he had not known a moment's hesitation. It was not the first time Paul had steered through treacherous waters.

How astonishingly easy it had all been; here he was, the thing done; and this time there would be no awakening, no figure at the top of the stairs. He watched the snow flakes whirling by his window until he fell asleep.

When he awoke, it was three o'clock in the afternoon. He bounded up with a start; half of one of his precious days gone already! He spent more than an hour in dressing, watching every stage of his toilet carefully in the mirror. Everything was quite perfect; he was exactly the kind of boy he had always wanted to be.

When he went downstairs, Paul took a carriage and drove up Fifth Avenue[4] toward the Park[5]. The snow had somewhat abated; carriages and tradesmen's wagons were hurrying soundlessly to and fro in the winter twilight; boys in woollen mufflers were shovelling off the doorsteps; the avenue stages made fine spots of color against the white street. Here and there on the corners were stands, with whole flower gardens blooming under glass cases, against the sides of which the snow flakes stuck and melted; violets, roses, carnations, lilies of the valley—somehow vastly more lovely and alluring that they blossomed thus unnaturally in the snow. The Park itself was a wonderful stage winter-piece.

When he returned, the pause of the twilight had ceased, and the tune of the streets had changed. The snow was falling faster, lights streamed from the hotels that reared their dozen stories fearlessly up into

---

1. in the traces:(马等)套着缰绳;(人)做着日常工作
2. leave the book to be balanced:保持账面收支平衡
3. deposit slip:存款单
4. Fifth Avenue:第五大道,位于纽约曼哈顿中心的一条大道
5. Park:此处指号称纽约"后花园"的中央公园(Central Park)。它坐落于摩天大楼耸立的曼哈顿正中,是纽约最大的都市公园,也是纽约第一个完全以园林学为设计准则建立的公园。

the storm, defying the raging Atlantic winds[1]. A long, black stream of carriages poured down the avenue, intersected here and there by other streams, tending horizontally. There were a score of cabs about the entrance of his hotel, and his driver had to wait. Boys in livery[2] were running in and out of the awning that was stretched across the sidewalk, up and down the red velvet carpet laid from the door to the street. Above, about, within it all was the rumble and roar, the hurry and toss of thousands of human beings as hot for pleasure as himself, and on every side of him towered the glaring affirmation of the omnipotence of wealth[3].

The boy set his teeth and drew his shoulders together in a spasm of realization; the plot of all dramas, the text of all romances, the nerve-stuff of all sensations was whirling about him like the snow flakes. He burnt like a faggot in a tempest.

When Paul went down to dinner, the music of the orchestra came floating up the elevator shaft to greet him. His head whirled as he stepped into the thronged corridor, and he sank back into one of the chairs against the wall to get his breath. The lights, the chatter, the perfumes, the bewildering medley of color—he had, for a moment, the feeling of not being able to stand it. But only for a moment; these were his own people, he told himself. He went slowly about the corridors, through the writing-rooms, smoking-rooms, reception-rooms, as though he were exploring the chambers of an enchanted palace, built and peopled for him alone.

When he reached the dining-room he sat down at a table near a window. The flowers, the white linen, the many-colored wine glasses, the gay toilettes of the women, the low popping of corks, the undulating repetitions of the *Blue Danube*[4] from the orchestra, all flooded Paul's dream with bewildering radiance. When the rosy tinge of his champagne was added—that cold, precious, bubbling stuff that creamed and foamed in his glass—Paul wondered that there were honest men in the world at all. This was what all the world was fighting for, he reflected; this was what all the struggle was about. He doubted the reality of his past. Had he ever known a place called Cordelia Street, a place where fagged-looking business men got on the early car; mere rivets in a machine, they seemed to Paul—sickening men, with combings of children's hair always hanging to their coats, and the smell of cooking in their clothes. Cordelia Street—Ah! that belonged to another time and country; had he not always been thus, had he not sat here night after night, from as far back as he could remember, looking pensively over just such shimmering textures and slowly twirling the stem of a glass like this one between his thumb and middle finger? He rather thought he had.

He was not in the least abashed or lonely. He had no especial desire to meet or to know any of these people; all he demanded was the right to look on and conjecture, to watch the pageant. The mere stage properties[5] were all he contended for. Nor was he lonely later in the evening, in his loge at the Metropolitan[6]. He was now entirely rid of his nervous misgivings, of his forced aggressiveness, of

---

1. Atlantic winds：从大西洋吹来的风
2. in livery：穿着制服
3. the omnipotence of wealth：财富万能
4. *Blue Danube*：《蓝色多瑙河》圆舞曲，由奥地利作曲家约翰·施特劳斯(Johann Strauss, 1825—1899)创作。
5. stage properties：舞台道具
6. the Metropolitan：大都市，这里指纽约。

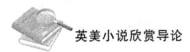

the imperative desire to show himself different from his surroundings. He felt now that his surroundings explained him. Nobody questioned the purple; he had only to wear it passively. He had only to glance down at his attire to reassure himself that here it would be impossible for anyone to humiliate him.

He found it hard to leave his beautiful sitting-room to go to bed that night, and sat long watching the raging storm from his turret window. When he went to sleep, it was with the lights turned on in his bedroom; partly because of his old timidity and partly so that, if he should wake in the night, there would be no wretched moment of doubt, no horrible suspicion of yellow wall-paper, or of Washington and Calvin above his bed.

Sunday morning the city was practically snowbound. Paul breakfasted late, and in the afternoon he fell in with[1] a wild San Francisco[2] boy, a freshman at Yale[3], who said he had run down for a "little flyer"[4] over Sunday. The young man offered to show Paul the night side of the town, and the two boys went out together after dinner, not returning to the hotel until seven o'clock the next morning. They had started out in the confiding warmth of a champagne friendship, but their parting in the elevator was singularly cool. The freshman pulled himself together to make his train and Paul went to bed. He awoke at two o'clock in the afternoon, very thirsty and dizzy, and rang for ice-water, coffee, and the Pittsburg papers.

On the part of the hotel management, Paul excited no suspicion. There was this to be said for him, that he wore his spoils with dignity[5] and in no way[6] made himself conspicuous. Even under the glow of his wine he was never boisterous, though he found the stuff like a magician's wand for wonder-building. His chief greediness lay in his ears and eyes, and his excesses were not offensive ones. His dearest pleasures were the gray winter twilights in his sitting-room; his quiet enjoyment of his flowers, his clothes, his wide divan, his cigarette, and his sense of power. He could not remember a time when he had felt so at peace with himself[7]. The mere release from the necessity of petty lying[8], lying every day and every day, restored his self-respect. He had never lied for pleasure, even at school, but to be noticed and admired, to assert his difference from other Cordelia Street boys; and he felt a good deal more manly, more honest even, now that he had no need for boastful pretensions, now that he could, as his actor friends used to say, "dress the part[9]." It was characteristic that remorse did not occur to him. His golden days went by without a shadow, and he made each as perfect as he could.

On the eighth day after his arrival in New York, he found the whole affair exploited in the Pittsburg papers, exploited with a wealth of detail which indicated that local news of a sensational nature was at a low ebb[10]. The firm of Denny & Carson announced that the boy's father had refunded the full amount of the theft, and that they had no intention of prosecuting. The Cumberland minister had been interviewed,

---

1. fell in with：偶然碰见
2. San Francisco：旧金山，美国加利福尼亚州西部港市
3. Yale：耶鲁大学
4. run down for a "little flyer"：来此体验一下"小小的冒险"
5. wore his spoils with dignity：穿戴着用诈骗的钱财买的衣饰，显得非常高贵
6. in no way：决不，一点不
7. at peace with himself：内心平静
8. petty lying：小小的谎言
9. dress the part：扮演好角色
10. local news of a sensational nature was at a low ebb：爆炸性的地方新闻逐渐减少

and expressed his hope of yet reclaiming the motherless boy[1], and his Sabbath-school teacher declared that she would spare no effort to that end[2]. The rumor had reached Pittsburg that the boy had been seen in a New York hotel, and his father had gone East to find him and bring him home.

Paul had just come in to dress for dinner; he sank into a chair, weak to the knees, and clasped his head in his hands. It was to be worse than jail, even; the tepid waters of Cordelia Street were to close over him finally and forever. The gray monotony stretched before him in hopeless, unrelieved years; Sabbath-school, Young People's Meeting, the yellow-papered room, the damp dish-towels; it all rushed back upon him with a sickening vividness. He had the old feeling that the orchestra had suddenly stopped, the sinking sensation that the play was over. The sweat broke out on his face[3], and he sprang to his feet, looked about him with his white, conscious smile, and winked at himself in the mirror. With something of the old childish belief in miracles with which he had so often gone to class, all his lessons unlearned, Paul dressed and dashed whistling down the corridor to the elevator.

He had no sooner entered the dining-room and caught the measure of the music than his remembrance was lightened by his old elastic power of claiming the moment, mounting with it, and finding it all sufficient. The glare and glitter about him, the mere scenic accessories had again, and for the last time, their old potency. He would show himself that he was game[4], he would finish the thing splendidly. He doubted, more than ever, the existence of Cordelia Street, and for the first time he drank his wine recklessly. Was he not, after all, one of those fortunate beings born to the purple, was he not still himself and in his own place? He drummed a nervous accompaniment to the *Pagliacci*[5] music and looked about him, telling himself over and over that it had paid.

He reflected drowsily, to the swell of the music and the chill sweetness of his wine, that he might have done it more wisely. He might have caught an outbound steamer and been well out of their clutches before now. But the other side of the world had seemed too far away and too uncertain then; he could not have waited for it; his need had been too sharp. If he had to choose over again, he would do the same thing tomorrow. He looked affectionately about the dining-room, now gilded with a soft mist. Ah, it had paid indeed!

Paul was awakened next morning by a painful throbbing in his head and feet. He had thrown himself across the bed without undressing, and had slept with his shoes on. His limbs and hands were lead heavy, and his tongue and throat were parched and burnt. There came upon him one of those fateful attacks of clear-headedness[6] that never occurred except when he was physically exhausted and his nerves hung loose[7]. He lay still and closed his eyes and let the tide of things wash over him.

His father was in New York; "stopping at some joint or other," he told himself. The memory of successive summers on the front stoop[8] fell upon him like a weight of black water. He had not a hundred

---

1. reclaiming the motherless boy:找回早年丧母的男孩
2. spare no effort to that end:不遗余力将此事进行到底,即找回这个孩子
3. The sweat broke out on his face:他满脸是汗
4. game:勇敢的
5. *Pagliacci*:雷翁卡伐洛的歌剧《丑角》
6. clear-headedness:头脑清醒
7. his nerves hung loose:神经放松
8. on the front stoop:即将来临的

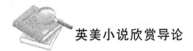

dollars left; and he knew now, more than ever, that money was everything, the wall that stood between all he loathed and all he wanted. The thing was winding itself up[1]; he had thought of that on his first glorious day in New York, and had even provided a way to snap the thread. It lay on his dressing-table now; he had got it out last night when he came blindly up from dinner, but the shiny metal hurt his eyes, and he disliked the looks of it.

    He rose and moved about with a painful effort, succumbing now and again to attacks of nausea. It was the old depression exaggerated; all the world had become Cordelia Street. Yet somehow, he was not afraid of anything, was absolutely calm; perhaps because he had looked into the dark corner at last and knew. It was bad enough, what he saw there, but somehow not so bad as his long fear of it had been. He saw everything clearly now. He had a feeling that he had made the best of it, that he had lived the sort of life he was meant to live, and for half an hour he sat staring at the revolver. But he told himself that was not the way, so he went down stairs and took a cab to the ferry.

    When Paul arrived at Newark, he got off the train and took another cab, directing the driver to follow the Pennsylvania[2] tracks out of the town. The snow lay heavy on the roadways and had drifted deep in the open fields. Only here and there the dead grass or dried weed stalks projected, singularly black, above it. Once well into the country, Paul dismissed the carriage and walked, floundering along the tracks, his mind a medley of irrelevant things. He seemed to hold in his brain an actual picture of everything he had seen that morning. He remembered every feature of both his drivers, of the toothless old woman from whom he had bought the red flowers in his coat, the agent from whom he had got his ticket, and all of his fellow-passengers on the ferry. His mind, unable to cope with vital matters near at hand, worked feverishly and deftly at sorting and grouping these images. They made for him a part of the ugliness of the world, of the ache in his head, and the bitter burning on his tongue. He stooped and put a handful of snow into his mouth as he walked, but that, too, seemed hot. When he reached a little hillside, where the tracks ran through a cut some twenty feet below him, he stopped and sat down.

    The carnations in his coat were drooping with the cold, he noticed; their red glory all over. It occurred to him that all the flowers he had seen in the glass cases that first night must have gone the same way, long before this. It was only one splendid breath they had, in spite of their brave mockery at the winter outside the glass, and it was a losing game in the end, it seemed, this revolt against the homilies by which the world is run. Paul took one of the blossoms carefully from his coat and scooped a little hole in the snow, where he covered it up. Then he dozed a while, from his weak condition, seemingly insensible to the cold.

    The sound of an approaching train awoke him, and he started to his feet, remembering only his resolution, and afraid lest he should be too late. He stood watching the approaching locomotive, his teeth chattering, his lips drawn away from them in a frightened smile; once or twice he glanced nervously sidewise, as though he were being watched. When the right moment came, he jumped. As he fell, the folly of his haste occurred to him with merciless clearness[3], the vastness of what he had left undone.

---

1. winding itself up：结束
2. Pennsylvania：宾夕法尼亚州，位于美国东部
3. with merciless clearness：清晰而残忍地

There flashed through his brain, clearer than ever before, the blue of Adriatic[1] water, the yellow of Algerian sands.

He felt something strike his chest, and that his body was being thrown swiftly through the air, on and on, immeasurably far and fast, while his limbs were gently relaxed. Then, because the picture-making mechanism[2] was crushed, the disturbing visions flashed into black, and Paul dropped back into the immense design of things.

Understanding the Text

Paul is a suspended middle school student in Pittsburgh. "Paul's Case" is the way Paul's teachers and father refer to him concerning his disinterest in school. The story is entitled in such a way that it enables the author to tell the story in the voice of medical authority. In other words the whole story is just like a medical analysis of Paul, the "patient," whose restlessness with his life and alienation from the society both in psychology and behaviour lead to his death, although we cannot say he is a patient in strict meaning because the young man just has a strong desire to live in his dream world. The subtitle of this story "A Study in Temperament" suggests that this story focuses on the temperament of the main character Paul.

The story is narrated chronologically. The two parts of the story relate what happens in Pittsburg and New York separately. The story begins with Paul's meeting after a week's suspense with the Principal and his teachers from the Pittsburgh High School who verbally attacked his demeanor within the bare, ugly walls of the school, with brief exposition of the setting of the story, background information for this meeting, and detailed description of Paul's clothes and bearing, especially "an opal pin in his neatly knotted black four-in-hand, and a red carnation in his buttonhole," which makes him look "something of the dandy" and "not properly significant of the contrite spirit befitting a boy under the ban of suspension." These expositions pave for the reader's understanding of what will happen next. At the meeting Paul always has a smile when his teachers complain of his agitation in class, and of his apparent aversion of other people's bodies. "His teachers were in despair" and believes that "There is something wrong about the fellow." After the meeting Paul "ran down the hill whistling the Soldiers' Chorus from Faust, looking wildly behind him, now and then, to see whether some of his teachers were not there to writhe under his light-heartedness." He goes to Carnegie Hall because he is on duty that evening as usher. He is early, so he loiters in the picture gallery, where he loses himself in pictures which "always exhilarated him." He then proceeds to usher the audience in; one of them is his English teacher. When the symphony begins, "the first sigh of the instruments seemed to free some hilarious and potent spirit within him" and

> *he felt a sudden zest of life; the lights danced before his eyes and the concert hall blazed into unimaginable splendor. When the soprano soloist came on, Paul forgot even the nastiness of*

---

1. Adriatic: 亚得里亚海的
2. picture-making mechanism: 编制图画的机器,这里指他的头。

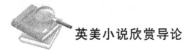

his teacher's being there and gave himself up to the peculiar stimulus such personages always had for him.

After the concert he follows some of the singers and marvels at their glamour. He then walks back to his house but decides to sneak into the basement and spend the night there so he doesn't have to explain to his father why he is late.

Paul's home and Cordelia Street make him feel frustrated and despondent, helpless to change the situation. At home he cannot gain his father's understanding and emotional support, and cannot stand "the sight of it all; his ugly sleeping chamber; the cold bathroom with the grimy zinc tub, the cracked mirror, the dripping spigots." Paul despises the "burghers" on his respectable but drab street, and is unimpressed by a plodding young man who works for a great steel corporation and is married with four children, although Paul's father would like to use him as a role model for Paul. These feelings are threatening to Paul, reflecting cowardice and fear. Paul, fearless of his teachers and the burghers of Cordelia Street, is frightened of being weak, terrified of becoming just like the people he has grown to detest!

Paul escapes his humdrum life through visiting Charley Edwards, a young actor who works at Carnegie Hall, where he fantasizes about the opera, romance, and the finer things that do not exist in his own life, and where music and art rapture Paul's soul and set it free. However, the dream world eventually makes it impossible for Paul to endure life in Pittsburgh and causes him to take drastic measures to fulfill his fantasies. Therefore sometime later, as Paul made it clear to one of his teachers that his job there was more important than his lessons, and his father prevents him from continuing to work there. Paul cannot endure the humdrum life at Pittsburg and takes a train to New York City.

He now works for Denny & Carson's and has stolen $2,000 for his trip. He checks in an expensive hotel, buys expensive clothes, wanders around the city, and meets a young San Franciscan who shows him around the nightlife until morning. His few days of living as a rich, privileged young man bring him more contentment than he has ever known before. On the eighth day, however, Paul reads in the Pittsburgh newspapers that the theft has been made public, and that his father has returned the money and is now on his way to New York City to fetch his son. Unable to face a return to his dull, middle class life in Pittsburgh, Paul decides to take a train and a cab in Pennsylvania and kills himself by jumping in front of a train. At this moment the story comes to its climax and the tension is momentarily resolved and the outcome is to be decided.

The story line is not complicated. When the story is narrated in chronological order, contrasts are made between Paul's feelings at school and home, and those in Carneigie Hall, and his life in New York and that in Pittsburg. Paul is depressed all the time when he is at school and home in Pittsburg, where his feelings of superiority and desire for the finer things in life make him a misfit in his own world and isolates him from the common, small-minded people he despises; and he is rapturous when he is at Carnegie Hall and New York, where he lives in his dream world. Paul has finally become the man of his dreams and truly believes this is the society in which he deserves to live the new life. Paul can now accept himself in his new role of nobility, which carries a unique sense of importance and power. Once the money runs out and "the orchestra had suddenly stopped," he knows "that the play was over." Paul stands alone at the dark fork in the road as the burden of his misfit life weighs heavily on his thin shoulders. He can no longer endure his drab existence and decides to "finish the thing splendidly." Darkness envelopes Paul as the gloomy shadow of fear comes back to haunt him, catching him unprepared:

The memory of successive summers on the front stoop fell upon him like a weight of black water. He had not a hundred dollars left; and he knew now, more than ever, that money was everything, the wall that stood between all he loathed and all he wanted... It was the old depression exaggerated; all the world had become Cordelia Street.

At this time, the power of free will holds hands with death. Paul takes a profound glimpse into his soul when the red flowers he is wearing are fading and his brave mockery against society fails to make a permanent change in his life:

The carnations in his coat were drooping with the cold, he noticed; their red glory all over. It occurred to him that all the flowers he had seen in the glass cases that first night must have gone the same way, long before this. It was only one splendid breath they had, in spite of their brave mockery at the winter outside the glass; and it was a losing game in the end, it seemed, this revolt against the homilies by which the world is run.

Paul stands shivering in the snow and waits for the coming of the train. "When the right moment came, he jumped." As his body flies through the air and falls, he instantly visualizes all the things he will never get to do, and "there flashed through his brain, clearer than ever before, the blue of Adriatic water, the yellow of Algerian sands." Even up to the end of his life, his ability to dream is still in motion in vivid colors.

Further Reading

Plot

Abrams, M. H. *A Glossary of Literary Terms*. Beijing: Foreign Language Teaching and Research Press, 2004.

Forester, E. M. *Aspects of the Novel*. Beijing: China Translation & Publishing Corporation, 2002.

Guerin, Wilfred L., et al. *A Handbook of Critical Approaches to Literature*. Beijing: Foreign Language Teaching and Research Press, 2004.

Gwynn, R. S. ed. *Literature: A Pocket Anthology*. New York: Addison-Wesley Educational Publishers Inc., 2002.

Hawthorn, Jeremy. *Studying the Novel: An Introduction*. London: Arnold, 1985.

Kennedy, X. J. and Diana Gioia. *Literature: An Introduction to Fiction, Poetry, and Drama*. 8th

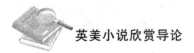

ed. New York: Longman, 2002.

Michael Meyer. *The Bedford Introduction to Literature*. 8th ed. Bedford/St. Martin's, 2008.

Shao Jindi and Bai Jinpeng. *An Introduction to Literature*. Shanghai: Shanghai Foreign Languages Education Press, 2002.

Scholes, Robert E, ed. *Elements of Fiction: An Anthology*. New York: Oxford University Press, 1981.

Paul's Case

Arnold, Marilyn. *Willa Cather's Short Fiction*. Athens: Ohio University Press, 1984.

Cather, Willa. *Willa Cather's Collected Short Fiction 1892—1912*. Ed. Virginia Faulkner. Lincoln: University of Nebraska Press, 1970.

Robinson, Phyllis. *Willa: The Life of Willa Cather*. New York: Doubleday, 1983.

Rubin, Larry. "The Homosexual Motif in Willa Cather's 'Paul's Case.'" *Studies in Short Fiction* 12.2 (Spring 1975): 127—31.

Summers, Claude J. "'A Losing Game in the End': Aestheticism and Homosexuality in Cather's 'Paul's Case.'" *Modern Fiction Studies* 36.1 (Spring 1990):103—19.

Chapter Two
Setting

Setting is also one of the fundamental components of fiction. It is the context in which the action of a story occurs. The major elements of setting include **time, place,** and **social and historical circumstances** that shape the characters. In most cases they provide the main backdrop and mood for a story. If we are sensitive to the contexts provided by setting, we are better able to understand the characters and their actions.

Some stories heavily depend on their locale or time setting and thus demand full exposition of setting. Historical fiction usually pays much attention to the altered landscapes and customs of bygone eras. Local color fiction depends heavily on the unique characteristics of a particular area, usually a rural one. Some southern writers, like William Faulkner or Flannery O'Connor, first established their reputations as practitioners of regionalism, setting most of their work in a particular area or country.

Setting is simply the time and place of a story, and in most cases a story may employ multiple locations in its different scenes, and its time structure may cover a few hours or many years. Novelists can give pages of details of setting, but short story writers, limited by space, must limit themselves to very selective descriptions of time and place. Some stories even have no particularly significant setting. "Reunion" has relatively few details of setting because Cheever wrote this story for *The New Yorker*, and the readers of this story are doubtlessly familiar with Grand Central Station, the famous landmark of New York. Similarly, he just gives brief descriptions of each of the restaurants with one or two sentences: One has "a lot of horse tack on the wall," one is "Italian," and the other two are not described at all. And the time setting is little mentioned. "Reunion" could be taking place today or twenty years from now. If, however, a shift in setting would make a serious difference to our understanding of a story, then the setting is probably an important element in the work.

Setting can be used to produce a mood or atmosphere that will prepare the reader for what is to come. Edgar Allan Poe makes enough detailed descriptions in "The Fall of the House of Usher" to produce the emotional atmosphere. In "Young Goodman Brown" Nathaniel Hawthorne describes in great detail a New England forest near the site of the seventeenth-century witch trials, where his protagonist leaves his wife and village one night to keep an appointment. The somber and threatening atmosphere is produced in his descriptive setting of Brown entering the forest:

> *He had taken a dreary road, darkened by all the gloomiest trees of the forest, which barely stood aside to let the narrow path creep through, and closed immediately behind. It was all as lonely as could be; and there is this peculiarity in such a solitude, that the traveler knows not who may be concealed by the innumerable trunks and the thick boughs overhead; so that he may yet be passing through an unseen multitude.*

Careful reading makes us aware "that the forest is not simply the woods, and it is a moral wilderness, where anything can happen"(Meyer, 183).

Besides specific settings, such as time, location, and the physical features, where the action takes place, the general setting of a story, what is called **enveloping action**, is also relevant to the overall purpose of a story. The general setting shows its sense of the "times" and how its characters interact with events and social currents in the larger world. In Faulkner's "A Rose for Emily," the setting—the changes in her southern town—is highly significant to the themes, characters, and events of the short story. It serves as a foil for Emily's firm hold on a lost past. Miss Emily is regarded as a relic from the past, as old-fashioned and peculiar as the "stubborn and coquettish decay" of her house. Refusing to accept modernity and change, she, along with her house, does not fits into the modern changes that are paving and transforming the town. Without the social context, you would probably consider this story "an account of a bizarre murder rather than an exploration of the conflicts Faulkner associated with the changing South"(Meyer, 183). Setting enlarges and deepens the meaning of Emily's actions. It is also impossible to read stories by Flannery O'Connor and not be made aware of the social changes that have transformed the rural South in the last thirty years of the 20th century.

William Faulkner (1897—1962)

William Faulkner was born of an old and important southern family, and grew up in Oxford, Mississippi. He spent most of his youth hunting, fishing, and playing baseball. But he was gifted at drawing and telling stories and wanted to be a writer. During World War I he was rejected from the U. S. Army Corps because he was too short, but was accepted for flight training in the Royal Canadian Air Force. He wanted to fly in combat, but gained no chance because the war was over before he could make his first solo flight.

Returning to Oxford, Mississippi, Faulkner continued to read and to write poetry, and studied for a while at the University of Mississippi. However, he was "a failed poet," just as Faulkner spoke of himself, and turned to fiction.

In 1925 he moved to New Orleans, where he knew Sherwood Anderson and his circle, and began to publish sketches in the Sunday feature section of the New Orleans Time-Picayune. Then, with the help of Anderson, he published his first novel, *Soldier's Pay* (1926). Except for some trips to Europe and Asia, and a few brief stays in Hollywood as a scriptwriter, he worked on his novels and short stories on a farm in Oxford.

Faulkner is best known for his Yoknapatawpha cycle, a series of novels of the decaying old American South, which started in 1929 with *Sartoris / Flags in the Dust* and completed with *The Mansion* in 1959. These novels, based on the history of the area around his home in Oxford, Mississippi, focus on an imaginary Mississippi county, Yoknapatawpha County, as represented by the Sartoris and Compson families, and the emergence of ruthless and brash newcomers, the Snopeses. Among his most highly regarded works are *Light in August* (1932), *Absalom, Absalom!* (1936), and two collections of short fiction: *The Unvanquished* (1938) and *Go Down, Moses* (1942). Faulkner was awarded the Nobel

Prize for Literature in 1949.

"A Rose for Emily" is Faulkner's first short story published in a national magazine. It was first published in the April 30, 1930 issue of *Forum*. This story takes place in Faulkner's fictional city, Jefferson, in his fictional county of Yoknapatawpha County, Mississippi.

 *Text*

A Rose for Emily

I

When Miss Emily Grierson died, our whole town went to her funeral: the men through a sort of respectful affection for a fallen monument[1], the women mostly out of curiosity to see the inside of her house, which no one save an old manservant—a combined gardener and cook—had seen in at least ten years.

It was a big, squarish frame house that had once been white, decorated with cupolas and spires and scrolled balconies in the heavily lightsome style of the seventies, set on what had once been our most select street[2]. But garages and cotton gins had encroached and obliterated even the august names of that neighborhood; only Miss Emily's house was left, lifting its stubborn and coquettish decay above the cotton wagons and the gasoline pumps—an eyesore among eyesores. And now Miss Emily had gone to join the representatives of those august names where they lay in the cedar-bemused cemetery among the ranked and anonymous graves of Union and Confederate[3] soldiers who fell at the battle of Jefferson[4].

Alive, Miss Emily had been a tradition, a duty, and a care; a sort of hereditary obligation upon the town, dating from that day in 1894 when Colonel Sartoris, the mayor—he who fathered the edict that no Negro woman should appear on the streets without an apron—remitted her taxes[5], the dispensation dating from the death of her father on into perpetuity. Not that Miss Emily would have accepted charity. Colonel Sartoris invented an involved tale to the effect that[6] Miss Emily's father had loaned money to the town, which the town, as a matter of business, preferred this way of repaying. Only a man of Colonel Sartoris' generation and thought could have invented it, and only a woman could have believed it.

When the next generation, with its more modern ideas, became mayors and aldermen[7], this arrangement created some little dissatisfaction. On the first of the year they mailed her a tax notice. February came, and there was no reply. They wrote her a formal letter, asking her to call at the sheriff's office at her convenience. A week later the mayor wrote her himself, offering to call or to send his car

---

1. the men through a sort of respectful affection for a fallen monument:男子们是出于敬慕之情,因为一个纪念碑倒下了。
2. most select street:最考究的街道
3. Union and Confederate:美国内战中的北部联邦军队和南方联盟军队
4. the battle of Jefferson:杰斐逊战役,美国内战中发生在 Port Jefferson 城的一场重要战役
5. remitted her taxes:免她的税
6. to the effect that:大意是,意思是
7. alderman:市议员

for her, and received in reply a note on paper of an archaic shape, in a thin, flowing calligraphy in faded ink, to the effect that she no longer went out at all. The tax notice was also enclosed, without comment.

They called a special meeting of the Board of Aldermen. A deputation waited upon her, knocked at the door through which no visitor had passed since she ceased giving china-painting lessons eight or ten years earlier. They were admitted by the old Negro into a dim hall from which a stairway mounted into still more shadow. It smelled of dust and disuse—a close, dank smell. The Negro led them into the parlor. It was furnished in heavy, leather-covered furniture. When the Negro opened the blinds of one window, they could see that the leather was cracked; and when they sat down, a faint dust rose sluggishly about their thighs, spinning with slow motes[1] in the single sun-ray. On a tarnished gilt easel[2] before the fireplace stood a crayon portrait of Miss Emily's father.

They rose when she entered—a small, fat woman in black, with a thin gold chain descending to her waist and vanishing into her belt, leaning on an ebony cane with a tarnished gold head. Her skeleton was small and spare[3]; perhaps that was why what would have been merely plumpness in another was obesity in her. She looked bloated, like a body long submerged in motionless water, and of that pallid hue. Her eyes, lost in the fatty ridges of her face, looked like two small pieces of coal pressed into a lump of dough as they moved from one face to another while the visitors stated their errand[4].

She did not ask them to sit. She just stood in the door and listened quietly until the spokesman came to a stumbling halt. Then they could hear the invisible watch ticking at the end of the gold chain.

Her voice was dry and cold. "I have no taxes in Jefferson. Colonel Sartoris explained it to me. Perhaps one of you can gain access to the city records and satisfy yourselves."

"But we have. We are the city authorities, Miss Emily. Didn't you get a notice from the sheriff, signed by him?"

"I received a paper, yes," Miss Emily said. "Perhaps he considers himself the sheriff . . . I have no taxes in Jefferson."

"But there is nothing on the books to show that, you see. We must go by the—"

"See Colonel Sartoris. I have no taxes in Jefferson."

"But, Miss Emily—"

"See Colonel Sartoris." (Colonel Sartoris had been dead almost ten years.) "I have no taxes in Jefferson. Tobe!" The Negro appeared. "Show these gentlemen out[5]."

II

So she vanquished them, horse and foot[6], just as she had vanquished their fathers thirty years before

---

1. mote:微尘,尘埃
2. on a tarnished gilt easel:在已经失去光泽的镀金画架上面
3. spare:瘦的
4. stated their errand:说明来意
5. Show these gentlemen out:送这些先生们出去
6. horse and foot:(常用作状语)骑兵和步兵共同地,全军地;全部地,彻底地

about the smell. That was two years after her father's death and a short time after her sweetheart—the one we believed would marry her—had deserted her. After her father's death she went out very little; after her sweetheart went away, people hardly saw her at all. A few of the ladies had the temerity to call, but were not received, and the only sign of life about the place was the Negro man—a young man then—going in and out with a market basket.

"Just as if a man—any man—could keep a kitchen properly," the ladies said; so they were not surprised when the smell developed. It was another link between the gross, teeming world and the high and mighty Griersons[1].

A neighbor, a woman, complained to the mayor, Judge Stevens, eighty years old.

"But what will you have me do about it, madam?" he said.

"Why, send her word to stop it," the woman said. "Isn't there a law?"

"I'm sure that won't be necessary," Judge Stevens said. "It's probably just a snake or a rat that nigger of hers killed in the yard. I'll speak to him about it."

The next day he received two more complaints, one from a man who came in diffident deprecation. "We really must do something about it, Judge. I'd be the last one in the world to bother Miss Emily[2], but we've got to do something." That night the Board of Aldermen met—three graybeards and one younger man, a member of the rising generation.

"It's simple enough," he said. "Send her word to have her place cleaned up. Give her a certain time to do it in, and if she don't..."

"Dammit[3], sir," Judge Stevens said, "will you accuse a lady to her face of smelling bad?"

So the next night, after midnight, four men crossed Miss Emily's lawn and slunk about the house like burglars, sniffing along the base of the brickwork and at the cellar openings while one of them performed a regular sowing motion with his hand out of a sack slung from his shoulder. They broke open the cellar door and sprinkled lime there, and in all the outbuildings. As they recrossed the lawn, a window that had been dark was lighted and Miss Emily sat in it, the light behind her, and her upright torso[4] motionless as that of an idol. They crept quietly across the lawn and into the shadow of the locusts that lined the street. After a week or two the smell went away.

That was when people had begun to feel really sorry for her. People in our town, remembering how old lady Wyatt, her great-aunt, had gone completely crazy at last, believed that the Griersons held themselves a little too high for what they really were. None of the young men were quite good enough for Miss Emily and such[5]. We had long thought of them as a tableau, Miss Emily a slender figure in white in the background, her father a spraddled silhouette in the foreground, his back to her and clutching a horsewhip, the two of them framed by the backflung front door. So when she got to be thirty and was still single, we were not pleased exactly, but vindicated; even with insanity in the family she wouldn't

---

1. Griersons: 指艾米丽所在的格里尔生家族
2. I'd be the last one in the world to bother Miss Emily: 我是最不愿意打扰艾米丽小姐的人。
3. Dammit: 该死的, 真他妈的
4. torso: (人体的)躯干
5. such: 艾米丽小姐这一类的女子

have turned down all of her chances if they had really materialized¹.

When her father died, it got about that the house was all that was left to her; and in a way, people were glad. At last they could pity Miss Emily. Being left alone, and a pauper, she had become humanized. Now she too would know the old thrill and the old despair of a penny more or less².

The day after his death all the ladies prepared to call at the house and offer condolence and aid, as is our custom. Miss Emily met them at the door, dressed as usual and with no trace of grief on her face. She told them that her father was not dead. She did that for three days, with the ministers calling on her, and the doctors, trying to persuade her to let them dispose of the body. Just as they were about to resort to law and force³, she broke down⁴, and they buried her father quickly.

We did not say she was crazy then. We believed she had to do that. We remembered all the young men her father had driven away, and we knew that with nothing left, she would have to cling to that which had robbed her, as people will.

III

She was sick for a long time. When we saw her again, her hair was cut short, making her look like a girl, with a vague resemblance to those angels in colored church windows—sort of tragic and serene⁵.

The town had just let the contracts for paving the sidewalks, and in the summer after her father's death they began the work. The construction company came with riggers and mules and machinery, and a foreman named Homer Barron, a Yankee⁶—a big, dark, ready man, with a big voice and eyes lighter than his face. The little boys would follow in groups to hear him cuss the niggers, and the niggers singing in time to the rise and fall of picks. Pretty soon he knew everybody in town. Whenever you heard a lot of laughing anywhere about the square, Homer Barron would be in the center of the group. Presently we began to see him and Miss Emily on Sunday afternoons driving in the yellow-wheeled buggy and the matched team of bays from the livery stable⁷.

At first we were glad that Miss Emily would have an interest, because the ladies all said, "Of course a Grierson would not think seriously of a Northerner, a day laborer." But there were still others, older people, who said that even grief could not cause a real lady to forget *noblesse oblige*⁸—without calling it *noblesse oblige*. They just said, "Poor Emily. Her kinsfolk should come to her." She had some

---

1. with insanity in the family she wouldn't have turned down all of her chances if they had really materialized:即使有疯癫的基因吧,可如果真有机会摆在她面前,她也不至于全部都拒绝吧。
2. Now she too would know the old thrill and the old despair of a penny more or less:她现在也能体会到那种多一便士便喜悦激动,少一便士便伤心绝望的感受了。即她现在该知道穷日子的感受了。
3. resort to law and force:诉诸法律和武力
4. break down:(精神等)垮掉,崩溃
5. sort of tragic and serene:带有几分悲怆和肃穆
6. Yankee:北方佬;(美国南北战争时期)北军士兵
7. driving in the yellow-wheeled buggy and the matched team of bays from the livery stable:驾着一辆轻便马车出游了。那辆黄轮车配上从马房中挑出的栗色骏马十分相称。
8. *noblesse oblige*:〈法语〉贵族的举止

kin in Alabama[1]; but years ago her father had fallen out with them over the estate of old lady Wyatt, the crazy woman, and there was no communication between the two families. They had not even been represented at the funeral.

And as soon as the old people said, "Poor Emily," the whispering began. "Do you suppose it's really so?" they said to one another. "Of course it is. What else could..." This behind their hands; rustling of craned silk and satin behind jalousies closed upon the sun of Sunday afternoon as the thin, swift clop-clop-clop of the matched team passed: "Poor Emily."

She carried her head high enough—even when we believed that she was fallen. It was as if she demanded more than ever the recognition of her dignity as the last Grierson; as if it had wanted that touch of earthiness to reaffirm her imperviousness[2]. Like when she bought the rat poison, the arsenic[3]. That was over a year after they had begun to say "Poor Emily," and while the two female cousins were visiting her.

"I want some poison," she said to the druggist. She was over thirty then, still a slight woman, though thinner than usual, with cold, haughty black eyes in a face the flesh of which was strained across the temples and about the eye-sockets as you imagine a lighthouse-keeper's face ought to look. "I want some poison," she said.

"Yes, Miss Emily. What kind? For rats and such? I'd recom—"

"I want the best you have. I don't care what kind."

The druggist named several. "They'll kill anything up to an elephant. But what you want is—"

"Arsenic," Miss Emily said. "Is that a good one?"

"Is... arsenic? Yes, ma'am. But what you want—"

"I want arsenic."

The druggist looked down at her. She looked back at him, erect, her face like a strained flag. "Why, of course," the druggist said. "If that's what you want. But the law requires you to tell what you are going to use it for."

Miss Emily just stared at him, her head tilted back in order to look him eye for eye, until he looked away and went and got the arsenic and wrapped it up. The Negro delivery boy brought her the package; the druggist didn't come back. When she opened the package at home there was written on the box, under the skull and bones: "For rats."

IV

So the next day we all said, "She will kill herself"; and we said it would be the best thing. When she had first begun to be seen with Homer Barron, we had said, "She will marry him." Then we said, "She will persuade him yet," because Homer himself had remarked—he liked men, and it was known

---

1. Alabama: 亚拉巴马州，位于美国南部，北接田纳西州，东界佐治亚州，南邻佛罗里达州，西与密西西比州接壤，西南濒墨西哥湾。
2. as if it had wanted that touch of earthiness to reaffirm her imperviousness: 仿佛她需要通过人性的那点弱点来重新肯定她那不受任何影响的尊严。
3. arsenic: 砒霜

that he drank with the younger men in the Elks' Club—that he was not a marrying man. Later we said, "Poor Emily" behind the jalousies as they passed on Sunday afternoon in the glittering buggy, Miss Emily with her head high and Homer Barron with his hat cocked and a cigar in his teeth, reins and whip in a yellow glove.

Then some of the ladies began to say that it was a disgrace to the town and a bad example to the young people. The men did not want to interfere, but at last the ladies forced the Baptist[1] minister—Miss Emily's people were Episcopal[2]—to call upon her. He would never divulge what happened during that interview, but he refused to go back again. The next Sunday they again drove about the streets, and the following day the minister's wife wrote to Miss Emily's relations in Alabama.

So she had blood-kin under her roof again and we sat back to watch developments. At first nothing happened. Then we were sure that they were to be married. We learned that Miss Emily had been to the jeweler's and ordered a man's toilet set in silver, with the letters H. B. on each piece. Two days later we learned that she had bought a complete outfit of men's clothing, including a nightshirt, and we said, "They are married." We were really glad. We were glad because the two female cousins were even more Grierson than Miss Emily had ever been.

So we were not surprised when Homer Barron—the streets had been finished some time since[3]—was gone. We were a little disappointed that there was not a public blowing-off, but we believed that he had gone on to prepare for Miss Emily's coming, or to give her a chance to get rid of the cousins. (By that time it was a cabal, and we were all Miss Emily's allies to help circumvent the cousins.) Sure enough, after another week they departed. And, as we had expected all along, within three days Homer Barron was back in town. A neighbor saw the Negro man admit him at the kitchen door at dusk one evening.

And that was the last we saw of Homer Barron. And of Miss Emily for some time. The Negro man went in and out with the market basket, but the front door remained closed. Now and then we would see her at a window for a moment, as the men did that night when they sprinkled the lime, but for almost six months she did not appear on the streets. Then we knew that this was to be expected too; as if that quality of her father which had thwarted her woman's life so many times had been too virulent and too furious to die[4].

When we next saw Miss Emily, she had grown fat and her hair was turning gray. During the next few years it grew grayer and grayer until it attained an even pepper-and-salt iron-gray, when it ceased turning. Up to the day of her death at seventy-four it was still that vigorous iron-gray, like the hair of an active man.

From that time on her front door remained closed, save for a period of six or seven years[5], when she was about forty, during which she gave lessons in china-painting. She fitted up[6] a studio in one of the

---

1. Baptist：浸信会，又称浸礼会，基督新教主要宗派之一，以《圣经》作为信仰和实践的最高权威。
2. Episcopal：圣公会，属于英国国教，是基督教新教的一个教派。
3. the streets had been finished some time since：街道铺路工程已经竣工好一阵子了。
4. which had thwarted her woman's life so many times had been too virulent and too furious to die：(她父亲的性格)使她作为女性的一生波折不断。这种性格太激烈，太狂暴，难以改变。
5. save for a period of six or seven years：除了六七年的时间
6. fit up：布置

downstairs rooms, where the daughters and granddaughters of Colonel Sartoris' contemporaries were sent to her with the same regularity and in the same spirit that they were sent to church on Sundays with a twenty-five-cent piece for the collection plate. Meanwhile her taxes had been remitted.

Then the newer generation became the backbone and the spirit of the town, and the painting pupils grew up and fell away and did not send their children to her with boxes of color and tedious brushes and pictures cut from the ladies' magazines. The front door closed upon the last one and remained closed for good[1]. When the town got free postal delivery, Miss Emily alone refused to let them fasten the metal numbers above her door and attach a mailbox to it. She would not listen to them.

Daily, monthly, yearly we watched the Negro grow grayer and more stooped, going in and out with the market basket. Each December we sent her a tax notice, which would be returned by the post office a week later, unclaimed. Now and then we would see her in one of the downstairs windows—she had evidently shut up the top floor of the house—like the carven torso of an idol in a niche, looking or not looking at us, we could never tell which. Thus she passed from generation to generation—dear, inescapable, impervious, tranquil, and perverse.

And so she died. Fell ill in the house filled with dust and shadows, with only a doddering Negro man to wait on her. We did not even know she was sick; we had long since given up trying to get any information from the Negro. He talked to no one, probably not even to her, for his voice had grown harsh and rusty, as if from disuse.

She died in one of the downstairs rooms, in a heavy walnut bed with a curtain, her gray head propped on a pillow yellow and moldy with age and lack of sunlight.

V

The Negro met the first of the ladies at the front door and let them in, with their hushed, sibilant voices and their quick, curious glances, and then he disappeared. He walked right through the house and out the back and was not seen again.

The two female cousins came at once. They held the funeral on the second day, with the town coming to look at Miss Emily beneath a mass of bought flowers, with the crayon face of her father musing profoundly above the bier and the ladies sibilant and macabre; and the very old men— some in their brushed Confederate uniforms—on the porch and the lawn, talking of Miss Emily as if she had been a contemporary of theirs, believing that they had danced with her and courted her perhaps, confusing time with its mathematical progression, as the old do, to whom all the past is not a diminishing road but, instead, a huge meadow which no winter ever quite touches, divided from them now by the narrow bottle-neck of the most recent decade of years.

Already we knew that there was one room in that region above stairs which no one had seen in forty years, and which would have to be forced[2]. They waited until Miss Emily was decently in the

---

1. The front door closed upon the last one and remained closed for good: 最后一个学生离开后，前门就关上了，而且永远关上了。
2. have to be forced: 需要被撬开

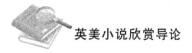

ground before they opened it.

The violence of breaking down the door seemed to fill this room with pervading dust. A thin, acrid pall as of the tomb seemed to lie everywhere upon this room decked and furnished as for a bridal: upon the valance curtains of faded rose color, upon the rose-shaded lights, upon the dressing table, upon the delicate array of crystal and the man's toilet things backed with tarnished silver, silver so tarnished that the monogram was obscured. Among them lay a collar and tie, as if they had just been removed, which, lifted, left upon the surface a pale crescent in the dust. Upon a chair hung the suit, carefully folded; beneath it the two mute shoes and the discarded socks.

The man himself lay in the bed.

For a long while we just stood there, looking down at the profound and fleshless grin. The body had apparently once lain in the attitude of an embrace, but now the long sleep that outlasts love, that conquers even the grimace of love, had cuckolded him. What was left of him, rotted beneath what was left of the nightshirt, had become inextricable from the bed in which he lay; and upon him and upon the pillow beside him lay that even coating of the patient and biding dust.

Then we noticed that in the second pillow was the indentation of a head. One of us lifted something from it, and leaning forward, that faint and invisible dust dry and acrid in the nostrils, we saw a long strand of iron-gray hair.

Understanding the Text

The setting established by William Faulkner in "A Rose for Emily" is highly successful. It provides the reader with background about the values and beliefs of the characters, helping the reader to understand the motivations, actions and reactions of Miss Emily and the rest of the town, and changing the mood or tone in the story. Thus it contributes to the theme of the story.

Faulkner sets the story in his fictitious post-Civil War Jefferson, a small town in the deep south of the United States. Faulkner's use of this particular time-period successfully gives the reader a background to understand the events, and values and beliefs of the characters in the story. The town of Jefferson is a fallen legacy. The town for which Colonel Sartoris, the Mayor, "fathered the edict that no Negro woman should appear on the streets without an apron" now has been faced with large social changes. Faulkner's contrast description of Miss Emily's house against the encroaching and inevitable forces of modernity reveals the social context in which Jefferson is located:

> It was a big, squarish frame house that had once been white, decorated with cupolas and spires and scrolled balconies in the heavily lightsome style of the seventies, set on what had once been our most select street. But garages and cotton gins had encroached and obliterated even the august names of that neighborhood; only Miss Emily's house was left, lifting its stubborn and coquettish decay above the cotton wagons and the gasoline pumps—an eyesore among eyesores.

Chapter Two Setting

Just as the town of Jefferson has now been encroached and obliterated and Miss Emily's house is becoming "an eyesore among eyesores," Miss Emily, the spinster daughter of the Griersons, one of the town's first families, who lives alone except for her lone servant, has become the only remnant of that greater time. This historical and social background gives the reader an understanding of the mindset of the "townspeople" who are telling us Miss Emily's story in a manner resembling a gossip circle.

Miss Emily has some eccentric or absurd actions. However, the reader's understanding of the setting keeps the story believable. Miss Emily becomes reclusive and introverted after the death of her father. She refuses to pay taxes and to have a mailbox or street numbers fastened to her house when the town of Jefferson receives free postal service. At the end of the story she goes as far as poisoning Barron Homer, a former beau who jilted her, keeping his dead body in her house, and sleeping next to him. All her eccentric or absurd actions actually betray her responses to the pressures placed on her by the town and her attempts to maintain the role of the southern women, dignified and proper while struggling with all the other issues in her life and dealing with the changes in the society.

Faulkner's setting also helps the reader understand the mentality and actions of the town. The townspeople seem oddly fascinated with Miss Emily as a relic of an older time. They have put her in a special position among the others. Although they have not maintained any direct contact with her for many years, they are still curious even after her death about her mystery. "When Miss Emily Grierson died, our whole town went to her funeral; the men through a sort of respectful affection for a fallen monument, the women mostly out of curiosity to see the inside of her house." There is one reason for this: As the times are changing, they need someone to uphold their southern majesty; as she is a Grierson, she is their only link to that past. When Emily was involved with Homer, they tried to correct her mistakes by calling on her cousins. For them Emily who was supposed to be of a higher class epitomizes morals and decency in the changing south. Since Emily is setting a bad example, they believed, they should do something to restore her moral standing for her. Therefore Miss Emily "had been a tradition, a duty, and a care." The townspeople protect her, and bend to her strong will. This enables her to behave in an imperious, high-handed way and refuse to be responsible for the murder of Homer.

Besides helping the reader understand the motivations and events in the story, the setting also changes the tone of the story. The descriptions that Faulkner gives and the images he conjures give the story gothic overtones. The following two quotations along with the first quotation above really produce such an effect:

> *They were admitted by the old Negro into a dim hall from which a stairway mounted into still more shadow. It smelled of dust and disuse—a close, dank smell. The Negro led them into the parlor. It was furnished in heavy, leather-covered furniture. When the Negro opened the blinds of one window they could see that the leather was cracked..., a faint dust rose sluggishly about their thighs...*
>
> *The violence of breaking down the door seemed to fill this room with pervading dust. A thin, acrid pall as the tomb seemed to lie everywhere upon this room decked and furnished as for a bridal: upon the valance curtains of faded red color, ...with tarnished silver, silver so tarnished that the monogram was obscured.*

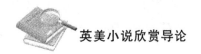

The image of the Grierson house which has the out-of-date structure and furnishings, the author's account of plumes of dust, cracked leather, and faded colors, the descriptions of lack of sunlight, varnished silver, molded material, and the mere fact that rotting corpses are left in household help to create a dreary environment and the gothic overtones. The physical setting parallel to the social change at the time can be used to symbolize the breakdown of the old structures of systems and the degradation and decay of its owner. And thus the theme of the story is revealed that privilege, constraining rather than liberating our true selves, can sometimes be a prison.

Further Reading

Setting

Abrams, M. H. *A Glossary of Literary Terms*. Beijing: Foreign Language Teaching and Research Press, 2004.

Forester, E. M. *Aspects of the Novel*. Beijing: China Translation & Publishing Corporation, 2002.

Guerin, Wilfred L., et al. *A Handbook of Critical Approaches to Literature*. Beijing: Foreign Language Teaching and Research Press, 2004.

Gwynn, R. S. ed. *Literature: A Pocket Anthology*. New York: Addison-Wesley Educational Publishers Inc., 2002.

Hawthorn, Jeremy. *Studying the Novel: An Introduction*. London: Arnold, 1985.

Kennedy, X. J. and Diana Gioia. *Literature: An Introduction to Fiction, Poetry, and Drama*. 8th ed. New York: Longman, 2002.

Michael Meyer. *The Bedford Introduction to Literature*. 8th ed. Bedford/St. Martin's, 2008.

Shao Jindi and Bai Jinpeng. *An Introduction to Literature*. Shanghai: Shanghai Foreign Languages Education Press, 2002.

Scholes, Robert E, ed. *Elements of Fiction: An Anthology*. New York: Oxford University Press, 1981.

A Rose for Emily

Allen, Dennis W. "Horror and Perverse Delight: Faulkner's 'A Rose for Emily.'" *Modern Fiction Studies* 30.4 (Winter 1984): 685—96.

Blotner, Joseph. *Faulkner: A Biography*. New York: Random House, 1974.

Gray, Richard J. *The life of William Faulkner*: A Critical Biography. Oxford; Cambridge, Mass.: Blackwell, 1994.

Volpe, Edmond Loris. *A Reader's Guide to William Faulkner*. New York: Octagon Books, 1983.

Watkins, Floyd C. "The Structure of 'A Rose for Emily.'" *Modern Language Notes* 69.7 (1954): 508—10.

Weinstein, Philip M. *The Cambridge Companion to William Faulkner*. Cambridge: Cambridge University Press, 1995.

Wilson, G. R., Jr. "The Chronology of Faulkner's 'A Rose for Emily' Again." *Notes on Mississippi Writers* 5.2(Fall 1972):43—62.

Chapter Three
Character

Character is essential to a literary story, and most writers attempt to create unique characters. The methods by which a writer creates people in a story who seem actually to exist are called **characterization**. A good writer gives us the illusion that a character is real, but we should remember that a character is not an actual person but instead has been imagined and created by the author. Huck Finn never lived, yet when we read Mark Twain's novel about his adventures along the Mississippi River we feel as if we knew him, just because in him we recognize human personalities that are familiar to us, and what he experiences with cheaters, lovers, and murderers nearly always are part of ourselves. However, we would not throw away the book in a fit of anger when we read Huck Finn's Pap talks about racist nonsense.

The main character of a story is called **protagonist**, a term drawn from ancient Greek tragedy. An opposing character, with whom the protagonist is drawn into conflict, is **antagonist**. In traditional stories a protagonist is usually a hero; in many modern stories, however, there is little, in any traditional sense, that is heroic about the protagonist; many a recent story has featured an **anti-hero**, who occupies center stage but seems incapable of fitting the traditional heroic mold. For example, the title character of "Paul's Case" is a social misfit, a thief, and finally suicidal.

Development and **motivation** are also important in any consideration of a story's characters. In a story which seems "true to life," its characters act in a reasonably consistent manner because its author has provided them with motivation: sufficient reason for a character's actions. This does not mean that all authors insist that their characters behave with absolute consistency, for certain contemporary stories feature characters who sometimes act without any apparent reason. If a character should behave in a sudden and unexpected way, seeming to deny that he had a reason, sooner or later we will discover it. In general, development in a character is usually clear in a story, but motivation may not be so obvious. In many cases, an author will simply tell usually what is going on in a character's mind, but in others we are denied access to this level of understanding. In some stories, writers may try to give a direct presentation of a character's thoughts by using interior monologue or stream-of-consciousness.

Characters can be either **static** or **dynamic** depending on the degree to which they change or develop in the course of the story. Some critics call a **fixed** character static; a **changing** one, dynamic. In "Reunion," the father is a static character. There is no change in his personality which was fixed long before the story opens. But Charlie does attain some understanding after he experiences disillusionments with his father.

Characters in a story may seem **flat** or **round**, depending on the depth of detail the writer supplies. Flat characters in stories are often **stock characters, stereotypes,** who may be necessary just for the development of the plot, and they usually have only one or at most a few outstanding features, and tend to stay the same throughout a story. Round characters, however, present us with more facets, some of which may even seem contradictory and are explored in depth as the author portrays them in more generous detail and delves into the characters, past and even into their unconscious mind. Such a round character may appear to us only as he appears to the other characters in the story. If their views of him differ, we will see him from more than one side. Moreover, round characters often change—learn or become enlightened, grow or deteriorate. This is not to regard a flat character as an inferior work of art. In most fiction—even the greatest—minor characters tend to be flat instead of round. This is because rounding them would cost time and space and their being enlarged might only distract us from the central characters. In "Reunion," the father is essentially a flat character who is given a few quick strokes of the pen and reduced to a single personality trait—his alcoholic rudeness while Charlie is a round character who becomes enlightened and grows.

Description of characters helps usually to understand the author's intent. In fiction, physical description invariably discloses what lurks beneath the surface. Considering the brevity of most short stories the authors just select the particular physical details. Cheever has Charlie describe his father at first as only "a big good-looking man." Then he uses his protagonist's sense of smell to make the character vivid: Charlie breathes in "a rich compound of whiskey, aftershave lotion, shoe, polish, woolens, and the rankness of a mature male." Similarly, actions in the story such as speech patterns and mannerisms may also reveal personality traits of a character. A character's misuse of grammar or stilted vocabulary can show usually a great deal more about his or her background and self-image than a whole page of background information or analysis. Charlie's father's gestures and loud attempts at ordering in various foreign languages come as a grotesque joke on himself.

A character is usually a person, but there are a few exceptions. In Jack London's *Call of the Wild*, the protagonist is a devoted sled dog, and in George Stewart's novel *Storm*, the protagonist is the wind; in Herman Melville's *Moby-Dick*, the antagonist is a whale; and in Richard Adams's *Watership Down*, the central characters are rabbits. Whatever the character is—whether an animal or even an inanimate object—it must have some recognizable human qualities. When we read a literary story we care about what happens to the characters and what they do; we may identify with a character's desires and aspirations, or we may be disgusted with his or her viciousness and selfishness. To understand our response to a story, we should be able to recognize the methods of characterization the author uses.

Flannery O'Connor (1925—1964)

Flannery O'Connor was born in Savannah, Georgia, the only child of a Catholic family of the Southern States. She graduated from the Peabody Laboratory School in 1942, and got a Social Sciences degree from Georgia State College for Women in 1945. In 1946 she was accepted into the prestigious Iowa Writers' Workshop. In 1951 she was diagnosed with disseminated lupus, of which her father died on February 1, 1941 when she was 15, and subsequently returned to her ancestral farm, Andalusia, in Milledgeville, Georgia, where she raised and nurtured ducks,

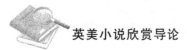

hens, geese, peacocks, and any sort of exotic bird she could obtain. She incorporates images of peacocks into her books and describes her peacocks in an essay entitled "The King of Birds." She died, at the age of 39, of complications from lupus at Baldwin County Hospital and was buried in Milledgeville, Georgia, at Memory Hill Cemetery. She never married, relying for companionship on her correspondence with such famous writers as Robert Lowell and Elizabeth Bishop and on her close relationship with her mother, Regina Cline O'Connor, while battling lupus.

O'Connor wrote two novels and 32 short stories, as well as a number of reviews, commentaries and letters, which earned her an important voice in American literature. As a Southern Catholic writer living in the "Bible Belt," the Protestant South, she often wrote in a Southern Gothic style and relied heavily on regional settings and grotesque characters, and her writings reflected her own Roman Catholic faith and frequently examined questions of morality and ethics.

O'Connor's short stories have been considered her finest work. With *A Good Man Is Hard to Find and Other Stories* (1955), she came to be regarded as a master of the form. *A Good Man Is Hard to Find and Other Stories* is a collection of short stories by O'Connor, whose subjects range from baptism to serial killers to human greed and exploitation. The short story "A Good Man Is Hard to Find" appears in this collection. The story title was taken from the blues song, "A Good Man Is Hard to Find," written by Eddie Green and popularized by singer Bessie Smith in 1927.

 *Text*

A Good Man Is Hard to Find

The grandmother didn't want to go to Florida. She wanted to visit some of her connections[1] in east Tennessee[2] and she was seizing at every chance to change Bailey's mind. Bailey was the son she lived with, her only boy. He was sitting on the edge of his chair at the table, bent over the orange sports section of the *Journal*. "Now look here, Bailey," she said, "see here, read this," and she stood with one hand on her thin hip and the other rattling the newspaper at his bald head. "Here this fellow that calls himself The Misfit[3] is aloose from the Federal Pen[4] and headed toward Florida[5] and you read here what it says he did to these people. Just you read it. I wouldn't take my children in any direction with a criminal like that aloose in it. I couldn't answer to my conscience[6] if I did."

Bailey didn't look up from his reading so she wheeled around then and faced the children's mother, a young woman in slacks, whose face was as broad and innocent as a cabbage and was tied round with a green head-kerchief that had two points on the top like rabbit's ears. She was sitting on the

---

1. connections: 亲戚
2. Tennessee: 田纳西州, 位于美国南部
3. The Misfit: 不适应环境的人, 与社会格格不入的人
4. aloose from the Federal Pen: 从联邦监狱中逃出来。Pen 为 Penitentiary 的缩写。
5. Florida: 佛罗里达州, 美国南部一州
6. I couldn't answer to my conscience: 我的良心上过不去。

sofa, feeding the baby his apricots out of a jar. "The children have been to Florida before," the old lady said. "You all ought to take them somewhere else for a change so they would see different parts of the world and be broad. They never have been to east Tennessee."

The children's mother didn't seem to hear her but the eight-year-old boy, John Wesley, a stocky child with glasses, said, "If you don't want to go to Florida, why dontcha[1] stay at home?" He and the little girl, June Star, were reading the funny papers on the floor.

"She wouldn't stay at home to be queen for a day," June Star said without raising her yellow head.

"Yes and what would you do if this fellow, The Misfit, caught you?" the grandmother asked.

"I'd smack his face," John Wesley said.

"She wouldn't stay at home for a million bucks[2]," June Star said. "Afraid she'd miss something. She has to go everywhere we go."

"All right, Miss," the grandmother said. "Just remember that the next time you want me to curl your hair."

June Star said her hair was naturally curly.

The next morning the grandmother was the first one in the car, ready to go. She had her big black valise that looked like the head of a hippopotamus in one corner, and underneath it she was hiding a basket with Pitty Sing, the cat, in it. She didn't intend for the cat to be left alone in the house for three days because he would miss her too much and she was afraid he might brush against one of the gas burners and accidentally asphyxiate[3] himself. Her son, Bailey, didn't like to arrive at a motel with a cat.

She sat in the middle of the back seat with John Wesley and June Star on either side of her. Bailey and the children's mother and the baby sat in front and they left Atlanta[4] at eight forty-five with the mileage on the car at 55890. The grandmother wrote this down because she thought it would be interesting to say how many miles they had been when they got back. It took them twenty minutes to reach the outskirts[5] of the city.

The old lady settled herself comfortably, removing her white cotton gloves and putting them up with her purse on the shelf in front of the back window. The children's mother still had on slacks and still had her head tied up in a green kerchief, but the grandmother had on a navy blue straw sailor hat with a bunch of white violets on the brim and a navy blue dress with a small white dot in the print. Her collars and cuffs were white organdy trimmed with lace and at her neckline she had pinned a purple spray of cloth violets containing a sachet. In case of an accident, anyone seeing her dead on the highway would know at once that she was a lady.

She said she thought it was going to be a good day for driving, neither too hot nor too cold, and she cautioned Bailey that the speed limit was fifty-five miles an hour and that the patrolmen hid themselves behind billboards and small clumps of trees and sped out after you before you had a chance to slow

---

1. dontcha：口语体，相当于 don't you
2. bucks：〈口〉美元
3. asphyxiate：使窒息
4. Atlanta：亚特兰大，美国佐治亚州首府
5. outskirts：边界

down. She pointed out interesting details of the scenery: Stone Mountain[1]; the blue granite that in some places came up to both sides of the highway; the brilliant red clay banks slightly streaked with purple; and the various crops that made rows of green lace-work on the ground. The trees were full of silver-white sunlight and the meanest of them sparkled. The children were reading comic magazines and their mother had gone back to sleep.

"Let's go through Georgia[2] fast so we won't have to look at it much," John Wesley said.

"If I were a little boy," said the grandmother, "I wouldn't talk about my native state that way. Tennessee has the mountains and Georgia has the hills."

"Tennessee is just a hillbilly dumping ground," John Wesley said, "and Georgia is a lousy state too."

"You said it," June Star said.

"In my time," said the grandmother, folding her thin veined fingers, "children were more respectful of their native states and their parents and everything else. People did right then. Oh look at the cute little pickaninny[3]!" she said and pointed to a Negro child standing in the door of a shack. "Wouldn't that make a picture, now?" she asked and they all turned and looked at the little Negro out of the back window. He waved.

"He didn't have any britches[4] on," June Star said.

"He probably didn't have any," the grandmother explained. "Little niggers[5] in the country don't have things like we do. If I could paint, I'd paint that picture," she said.

The children exchanged comic books.

The grandmother offered to hold the baby and the children's mother passed him over the front seat to her. She set him on her knee and bounced him and told him about the things they were passing. She rolled her eyes and screwed up her mouth and stuck her leathery thin face into his smooth bland one. Occasionally he gave her a faraway[6] smile. They passed a large cotton field with five or six graves fenced in the middle of it, like a small island. "Look at the graveyard!" the grandmother said, pointing it out. "That was the old family burying ground. That belonged to the plantation."

"Where's the plantation?" John Wesley asked.

"Gone With the Wind[7]," said the grandmother. "Ha. Ha."

When the children finished all the comic books they had brought, they opened the lunch and ate it. The grandmother ate a peanut butter sandwich and an olive and would not let the children throw the box and the paper napkins out the window. When there was nothing else to do they played a game by choosing a cloud and making the other two guess what shape it suggested. John Wesley took one the shape of a cow and June Star guessed a cow and John Wesley said, no, an automobile, and June Star said

---

1. Stone Mountain：石山公园，位于美国佐治亚州亚特兰大市东部。园中有石山，海拔1683英尺，自地面高出825英尺，为灰色花岗石。其北侧有世界上最大的峭壁浮雕，雕刻的是南北战争时期南方三位伟人骑马的英姿。
2. Georgia：佐治亚州，位于美国南部。
3. pickaninny：〈贬〉黑人小孩
4. britches：〈口〉裤子
5. nigger：对黑人的蔑称
6. faraway：朦胧的；心不在焉的
7. Gone With the Wind：双关语。美国作家玛格丽特·米切尔(Margaret Mitchell)的小说《飘》(Gone With the Wind)以南北战争为背景，反映了南方种植园的兴衰。这里祖母借用小说的名字表达"一切随风而去"的意思。

he didn't play fair¹, and they began to slap each other over the grandmother.

The grandmother said she would tell them a story if they would keep quiet. When she told a story, she rolled her eyes and waved her head and was very dramatic. She said once when she was a maiden lady she had been courted by a Mr. Edgar Atkins Teagarden from Jasper², Georgia. She said he was a very good-looking man and a gentleman and that he brought her a watermelon every Saturday afternoon with his initials cut in it, E. A. T. Well, one Saturday, she said, Mr. Teagarden brought the watermelon and there was nobody at home and he left it on the front porch and returned in his buggy³ to Jasper, but she never got the watermelon, she said, because a nigger boy ate it when he saw the initials, E. A. T.! This story tickled John Wesley's funny bone and he giggled and giggled but June Star didn't think it was any good. She said she wouldn't marry a man that just brought her a watermelon on Saturday. The grandmother said she would have done well to marry Mr. Teagarden because he was a gentleman and had bought Coca-Cola stock⁴ when it first came out and that he had died only a few years ago, a very wealthy man.

They stopped at The Tower⁵ for barbecued sandwiches. The Tower was a part stucco and part wood filling station and dance hall set in a clearing outside of Timothy⁶. A fat man named Red Sammy Butts ran it and there were signs stuck here and there on the building and for miles up and down the highway saying, TRY RED SAMMY'S FAMOUS BARBECUE. NONE LIKE FAMOUS RED SAMMY'S! RED SAM! THE FAT BOY WITH THE HAPPY LAUGH. A VETERAN! RED SAMMY'S YOUR MAN!

Red Sammy was lying on the bare ground outside The Tower with his head under a truck⁷ while a gray monkey about a foot high, chained to a small chinaberry tree, chattered nearby. The monkey sprang back into the tree and got on the highest limb as soon as he saw the children jump out of the car and run toward him.

Inside, The Tower was a long dark room with a counter at one end and tables at the other and dancing space in the middle. They all sat down at a board table next to the nickelodeon⁸ and Red Sam's wife, a tall burnt-brown woman with hair and eyes lighter than her skin, came and took their order. The children's mother put a dime in the machine and played "The Tennessee Waltz⁹," and the grandmother said that tune always made her want to dance. She asked Bailey if he would like to dance but he only glared at her. He didn't have a naturally sunny disposition like she did and trips made him nervous. The grandmother's brown eyes were very bright. She swayed her head from side to side and pretended she was dancing in her chair. June Star said play something she could tap to so the children's mother put in another dime and played a fast number and June Star stepped out onto the dance floor and

---

1. play fair:公平地比赛,做事公允
2. Jasper:佐治亚州皮肯斯县(Pickens County)的一个城市,也是皮肯斯县的县府所在地
3. buggy:(俚)双轮单座的轻马车
4. Coca-Cola stock:"可口可乐"公司的股票
5. The Tower:餐馆名
6. Timothy:佐治亚州一城市
7. with his head under a truck:正在车下面修车
8. nickelodeon:五分钱娱乐场,一种旧式自动点唱机
9. The Tennessee Waltz:《田纳西华尔兹》(有译作《田纳西圆舞曲》)。美国著名乡村歌手帕蒂·佩奇(Patti Page)的名曲,1951年全美十大畅销歌曲之首,20世纪50年代舞会必播经典曲目,被田纳西州选为州歌。

did her tap routine¹.

"Ain't she cute?" Red Sam's wife said, leaning over the counter. "Would you like to come be my little girl?"

"No I certainly wouldn't," June Star said. "I wouldn't live in a broken-down place like this for a million bucks!" and she ran back to the table.

"Ain't she cute?" the woman repeated, stretching her mouth politely.

"Aren't you ashamed?" hissed the grandmother.

Red Sam came in and told his wife to quit lounging on the counter and hurry up with these people's order. His khaki trousers reached just to his hip bones and his stomach hung over them like a sack of meal swaying under his shirt. He came over and sat down at a table nearby and let out a combination sigh and yodel². "You can't win," he said. "You can't win," and he wiped his sweating red face off with a gray handkerchief. "These days you don't know who to trust," he said. "Ain't that the truth?"

"People are certainly not nice like they used to be," said the grandmother.

"Two fellers come in here last week," Red Sammy said, "driving a Chrysler³. It was a⁴ old beat-up car but it was a good one and these boys looked all right to me. Said they worked at the mill and you know I let them fellers charge the gas they bought? Now why did I do that?"

"Because you're a good man!" the grandmother said at once.

"Yes'm⁵, I suppose so," Red Sam said as if he were struck with this answer.

His wife brought the orders, carrying the five plates all at once without a tray, two in each hand and one balanced on her arm. "It isn't a soul in this green world⁶ of God's that you can trust," she said. "And I don't count nobody out of that, not nobody," she repeated, looking at Red Sammy.

"Did you read about that criminal, The Misfit, that's escaped?" asked the grandmother.

"I wouldn't be a bit surprised if he didn't attact this place right here," said the woman. "If he hears about it being here, I wouldn't be none surprised to see him. If he hears it's two cent in the cash register, I wouldn't be a tall⁷ surprised if he..."

"That'll do," Red Sam said. "Go bring these people their Co'-Colas," and the woman went off to get the rest of the order.

"A good man is hard to find," Red Sammy said. "Everything is getting terrible. I remember the day you could go off and leave your screen door unlatched. Not no more."

He and the grandmother discussed better times. The old lady said that in her opinion Europe was entirely to blame for the way things were now. She said the way Europe acted you would think we were made of money and Red Sam said it was no use talking about it, she was exactly right. The children ran outside into the white sunlight and looked at the monkey in the lacy chinaberry tree. He was busy

---

1. tap routine: 踢踏舞舞步
2. yodel: 岳德尔歌,一种流行于瑞士和奥地利山民间的民歌,用真假嗓音反复变换唱法。
3. Chrysler: 克莱斯勒汽车,由美国克莱斯勒汽车公司生产
4. a: 应为 an。讲话人的文化程度不高,所以,语法和发音都不很规范。下文还有类似错误。
5. Yes'm: "Yes Madam"的口语形式
6. It isn't a soul in this green world: There isn't a soul in this good world.
7. a tall: 相当于 at all

catching fleas on himself and biting each one carefully between his teeth as if it were a delicacy[1].

They drove off again into the hot afternoon. The grandmother took cat naps[2] and woke up every few minutes with her own snoring. Outside of Toombsboro[3] she woke up and recalled an old plantation that she had visited in this neighborhood once when she was a young lady. She said the house had six white columns across the front and that there was an avenue of oaks leading up to it and two little wooden trellis arbors on either side in front where you sat down with your suitor after a stroll in the garden. She recalled exactly which road to turn off to get to it. She knew that Bailey would not be willing to lose any time looking at an old house, but the more she talked about it, the more she wanted to see it once again and find out if the little twin arbors were still standing. "There was a secret panel in this house," she said craftily, not telling the truth but wishing that she were, "and the story went that all the family silver was hidden in it when Sherman[4] came through but it was never found..."

"Hey!" John Wesley said. "Let's go see it! We'll find it! We'll poke all the woodwork and find it! Who lives there? Where do you turn off at? Hey Pop, can't we turn off there?"

"We never have seen a house with a secret panel!" June Star shrieked. "Let's go to the house with the secret panel! Hey, Pop, can't we go see the house with the secret panel!"

"It's not far from here, I know," the grandmother said. "It wouldn't take over twenty minutes."

Bailey was looking straight ahead. His jaw was as rigid as a horseshoe. "No," he said.

The children began to yell and scream that they wanted to see the house with the secret panel. John Wesley kicked the back of the front seat and June Star hung over her mother's shoulder and whined desperately into her ear that they never had any fun even on their vacation, that they could never do what THEY wanted to do. The baby began to scream and John Wesley kicked the back of the seat so hard that his father could feel the blows in his kidney.

"All right!" he shouted and drew the car to a stop at the side of the road. "Will you all shut up[5]? Will you all just shut up for one second? If you don't shut up, we won't go anywhere."

"It would be very educational for them," the grandmother murmured.

"All right," Bailey said, "but get this: this is the only time we're going to stop for anything like this. This is the one and only time."

"The dirt road that you have to turn down is about a mile back," the grandmother directed. "I marked it when we passed."

"A dirt road," Bailey groaned.

After they had turned around and were headed toward the dirt road, the grandmother recalled other points about the house, the beautiful glass over the front doorway and the candle-lamp in the hall. John Wesley said that the secret panel was probably in the fireplace.

"You can't go inside this house," Bailey said. "You don't know who lives there."

"While you all talk to the people in front, I'll run around behind and get in a window," John

---

1. delicacy: 美味佳肴
2. cat naps: 打瞌睡
3. Toombsboro: 一镇名
4. Sherman: William Tecumseh Sherman (1820—1891), 美国南北战争中北方军的将军
5. shut up: 闭嘴

Wesley suggested.

"We'll all stay in the car," his mother said.

They turned onto the dirt road and the car raced roughly along in a swirl of pink dust. The grandmother recalled the times when there were no paved roads and thirty miles was a day's journey. The dirt road was hilly and there were sudden washes[1] in it and sharp curves on dangerous embankments. All at once they would be on a hill, looking down over the blue tops of trees for miles around, then the next minute, they would be in a red depression with the dust-coated trees looking down on them.

"This place had better turn up in a minute," Bailey said, "or I'm going to turn around."

The road looked as if no one had traveled on it for months.

"It's not much farther," the grandmother said and just as she said it, a horrible thought came to her. The thought was so embarrassing that she turned red in the face and her eyes dilated and her feet jumped up, upsetting her valise in the corner. The instant the valise moved, the newspaper top she had over the basket under it rose with a snarl and Pitty Sing, the cat, sprang onto Bailey's shoulder.

The children were thrown to the floor and their mother, clutching the baby, was thrown out the door onto the ground; the old lady was thrown into the front seat. The car turned over once and landed right-side-up in a gulch[2] off the side of the road. Bailey remained in the driver's seat with the cat—gray-striped with a broad white face and an orange nose—clinging to his neck like a caterpillar.

As soon as the children saw they could move their arms and legs, they scrambled out of the car, shouting, "We've had an ACCIDENT!" The grandmother was curled up under the dashboard, hoping she was injured so that Bailey's wrath would not come down on her all at once. The horrible thought she had had before the accident was that the house she had remembered so vividly was not in Georgia but in Tennessee.

Bailey removed the cat from his neck with both hands and flung it out the window against the side of a pine tree. Then he got out of the car and started looking for the children's mother. She was sitting against the side of the red gutted ditch, holding the screaming baby, but she only had a cut down her face and a broken shoulder. "We've had an ACCIDENT!" the children screamed in a frenzy of delight.

"But nobody's killed," June Star said with disappointment as the grandmother limped out of the car, her hat still pinned to her head but the broken front brim standing up at a jaunty angle and the violet spray hanging off the side. They all sat down in the ditch, except the children, to recover from the shock. They were all shaking.

"Maybe a car will come along," said the children's mother hoarsely

"I believe I have injured an organ," said the grandmother, pressing her side, but no one answered her. Bailey's teeth were clattering. He had on a yellow sport shirt with bright blue parrots designed in it and his face was as yellow as the shirt. The grandmother decided that she would not mention that the house was in Tennessee.

The road was about ten feet above and they could see only the tops of the trees on the other side of

---

1. washes: 洼地
2. gulch: 峡谷

it. Behind the ditch they were sitting in there were more woods, tall and dark and deep. In a few minutes they saw a car some distance away on top of a hill, coming slowly as if the occupants were watching them. The grandmother stood up and waved both arms dramatically to attract their attention. The car continued to come on slowly, disappeared around a bend and appeared again, moving even slower, on top of the hill they had gone over. It was a big black battered hearse-like automobile. There were three men in it.

It came to a stop just over them and for some minutes, the driver looked down with a steady expressionless gaze to where they were sitting, and didn't speak. Then he turned his head and muttered something to the other two and they got out. One was a fat boy in black trousers and a red sweat shirt with a silver stallion embossed on the front of it. He moved around on the right side of them and stood staring, his mouth partly open in a kind of loose grin. The other had on khaki pants and a blue striped coat and a gray hat pulled down very low, hiding most of his face. He came around slowly on the left side. Neither spoke.

The driver got out of the car and stood by the side of it, looking down at them. He was an older man than the other two. His hair was just beginning to gray and he wore silver-rimmed spectacles that gave him a scholarly look. He had a long creased face and didn't have on any shirt or undershirt. He had on blue jeans that were too tight for him and was holding a black hat and a gun. The two boys also had guns.

"We've had an ACCIDENT!" the children screamed.

The grandmother had the peculiar feeling that the bespectacled man was someone she knew. His face was as familiar to her as if she had known him all her life but she could not recall who he was. He moved away from the car and began to come down the embankment, placing his feet carefully so that he wouldn't slip. He had on tan and white shoes and no socks, and his ankles were red and thin. "Good afternoon," he said. "I see you all had you a little spill."

"We turned over twice!" said the grandmother.

"Oncet[1]," he corrected. "We seen it happen. Try their car and see will it run, Hiram," he said quietly to the boy with the gray hat.

"What you got that gun for?" John Wesley asked. "Whatcha gonna do with that gun[2]?"

"Lady," the man said to the children's mother, "would you mind calling them children to sit down by you? Children make me nervous. I want all you all to sit down right together there where you're at."

"What are you telling US what to do for?" June Star asked.

Behind them the line of woods gaped like a dark open mouth. "Come here," said their mother.

"Look here now," Bailey began suddenly, "we're in a predicament! We're in..."

The grandmother shrieked. She scrambled to her feet and stood staring. "You're The Misfit!" she said. "I recognized you at once!"

"Yes'm," the man said, smiling slightly as if he were pleased in spite of himself to be known, "but it would have been better for all of you, lady, if you hadn't of reckernized me[3]."

---

1. oncet = once
2. Whatcha gonna do with that gun?=What are you going to do with that gun
3. you hadn't of reckernized me=you hadn't recognizd me

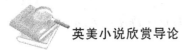

Bailey turned his head sharply and said something to his mother that shocked even the children. The old lady began to cry and The Misfit reddened.

"Lady," he said, "don't you get upset. Sometimes a man says things he don't mean. I don't reckon he meant to talk to you thataway[1]."

"You wouldn't shoot a lady, would you?" the grandmother said and removed a clean handkerchief from her cuff and began to slap at her eyes with it.

The Misfit pointed the toe of his shoe into the ground and made a little hole and then covered it up again. "I would hate to have to," he said.

"Listen," the grandmother almost screamed, "I know you're a good man. You don't look a bit like you have common blood[2]. I know you must come from nice people!"

"Yes mam," he said, "finest people in the world." When he smiled he showed a row of strong white teeth. "God never made a finer woman than my mother and my daddy's heart was pure gold," he said. The boy with the red sweat shirt had come around behind them and was standing with his gun at his hip. The Misfit squatted down on the ground. "Watch them children, Bobby Lee," he said. "You know they make me nervous." He looked at the six of them huddled together in front of him and he seemed to be embarrassed as if he couldn't think of anything to say. "Ain't a cloud in the sky," he remarked, looking up at it. "Don't see no sun but don't see no cloud neither."

"Yes, it's a beautiful day," said the grandmother. "Listen," she said, "you shouldn't call yourself The Misfit because I know you're a good man at heart. I can just look at you and tell."

"Hush!" Bailey yelled. "Hush! Everybody shut up and let me handle this!" He was squatting in the position of a runner about to sprint forward but he didn't move.

"I pre-chate[3] that, lady," The Misfit said and drew a little circle in the ground with the butt of his gun.

"It'll take a half a hour to fix this here car," Hiram called, looking over the raised hood of it.

"Well, first you and Bobby Lee get him and that little boy to step over yonder with you," The Misfit said, pointing to Bailey and John Wesley. "The boys want to ask you something," he said to Bailey. "Would you mind stepping back in them woods there with them?"

"Listen," Bailey began, "we're in a terrible predicament! Nobody realizes what this is," and his voice cracked. His eyes were as blue and intense as the parrots in his shirt and he remained perfectly still.

The grandmother reached up to adjust her hat brim as if she were going to the woods with him but it came off in her hand. She stood staring at it and after a second she let it fall to the ground. Hiram pulled Bailey up by the arm as if he were assisting an old man. John Wesley caught hold of his father's hand and Bobby Lee followed. They went off toward the woods and just as they reached the dark edge, Bailey turned and supporting himself against a gray naked pine trunk, he shouted, "I'll be back in a minute, Mamma, wait on me[4]!"

---

1. thataway=that way
2. You don't look a bit like you have common blood：你看上去一点也不像出身卑微的人。
3. pre-chate=appreciate
4. wait on me=wait for me

Chapter Three Character

"Come back this instant!" his mother shrilled but they all disappeared into the woods.

"Bailey Boy!" the grandmother called in a tragic voice but she found she was looking at The Misfit squatting on the ground in front of her. "I just know you're a good man," she said desperately. "You're not a bit common!"

"Nome, I ain't a good man," The Misfit said after a second as if he had considered her statement carefully, "but I ain't the worst in the world neither. My daddy said I was a different breed of dog from my brothers and sisters. 'You know,' Daddy said, 'it's some that can live their whole life out without asking about it and it's others has to know why it is, and this boy is one of the latters[1]. He's going to be into everything!'" He put on his black hat and looked up suddenly and then away deep into the woods as if he were embarrassed again. "I'm sorry I don't have on a shirt before you ladies," he said, hunching his shoulders slightly. "We buried our clothes that we had on when we escaped and we're just making do until we can get better. We borrowed these from some folks we met," he explained.

"That's perfectly all right," the grandmother said. "Maybe Bailey has an extra shirt in his suitcase."

"I'll look and see terrectly[2]," The Misfit said.

"Where are they taking him?" the children's mother screamed.

"Daddy was a card[3] himself," The Misfit said. "You couldn't put anything over on him[4]. He never got in trouble with the Authorities though. Just had the knack of handling them."

"You could be honest too if you'd only try," said the grandmother. "Think how wonderful it would be to settle down and live a comfortable life and not have to think about somebody chasing you all the time."

The Misfit kept scratching in the ground with the butt of his gun as if he were thinking about it. "Yes'm, somebody is always after you," he murmured.

The grandmother noticed how thin his shoulder blades were just behind his hat because she was standing up looking down on him. "Do you ever pray?" she asked.

He shook his head. All she saw was the black hat wiggle between his shoulder blades. "Nome," he said.

There was a pistol shot from the woods, followed closely by another. Then silence. The old lady's head jerked around. She could hear the wind move through the tree tops like a long satisfied insuck of breath. "Bailey Boy!" she called.

"I was a gospel singer for a while," The Misfit said. "I been most everything. Been in the arm service, both land and sea, at home and abroad, been twict married, been an undertaker, been with the railroads, plowed Mother Earth, been in a tornado, seen a man burnt alive oncet," and he looked up at the children's mother and the little girl who were sitting close together, their faces white and their eyes glassy; "I even seen a woman flogged," he said.

"Pray, pray," the grandmother began, "pray, pray..."

---

1. It's some that can live their whole life out without asking about it and it's others has to know why it is, and this boy is one of the latters:有些人一辈子也不会对生活提出任何问题,而另一些人,他们一定要知道生活是什么,这个孩子属于后者。
2. terrectly=directly
3. a card:一个精明人
4. You couldn't put anything over on him:你捉弄不了他。

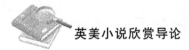

"I never was a bad boy that I remember of," The Misfit said in an almost dreamy voice, "but somewheres along the line I done something wrong and got sent to the penitentiary. I was buried alive," and he looked up and held her attention to him by a steady stare.

"That's when you should have started to pray," she said. "What did you do to get sent to the penitentiary that first time?"

"Turn to the right, it was a wall," The Misfit said, looking up again at the cloudless sky. "Turn to the left, it was a wall. Look up it was a ceiling, look down it was a floor. I forget what I done, lady. I set there and set there, trying to remember what it was I done and I ain't recalled it to this day. Oncet in a while, I would think it was coming to me, but it never come."

"Maybe they put you in by mistake." the old lady said vaguely.

"Nome," he said. "It wasn't no mistake. They had the papers on me."

"You must have stolen something," she said.

The Misfit sneered slightly. "Nobody had nothing I wanted," he said. "It was a head-doctor at the penitentiary said what I had done was kill my daddy but I known that for a lie. My daddy died in nineteen ought nineteen[1] of the epidemic flu and I never had a thing to do with it. He was buried in the Mount Hopewell Baptist churchyard and you can go there and see for yourself."

"If you would pray," the old lady said, "Jesus would help you."

"That's right," The Misfit said.

"Well then, why don't you pray?" she asked trembling with delight suddenly.

"I don't want no hep[2]," he said. "I'm doing all right by myself."

Bobby Lee and Hiram came ambling back from the woods. Bobby Lee was dragging a yellow shirt with bright blue parrots in it.

"Throw me that shirt, Bobby Lee," The Misfit said. The shirt came flying at him and landed on his shoulder and he put it on. The grandmother couldn't name what the shirt reminded her of. "No, lady," The Misfit said while he was buttoning it up, "I found out the crime don't matter. You can do one thing or you can do another, kill a man or take a tire off his car, because sooner or later you're going to forget what it was you done[3] and just be punished for it."

The children's mother had begun to make heaving noises as if she couldn't get her breath. "Lady," he asked, "would you and that little girl like to step off yonder with Bobby Lee and Hiram and join your husband?"

"Yes, thank you," the mother said faintly. Her left arm dangled helplessly and she was holding the baby, who had gone to sleep, in the other. "Hep that lady up, Hiram," The Misfit said as she struggled to climb out of the ditch, "and Bobby Lee, you hold onto that little girl's hand."

"I don't want to hold hands with him," June Star said. "He reminds me of a pig."

The fat boy blushed and laughed and caught her by the arm and pulled her off into the woods after Hiram and her mother.

---

1. nineteen ought nineteen:1919 年
2. I don't want no hep=I don't want help at all.
3. done=did

Chapter Three Character

Alone with The Misfit, the grandmother found that she had lost her voice. There was not a cloud in the sky nor any sun. There was nothing around her but woods. She wanted to tell him that he must pray. She opened and closed her mouth several times before anything came out. Finally she found herself saying, "Jesus. Jesus," meaning, Jesus will help you, but the way she was saying it, it sounded as if she might be cursing.

"Yes'm," The Misfit said as if he agreed. "Jesus thown[1] everything off balance. It was the same case with Him as with me except He hadn't committed any crime and they could prove I had committed one because they had the papers on me. Of course," he said, "they never shown me my papers. That's why I sign myself now. I said long ago, you get you a signature and sign everything you do and keep a copy of it. Then you'll know what you done and you can hold up the crime to the punishment and see do they match and in the end you'll have something to prove you ain't been treated right. I call myself The Misfit," he said, "because I can't make what all I done wrong fit what all I gone through in punishment[2]."

There was a piercing scream from the woods, followed closely by a pistol report. "Does it seem right to you, lady, that one is punished a heap and another ain't punished at all[3]?"

"Jesus!" the old lady cried. "You've got good blood! I know you wouldn't shoot a lady! I know you come from nice people! Pray! Jesus, you ought not to shoot a lady. I'll give you all the money I've got!"

"Lady," The Misfit said, looking beyond her far into the woods, "there never was a body that give the undertaker a tip."

There were two more pistol reports and the grandmother raised her head like a parched old turkey hen crying for water and called, "Bailey Boy, Bailey Boy!" as if her heart would break.

"Jesus was the only One that ever raised the dead[4]," The Misfit continued, "and He shouldn't have done it. He thown everything off balance. If He did what He said, then it's nothing for you to do but thow away everything and follow Him, and if He didn't, then it's nothing for you to do but enjoy the few minutes you got left the best way you can—by killing somebody or burning down his house or doing some other meanness to him. No pleasure but meanness," he said and his voice had become almost a snarl.

"Maybe He didn't raise the dead," the old lady mumbled, not knowing what she was saying and feeling so dizzy that she sank down in the ditch with her legs twisted under her.

"I wasn't there so I can't say He didn't," The Misfit said. "I wisht I had of been there[5]," he said, hitting the ground with his fist. "It ain't right I wasn't there because if I had of been there I would of known[6]. Listen lady," he said in a high voice, "if I had of been there I would of known and I wouldn't be like I am now." His voice seemed about to crack and the grandmother's head cleared for an instant. She saw the man's face twisted close to her own as if he were going to cry and she murmured, "Why

---

1. thown=threw
2. I can't make what all I done wrong fit what all I gone through in punishment=I can't make what all I have done wrong fit what all I have gone through in punishment：我无法把我所干的坏事与我所受的惩罚对应起来。
3. one is punished a heap and another ain't punished at all=one is punished a lot and another isn't punished at all
4. Jesus was the only One that ever raised the dead：耶稣是唯一能使死人复活的人。
5. I wisht I had of been there= I wished I had been there
6. if I had of been there I would of known=if I had been there I would have known

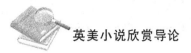

you're one of my babies. You're one of my own children!" She reached out and touched him on the shoulder. The Misfit sprang back as if a snake had bitten him and shot her three times through the chest. Then he put his gun down on the ground and took off his glasses and began to clean them.

Hiram and Bobby Lee returned from the woods and stood over the ditch, looking down at the grandmother who half sat and half lay in a puddle of blood with her legs crossed under her like a child's and her face smiling up at the cloudless sky.

Without his glasses, The Misfit's eyes were red-rimmed and pale and defenseless-looking. "Take her off and thow her where you thown the others," he said, picking up the cat that was rubbing itself against his leg.

"She was a talker, wasn't she?" Bobby Lee said, sliding down the ditch with a yodel.

"She would of been a good woman," The Misfit said, "if it had been somebody there to shoot her every minute of her life."

"Some fun!" Bobby Lee said.

"Shut up, Bobby Lee," The Misfit said. "It's no real pleasure in life."

Understanding the Text

"A Good Man Is Hard to Find" is a short story about an American family's journey to Florida. It is characteristic of O'Connor's stories which never give a specific reason for the trip. However, her message seems clear: the family's journey is nonspiritual; and modern Americans have lost their spiritual direction because of the declining role of religion in the 20th century society.

The characters in the story consists of the grandmother, Bailey Boy, the son of the grandmother, the mother, wife of Bailey, John Wesley and June Star, son and daughter of Bailey, and The Misfit, and his accomplices, Bobby Lee and Hiram. Of the characters, the grandmother and The Misfit are given more focus on than the other characters. They are the protagonist and antagonist of the story. The other characters are just flat and static characters which help with the development of the story. However, these minor characters have their roles in the representation of the theme of the story.

Hal Blythe makes a comparison in his "O'Connor's 'A Good Man Is Hard to Find'" between "A Goodman Is Hard to Find" and Chaucer's *The Canterbury Tales* in character, theme, and frame, and claims that "there is a possible parallel" between them. But he points out that O'Connor produces quite different characters and motifs from Chaucer's though both works "attempt to define the good man and good woman of their age within a Christian context." Whereas Chaucer's pilgrims contain all classes of church and secular personages, O'Connor limits her "pilgrims" to one lower-class family. Whereas Chaucer's pilgrims journey to Canterbury, a religious shrine, O'Connor's pilgrims journey to Florida, America's traditional vacation spot. Therefore, in contrast to Chaucer's pilgrims who search for the spiritual renewal, O'Connor's pilgrims are searching for the materialistic content.

The family's pilgrimage is directed by the host Bailey Boy. Contrast to Harry Bailly in *The Canterbury Tales*, who "is a forceful, humorous, manly individual"(Blythe) in charge of the pilgrims, Bailey Boy is "a nondescript, dour and submissive male in a laughable, parrot-covered shirt." "[H]e didn't have a naturally sunny disposition" and is manipulated by his mother and screaming children. The decline of authority of Bailey, to some extent, conveys the message of the decline of the role of spirit in the 20th century.

Each member of Bailey's family is driven by selfishness. And they just pursue their materials. The story opens with an unnamed grandmother complaining to her son, Bailey, and his family that she would rather go to Tennessee for vacation than Florida, the family's planned destination. When she tries to persuade her son and daughter-in-law into changing their plan, neither of them seems to hear her. And even her grandson John says, "If you don't want to go to Florida, why dontcha stay at home?" and her granddaughter says, "She[grandmother] wouldn't stay at home to be queen for a day."

When the family stops at The Tower, a "filling station and dance hall set in a clearing outside of Timonthy" and "beyond the influence of organized religion,"

"Bailey glares, the children whine, and the grandmother and Red Sam lament the passing of better times and better people." "Instead of communal wine, they drink Co'Colas, the recurring symbol of the materialistic New South (Ellis)." And Red Sam's wife sums up the cynical nature of the modern world: "It isn't a soul in the green world of God that you can trust." (Blythe)

As the trip progresses, the children reveal themselves as brats and June Star and her brother begin slapping each other. When the family passes through the town "Toombsboro," the grandmother makes the mistake of telling the children about a house with secret panels nearby. The children scream until Bailey concedes to take a detour and to visit the house. From all these, we cannot see love among the family members and may easily note the absence of respect and reverence for the family, and the elders. Each of the family members is driven by selfishness and pursuit of mammon. These minor characters without spiritual and moral consideration foreshadow what is later to come: ultimately, Bailey's family die because they have gone in search of a house filled with hidden "family silver" that has never been found.

In contrast to the flat characters, the grandmother is a round character who has more facets and is changing with the story. O'Connor gives much more information and description about her than any other character in the story. The grandmother, who exemplifies the southern women, is ruthlessly manipulative, selfish and materialistic. As the story begins, she wants to take the vacation to Tennessee instead of Florida. In order to force her son to change their plan, she even warns her son that if they go south, they'll run into the crazed killer, The Misfit, on the run heading for Florida, about whom she has read in a newspaper. Against his son, she takes her cat with her in the car. Trying to detour the family away from Florida, she tells stories about her childhood home, and incites her grandchildren to riotous defiance of their father until he gives in and agrees to follow the grandmother's directions to the house with secret panels that conceal treasure. When the grandmother's directions lead the family down an abandoned dirt road, she realizes that the house is, in fact, in Tennessee and not Georgia. Flustered, she upsets her cat, which attacks Bailey out of panics, resulting in the car being out of control and overturned into a ditch. Not wanting to face the consequences for giving the family improper information, the grandmother pretends to be injured in order to gain their sympathy. Though all these demonstrate that she is selfish and materialistic, what more straightly reveals that she is highly materialistic as well as selfish in moral is her tale about Mr. Teagarden—she regrets that she married the wrong beau because Teagarden became wealthy.

The grandmother is moralistic and self-righteously superior. While she makes the conversation with The Misfit, she repeatedly instructs him to pray and mentions Jesus. It easily reveals that the grandmother looks superior because she believes that she knows much more about religion even if she is thoroughly at the mercy of The Misfit. However, it turns out that she is no match for the Misfit, who has quicker wits and much deeper understanding of religion and his belief system. Therefore, no plead by the grandmother to save her own life when her family member is killed one by one has affected The Misfit. As The Misfit asks the grandmother if it seems right that Jesus was punished and he has escaped punishment in reply to her instructions of prayer, the grandmother responds in the only way she knows by clinging to her superficial beliefs about "good blood" and behaving as a gentleman would. The Misfit is angry with Christ for having given no physical evidence for His existence, therefore casting doubt about the legitimacy of Christianity. He explains that he does not want to waste his life serving a figure who may not exist, nor does he want to displease an almighty God who may exist. And actually The Misfit's deep frustration does not lie in whether Jesus does really personify the metaphysical, but in the fact that when we live in a world where the religious and spiritual doctrines of yesterday are no match for the scientific, coldly observation-based and amoral context of the modern world, we have no means with which to answer the animal violence of someone like The Misfit.

It is obvious that the grandmother has always been more concerned about looking like a good Christian than being a good Christian. However, the conversation between the grandmother and The Misfit gets the grandmother to realize that she helped to create The Misfit and that they are bound by kinship. In this way she gains grace in her own life and extends it to another. Before she is brutally shot to death by The Misfit, she reaches out to her killer, The Misfit, remarking, "Why you're one of my babies. You're one of my own children." "Even though she fails, her attempt is not lost on The Misfit, who remarks that through enduring a constant of violence, she would have been a good woman" (as opposed to a lady) (Desmond). And just as O'Connor explains, "at this point, she does the right thing, makes the right gesture..."

Further Reading

Character

Abrams, M. H. *A Glossary of Literary Terms*. Beijing: Foreign Language Teaching and Research Press, 2004.

Forester, E. M. *Aspects of the Novel*. Beijing: China Translation & Publishing Corporation, 2002.

Guerin, Wilfred L., et al. *A Handbook of Critical Approaches to Literature*. Beijing: Foreign Language Teaching and Research Press, 2004.

Gwynn, R. S. ed. *Literature: A Pocket Anthology*. New York: Addison-Wesley Educational Publishers Inc., 2002.

Hawthorn, Jeremy. *Studying the Novel: An Introduction*. London: Arnold, 1985.

Kennedy, X. J. and Diana Gioia. *Literature: An Introduction to Fiction, Poetry, and Drama*. 8th ed. New York: Longman, 2002.

Michael Meyer. *The Bedford Introduction to Literature*. 8th ed. Bedford/St. Martin's, 2008.

Shao Jindi and Bai Jinpeng. *An Introduction to Literature*. Shanghai: Shanghai Foreign Languages Education Press, 2002.

Scholes, Robert E, ed. *Elements of Fiction: An Anthology*. New York: Oxford University Press, 1981.

A Good Man Is Hard to Find

Blythe, Hal. "O'Connor's 'A Good Man Is Hard to Find'". *Explicator 55.1*(Fall 1996):49—51.

Bonney, William. "The Moral Structure of Flannery O'Connor's 'A Good Man Is Hard to Find.'" *Studies in Short Fiction* 27.3(Summer 1990):347—56.

Cash, W. J. *Flannery O'Connor: A Life*. Knoxville: University of Tennessee Press, 2002.

Doxey, William S. "A Dissenting Opinion of Flannery O'Connor's 'A Good Man Is Hard to Find'". *Studies in Short Fiction* 10.2(Spring 1973):199—204.

Flanner O'Connor. *Flannery O'Connor: The Complete Stories*. Ed. Robert Giroux. New York: Ferrar, Strauss, and Giroux, 1972.

Grimshaw, James A. *The Flannery O'Connor Companion*. Westport: Greenwood Press, 1981.

Paulson, S. M. *Flannery O'Connor: A Study of the Short Fiction*. Boston: Twayne Publishers, 1988.

Chapter Four
Point of View

Different from a politician's point of view on an issue which refers to his or her attitude toward an issue, **point of view** in fiction refers to the question of authority in the story, that is, who tells the story and how it is told. The teller of a story is termed as narrator. The **narrator** provides the reader with information about insight into characters and incidents, which are filtered through his or her own perspective, thus affecting the reader's understanding of the characters' actions. However, the narrator of a story is not the same person as the "real life" author. Mark Twain wrote the novel *Adventures of Huckleberry Finn*, but the narrator is Huck Finn.

The various points of view that storytellers draw on can be conveniently grouped into two broad categories: the first-person narrator and the thind-person narrator. The **first-person narrator** uses "I" or "we" to tell the story and is a participant in the action. The first-person narrator "I" presents the point of view of only one character's consciousness. The reader is restricted to the perceptions, thoughts, and feelings of that single character. Such a narrator may be a major character (Huck Finn, and Charlie in "Reunion") who may be close to the event in time.

A first-person narrator can, however, also be a minor character, an observer, who stands a little to one side, watching a story unfold that mainly concerns someone else. Faulkner uses an observer in "A Rose for Emily." In the story, we, the first-person narrator in the plural, represents the town people's view of Emily.

The ability of the narrator to tell the story accurately is very important. However, a narrator can be unreliable for a variety of reasons. Sometimes he might be innocent and inexperienced such as Huck Finn, whose youthful innocence characterizes a naive narrator. Huck Finn is too young to understand what happens around him and to interpret accurately what he sees. Sometimes he might lack self-knowledge or have mental problems. In whatever case, an **unreliable narrator** relates events in such a distorted manner that the reader, who has come to recognize the narrator's unreliability, literally has to go beyond the character's reporting to comprehend the situations described. Contemporary writers have been particularly fond of unreliable narrators.

The **third-person narrator** uses "he," "she," or "they" to tell the story and does not participate in the action as a character. In third-person stories the question of reliability is rarely an issue, but the matter of omniscience, the degree to which the "all-knowing" narrator can reveal the thoughts of characters, is. The omniscient narrator is all-knowing. The narrator knows everything about the characters' lives— their pasts, presents, and future—and may reveal their thoughts and feelings, and report their action and dialogue. The **limited omniscient narrator** is much confined than the omniscient narrator. The **limited omniscience** or **selective omniscience**, restricts the narrator to the thoughts and perceptions of either a major or a minor character. This point of view is perhaps the most flexible of all because it allows the writer to compromise between the immediacy of first-person narration and the mobility of third-person narration. Sometimes a narrator can see into more than one character, particularly in a long work that focuses on two or more characters alternately from one chapter to the next. The way people, places, and events appear to that character is the way they appear to the reader. The reader has access to the thoughts and feelings of the characters revealed by the narrator, but neither the reader nor the character has access to the inner lives of any of the other characters in the story.

Modern writers of fiction have developed many strategies in seeing into the character's mind. One is the technique of **stream of consciousness**, a phrase coined by psychologist William James to describe the procession of thoughts passing through the mind. This technique developed by modern writers such as James Joyce, Virginia Woolf, and William Faulkner takes the reader inside a character's mind to see his perceptions, thoughts, and sense impressions on a conscious or unconscious level which are not arranged by logic, but mingled randomly. Stream of consciousness writing usually occurs in relatively short passages, but modern writers like Joyce also makes an extended use of it in his novels. And his *Ulysses* is famous for its use of this technique.

Similar in method, an **interior monologue** is an extended presentation of a character's thoughts. Unlike the stream-of-consciousness method without order and logic, it might take the reader to stand behind the character who is speaking out loud to himself, for us to overhear.

In contrast to the limited omniscient point of view, the **dramatic point of view** or the **objective point of view** employs a narrator who does not enter the mind of any character but describes events from the outside. Reporting dialogue and action, and describing external details, he leaves us to infer their thoughts and feelings. So inconspicuous is the narrator that this point of view has been called "the fly on the wall."

Besides the common points of view just listed, uncommon points of view are possible. Possible also, but rarely used, is a story written in the second person, "you." Theoretically, in a story, it is usual for the writer to maintain one point of view from beginning to end, but it is also possible for the author to introduce more than one point of view into a single story. And he freely shifts the point of view in and out of the minds of many characters. In this way a writer may illustrates how the "truth" of any incident is always relative to the way in which it is witnessed.

Every point of view has its advantages and disadvantages. Writers choose a particular point of view to achieve particular effects because point of view determines what we know about the characters and events in a story. We should, therefore, be aware of who is telling the story and whether the narrator is reliable.

John Cheever (1912—1982)

John Cheever was an American novelist and short story writer, called "the Chekhov of the suburbs." His fiction is mostly set in the Upper East Side of Manhattan, the Westchester suburbs, old New England villages based on various South Shore towns around Quincy, Massachusetts, where he was born. Describing manners and morals of middle-class, suburban Americans, with an ironic humour is characteristic of

Cheever's fictions, whose main theme was the spiritual and emotional emptiness of life. Although it was his novels such as *The Wapshot Chronicle* (National Book Award, 1958), *The Wapshot Scandal* (William Dean Howells Medal, 1965), *Bullet Park* (1969), and *Falconer* (1977) that brought him to the attention of large audience, he is best remembered for his short stories, including "The Enormous Radio," "Goodbye, My Brother," "The Five-Forty-Eight," "The Country Husband," and "The Swimmer." And he is now recognized as one of the most important short fiction writers of the 20th century. The compilation of his short stories, *The Stories of John Cheever*, won the 1979 Pulitzer Prize for Fiction and the National Book Critics Circle Award. In this collection appears "Reunion."

"Reunion" is a story first published in the October 27th, 1962 issue of *The New Yorker*. It is set in New York where Charlie, a young boy's father lives. The story is told through the eyes of Charlie, who is recalling a meeting with his father who he hasn't seen since his mother divorced him three years ago. He meets up with his father during a stop over between trains.

Text

Reunion

The last time I saw my father was in Grand Central Station[1]. I was going from my grandmother's in the Adirondacks[2] to a cottage on the Cape[3] that my mother had rented, and I wrote my father that I would be in New York between trains for an hour and a half, and asked if we could have lunch together. His secretary wrote to say that he would meet me at the information booth at noon, and at twelve o'clock sharp I saw him coming through the crowd. He was a stranger to me—my mother divorced him three years ago and I hadn't been with him since—but as soon as I saw him I felt that he was my father, my flesh and blood, my future and my doom. I knew that when I was grown I would be something like him; I would have to plan my campaigns within his limitations[4]. He was a big, good-looking man, and I was terribly happy to see him again. He struck me on the back and shook my hand. "Hi, Charlie," he said. "Hi, boy. I'd like to take you up to my club, but it's in the Sixties, and if you have to catch an early train I guess we'd better get something to eat around here." He put his arm around me, and I smelled my father the way my mother sniffs a rose. It was a rich compound of whiskey, after-shave lotion, shoe, polish, woolens, and the rankness of a mature male. I hoped that someone would see us together. I wished that we could be photographed. I wanted some record of our having been together.

We went out of the station and up a side street to a restaurant. It was still early, and the place was empty. The bartender was quarreling with a delivery boy, and there was one very old waiter in a red coat

---

1. Grand Central Station: 中央车站,位于纽约曼哈顿
2. Adirondacks: 阿迪伦达克山区,美国纽约州东北部的一处山地
3. Cape: 科德角,位于美国马萨诸塞州东南部
4. I would have to plan my campaigns within his limitations: 我再怎么努力也就只能达到他那个程度了。

down by the kitchen door. We sat down, and my father hailed the waiter in a loud voice. "*Kellner*[5]!" he shouted. "*Garçon*[2]! *Camérière*[3]! You!" His boisterousness[4] in the empty restaurant seemed out of place[5]. "Could we have a little service here!" he shouted. "Chop-chop[6]." Then he clapped his hands. This caught the waiter's attention, and he shuffled over to our table.

"Were you clapping your hands at me?" he asked.

"Calm down, calm down, sommelier[7]," my father said. "If it isn't too much to ask of you—if it wouldn't be too much above and beyond the call of duty, we would like a couple of Beefeater Gibsons."

"I don't like to be clapped at," the waiter said.

"I should have brought my whistle," my father said. "I have a whistle that is audible only to the ears of old waiters. Now, take out your little pad and your little pencil and see if you can get this straight[8]: two Beefeater Gibsons. Repeat after me: two Beefeater Gibsons."

"I think you'd better go somewhere else," the waiter said quietly.

"That," said my father, "is one of the most brilliant suggestions I have ever heard. Come on, Charlie, let's get the hell out of here[9]!"

I followed my father out of that restaurant into another. He was not so boisterous this time. Our drinks came, and he cross-questioned me about the baseball season. He then struck the edge of his empty glass with his knife and began shouting again. "*Garçon*,! *Kellner*! *Camérière*! You! Could we trouble you to bring us two more of the same."

"How old is the boy?" the waiter asked.

"That," my father said, "is none of your God-damned business."

"I'm sorry, sir," the waiter said, "but I won't serve the boy another drink."

"Well, I have some news for you," my father said. "I have some very interesting news for you. This doesn't happen to be the only restaurant in New York. They've opened another on the corner. Come on, Charlie."

He paid the bill, and I followed him out of that restaurant into another. Here the waiters wore pink jackets like hunting coats, and there was a lot of horse tack on the walls. We sat down, and my father began to shout again. "Master of the hounds[10]! Tallyhoo[11] and all that sort of thing. We'd like a little something in the way of a stirrup cup. Namely, two Bibson Geefeaters."

"Two Bibson Geefeaters?" the waiter asked, smiling.

"You know damned well what I want," my father said angrily. "I want two Beefeater Gibsons, and make it snappy. Things have changed in jolly old England. So my friend the duke tells me. Let's see

---

1. kellner: 饭店服务员
2. *garçon*: 〈法语〉侍者, 服务员
3. *camérière*: 〈法语〉侍者, 服务员
4. boisterousness: 喧闹, 吵吵嚷嚷
5. out of place: 不合适, 格格不入
6. chop-chop: 快点, 赶快
7. *sommelier*: 〈法语〉斟酒服务生
8. get this straight: 把这个搞清楚, 把这个弄明白
9. Let's get the hell out of here: 我们快点离开这个鬼地方。
10. Master of the hounds: 猎狐队的头。此处是查理父亲对服务员的戏谑之词。
11. tallyhoo: 呔唷! (猎人发现狐狸时嗾使猎狗追逐所发出的叫喊)

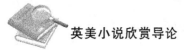

what England can produce in the way of a cocktail."

"This isn't England," the waiter said.

"Don't argue with me," my father said. "Just do as you're told."

"I just thought you might like to know where you are," the waiter.

"If there is one thing I cannot tolerate," my father said, "it is an impudent domestic[1]. Come on, Charlie."

The fourth place we went to was Italian. "*Buon giorno*[2]," my father said. "*Per favore, possiamo avere due cocktail americani, forti, forti. Molto gin, poco vermut*[3]."

"I don't understand Italian," the waiter said.

"Oh, come off it[4]," my father said. "You understand Italian, and you know damned well you do. V*ogliamo due cocktail americani. Subito*[5]."

The waiter left us and spoke with the captain[6], who came over to our table and said, "I'm sorry, sir, but this table is reserved."

"All right," my father said. "Get us another table."

"All the tables are reserved," the captain said.

"I get it," my father said. "You don't desire our patronage[7]. Is that it? Well, the hell with you[8]. *Vada all' inferno*[9]. Let's go, Charlie."

"I have to get my train," I said.

"I'm sorry, sonny," my father said. "I'm terribly sorry." He put his arm around me and pressed me against him. "I'll walk you back to the station. If there had only been time to go up to my club[10]."

"That's all right, Daddy," I said.

"I'll get you a paper," he said. "I'll get you a paper to read on the train."

Then he went up to a newsstand and said, "Kind sir, will you be good enough to favor me with one of your God-damned, no-good, ten cent afternoon papers?" The clerk turned away from him and stared at a magazine cover. "Is it asking too much, kind sir," my father said, "is it asking too much for you to sell me one of your disgusting specimens of yellow journalism?"

"I have to go, Daddy," I said. "It's late."

"Now, just wait a second, sonny," he said. "I want to get a rise out of this chap[11]."

"Goodbye, Daddy," I said, and I went down the stairs and got my train, and that was the last time I saw my father.

---

1. impudent domestic：无礼的家佣
2. *Buon giorno*：〈意大利语〉早上好。
3. *Per favore, possiamo avere due cocktail americani, forti, forti. Molto gin, poco vermut*：〈意大利语〉请给我们两杯美式烈鸡尾酒。多放点杜松子酒，少放些苦艾酒。
4. come off it：好了，住口
5. *Vogliamo due cocktail americani. Subito*：〈意大利语〉两杯美式鸡尾酒。快点。
6. the captain：领班
7. You don't desire our patronage：你们不希望我们光顾。
8. the hell with you：见鬼去吧
9. *Vada all' inferno*：〈意大利语〉下地狱去吧。
10. If there had only been time to go up to my club：要是有时间去我的俱乐部就好了。
11. get a rise out of this chap：去招惹一下这个家伙

Chapter Four   Point of View

Understanding the Text

"Reunion" is told by the first-person narrator, Charlie, a young boy, who is recalling a meeting with his father who he hasn't seen for more than three years. With its being narrated from his point of view, we are only restricted to Charlie's consciousness—his perceptions, emotions and feelings.

From the very beginning of the story we begin to be influenced by Charlie, and feel Charlie's strong expectation of the meeting with his father during a stop-over between trains, and his respect, admiration, and awe for his unknown father figure. This can be seen in the introduction to Charlie and his father in the first paragraph. Charlie goes to the trouble of writing his father and asking if they can have lunch together. "His[Father's] secretary wrote to say that he would meet me at the information booth at noon." The use of formal language during the communications between Charlie and his father produces the image of an ambitious businessman in the reader's mind, which is strengthened by his father's punctuality— "at 12 o'clock sharp I saw him coming." Charlie is anxious about his upcoming meeting with his father when he states "He was a stranger to me," which shows a distance between them. "But as soon as I saw him I felt he was my father" obviously implies to the reader that Charlie is a little more relaxed when he sees his father, because the word "father" powerfully expresses the relationship between the two characters. And quotes such as "I smelled my father the way my mother sniffs a rose... I hoped that someone would see us together. I wished that we could be photographed. I wanted some record of our having been together," "I was terribly happy to see him again," and " Hi Charlie, Hi boy!" lead us to believe how desperately Charlie hopes that the moment of the reunion is preserved in his memory and that he and his father are happy to see each other and have a good relationship.

However, the narrator's statements "he was my father, my flesh and blood, my future and my doom" allude to a severely depressed narrative viewpoint that has some apocalyptic suggestion while they indicate Charlie's strong wish for the close relationship with his father. And towards the end of the first paragraph we begin to get more of an insight into what Charlie's father is really like when he tells Charlie "I'd like to take you up to my club, but it's in the Sixties, and if you have to catch an early train I guess we'd better get something around here." What is evidently suggested in these statements is the father's snobbish tone which becomes more noticeable in the following paragraphs as he shows off to Charlie in the restaurants. And this threatens to waken Charlie from his perfect dream of the meeting with his father and influences the reader's attitude toward Charlie and his father.

Charlie experiences a state of confusion and shock when he and his father go to the first restaurant. Though the restaurant is almost entirely empty, his father uses such a loud and commanding voice that even Charlie observes that his father's "boisterousness in the empty restaurant seemed out of place." His father's sarcastic and rude behaviour reinforces Charlie's feeling of embarrassment and confusion when his father shouts at the waiter "'I have a whistle that is audible only to the ears of old waiters. Now, take out your little pad and your little pencil and see if you can get this straight...'" and "get the hell out" in response to the waiter's statement "I think you'd better go somewhere else."

And before Charlie spares time to get out of the embarrassment and shock, he has to encounter his

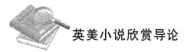

father's ignorance of him in the next restaurant. In this restaurant, when the waiter asks, "How old is the boy?" and Charlie's father responds, "That is none of your G (smudge) damned business." The father's response can be interpreted as his true ignorance of Charlie's age as well as his lack of involvement in Charlie's upbringing though it may be interpreted as the father's playing on the issue of Charlie's age. Whatever the case may be, Charlie at this point in the story is slowly beginning to realize what his father is like.

What Charlie sees in the third restaurant into which he is dragged is his father's authoritarian and almost paternal-like nature when his father retorts angrily to the waiter, "Don't argue with me. Just do as you're told." It is believed that Charlie would prefer to be a child of a divorced family than a child of a tyrannical father.

As Charlie and his father are denied service again in an Italian restaurant, in which they have their final chance to fill their stomachs, Charlie's father tells the waiters to "*Vada all' inferno*," which means "Go to hell." At this moment, Charlie is clearly aware of the similarity between the pattern of being booted from the restaurants and the role his father played in his life. Just as their experiences in restaurants represent an endless cycle of failure, disappointment, and rejections, Charlie has lived with disappointment and rejection from his father because his father failed to keep his marriage intact and was not involved in Charlie's life through that period of three years while he moved on with his life. Rejection is most damaging to Charlie's psyche because it is truly painful to feel insignificant and worthless in the eyes of his father.

As the whole story is told from Charlie's point of view, the reader is deeply involved in what Charlie genuinely experiences and feels, and how his feelings with his father are changing in the course of their meeting. Thus, the reader's attitudes towards the characters change: We begin to feel sorry for poor Charlie and show resent towards his father for ruining the time Charlie is spending with him. Though the development of the characters may be bias when it is told from the first-person narrator Charlie, we are allowed to subtly perceive the mix of Charlie's emotions: expectation and disappointment from his father. This effect cannot be created otherwise.

Therefore, at the end of the story, when Charlie has to leave for the train, he refers to his father as "Daddy" instead of "my father" which throughout the entire narration Charlie's dad is always referred to until the final moments of departure. The use of the intimate name of Daddy suggests that Charlie strongly hopes that he will finally find the ideal father that he yearned for during the lonesome years of his life, for he believes that if he believes in his dreams, they will come true.

Further Reading

Point of View

Abrams, M. H. *A Glossary of Literary Terms*. Beijing: Foreign Language Teaching and Research Press, 2004.

Forester, E. M. *Aspects of the Novel*. Beijing: China Translation & Publishing Corporation, 2002.

Guerin, Wilfred L., et al. *A Handbook of Critical Approaches to Literature*. Beijing: Foreign Language Teaching and Research Press, 2004.

Gwynn, R. S. ed. *Literature: A Pocket Anthology*. New York: Addison-Wesley Educational Publishers Inc., 2002.

Hawthorn, Jeremy. *Studying the Novel: An Introduction*. London: Arnold, 1985.

Kennedy, X. J. and Diana Gioia. *Literature: An Introduction to Fiction, Poetry, and Drama*. 8th ed. New York: Longman, 2002.

Michael Meyer. *The Bedford Introduction to Literature*. 8th ed. Bedford/St. Martin's, 2008.

Shao Jindi and Bai Jinpeng. *An Introduction to Literature*. Shanghai: Shanghai Foreign Languages Education Press, 2002.

Scholes, Robert E, ed. *Elements of Fiction: An Anthology*. New York: Oxford University Press, 1981.

Reunion

Booth, Wayne C. *A Rhetoric of Irony*. Chicago: University of Chicago Press, 1974.

Boscha, Francis J., ed. *The Critical Response to John Cheever*. Westport: Greenwood Press, 1994.

Cheever, John. *The Collected Stories of John Cheever*. New York: Ballantine, 1978.

Donaldson, Scott. *John Cheever: A Biography*. New York: Delta, 1988.

Shannon, Patrick. "Metonymy and Metaphor in the Fiction of John Cheever". Dissertation. Concordia University, 1998.

Waldeland, Lynn. *John Cheever*. Boston: Twayne Publishers, 1979.

Chapter Five
Theme

Theme in literary fiction refers to the central idea or the overall meaning the entire story reveals. It provides a unifying vision around which the plot, characters, setting, point of view, symbols, and other elements of a story are organized. In some stories the theme is unmistakable. However, a theme is not always so obvious, and determining the underlying meaning of a work often requires much effort because its theme is fused into the elements of the story and only a close reading and analysis of all the elements of the work as a whole can achieve sharp insights into the work. When we come to the end of a finely wrought short story such as "The Country of the Blind" by H. G. Wells, it may be easy to sum up the plot, but it may be difficult to sum up in a sentence the story's main idea.

Although themes are not always easy to express, some principles can help us express the central meaning of a work. First, distinguish between the theme of a story and its **subject**. Many stories share identical subjects, such as fate, death, innocence, youth, love and racial prejudice. Yet each story usually makes its own statement about the subject and expresses some view of life. "Hills like White Elephants" and "A Dill Pickle" both describe the relationship between lovers, but the meaning of each story is quite different. A thematic generalization about "Hills like White Elephants" could be something like this: The conflict between the romantic relationship and its responsibility for the family is usually the critical issue lovers have to be faced with. The theme of "A Dill Pickle" could be stated this way: The woman's sensitivity and the man's insensitivity to feelings, attitudes and inner motivations of the other frequently lead to the failure of their love affairs. Although the title of Isaac Bashevis Singer's "Gimple the Fool" focuses on the central character and suggests the subject—his foolishness, the theme of the story has less to do with foolishness than with how to be wise.

A literary work often contains more than one theme. There is no single, absolute way of expressing a work's theme. People have different responses to life and therefore it is not surprising that responses to a literary work are different. Furthermore, interpretations of themes of complex works are always subject to revision because cultural and ideological differences in different countries and historical periods, and new critical methods and theories are frequently modifying and expanding these interpretations.

Although readers may differ in their interpretations of a story, it does not mean that any interpretation is valid. To be valid, the statement of the theme must be based on evidence within a story rather than only on experiences, or values the reader brings to the work. The reader's experience with a war and his attitudes towards the war should not stand in the way of seeing the author's perspective.

Sometimes readers believe that a story's theme always consists of a moral. There are stories that do this—Hawthorne's "Young Goodman Brown," for example. And a moralist like Flannery O'Connor perceives her characters' shortcomings and judges them according to her own Roman Catholic moral standards. In fact, many stories go beyond traditional moral values to explore human behaviour instead of condemning or endorsing it.

Determining the theme of a story can be a difficult task because all the story's elements may contribute to its central idea. And there is no formula that can take us to the central meaning of a story and help us to state it accurately and clearly. However, we may find the following strategies practical and useful once we have read the story:

1. Look back once more at the title of the story. It often indicates the major symbol and the subject around which the theme develops.

2. Decide whether the main character in any way changes in the course of the story, and whether this character arrives at any eventual realization or understanding.

3. Pay attention to details in the story that may have symbolic meanings. Carefully consider curious objects, mysterious flat characters, significant animals, repeated names, song titles, and incidents that hint toward meanings larger than such things ordinarily have. This can lead you to the central theme.

4. Decide whether the author or the characters make any general observations about life or human nature.

5. Make sure that your expression of the theme is a general statement rather than just a plot summary, or a specific description of particular people, places, and incidents in the story.

6. Be certain that your statement hold true for the story.

Katherine Mansfield (1888—1923)

Katherine Mansfield, an outstanding short story writer, was born in Wellington, New Zealand. As the daughter of the successful businessman, Harold Beauchamp, she was educated at Queens College, London, where she met John Middleton Murry, a famous critic, whom she later married, and who introduced her to other important figures in the literary world such as D. H. Lawrence, Bertrand Russell, Ottoline Morrell, Leonard Woolf and Virginia Woolf. After the success of Mansfield's first collection of stories, *In the German Pension* (1911), she wrote regularly in London for the periodical *The New Age*. Mansfield did her best work in the early 1920s, and *Bliss and Other Stories* (1920) and *The Garden Party* (1922) secured her reputation as an important writer. Just as she won world fame, however, her health grew worse, and she died of tuberculosis in 1923. After her death two further collections of her short stories were published: *The Dove's Nest* (1923) and *Something Childish* (1924). John Middleton Murry edited and arranged for the publication of her *Journals* (1927) and *The Letters of Katherine Mansfield* (1928).

Mansfield was greatly influenced by Anton Chekhov, and was praised for her capturing the essence of Chekhov's art for stories. Just like Chekhov, her stories emphasize atmosphere and actual life rather than exciting plot, focus on depiction of trivial events and pay much attention to small details of human behavior. Her short stories are also notable for their use of stream of consciousness. Mansfield's creative years were burdened with loneliness, illness, jealousy, alienation—all of which are reflected in her work with the bitter depiction of marital and family

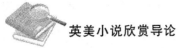

relationships of her middle-class characters.

"A Dill Pickle," a short story by Katherine Mansfield, was first published in *The New Age* on 4 October 1917 under the title "An Album Leaf." It was revised later and appeared in *Bliss and Other Stories*.

 Text

A Dill Pickle

And then, after six years, she saw him again. He was seated at one of those little bamboo tables decorated with a Japanese vase of paper daffodils. There was a tall plate of fruit in front of him, and very carefully, in a way she recognized immediately as his "special" way, he was peeling an orange.

He must have felt that shock of recognition in her for he looked up and met her eyes. Incredible! He didn't know her! She smiled; he frowned. She came towards him. He closed his eyes an instant, but opening them his face lit up as though he had struck a match in a dark room. He laid down the orange and pushed back his chair[1], and she took her little warm hand out of her muff and gave it to him.

"Vera!" he exclaimed. "How strange. Really, for a moment I didn't know you. Won't you sit down? You've had lunch? Won't you have some coffee?"

She hesitated, but of course she meant to.

"Yes, I'd like some coffee." And she sat down opposite him.

"You've changed. You've changed very much," he said, staring at her with that eager, lighted look. "You look so well. I've never seen you look so well before."

"Really?" She raised her veil and unbuttoned her high fur collar. "I don't feel very well. I can't bear this weather, you know."

"Ah, no. You hate the cold..."

"Loathe it[2]." She shuddered. "And the worst of it is that the older one grows..."

He interrupted her. "Excuse me," and tapped on the table for the waitress. "Please bring some coffee and cream." To her: "You are sure you won't eat anything? Some fruit, perhaps. The fruit here is very good."

"No, thanks. Nothing."

"Then that's settled[3]." And smiling just a hint too broadly he took up the orange again. "You were saying—the older one grows—"

"The colder," she laughed. But she was thinking how well she remembered that trick of his—the trick of interrupting her—and of how it used to exasperate her six years ago. She used to feel then as

---

1. pushed back his chair: 把椅子往后推了推
2. Loathe it: 讨厌寒冷的天气。"it"这里指"the cold"。
3. Then that's settled: 那就这些了

Chapter Five Theme

though he, quite suddenly, in the middle of what she was saying, put his hand over her lips, turned from her, attended to something different, and then took his hand away, and with just the same slightly too broad smile, gave her his attention again... Now we are ready. That is settled.

"The colder!" He echoed her words, laughing too. "Ah, ah. You still say the same things. And there is another thing about you that is not changed at all—your beautiful voice—your beautiful way of speaking." Now he was very grave; he leaned towards her, and she smelled the warm, stinging scent of the orange peel. "You have only to say one word and I would know your voice among all other voices. I don't know what it is—I've often wondered—that makes your voice such a—haunting memory[1]... Do you remember that first afternoon we spent together at Kew Gardens[2]? You were so surprised because I did not know the names of any flowers. I am still just as ignorant for all your telling me. But whenever it is very fine and warm, and I see some bright colours—it's awfully strange—I hear your voice saying: 'Geranium, marigold, and verbena.' And I feel those three words are all I recall of some forgotten, heavenly language... You remember that afternoon?"

"Oh, yes, very well." She drew a long, soft breath, as though the paper daffodils between them were almost too sweet to bear. Yet, what had remained in her mind of that particular afternoon was an absurd scene over the tea table. A great many people taking tea in a Chinese pagoda, and he behaving like a maniac about the wasps[3]—waving them away, flapping at them with his straw hat, serious and infuriated out of all proportion to the occasion[4]. How delighted the sniggering tea drinkers had been. And how she had suffered.

But now, as he spoke, that memory faded. His was the truer. Yes, it had been a wonderful afternoon, full of geranium and marigold and verbena, and—warm sunshine. Her thoughts lingered over the last two words as though she sang them.

In the warmth, as it were, another memory unfolded. She saw herself sitting on a lawn. He lay beside her, and suddenly, after a long silence, he rolled over and put his head in her lap.

"I wish," he said, in a low, troubled voice, "I wish that I had taken poison and were about to die—here now!"

At that moment a little girl in a white dress, holding a long, dripping water lily, dodged from behind a bush, stared at them, and dodged back again. But he did not see. She leaned over him.

"Ah, why do you say that? I could not say that."

But he gave a kind of soft moan, and taking her hand he held it to his cheek.

"Because I know I am going to love you too much—far too much. And I shall suffer so terribly, Vera, because you never, never will love me."

He was certainly far better looking now than he had been then. He had lost all that dreamy vagueness and indecision. Now he had the air of a man who has found his place in life, and fills it with a confidence

---

1. haunting memory: 不易忘怀的记忆
2. Kew Gardens: 英国皇家植物园。该园位于伦敦东南部的里奇蒙德和邱之间，濒临泰晤士河。这里生长着3万多种植物，2003年被联合国教科文组织列入世界自然遗产名录。
3. wasps: 黄蜂
4. out of all proportion to the occasion: 不合场合地

and an assurance which was, to say the least, impressive. He must have made money, too. His clothes were admirable, and at that moment he pulled a Russian cigarette case out of his pocket.

"Won't you smoke?"

"Yes, I will." She hovered over them. "They look very good."

"I think they are. I get them made for me by a little man in St. James's Street. I don't smoke very much. I'm not like you—but when I do, they must be delicious, very fresh cigarettes. Smoking isn't a habit with me; it's a luxury—like perfume. Are you still so fond of perfumes? Ah, when I was in Russia..."

She broke in: "You've really been to Russia?"

"Oh, yes. I was there for over a year. Have you forgotten how we used to talk of going there?"

"No, I've not forgotten."

He gave a strange half laugh and leaned back in his chair. "Isn't it curious. I have really carried out all those journeys that we planned. Yes, I have been to all those places that we talked of, and stayed in them long enough to—as you used to say, 'air oneself' in them. In fact, I have spent the last three years of my life travelling all the time. Spain, Corsica[1], Siberia[2], Russia, Egypt. The only country left is China, and I mean to go there, too, when the war is over."

As he spoke, so lightly, tapping the end of his cigarette against the ash-tray, she felt the strange beast that had slumbered so long within her bosom stir, stretch itself, yawn, prick up its ears, and suddenly bound to its feet, and fix its longing, hungry stare upon those far away places. But all she said was, smiling gently: "How I envy you."

He accepted that. "It has been," he said, "very wonderful—especially Russia. Russia was all that we had imagined, and far, far more. I even spent some days on a river boat on the Volga[3]. Do you remember that boatman's song that you used to play?"

"Yes." It began to play in her mind as she spoke.

"Do you ever play it now?"

"No, I've no piano."

He was amazed at that. "But what has become of your beautiful piano[4]?"

She made a little grimace[5]. "Sold. Ages ago."

"But you were so fond of music," he wondered.

"I've no time for it now," said she.

He let it go at that[6]. "That river life," he went on, "is something quite special. After a day or two you cannot realize that you have ever known another. And it is not necessary to know the language—the life of the boat creates a bond between you and the people that's more than sufficient. You eat with them, pass the day with them, and in the evening there is that endless singing."

She shivered, hearing the boatman's song break out again loud and tragic, and seeing the boat

---

1. Corsica：科西嘉，法国东南部一省
2. Siberia：西伯利亚，俄罗斯一地区
3. the Volga：伏尔加河，位于俄罗斯西部，是欧洲第一大河
4. what has become of your beautiful piano：你的漂亮的钢琴哪儿去了？
5. made a little grimace：做了个鬼脸，面露苦色
6. let it go at that：这个话题就此打住了

floating on the darkening river with melancholy trees on either side... "Yes, I should like that," said she, stroking her muff.

"You'd like almost everything about Russian life," he said warmly. "It's so informal, so impulsive, so free without question. And then the peasants are so splendid. They are such human beings—yes, that is it. Even the man who drives your carriage has—has some real part in what is happening. I remember the evening a party of us, two friends of mine and the wife of one of them, went for a picnic by the Black Sea[1]. We took supper and champagne and ate and drank on the grass. And while we were eating the coachman came up. 'Have a dill pickle,' he said. He wanted to share with us. That seemed to me so right, so—you know what I mean?"

And she seemed at that moment to be sitting on the grass beside the mysteriously Black Sea, black as velvet, and rippling against the banks in silent, velvet waves. She saw the carriage drawn up to one side of the road, and the little group on the grass, their faces and hands white in the moonlight. She saw the pale dress of the woman outspread and her folded parasol, lying on the grass like a huge pearl crochet hook. Apart from them, with his supper in a cloth on his knees, sat the coachman. "Have a dill pickle," said he, and although she was not certain what a dill pickle was, she saw the greenish glass jar with a red chili like a parrot's beak glimmering through. She sucked in her cheeks; the dill pickle was terribly sour...

"Yes, I know perfectly what you mean," she said.

In the pause that followed they looked at each other. In the past when they had looked at each other like that they had felt such a boundless understanding between them that their souls had, as it were, put their arms round each other and dropped into the same sea, content to be drowned, like mournful lovers. But now, the surprising thing was that it was he who held back. He who said:

"What a marvellous listener you are. When you look at me with those wild eyes I feel that I could tell you things that I would never breathe to another human being."

Was there just a hint of mockery in his voice or was it her fancy? She could not be sure.

"Before I met you," he said, "I had never spoken of myself to anybody. How well I remember one night, the night that I brought you the little Christmas tree, telling you all about my childhood. And of how I was so miserable that I ran away and lived under a cart in our yard for two days without being discovered. And you listened, and your eyes shone, and I felt that you had even made the little Christmas tree listen too, as in a fairy story."

But of that evening she had remembered a little pot of caviare. It had cost seven and sixpence. He could not get over it. Think of it—a tiny jar like that costing seven and sixpence. While she ate it he watched her, delighted and shocked.

"No, really, that is eating money. You could not get seven shillings into a little pot that size. Only think of the profit they must make..." And he had begun some immensely complicated calculations... But now good-bye to the caviare. The Christmas tree was on the table, and the little boy lay under the cart with his head pillowed on the yard dog.

"The dog was called Bosun," she cried delightedly.

---

1. the Black Sea: 黑海，欧亚大陆的一个内海，是连接东欧内陆和中亚、高加索地区出地中海的主要海路。

But he did not follow. "Which dog? Had you a dog? I don't remember a dog at all."

"No, no. I meant the yard dog when you were a little boy." He laughed and snapped the cigarette case.

"Was he? Do you know I had forgotten that. It seems such ages ago. I cannot believe that it is only six years. After I had recognized you today—I had to take such a leap—I had to take a leap over my whole life to get back to that time. I was such a kid then." He drummed on the table. "I've often thought how I must have bored you. And now I understand so perfectly why you wrote to me as you did—although at the time that letter nearly finished my life. I found it again the other day, and I couldn't help laughing as I read it. It was so clever—such a true picture of me." He glanced up. "You're not going?"

She had buttoned her collar again and drawn down her veil.

"Yes, I am afraid I must," she said, and managed a smile. Now she knew that he had been mocking.

"Ah, no, please," he pleaded. "Don't go just for a moment," and he caught up one of her gloves from the table and clutched at it as if that would hold her. "I see so few people to talk to nowadays, that I have turned into a sort of barbarian," he said. "Have I said something to hurt you?"

"Not a bit," she lied. But as she watched him draw her glove through his fingers, gently, gently, her anger really did die down, and besides, at the moment he looked more like himself of six years ago....

"What I really wanted then," he said softly, "was to be a sort of carpet—to make myself into a sort of carpet for you to walk on so that you need not be hurt by the sharp stones and mud that you hated so. It was nothing more positive than that[1]—nothing more selfish. Only I did desire, eventually, to turn into a magic carpet and carry you away to all those lands you longed to see."

As he spoke she lifted her head as though she drank something; the strange beast in her bosom began to purr...

"I felt that you were more lonely than anybody else in the world," he went on, "and yet, perhaps, that you were the only person in the world who was really, truly alive. Born out of your time[2]," he murmured, stroking the glove, "fated."

Ah, God! What had she done! How had she dared to throw away her happiness like this. This was the only man who had ever understood her. Was it too late? Could it be too late? She was that glove that he held in his fingers...

"And then the fact that you had no friends and never had made friends with people. How I understood that, for neither had I. Is it just the same now?"

"Yes," she breathed. "Just the same. I am as alone as ever."

"So am I," he laughed gently, "just the same."

Suddenly with a quick gesture he handed her back the glove and scraped his chair on the floor. "But what seemed to me so mysterious then is perfectly plain to me now. And to you, too, of course... It simply was that we were such egoists, so self-engrossed, so wrapped up in ourselves that we hadn't a corner in our hearts for anybody else. Do you know," he cried, naive and hearty, and dreadfully like another side of that old self again, "I began studying a Mind System when I was in Russia, and I found

---

1. nothing more positive than that：没有比这样做更好的了。"that"这里指将自己变成地毯让她在上面走这件事。
2. Born out of your time：不是你那个时代的人，与你的时代格格不入。

that we were not peculiar at all. It's quite a well-known form of..."

She had gone. He sat there, thunder-struck, astounded beyond words[1]... And then he asked the waitress for his bill.

"But the cream has not been touched," he said. "Please do not charge me for it."

Understanding the Text

"A Dill Pickle" is a story about Vera and an unnamed man who used to be lovers and meet at a restaurant after a six-year separation. The story is written in the modernist mode, without a set structure, and with many shifts in the narrative and human experiences in fragments. While readers are led to jump back and forth between now and six years ago, they have to piece together the fragments in their minds to come up with the overall meaning of the story, and one of the themes of this story: in the relationship between lovers, the woman's sensitivity and the man's insensitivity to feelings, attitudes and inner motivations of the other frequently lead to the failure of their love affair.

In the story, the author never states what either of the characters—Vera and the man—is really thinking about. From their reactions and movements, readers could derive things about the characters, their past relationship, and the places that they are at in their lives today. Therefore, right from the very beginning, readers act as being merely another patron sitting at the next table, watching and listening to everything that is happening between the two main characters. This theme is represented in the author's description of fine details of the two characters' changes in appearance, experience and career.

Six years ago Vera was a beautiful and happy girl and she seemed to have nothing to worry about; as one of the well-educated middle-class, she used to know a lot of flowers and enjoy the life of the leisure class. In contrast to Vera, the young man was poor, and absurd sometimes, with no confidence. When they spent the first afternoon at Kew Gardens he "did not know the names of any flowers" and behaved in an absurd manner: he behaved "like a maniac about the wasps—waving them away, flapping at them with his straw hat, serious and infuriated out of all proportion to the occasion." Therefore, Vera suffered much of the sniggering from tea drinkers in a Chinese pagoda. However, he was not sensitive to Vera's feeling at that time, but cared too much about his future sufferings from their love. When they were on a lawn, the man lay beside Vera, telling her that he would suffer so terribly because she would never love him. On a Christmas evening, a little pot of caviare costing seven and sixpence made him think "that is eating money."

Six years goes by, and both Vera and the man have changed much. The young man, who was handsome, but unpractical, dreamy, indecisive and vague about future and life, has grown to be a man with confidence and assurance; he has found his place in life, looking far better, wearing admirable clothes, and smoking Russian cigarette made for him "by a little man in St. James's Street." Although he is attractive, wealthy, experienced, and very sophisticated, he is as self-centered, insensitive, talkative, conceited, and inconsiderate as he was six years ago. For love, the man has ignored a lot and has

---

1. thunder-struck, astounded beyond words: 感到像五雷轰顶一样震惊，无法用语言来描述

forgotten even the woman he has once loved. He cannot recognize Vera immediately, and frowns at shock of recognition in her when she smiles at him. As for the important things for the love, he has "to take a leap over my whole life to get back to that time." Recognizing Vera, he shows no care about Vera, exaggerating "with that eager, lighted look" that "You've changed very much" and "I've never seen you look so well before," while Vera does not "feel well now." During the talk, he is in the dominant position all the time. Instead of being ready to listen to Vera, he repeats his "trick of interrupting her," telling Vera, lightly "tapping the end of his cigarette against the ash-tray," a long story of his own wonderful experience in Russia and other countries, which they planned to do together six years ago. All the talk he shows off his experience, even telling Vera he regards smoking as a luxury like perfume; he speaks with "a hint of mockery in his voice" which Vera perceives, and takes no notice of Vera's feelings and shows no care about how Vera lived her life during the past six years even if Vera says how she envies him for his experiences in Russia and that she has sold her piano because she has no time for it now. Therefore, readers cannot see his seriousness in dealing with his love with Vera and his genuine love for Vera.

While the man rises up, Vera, still one of the well-educated middle-class, declines. She "does not feel well" and is in a very difficult situation (she sold her piano despite her love of music). However, something in her has not changed. She says the same things, and her voice does not change at all. She treats love and her lover seriously and they are unforgettable in her mind. She still remembers "the warm sunshine" at Kew Garden, the "little girl in a white dress, holding a long, dripping water lily" and even the name of the dog the man told her of, but forgets now. She is still as considerate and sensitive to others' feelings as ever, not willing to hurt others. She does not tell the man her feelings although she is hurt all the time of their talk. When the man interrupts her and tells his wonderful experience in Russia, she says gently "How I envy you." When the man "caught up one of her gloves from the table and clutched at it" she suppresses her anger.

Vera is as romantic as ever, but she is more strong-willed and mature than ever, and knows what love is and what love means. She focuses much on spiritual life and resists the temptation. For her, without spiritual satisfaction, she would give up. Vera's life is very dull. She is looking forward to the meeting with the man, but it turns out to be no satisfaction at all. Her meeting with the man is just like the bitter dill pickle which can be only used as an appetizer rather than a main course. A dill pickle is rather bitter in taste, and the reader gets the impression, throughout the whole conversation, that Vera is sort of bitter towards the man she is talking to. When he looks back on all of the fond memories he has had with Vera, Vera is bitter about something that happened there. However, the meeting serves as an appetizer just as a stone is thrown into the motionless water and stirs up various desires to break the dull life of Vera.

As he spoke, so lightly, tapping the end of his cigarette against the ash-tray, she felt the strange beast that had slumbered so long within her bosom stir, stretch itself, yawn, prick up its ears, and suddenly bound to its feet, and fix its longing, hungry stare upon those far away places.

Her strong long-cherished desire to travel to all those distant and mysterious places was hidden deep in her heart for quite a long time because it was impossible for her to realize it given her financial and health conditions. But now this old wish seems to be suddenly awakened. Her long-buried love for the man seems to wake up again. However, after hearing the man's story about the Russian coachman, Vera conjures up a false image of a dill pickle ("a red chili like a parrot's beak"), which symbolizes the false impression Vera also formed of this man and implies that the meeting will not bring Vera full satisfaction and a rekindling of their romance will never occur. Although the man tries to hold Vera back by clutching her glove, he holds the wrong thing, for a glove was not strong enough to keep her. Now he still does not know how to keep her just as he did six years ago, for he seems to be unaware that Vera is just an appetizer, a person that only makes his dull life a little colorful, not a main course, a person that he would like to spend the whole life with. So it is not surprising that Vera buttons her collar again and draws down her veil and leaves for a second time.

However, Vera's leaving is not because both of them are "such egoists, so self-engrossed, so wrapped up in ourselves that we hadn't a corner in our hearts for anybody else" as the man says, but because Vera has grown mature enough in spirit to dare to "throw away her happiness like this."

Further Reading

Theme

Abrams, M. H. *A Glossary of Literary Terms*. Beijing: Foreign Language Teaching and Research Press, 2004.

Forester, E. M. *Aspects of the Novel*. Beijing: China Translation & Publishing Corporation, 2002.

Guerin, Wilfred L., et al. *A Handbook of Critical Approaches to Literature*. Beijing: Foreign Language Teaching and Research Press, 2004.

Gwynn, R. S. ed. Literature: *A Pocket Anthology*. New York: Addison-Wesley Educational Publishers Inc., 2002.

Hawthorn, Jeremy. *Studying the Novel: An Introduction*. London: Arnold, 1985.

Kennedy, X. J. and Diana Gioia. *Literature: An Introduction to Fiction, Poetry, and Drama*. 8th ed. New York: Longman, 2002.

Michael Meyer. *The Bedford Introduction to Literature*. 8th ed. Bedford/St. Martin's, 2008.

Shao Jindi and Bai Jinpeng. *An Introduction to Literature*. Shanghai: Shanghai Foreign Languages Education Press, 2002.

Scholes, Robert E, ed. *Elements of Fiction: An Anthology*. New York: Oxford University Press, 1981.

A Dill Pickle

Dunbar, Pamela. *Radical Mansfield: Double Discourse in Catherine Mansfield's Short Stories*. Basingstoke: Macmillan, 1997.

Kaplan, Sydney Janet. *Katherine Mansfield and the Origins of Modernist Fiction*. Ithaca and London: Cornell University Press, 1991.

Mansfield, Katherine. *The Collected Stories of Katherine Mansfield*. Harmondsworth: Penguin, 1981.

Smith, Angela. *Katherine Mansfield and Virginia Woolf: A Public of Two*. Oxford: Clarendon Press, 1999.

——*Katherine Mansfield: A Literary Life*. Basingstoke: Palgrave, 2000.

Chapter Six
Style and Tone

    Style in fiction refers to the distinctive manner in which a writer uses the language to achieve particular effects. It either refers to characteristics of language in a particular story or to the same characteristics in a writer's complete works. A distinctive style clearly marks the work of a fine writer: we can tell his work from that of anyone else. From one story to another, however, the writer may fittingly modify his style, and in some stories, style may be altered meaningfully as the story goes along. A detailed analysis of the style in an individual story might include such matters as sentence structure, length of sentences, punctuation, and diction (choice of words: abstract or concrete, bookish or close to speech, standard or slang). Involved in the style, too, is any habitual use of imagery, patterns of sound, figurative language, or other devices.

    When it comes to style, Hemingway must be the first that comes to our mind. His terse, economical sentences are frequently noted and perceived. His sentences include both short sentences, and long sentences which tend to be relatively simple in construction. The effect is like listening to speech. Hemingway is a master of swift, terse dialogue, and often big part of his story is done in the form of conversation. The narrator of Hemmingway's story is always a closemouthed speaker unwilling to let his feelings loose, allowing the characters to speak for themselves free of the narrator's subjective observations. "Hills like White Elephants" is a good example of Hemingway's style.

    Style reveals **tone**, the author's implicit attitude towards the people, places, and events in a story. When we speak, tone is conveyed by our voice and gestures. In a literary work that spoken voice is not available, we must rely on the context in which a statement appears to interpret it correctly.

    In Chopin's "The Story of an Hour," for example, we can perceive that the author shows sympathy with Mrs. Mallard despite the fact that her grief over her husband's assumed death is mixed with joy. When Mrs. Mallard's husband is announced dead in an accident, she is relieved because she feels free from an oppressive male-dominated life. That's why she dies suddenly when she sees her husband alive at the end of the story. Chopin makes clear by the tone of the final line ("When the doctors came they said she had died of heart disease—of joy that kills") that she may not have died of a shock of joy but of a recognition of her lost freedom.

    In many Victorian novels it was customary for some commentator to interpret the story from time to time, remarking upon the action, offering philosophic ideas. Although we can not say the voice of this commentator was not identical with that of the "real life" author, the author in effect created the character of a commentator to speak for him. However, such intrusions are rare today.

    Modern storytellers, carefully keeping out of sight, seldom comment on their plots and characters. We must infer the author's attitude from his choice of details, characters, events, situations, and words.

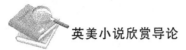

When the narrator of Joseph Conrad's *Heart of Darkness* comes upon an African outpost littered with abandoned machines and notices "a boiler wallowing in the grass," the exact word "wallowing" conveys an attitude: there is something swinish about this scene of careless waste. In "Reunion," there are points where we may laugh, but it is an uncomfortable laugh at which we probably feel a little guilty just because we feel sorry for Charlie whose father's actions make him embarrassed.

Like a tone of voice, the tone of a story may convey not simply one attitude, but a medley: amusement, anger, affection, sorrow, contempt, sympathy. These feelings of the author may be similar to feelings expressed by the narrator of the story (or any character), but sometimes they may be dissimilar, even sharply opposed. The characters in a story may regard an event as sad, but we sense that the author regards it as funny. To understand the tone of the story, then, is to understand some attitude more fundamental to the story than whatever attitude the characters explicitly declare. Reading "Gimple of the Fool" we have mingled feelings toward Gimple and his "foolishness": amusement that Gimple is so easily deceived; sympathy for his excessive innocence; admiration for his firm faith in God and fellow man. Often the tone of a literary story will be too rich and complicated to sum up in one or two words. But to try to describe the tone of such a story may be a useful way to penetrate its center and to grasp the whole of it.

The tone is frequently an important element for interpreting a story. An insensitivity to tone can lead a reader astray in determining the theme of a work. Regardless of who is speaking in a story, it is wise to listen to the author's voice.

David Herbert Lawrence (1885—1930)

David Herbert Lawrence was the fourth child of Arthur John Lawrence, an illiterate coal miner in the Nottinghamshire area of England, and Lydia Beardsall Lawrence, a schoolteacher. Lawrence's boyhood was dominated by poverty and tensions between his parents which resulted from their different backgrounds. Lawrence had a close relationship with his mother and, with her encouragement, he studied at Nottingham University, where he began writing poems and short stories. In 1908, he left his home town for Croyden, just south of London, and began teaching. In 1910, his mother died of cancer. In 1911, because he had developed tuberculosis, Lawrence quit teaching and wrote full time. In March 1912 Lawrence eloped to Germany with Frieda Weekley, the wife of his former modern language professor from Nottingham University, and they got married two years later. He and Frieda returned to England just before the beginning of World War I, but they endured continual harassment from the English government due to Lawrence's objections to the war and Frieda's German ancestry. After the war, the Lawrences lived an itinerant life in Germany, Austria, Italy, Sicily, England, France, Australia, and Mexico, before finally settling in Taos, New Mexico. All this travelling provided the settings for many of the stories and novels that Lawrence wrote in the 1920s and also inspired his four books of travel sketches. Lawrence died in 1930 at a hospital in France, where he attempted to cure the tuberculosis that had plagued him most of his life.

Chapter Six Style and Tone

Lawrence was a prolific novelist. His first novel, *The White Peacock* (1911), was well received by critics and launched him as a writer at the age of 25. Two years later Lawrence's novel *Sons and Lovers* appeared. It is based on his childhood and contains a portrayal of Jessie Chambers, his childhood sweetheart, the Miriam in the novel. In 1915 Lawrence published his novel, *The Rainbow*, which is about two sisters growing up in the north of England. The novel describes frankly sexual relations between men and women, which upset a great many people, and was judged obscene and banned in England. The banning created further difficulties for him in getting anything published. *The Lost Girl* (1920), which Lawrence started to write in Italy, deals with one of Lawrence's favorite subjects—a girl marries a man of a much lower social status, against the advice of friends, and finds compensation in his superior warmth and understanding. Lawrence's best known work is *Lady Chatterley's Lover*, first published privately in Florence in 1928, and was banned for a time in both the UK and the US as pornographic. It tells of the love affair between a wealthy, married woman, Constance Chatterley, whose husband has been left impotent and paralyzed by a war wound, and a man who works on her husband's estate. Among Lawrence's other famous novels is *Women in Love* (1920), a sequel to *Rainbow*. The characters are probably partially based on Lawrence and his wife, and John Middleton Murray and his wife Katherine Mansfield, who were friends and shared a house in England in 1914—1915. Lawrence was influenced deeply by Friedrich Nietzsche, whom Lawrence had read already in the 1910s. *Aaron's Road* (1922) reflects his belief in instincts and intuitions, and *Kangaroo* (1923) expresses his own idea of a "superman."

Although Lawrence's most famous works are novels, many critics agree that his short stories, including "The Rocking-Horse Winner" (1926) are better than his novels. His thematic focus on relationships between men and women, the destruction of relationships by the desire for wealth, and his explorations of psychological motivation in human behavior earned him an international reputation as an important 20th-century author.

Lawrence also was a critic. He expressed his unique literary ideas in his non-fiction works, including *Movements in European History* (1921), *Psychoanalysis and the Unconscious* (1922), *Studies in Classic American Literature* (1923) and *Apocalypse and the Writings on Revelation* (1931).

Lawrence's "The Rocking-Horse Winner" was first published in 1926 *Harper's Bazaar* magazine. It was published again that same year in a collection that was put together by Lady Cynthia Asquith, a friend of Lawrence's. Critics view "The Rocking-Horse Winner" as an example of Lawrence's most accomplished writing, and an example of modernist prose. The story with an omniscient narrator relates the tale of a boy whose family is always short of money and who has the gift for picking the winners in horse races.

The Rocking-Horse Winner

There was a woman who was beautiful, who started with all the advantages, yet she had no luck. She married for love, and the love turned to dust. She had bonny children, yet she felt they had been thrust upon her[1], and she could not love them. They looked at her coldly, as if they were finding fault with her. And hurriedly she felt she must cover up some fault in herself. Yet what it was that she must cover up she never knew. Nevertheless, when her children were present, she always felt the centre of her heart go hard. This troubled her, and in her manner she was all the more gentle and anxious for her children[2], as if she loved them very much. Only she herself knew that at the centre of her heart was a hard little place that could not feel love, no, not for anybody. Everybody else said of her: "She is such a good mother. She adores[3] her children." Only she herself, and her children themselves, knew it was not so. They read it in each other's eyes.

There were a boy and two little girls. They lived in a pleasant house, with a garden, and they had discreet servants, and felt themselves superior to anyone in the neighbourhood.

Although they lived in style[4], they felt always an anxiety in the house. There was never enough money. The mother had a small income, and the father had a small income, but not nearly enough for the social position which they had to keep up. The father went into town to some office. But though he had good prospects, these prospects never materialized[5]. There was always the grinding sense of the shortage of money, though the style was always kept up.

At last the mother said: "I will see if *I* can't make something." But she did not know where to begin. She racked her brains, and tried this thing and the other, but could not find anything successful. The failure made deep lines come into her face. Her children were growing up; they would have to go to school. There must be more money, there must be more money. The father, who was always very handsome and expensive in his tastes, seemed as if he never *would* be able to do anything worth doing. And the mother, who had a great belief in herself, did not succeed any better, and her tastes were just as expensive.

And so the house came to be haunted by the unspoken phrase: *There must be more money! There must be more money!* The children could hear it all the time, though nobody said it aloud. They heard it at Christmas, when the expensive and splendid toys filled the nursery. Behind the shining modern rocking-horse, behind the smart doll's house, a voice would start whispering: "There *must* be more money! There *must* be more money!" And the children would stop playing to listen for a moment. They would

---

1 they had been thrust upon her: 他们(孩子们)是硬塞给她的
2 in her manner she was all the more gentle and anxious for her children: 她对孩子们表现得更加和蔼可亲,更加关心
3 adore: 极其喜爱
4 live in style: 过着入时的生活
5 these prospects never materialized: 这些期望从未实现

look into each other's eyes, to see if they had all heard. And each one saw in the eyes of the other two that they too had heard. "There *must* be more money! There *must* be more money!"

It came whispering from the springs of the still-swaying rocking-horse, and even the horse, bending his wooden, champing head, heard it. The big doll, sitting so pink and smirking in her new pram, could hear it quite plainly, and seemed to be smirking all the more self-consciously because of it. The foolish puppy, too, that took the place of the teddy-bear, he was looking so extraordinarily foolish for no other reason but that he heard the secret whisper all over the house: "There *must* be more money!"

Yet nobody ever said it aloud. The whisper was everywhere, and therefore no one spoke it. Just as no one ever says: "We are breathing!" in spite of the fact that breath is coming and going all the time.

"Mother," said the boy Paul one day, "why don't we keep a car of our own? Why do we always use uncle's, or else a taxi?"

"Because we're the poor members of the family," said the mother.

"But why *are* we, mother?"

"Well—I suppose," she said slowly and bitterly, "it's because your father has no luck."

The boy was silent for some time.

"Is luck money, mother?" he asked, rather timidly.

"No, Paul. Not quite. It's what causes you to have money."

"Oh!" said Paul vaguely. "I thought when Uncle Oscar said *filthy-lucker*, it meant money."

"*Filthy Lucre* does mean money," said the mother. "But it's lucre, not luck."

"Oh!" said the boy. "Then what *is* luck, mother?"

"It's what causes you to have money. If you're lucky you have money. That's why it's better to be born lucky than rich. If you're rich, you may lose your money. But if you're lucky, you will always get more money."

"Oh! Will you? And is father not lucky?"

"Very unlucky, I should say," she said bitterly.

The boy watched her with unsure eyes.

"Why?" he asked.

"I don't know. Nobody ever knows why one person is lucky and another unlucky."

"Don't they? Nobody at all? Does *nobody* know?"

"Perhaps God. But He never tells."

"He ought to, then. And aren't you lucky either, mother?"

"I can't be, if I married an unlucky husband."

"But by yourself, aren't you?"

"I used to think I was, before I married. Now, I think I am very unlucky indeed."

"Why?"

"Well—never mind! Perhaps I'm not really," she said.

The child looked at her, to see if she meant it. But he saw, by the lines of her mouth[1], that she was only trying to hide something from him.

---

1 by the lines of her mouth: 从母亲嘴角的皱纹

"Well, anyhow," he said stoutly, "I'm a lucky person."

"Why?" said his mother, with a sudden laugh.

He stared at her. He didn't even know why he had said it.

"God told me," he asserted, brazening it out[1].

"I hope He did, dear!" she said, again with a laugh, but rather bitter.

"He did, mother!"

"Excellent!" said the mother, using one of her husband's exclamations.

The boy saw she did not believe him; or, rather, that she paid no attention to his assertion. This angered him somewhat, and made him want to compel her attention[2].

He went off by himself, vaguely, in a childish way, seeking for the clue to "luck." Absorbed, taking no heed of other people, he went about with a sort of stealth, seeking inwardly for luck. He wanted luck, he wanted it, he wanted it. When the two girls were playing dolls in the nursery, he would sit on his big rocking-horse, charging madly into space[3], with a frenzy that made the little girls peer at him uneasily. Wildly the horse careered[4], the waving dark hair of the boy tossed, his eyes had a strange glare in them. The little girls dared not speak to him.

When he had ridden to the end of his mad little journey, he climbed down and stood in front of his rocking-horse, staring fixedly into its lowered face. Its red mouth was slightly open, its big eye was wide and glassy-bright.

"Now!" he would silently command the snorting steed. "Now, take me to where there is luck! Now take me!"

And he would slash the horse on the neck with the little whip he had asked Uncle Oscar for. He *knew* the horse could take him to where there was luck, if only he forced it. So he would mount again, and start on his furious ride, hoping at last to get there. He knew he could get there.

"You'll break your horse, Paul!" said the nurse.

"He's always riding like that! I wish he'd leave off!" said his elder sister Joan.

But he only glared down on them in silence. Nurse gave him up. She could make nothing of him. Anyhow he was growing beyond her[5].

One day his mother and his Uncle Oscar came in when he was on one of his furious rides. He did not speak to them.

"Hallo, you young jockey! Riding a winner?" said his uncle.

"Aren't you growing too big for a rocking horse? You're not a very little boy any longer, you know," said his mother.

But Paul only gave a blue glare from his big, rather close-set eyes. He would speak to nobody when he was in full tilt. His mother watched him with an anxious expression on her face.

At last he suddenly stopped forcing his horse into the mechanical gallop, and slid down.

---

1 brazening it out：厚着脸皮说

2 compel her attention：迫使她关注

3 charging madly into space：疯狂地摇着

4 Wildly the horse careered：木马在疾驰

5 he was growing beyond her：他已经长大，她已经管不了他了

Chapter Six Style and Tone

"Well, I got there!" he announced fiercely, his blue eyes still flaring, and his sturdy long legs straddling apart.

"Where did you get to?" asked his mother.

"Where I wanted to go," he flared back at her.

"That's right, son!" said Uncle Oscar. "Don't you stop till you get there. What's the horse's name?"

"He doesn't have a name," said the boy.

"Gets on without all right[1]?" asked the uncle.

"Well, he has different names. He was called Sansovino last week."

"Sansovino, eh? Won the Ascot[2]. How did you know his name?"

"He always talks about horse-races with Bassett," said Joan.

The uncle was delighted to find that his small nephew was posted with all the racing news[3]. Bassett, the young gardener, who had been wounded in the left foot in the war and had got his present job through Oscar Cresswell, whose batman he had been, was a perfect blade of the "turf.[4]" He lived in the racing events, and the small boy lived with him.

Oscar Cresswell got it all from Bassett.

"Master Paul comes and asks me, so I can't do more than tell him, sir," said Bassett, his face terribly serious, as if he were speaking of religious matters.

"And does he ever put anything on a horse he fancies?"

"Well—I don't want to give him away—he's a young sport, a fine sport, sir. Would you mind asking him yourself? He sort of takes a pleasure in it, and perhaps he'd feel I was giving him away, sir, if you don't mind."

Bassett was serious as a church.

The uncle went back to his nephew, and took him off for a ride in the car.

"Say, Paul, old man, do you ever put anything on a horse?" the uncle asked.

The boy watched the handsome man closely.

"Why, do you think I oughtn't to?" he parried.

"Not a bit of it. I thought perhaps you might give me a tip for the Lincoln."

The car sped on into the country, going down to Uncle Oscar's place in Hampshire[5].

"Honour bright?" said the nephew.

"Honour bright, son!" said the uncle.

"Well, then, Daffodil."

"Daffodil! I doubt it, sonny. What about Mirza?"

"I only know the winner," said the boy. "That's Daffodil."

"Daffodil, eh?"

There was a pause. Daffodil was an obscure horse comparatively.

---

1 Gets on without all right：在比赛时真的没有名字
2 the Ascot：爱斯科赛马会，世界最著名的赛马比赛。
3 was posted with all the racing news：对所有赛事都很灵通
4 "turf"：赛马迷
5 Hampshire：汉普郡，英国南部的一个郡

"Uncle!"

"Yes, son?"

"You won't let it go any further, will you? I promised Bassett."

"Bassett be damned, old man! What's he got to do with it?"

"We're partners. We've been partners from the first. Uncle, he lent me my first five shillings, which I lost. I promised him, honour bright, it was only between me and him; only you gave me that ten-shilling note I started winning with, so I thought you were lucky. You won't let it go any further, will you?"

The boy gazed at his uncle from those big, hot, blue eyes, set rather close together. The uncle stirred and laughed uneasily.

"Right you are, son! I'll keep your tip private. Daffodil, eh? How much are you putting on him?"

"All except twenty pounds," said the boy. "I keep that in reserve[1]."

The uncle thought it a good joke.

"You keep twenty pounds in reserve, do you, you young romancer? What are you betting, then?"

"I'm betting three hundred," said the boy gravely. "But it's between you and me, Uncle Oscar! Honour bright?"

The uncle burst into a roar of laughter.

"It's between you and me all right, you young Nat Gould[2]," he said, laughing. "But where's your three hundred?"

"Bassett keeps it for me. We're partners."

"You are, are you! And what is Bassett putting on Daffodil?"

"He won't go quite as high as I do, I expect. Perhaps he'll go a hundred and fifty."

"What, pennies?" laughed the uncle.

"Pounds," said the child, with a surprised look at his uncle. "Bassett keeps a bigger reserve than I do."

Between wonder and amusement Uncle Oscar was silent. He pursued the matter no further, but he determined to take his nephew with him to the Lincoln races.

"Now, son," he said, "I'm putting twenty on Mirza, and I'll put five for you on any horse you fancy. What's your pick?"

"Daffodil, uncle."

"No, not the fiver on Daffodil!"

"I should if it was my own fiver," said the child.

"Good! Good! Right you are! A fiver for me and a fiver for you on Daffodil."

The child had never been to a race-meeting before, and his eyes were blue fire. He pursed his mouth tight[3], and watched. A Frenchman just in front had put his money on Lancelot. Wild with excitement, he flayed his arms up and down, yelling, *Lancelot! Lancelot!* " in his French accent.

---

1 I keep that in reserve:我存 20 英镑
2 Nat Gould:纳特·古尔德(1857—1919),英国作家、记者,著有一百多本有关赛马的通俗小说
3 pursed his mouth tight:他嘴唇紧闭

Daffodil came in first, Lancelot second, Mirza third. The child, flushed and with eyes blazing, was curiously serene. His uncle brought him four five-pound notes, four to one.

"What am I to do with these?" he cried, "waving them before the boy's eyes."

"I suppose we'll talk to Bassett," said the boy. "I expect I have fifteen hundred now; and twenty in reserve; and this twenty."

His uncle studied him for some moments.

"Look here, son!" he said. "You're not serious about Bassett and that fifteen hundred, are you?"

"Yes, I am. But it's between you and me, uncle. Honour bright!"

"Honour bright all right, son! But I must talk to Bassett."

"If you'd like to be a partner, uncle, with Bassett and me, we could all be partners. Only, you'd have to promise, honour bright, uncle, not to let it go beyond us three. Bassett and I are lucky, and you must be lucky, because it was your ten shillings I started winning with..."

Uncle Oscar took both Bassett and Paul into Richmond Park for an afternoon, and there they talked.

"It's like this, you see, sir," Bassett said. "Master Paul would get me talking about racing events, spinning yarns, you know, sir. And he was always keen on knowing if I'd made or if I'd lost. It's about a year since, now, that I put five shillings on Blush of Dawn for him—and we lost. Then the luck turned, with that ten shillings he had from you: that we put on Singhalese. And since that time, it's been pretty steady, all things considering. What do you say, Master Paul?"

"We're all right when we're sure," said Paul. "It's when we're not quite sure that we go down."

"Oh, but we're careful then," said Bassett.

"But when are you *sure*?" smiled Uncle Oscar.

"It's Master Paul, sir," said Bassett, in a secret, religious voice. "It's as if he had it from heaven. Like Daffodil, now, for the Lincoln. That was as sure as eggs."

"Did you put anything on Daffodil?" asked Oscar Cresswell.

"Yes, sir. I made my bit."

"And my nephew?"

Bassett was obstinately silent, looking at Paul.

"I made twelve hundred, didn't I, Bassett? I told uncle I was putting three hundred on Daffodil."

"That's right," said Bassett, nodding.

"But where's the money?" asked the uncle.

"I keep it safe locked up, sir. Master Paul he can have it any minute he likes to ask for it."

"What, fifteen hundred pounds?"

"And twenty! and *forty*, that is, with the twenty he made on the course."

"It's amazing!" said the uncle.

"If Master Paul offers you to be partners, sir, I would, if I were you; if you'll excuse me," said Bassett.

Oscar Cresswell thought about it.

"I'll see the money," he said.

They drove home again, and sure enough, Bassett came round to the garden-house with fifteen hundred pounds in notes. The twenty pounds reserve was left with Joe Glee, in the Turf Commission[1] deposit.

"You see, it's all right, uncle, when I'm *sure*! Then we go strong, for all we're worth. Don't we, Bassett!"

"We do that, Master Paul."

"And when are you sure?" said the uncle, laughing.

"Oh, well, sometimes I'm *absolutely* sure, like about Daffodil," said the boy, "and sometimes I have an idea; and sometimes I haven't even an idea, have I, Bassett? Then we're careful, because we mostly go down."

"You do, do you! And when you're sure, like about Daffodil, what makes you sure, sonny?"

"Oh, well, I don't know," said the boy uneasily. "I'm sure, you know, uncle; that's all."

"It's as if he had it from heaven, sir," Bassett reiterated.

"I should say so!" said the uncle.

But he became a partner. And when the Leger was coming on, Paul was "sure" about Lively Spark, which was a quite inconsiderable horse. The boy insisted on putting a thousand on the horse, Bassett went for five hundred, and Oscar Cresswell two hundred. Lively Spark came in first, and the betting had been ten to one against him. Paul had made ten thousand.

"You see," he said, "I was absolutely sure of him."

Even Oscar Cresswell had cleared two thousand[2].

"Look here, son," he said, "this sort of thing makes me nervous."

"It needn't, uncle! Perhaps I shan't be sure again for a longtime."

"But what are you going to do with your money?" asked the uncle.

Of course," said the boy, "I started it for mother. She said she had no luck, because father is unlucky, so I thought if I was lucky, it might stop whispering."

"What might stop whispering?"

"Our house. I *hate* our house for whispering."

"What does it whisper?"

"Why—why"—the boy fidgeted—"why, I don't know. But it's always short of money, you know, uncle."

"I know it, son, I know it."

"You know people send mother writs, don't you, uncle?"

"I'm afraid I do," said the uncle.

"And then the house whispers, like people laughing at you behind your back. It's awful, that is! I thought if I was lucky —"

"You might stop it," added the uncle.

The boy watched him with big blue eyes that had an uncanny cold fire in them, and he said never a word.

---

1 in the Turf Commission deposit:存在赛马委员会

2 cleared two thousand:净得了两千

"Well, then!" said the uncle. "What are we doing?"

"I shouldn't like mother to know I was lucky," said the boy.

"Why not, son?"

"She'd stop me."

"I don't think she would."

"Oh!"—and the boy writhed in an odd way— "I *don't* want her to know, uncle."

"All right, son! We'll manage it without her knowing."

They managed it very easily. Paul, at the other's suggestion, handed over five thousand pounds to his uncle, who deposited it with the family lawyer, who was then to inform Paul's mother that a relative had put five thousand pounds into his hands, which sum was to be paid out a thousand pounds at a time, on the mother's birthday, for the next five years.

"So she'll have a birthday present of a thousand pounds for five successive years," said Uncle Oscar. "I hope it won't make it all the harder for her later."

Paul's mother had her birthday in November. The house had been "whispering" worse than ever lately, and, even in spite of his luck, Paul could not bear up against it. He was very anxious to see the effect of the birthday letter, telling his mother about the thousand pounds.

When there were no visitors, Paul now took his meals with his parents, as he was beyond the nursery control. His mother went into town nearly every day. She had discovered that she had an odd knack of sketching furs and dress materials, so she worked secretly in the studio of a friend who was the chief "artist" for the leading drapers. She drew the figures of ladies in furs and ladies in silk and sequins for the newspaper advertisements. This young woman artist earned several thousand pounds a year, but Paul's mother only made several hundreds, and she was again dissatisfied. She so wanted to be first in something, and she did not succeed, even in making sketches for drapery advertisements.

She was down to breakfast on the morning of her birthday. Paul watched her face as she read her letters. He knew the lawyer's letter. As his mother read it, her face hardened and became more expressionless. Then a cold, determined look came on her mouth. She hid the letter under the pile of others, and said not a word about it.

"Didn't you have anything nice in the post for your birthday, mother?" said Paul.

"Quite moderately nice," she said, her voice cold and absent.

She went away to town without saying more.

But in the afternoon Uncle Oscar appeared. He said Paul's mother had had a long interview with the lawyer, asking if the whole five thousand could be advanced at once, as she was in debt.

"What do you think, uncle?" said the boy.

"I leave it to you, son."

"Oh, let her have it, then! We can get some more with the other," said the boy.

"A bird in the hand is worth two in the bush, laddie!" said Uncle Oscar.

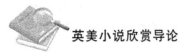

"But I'm sure to *know* for the Grand National[1]; or the Lincolnshire[2]; or else the Derby[3]. I'm sure to know for *one* of them," said Paul.

So Uncle Oscar signed the agreement, and Paul's mother touched the whole five thousand. Then something very curious happened. The voices in the house suddenly went mad, like a chorus of frogs on a spring evening. There were certain new furnishings, and Paul had a tutor. He was *really* going to *Eton*[4], his father's school, in the following autumn. There were flowers in the winter, and a blossoming of the luxury Paul's mother had been used to. And yet the voices in the house, behind the sprays of mimosa and almond blossom, and from under the piles of iridescent cushions, simply trilled and screamed in a sort of ecstasy: "There *must* be more money! Oh-h-h, there *must* be more money. Oh, now, now-w! Now-w-w—there *must* be more money!—more than ever! More than ever!"

It frightened Paul terribly. He studied away at his Latin and Greek with his tutors. But his intense hours were spent with Bassett. The Grand National had gone by: he had not "known," and had lost a hundred pounds. Summer was at hand. He was in agony for the Lincoln. But even for the Lincoln he didn't "know" and he lost fifty pounds. He became wild-eyed and strange, as if something were going to explode in him.

"Let it alone, son! Don't you bother about it!" urged Uncle Oscar. But it was as if the boy couldn't really hear what his uncle was saying.

"I've got to know for the Derby! I've got to know for the Derby!" the child reiterated, his big blue eyes blazing with a sort of madness.

His mother noticed how overwrought[5] he was.

"You'd better go to the seaside. Wouldn't you like to go now to the seaside, instead of waiting? I think you'd better," she said, looking down at him anxiously, her heart curiously heavy because of him.

But the child lifted his uncanny blue[6] eyes.

"I couldn't possibly go before the Derby, mother" he said. "I couldn't possibly!"

"Why not?" she said, her voice becoming heavy when she was opposed. "Why not? You can still go from the seaside to see the Derby with your Uncle Oscar, if that's what you wish. No need for you to wait here. Besides, I think you care too much about these races. It's a bad sign. My family has been a gambling family, and you won't know till you grow up how much damage it has done. But it has done damage. I shall have to send Bassett away, and ask Uncle Oscar not to talk racing to you, unless you promise to be reasonable about it; go away to the seaside and forget it. You're all nerves[7]!"

"I'll do what you like, mother, so long as you don't send me away till after the Derby," the boy said.

"Send you away from where? Just from this house?"

---

1 Grand National: (英国一年一度的)全国越野障碍赛马赛
2 Lincolnshire: 林肯郡赛马会
3 Derby: 英国的大赛马会。1780 年德贝伯爵所创立,每年六月的第一个星期三在伦敦附近的 Epsom 举行。参赛马龄平均为三岁,这天称为 Derby Day。
4 Eton: 伊顿,泰晤士河边的一个市镇,位于伦敦附近的白金汉郡,伊顿公学所在地。
5 overwrought: 过度紧张的
6 uncanny: 诡异的
7 You're all nerves: 你太紧张了。

Chapter Six Style and Tone

"Yes," he said, gazing at her.

"Why, you curious child, what makes you care about this house so much, suddenly? I never knew you loved it."

He gazed at her without speaking. He had a secret within a secret, something he had not divulged, even to Bassett or to his Uncle Oscar.

But his mother, after standing undecided and a little bit sullen for some moments, said:

"Very well then! Don't go to the seaside till after the Derby, if you don't wish it. But promise me you won't let our nerves go to pieces. Promise you won't think so much about horse-racing and *events*, as you call them!"

"Oh, no," said the boy casually. "I won't think much about them, mother. You needn't worry. I wouldn't worry, mother, if I were you."

"If you were me and I were you," said his mother, "I wonder what we *should* do!"

"But you know you needn't worry, mother, don't you?" the boy repeated.

"I should be awfully glad to know it," she said wearily.

"Oh, well, you *can*, you know. I mean, you *ought* to know you needn't worry," he insisted.

"Ought I? Then I'll see about it," she said.

Paul's secret of secrets was his wooden horse, that which had no name. Since he was emancipated from a nurse and a nursery-governess, he had had his rocking horse removed to his own bedroom at the top of the house.

"Surely, you're too big for a rocking horse!" his mother had remonstrated.

"Well, you see, mother, till I can have a *real* horse, I like to have *some* sort of animal about," had been his quaint answer.

"Do you feel he keeps you company?" she laughed.

"Oh, yes! He's very good, he always keeps me company, when I'm there," said Paul.

So the horse, rather shabby, stood in an arrested prance in the boy's bedroom.

The Derby was drawing near, and the boy grew more and more tense. He hardly heard what was spoken to him, he was very frail, and his eyes were really uncanny. His mother had sudden strange seizures of uneasiness about him[1]. Sometimes, for half-an-hour, she would feel a sudden anxiety about him that was almost anguish. She wanted to rush to him at once, and know he was safe.

Two nights before the Derby, she was at a big party in town, when one of her rushes of anxiety about her boy, her first-born, gripped her heart till she could hardly speak. She fought with the feeling, might and main[2], for she believed in common sense. But it was too strong. She had to leave the dance and go downstairs to telephone to the country. The children's nursery-governess was terribly surprised and startled at being rung up in the night.

"Are the children all right, Miss Wilmot?"

"Oh, yes, they are quite all right."

"Master Paul? Is he all right?"

---

1 His mother had sudden strange seizures of uneasiness about him: 他母亲突然对他有一种奇怪而不安的感觉。
2 might and main: 竭尽全力

"He went to bed as right as a trivet. Shall I run up and look at him?"

"No," said Paul's mother reluctantly. "No! Don't trouble. It's all right. Don't sit up. We shall be home fairly soon." She did not want her son's privacy intruded upon.

"Very good," said the governess.

It was about one o'clock when Paul's mother and father drove up to their house. All was still. Paul's mother went to her room and slipped off her white fur coat. She had told her maid not to wait up for her. She heard her husband downstairs, mixing a whisky-and-soda.

And then, because of the strange anxiety at her heart, she stole upstairs to her son's room. Noiselessly she went along the upper corridor. Was there a faint noise? What was it?

She stood, with arrested[1] muscles, outside his door, listening. There was a strange, heavy, and yet not loud noise. Her heart stood still. It was a soundless noise, yet rushing and powerful. Something huge, in violent, hushed motion. What was it? What in God's name was it? She ought to know. She felt that she knew the noise. She knew what it was.

Yet she could not place it. She couldn't say what it was. And on and on it went, like a madness.

Softly, frozen with anxiety and fear, she turned the door handle.

The room was dark. Yet in the space near the window, she heard and saw something plunging to and fro. She gazed in fear and amazement.

Then suddenly she switched on the light, and saw her son, in his green pyjamas, madly surging on the rocking horse. The blaze of light suddenly lit him up, as he urged the wooden horse, and lit her up, as she stood, blonde, in her dress of pale green and crystal, in the doorway.

"Paul!" she cried. "Whatever are you doing?"

"It's Malabar!" he screamed in a powerful, strange voice. "It's Malabar!"

His eyes blazed at her for one strange and senseless second, as he ceased urging his wooden horse. Then he fell with a crash to the ground, and she, all her tormented motherhood flooding upon her, rushed to gather him up.

But he was unconscious, and unconscious he remained, with some brain fever. He talked and tossed, and his mother sat stonily by his side.

"Malabar! It's Malabar! Bassett, Bassett, I *know* it! It's Malabar!"

So the child cried, trying to get to get up and urge the rocking horse that gave him his inspiration.

"What does he mean by Malabar?" asked the heart-frozen mother.

"I don't know," said the father stonily.

"What does he mean by Malabar?" she asked her brother Oscar.

"It's one of the horses running for the Derby," was the answer.

And, in spite of himself, Oscar Cresswell spoke to Bassett, and himself put a thousand on Malabar: at fourteen to one.

The third day of the illness was critical: they were waiting for a change. The boy, with his rather long, curly hair, was tossing ceaselessly on the pillow. He neither slept nor regained consciousness, and

---

1 arrested: 紧绷的

his eyes were like blue stones. His mother sat, feeling her heart had gone, turned actually into a stone.

In the evening, Oscar Cresswell did not come, but Bassett sent a message, saying could he come up for one moment, just one moment? Paul's mother was very angry at the intrusion, but on second thought she agreed. The boy was the same. Perhaps Bassett might bring him to consciousness.

The gardener, a shortish fellow with a little brown moustache, and sharp little brown eyes, tiptoed into the room, touched his imaginary cap to Paul's mother, and stole to the bedside, staring with glittering, smallish eyes, at the tossing, dying child.

"Master Paul!" he whispered. "Master Paul! Malabar came in first all right, a clean win[1]. I did as you told me. You've made over seventy thousand pounds, you have; you've got over eighty thousand. Malabar came in all right, Master Paul."

"Malabar! Malabar! Did I say Malabar, mother? Did I say Malabar? Do you think I'm lucky, mother? I knew Malabar, didn't I? Over eighty thousand pounds! I call that lucky, don't you, mother? Over eighty thousand pounds! I knew, didn't I know I knew? Malabar came in all right. If I ride my horse till I'm sure, then I tell you, Bassett, you can go as high as you like. Did you go for all you were worth, Bassett?"

"I went a thousand on it, Master Paul."

"I never told you, mother, that if I can ride my horse, and *get there*, then I'm absolutely sure—oh, absolutely! Mother, did I ever tell you? I *am* lucky!"

"No, you never did," said the mother.

But the boy died in the night.

And even as he lay dead, his mother heard her brother's voice saying to her: "My God, Hester, you're eighty-odd thousand to the good and a poor devil of a son to the bad[2]. But, poor devil, poor devil, he's best gone out of a life where he rides his rocking horse to find a winner."

Understanding the Text

"The Rocking-Horse Winner," an example of Lawrence's most accomplished writing, belongs to the group of stories D. H. Lawrence wrote in the last years of his life, during which period he abandoned the realism that characterizes his mid-career work, and turned toward a style of short story that more closely resembles the fable or folktale. Like Lawrence's other later stories, "The Rocking-Horse Winner" "employs devices of the fairy tale and a mockingly detached tone to moralize on the value of love and the dangers of money."(D. H. Lawrence Criticism)

"The Rocking-Horse Winner" begins with fable-like simplicity but ends with a serious message about wasted lives. The opening paragraphs of the story are written in a style similar to that of a fairy tale. The story begins with "There was a woman who was beautiful, who started with all the advantages, yet she had no luck." The distant, solemn tone of the narrator suggests that this is an old story like a legend. Lawrence also uses the supernatural elements of a fable, mainly Paul's ability to "know" the winners

---

1 a clean win: 大获全胜
2 you're eighty-odd thousand to the good and a poor devil of a son to the bad: 你净赚八万多，但你却赔上了儿子，你是个可怜虫。

just by riding his rocking horse. The style and tone of this story signals us that this story comes from the world of fable and legend. Therefore, it is necessary for us to understand the meaning of the story at different levels with consideration of the style and tone, as well as stylized characterization and the symbolic landscape that Lawrence creates in "The Rocking-Horse Winner."

In "The Rocking-Horse Winner," Lawrence seems to be offering a broad satire on rising consumerism and crass materialism in English culture, which are represented by those who equate love with money, luck with happiness. And Hester, Paul's mother, is the representative of them. The mother, who is obsessed with material possessions and the status that material wealth can provide, believes that money will make her happy despite the obvious fact that so far it has not. And it is her pursuit of material wealth that leads to her son's death.

In "The Rocking-Horse Winner," the husband's inadequacy is explicit. The narrator describes him as "one who was always very handsome and expensive in his tastes, [and] seemed as if he never would be able to do anything worth doing." The mother "bitterly" characterizes him as "very unlucky" and tries to make her feelings very clear to her young son. When she makes her son acutely aware of his mother's dissatisfaction with her husband and strong desire for money, the mother sets in motion the boy's futile quest to please her, to silence the voice that haunts him, the voice of the house itself whispering, "There must be more money! There must be more money," and to be the man she wants him/her husband to be.

When Paul begins to directly associates luck with money, and love with money, he starts his desperate search for values in a cash culture: gambling. As W. D. Snodgrass argues in "A Rocking-Horse: The Symbol, the Pattern, the Way to Live," an influential article written in 1958, there is a resemblance of "luck" to "lucre," and a vaguer resemblance of both to "love." Paul's strong desire "to be lucky" represents Paul's desire to earn money for the family, an unconscious desire to take his father's place to take care of the family's needs. The main way of his earning money—the rocking horse—is symbolically sexually oriented. It represents both Paul's desire to make money for his mother and his own sexuality. However, Paul's desire to satisfy his mother's love and win her love is doomed to futility. And he ultimately gives the most precious gift of all: his life.

Obsess with material items and wealth leads to the mother's greed, selfishness and irresponsibility, and make her heart "a hard little place that could not feel love, no, not for anybody." When the mother first receives the news from the lawyer that she has "inherited" 5,000 pounds from a long-lost relative which will be paid out to her in yearly increments of 1,000 pounds, she goes immediately to the lawyer and asks for the entire amount immediately. However, instead of paying off her debts and saving for the future, she spends foolishly the money on material things for the house. This results in an even greater need for more money. Throughout the story, the mother has no idea where all this money comes from and does not seem to care, and of course she does not express any thanks for this sudden windfall. Moreover she is so obsessed with wealth that she seems oblivious to Paul's concerns and does not show much care for him. Before he dies Paul asks "Mother, did I ever tell you? I'm lucky," she responds, "No, you never did." However, readers remember that Paul did tell her earlier in the story that he was lucky. Since she pays little attention to him, she does not remember this. At the end of the story the mother seems to become increasingly concerned about Paul's deteriorating health, but she still does not love him, even when he dies, for she sits by her son's bedside with her heart having gone, turned actually into a stone. Therefore readers have every reason to believe that when the mother finally receives the financial fortune she has always wanted but loses her son in the process, she will probably not feel the loss of her son and will probably waste all that money in record time. All of these details show that the mother is cold, unfeeling, wasteful, and shallow.

It is the responsibility of the parents to provide love for the children in a family. It is also the responsibility of the parents to spend money wisely and budget carefully so that the bills are paid and no one goes without food, clothing, or shelter. However, in this story, the parents are complete failures at financial dealings and giving children love. They seem completely unaware that Paul has overtaken responsibilities that are rightly theirs. Besides, all of the adults, Bassett, Uncle Oscar, and Paul's mother, seem to treat him like an adult even though Paul is still a child. When Uncle Oscar discovers that Paul has been gambling, he does not stop Paul from gambling further. No one anticipates that Paul will pay a huge price for playing this game. This emotionally distant style of parenting resulting from the new consumer culture in which luck and lucre mean the same thing popularly exist in England during the late 19th and early 20th centuries. And the fable-like quality of "The Rocking-Horse Winner" gives Lawrence an opportunity to make satires directed at a society that is dominated by a quest for cash, and at those who buy into the deadly equation of love equaling money.

Further Reading

Style and Tone

Abrams, M. H. *A Glossary of Literary Terms*. Beijing: Foreign Language Teaching and Research Press, 2004.

Forester, E. M. *Aspects of the Novel*. Beijing: China Translation & Publishing Corporation, 2002.

Guerin, Wilfred L., et al. *A Handbook of Critical Approaches to Literature*. Beijing: Foreign Language Teaching and Research Press, 2004.

Gwynn, R. S. ed. *Literature: A Pocket Anthology*. New York: Addison-Wesley Educational Publishers Inc., 2002.

Hawthorn, Jeremy. *Studying the Novel: An Introduction*. London: Arnold, 1985.

Kennedy, X. J. and Diana Gioia. *Literature: An Introduction to Fiction, Poetry, and Drama*. 8th ed. New York: Longman, 2002.

Michael Meyer. *The Bedford Introduction to Literature*. 8th ed. Bedford/St. Martin's, 2008.

Shao Jindi and Bai Jinpeng. *An Introduction to Literature*. Shanghai: Shanghai Foreign Languages Education Press, 2002.

Scholes, Robert E, ed. *Elements of Fiction: An Anthology*. New York: Oxford University Press, 1981.

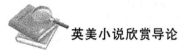

The Rocking-Horse Winner

Anne Fernihough, ed. *The Cambridge Companion to D.H. Lawrence*. Shanghai: Shanghai Foreign Languages Education Press, 2003.

Salgado, Gamini. *A Preface to D.H. Lawrence*. Beijing: Peking University Press, 2005.

Snodgrass, W. D. "A Rocking-Horse: The Symbol, the Pattern, the Way to Live". *The Hudson Review*, 11.2 (Summer 1958):191—200.

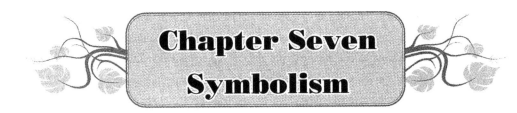

Chapter Seven
Symbolism

A **symbol** in literature is a person, object, or event that suggests more than its literal meaning. This basic definition is simple enough, but the use of symbol in literature is often a troublesome affair for beginning readers.

In fact, symbols appear all round us; anything can be given symbolic significance. Awareness of a writer's use of symbols is not all that different from the kinds of perceptions and interpretations that allow us to make sense of our daily lives. We know, for example, that a red rose a young man presents a lady with is more than just a rose because it frequently suggests a romantic love. The bride's and the bridegroom' clothes in China are always red because we tend to associate happiness and luck with that color. And the national flag of each country has its symbolic meaning. Symbols such as these that are instantly recognized by most members of a culture as possessing a shared symbolic meaning are called **conventional symbols**. Writers often use the conventional symbols, such as seasons, colors and the setting and rising of the sun, to reinforce meanings. Kate Chopin, for example, uses the spring setting in "The Story of an Hour" to suggest the renewed sense of life that Mrs. Mallard feels when she thinks herself free from her husband. Willar Cathy in "Paul's Case" uses different colors to symbolize Paul's frustrations, feelings and desires in life: Yellow (his upstairs bedroom is covered in dingy, old "horrible yellow wallpaper") illustrates the ugliness and fear in Paul's life at the beginning of the story; red (the proud purchase of a new "red robe" while in New York enables him to express his audacity in a daring way) not only provides Paul courage but also is a continual reminder of his own power of choice as he prepares for his grand finale; black (as his body flies through the air, he instantly visualizes all the things he will never get to do, and then "the disturbing visions flashed into black" as death directs the final scene of Paul's life) denotes darkness, loneliness, and death.(Carpenter-Houde)

A literary symbol can include traditional or conventional meanings, but it may also be established internally by the total context of the work in which it appears. It can be any of the elements discussed above, such as plot, character, setting, or an object, name, or anything else in a work. In "Reunion," the title, with its suggestions of emotional warmth, and the setting, a busy train station, give us the suggestion of both ironic and symbolic overtones.

Symbols generally do not "stand for" any one meaning, nor for anything absolutely definite; they are suggestive rather than definitive. In William Faulkner's "A Rose for Emily," "Miss Emily's invisible watch ticking at the end of a golden chain indicates not only the passage of time, but suggests that time passes without even being noticed by the owner of the watch, and the golden chain carries the suggestions of wealth and authority." (Kennedy, p.114)

Often the symbols we meet in fiction are inanimate objects, but other things also may function symbolically. In some novels and stories, characters suggest symbolic meanings. In "Rose for Emily" Miss Emily has symbolic hints: she seems to symbolize the vanishing aristocracy of the antebellum South, still maintaining a black servant and being betrayed by a moneymaking Yankee. In this story Miss Emily, who twice appears at a window of her house "like the carven torso of an idol in a niche," is not given a complicated description of the change of her character. Miss Emily is more a portrait than a person. Therefore a symbolic character, just like Miss Emily, tends not to be well-rounded and fully-known, but to remain slightly mysterious.

When a character, object, or incident indicates a single, fixed meaning, the writer is using **allegory** rather than a symbol. What an allegory primarily focuses on is the abstract idea called forth by the concrete object. It tends to be definitive rather than suggestive. In "Young Goodman Brown" Hawthorne uses the protagonist's and his wife's names to represent untested virtue and religious fidelity respectively, and the dark forest to mirror the confusion of Brown's soul.

To some extent, all stories are symbolic. Although there is probably little point in looking for symbolism in every word, in every object, in every minor character, to be on the alert for symbols when reading fiction is perhaps wiser than to ignore them. Some symbols are so subtle that they may escape us while some symbols are easily identified. Fortunately, the storyteller often gives the symbol particular emphasis. It may be mentioned repeatedly throughout the story; it may even supply the story with a title. Sometimes, a crucial symbol will open a story or end it. In whatever situation, if we treat stories like people—with tact and care—we can get access to them; and the context of the story can help us decide whether our reading is reasonable and appropriate.

Familiarity with an individual author's works may also help us to recognize a private symbol, a symbol that the author has made his or her own by repeated usage. Flannery O'Connor frequently uses bursts of bright light to indicate some kind of dawning spiritual revelation in the mind of one of her characters whereas Edgar Allan Poe draws on small, confined spaces to represent the personal horror.

Ernest Hemingway (1899—1961)

Ernest Hemingway, an American writer and journalist, has embodied the public image of the successful writer even until now. As the son of a doctor in Chicago, he was wounded as a volunteer ambulance driver at Italian front during World War I, and trained as a reporter on the *Kansas City Star*. Hemingway moved to Paris in the early 1920s, where he became part of American expatriate community. He spent much time in Spain and covered the Spanish Civil War. His wide travels and complexity of life provided materials for his novels and short stories, some of which reflected his being haunted by his war experience.

In Our Time (1925) is a collection of short stories that reflect Hemingway's attempts to readjust to life back home after World War I, and earned him the recognition in the world. *The Sun Also Rises* (1926), his first novel, *A Farewell to Arms* (1929) and *For Whom the Bell Tolls* (1940) are also about war and its impact on people's lives. He received the Pulitzer Prize in 1953 and the Nobel Prize in Literature in

Chapter Seven Symbolism

1954 for *The Old Man and the Sea*, which centers on Santiago, an aging Cuban fisherman who struggles with a giant marlin far out in the Gulf Stream. Santiago has become one of his typically stoical protagonists, who exhibit an ideal described as "grace under pressure."

"Hills like White Elephants" is a short story by Ernest Hemingway, which was first published in the 1927 collection *Men Without Women*. It earned him a reputation for daring subject matter "abortion" and made him one of the chief spokesmen for "the Lost Generation."

 *Text*

Hills like White Elephants

The hills across the valley of the Ebro[1] were long and white. On this side there was no shade and no trees and the station was between two lines of rails in the sun. Close against the side of the station there was the warm shadow of the building and a curtain, made of strings of bamboo beads, hung across the open door into the bar, to keep out flies. The American and the girl with him sat at a table in the shade, outside the building. It was very hot and the express from Barcelona[2] would come in forty minutes. It stopped at this junction for two minutes and went to Madrid.

"What should we drink?" the girl asked. She had taken off her hat and put it on the table.

"It's pretty hot," the man said.

"Let's drink beer."

"Dos cervezas[3]," the man said into the curtain.

"Big ones?" a woman asked from the doorway.

"Yes. Two big ones."

The woman brought two glasses of beer and two felt pads[4]. She put the felt pads and the beer glasses on the table and looked at the man and the girl. The girl was looking off at the line of hills. They were white in the sun and the country was brown and dry.

"They look like white elephants," she said.

"I've never seen one," the man drank his beer.

"No, you wouldn't have."

"I might have," the man said. "Just because you say I wouldn't have doesn't prove anything."

The girl looked at the bead curtain. "They've painted something on it," she said. "What does it say?"

"Anis del Toro[5]. It's a drink."

"Could we try it?"

---

1 the Ebro：埃布罗河，位于西班牙北部
2 Barcelona：巴塞罗那，西班牙东部港口城市
3 Dos cervezas：〈西班牙语〉两杯酒
4 felt pad：毛毡杯垫
5 Anis del Toro：〈西班牙语〉一种深色、甘草味的酒

The man called "Listen" through the curtain. The woman came out from the bar.

"Four reales."

"We want two Anis del Toro."

"With water?"

"Do you want it with water?"

"I don't know," the girl said. "Is it good with water?"

"It's all right."

"You want them with water?" asked the woman.

"Yes, with water."

"It tastes like liquorice[1]," the girl said and put the glass down.

"That's the way with everything."

"Yes," said the girl. "Everything tastes of liquorice. Especially all the things you've waited so long for, like absinthe[2]."

"Oh, cut it out[3]."

"You started it," the girl said. "I was being amused. I was having a fine time."

"Well, let's try and have a fine time."

"All right. I was trying. I said the mountains looked like white elephants. Wasn't that bright?"

"That was bright."

"I wanted to try this new drink. That's all we do, isn't it—look at things and try new drinks?"

"I guess so."

The girl looked across at the hills.

"They're lovely hills," she said. "They don't really look like white elephants. I just meant the colouring of their skin through the trees."

"Should we have another drink?"

"All right."

The warm wind blew the bead curtain against the table.

"The beer's nice and cool," the man said.

"It's lovely," the girl said.

"It's really an awfully simple operation, Jig," the man said. "It's not really an operation at all."

The girl looked at the ground the table legs rested on.

"I know you wouldn't mind it, Jig. It's really not anything. It's just to let the air in."

The girl did not say anything.

"I'll go with you and I'll stay with you all the time. They just let the air in and then it's all perfectly natural."

"Then what will we do afterward?"

"We'll be fine afterward. Just like we were before."

"What makes you think so?"

---

1 liquorice: 甘草

2 absinthe: 苦艾酒。当时,苦艾酒被认为可能导致幻觉和不孕,所以,在很多欧洲国家已被禁止。

3 cut it out: 别说了,住嘴

Chapter Seven Symbolism

"That's the only thing that bothers us. It's the only thing that's made us unhappy."

The girl looked at the bead curtain, put her hand out and took hold of two of the strings of beads.

"And you think then we'll be all right and be happy."

"I know we will. Yon don't have to be afraid. I've known lots of people that have done it."

"So have I," said the girl. "And afterward they were all so happy."

"Well," the man said, "if you don't want to you don't have to. I wouldn't have you do it if you didn't want to. But I know it's perfectly simple."

"And you really want to?"

"I think it's the best thing to do. But I don't want you to do it if you don't really want to."

"And if I do it you'll be happy and things will be like they were and you'll love me?"

"I love you now. You know I love you."

"I know. But if I do it, then it will be nice again if I say things are like white elephants, and you'll like it?"

"I'll love it. I love it now but I just can't think about it. You know how I get when I worry."

"If I do it you won't ever worry?"

"I won't worry about that because it's perfectly simple."

"Then I'll do it. Because I don't care about me."

"What do you mean?"

"I don't care about me."

"Well, I care about you."

"Oh, yes. But I don't care about me. And I'll do it and then everything will be fine."

"I don't want you to do it if you feel that way."

The girl stood up and walked to the end of the station. Across, on the other side, were fields of grain and trees along the banks of the Ebro. Far away, beyond the river, were mountains. The shadow of a cloud moved across the field of grain and she saw the river through the trees.

"And we could have all this," she said. "And we could have everything and every day we make it more impossible."

"What did you say?"

"I said we could have everything."

"No, we can't."

"We can have the whole world."

"No, we can't."

"We can go everywhere."

"No, we can't. It isn't ours any more."

"It's ours."

"No, it isn't. And once they take it away, you never get it back."

"But they haven't taken it away."

"We'll wait and see."

"Come on back in the shade," he said. "You mustn't feel that way."

"I don't feel any way," the girl said. "I just know things."

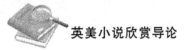

"I don't want you to do anything that you don't want to do—"

"Nor that isn't good for me," she said. "I know. Could we have another beer?"

"All right. But you've got to realize —"

"I realize," the girl said. "Can't we maybe stop talking?"

They sat down at the table and the girl looked across at the hills on the dry side of the valley and the man looked at her and at the table.

"You've got to realize," he said, "that I don't want you to do it if you don't want to. I'm perfectly willing to go through with it if it means anything to you."

"Doesn't it mean anything to you? We could get along."

"Of course it does. But I don't want anybody but you. I don't want anyone else. And I know it's perfectly simple."

"Yes, you know it's perfectly simple."

"It's all right for you to say that, but I do know it."

"Would you do something for me now?"

"I'd do anything for you."

"Would you please please please please please please please stop talking?"

He did not say anything but looked at the bags against the wall of the station. There were labels on them from all the hotels where they had spent nights.

"But I don't want you to," he said, "I don't care anything about it."

"I'll scream," the girl said.

The woman came out through the curtains with two glasses of beer and put them down on the damp felt pads. "The train comes in five minutes," she said.

"What did she say?" asked the girl.

"That the train is coming in five minutes."

The girl smiled brightly at the woman, to thank her.

"I'd better take the bags over to the other side of the station," the man said. She smiled at him.

"All right. Then come back and we'll finish the beer."

He picked up the two heavy bags and carried them around the station to the other tracks. He looked up the tracks but could not see the train. Coming back, he walked through the bar-room, where people waiting for the train were drinking. He drank an Anis at the bar and looked at the people. They were all waiting reasonably for the train. He went out through the bead curtain. She was sitting at the table and smiled at him.

"Do you feel better?" he asked.

"I feel fine," she said. "There's nothing wrong with me. I feel fine."

Understanding the Text

The story "Hills like White Elephants" takes place at a train station in the Ebro River valley of Spain on a hot and dry day. The time setting is not given, but is almost surely contemporary to the composition of the story (1920s). Most of the story is simply dialogue between two characters, the

American and his female companion, whom he calls Jig. The third-person narration reveals very few facts about the characters; it never explicitly states what it is that the couple is arguing about. As usual, Hemingway here leaves details of characters to the sensibilities of the reader, allowing the characters to speak for themselves free of an omniscient narrator's subjective observations. And the reader must infer their backgrounds and their attitudes towards the situation at hand, and their attitudes toward one another by resorting to their dialogue and body language. This leaves a good deal of room for the reader's interpretation. And thus there are rich interpretations of such themes as choices and consequences, doubt and ambiguity, conflict between personal responsibility and hedonism, and how men and women relate.

No matter how differently readers interpret the story, they are unlikely to take no notice of Hemmingway's powerful use of symbolism, which makes the reader doubtlessly understand what the two characters are arguing about, though the word "abortion" is nowhere in the story. Hemingway's symbolism in "Hills like White Elephants" can be found in descriptions of the setting, the hills themselves, and even the name of the character, Jig.

The setting is symbolically significant in the story. In the first paragraph the setting immediately introduces the tense atmosphere that will surround the rest of the story:

The hills across the valley of the Ebro were long and white. On this side there was no shade and no trees and the station was between two lines of rails in the sun. Close against the side of the station there was the warm shadow of the building and a curtain, made of strings of bamboo beads, hung across the open door into the bar, to keep out flies. The American and the girl with him sat at a table in the shade, outside the building. It was very hot and the express from Barcelona would come in forty minutes. It stopped at this junction for two minutes and went to Madrid.

The tense atmosphere Hemingway creates in this paragraph symbolically implies that the couple is at the critical point of making a drastic decision in which there are only two choices—two directions, just like the two rail lines that pass by the station. The landscape that encompasses the station plays a fundamental role in the conflict of the story through its extensive symbolism. The openness and barrenness around the railroad station and the oppressive hot and dry landscape suggest that the American and Jig must address the problem at hand now. And the contrasting sceneries on both sides of the train tracks—the barren land stretching toward the hills on one side and the green, fertile farmland on the other—represent the implication of the differing interpretations of what the two characters are arguing about. And the conflict between them is revealed as the story unfolds.

Throughout the story Jig is seen to look at the hills three times. When the girl sees the long and white hills in the sun for the first time she says that "they look like white elephants." As she refers to the hills as "white elephants," she is actually making a reply to the birth of her baby—something unique like the uncommon white elephant—who, Jig believes, will be an extraordinary addition to her mundane life of drinking and mindless traveling. The color white symbolizes the innocence and purity of her unborn child, and allegorically implies that Jig is innocent in her affair with the American who simply sees the pleasure in being with her in the flesh. Jig's ordering a drink called Anis del Toro that she has never had before and does not know the taste of, and her taste of her drink being like licorice can be exemplified as her innocence. Just as she lacks the experience in better expressing the flavor of the drink more accurately she has no much experience in better expressing her feelings of being pregnant, thus perceiving the hills as being like white elephants, which she is not aware has been disturbing the American. And therefore she is stopped with the American's "Oh cut it out."

When she again looks across at the "lovely" hills, they quickly drift to the subject of an operation which the American is attempting to convince Jig to undergo. After posing arguments to which the American is largely unresponsive, Jig eventually assents to the operation, giving the final justification: "I don't care about me." She attempts to drop the subject, but the American persists as if still unsure of Jig's intentions and mental state.

> The girl stood up and walked to the end of the station. Across, on the other side, were the fields of grain and trees along the banks of the Ebro. Far away, beyond the river, were mountains. The shadow of a cloud moved across the field of grain and she saw the river through the trees.

The fields of grain and trees represent fertility and fruitfulness, which symbolize Jig's current pregnant state and the life in her womb. The Ebro River also represents life, as it germinates the fields. Just as the girl appreciates the scenery and its connection to her unborn child, the "shadow of a cloud," which represents the abortion of the fetus, overcomes her happiness. "They sat down at the table and the girl looked across the hills on the dry side of the valley" whose being barren and sterile symbolizes her body after the abortion. She is so frustrated with this that she says to the American, "Would you please please please please please please please stop talking?"

"He did not say anything but looked at the bags against the wall of the station. There were labels on them from all the hotels where they had spent nights." The bags with all the hotel labels on them are symbolic of the American's vivacious spirit and the current lifestyle he and Jig have—traveling to see the world—which would have to be stopped with the coming of the baby.

The story ends with the couple expecting their train's arrival in five minutes. As the train approaches, the American carries their bags to the "other tracks" on the opposite side of the station. This can be interpreted in two ways: he has the sense of primacy in making the decision to give up their child, or it is viewed as a sign that the couple has changed their mind and their destination after the discussion they had.

When we interpret the symbolism in "Hills like White Elephants" we should not overlook the symbolic significance of Jig's name. In the story Jig's real name is never given except for the nickname "Jig." The word "Jig" associates with such tools as whiskey measurer, fishing lure, and woodworking tool in the public and cultural association, and "suggests a dance, the music for the dance, and the joke," which exposes the man's ultimately condescending attitude toward her: For the man, Jig is more a sexual object or tool for entertainment than a person with feelings and values to be respected.(O'Brien) This, to some degree, explains the inequality of these two characters in relationship and the American's primacy in making the decision of the fetus.

There is no resolution and there is no decision stated regarding the abortion. Hemmingway's interweaving of symbolism in the setting, white hills and Jig's name helps provide maximum detail and space for readers to conclude for themselves what will happen next.

Further Reading

Symbolism

Abrams, M. H. *A Glossary of Literary Terms*. Beijing: Foreign Language Teaching and Research Press, 2004.

Forester, E. M. *Aspects of the Novel*. Beijing: China Translation & Publishing Corporation, 2002.

Guerin, Wilfred L., et al. *A Handbook of Critical Approaches to Literature*. Beijing: Foreign Language Teaching and Research Press, 2004.

Gwynn, R. S. ed. *Literature: A Pocket Anthology*. New York: Addison-Wesley Educational Publishers Inc., 2002.

Hawthorn, Jeremy. *Studying the Novel: An Introduction*. London: Arnold, 1985.

Kennedy, X. J. and Diana Gioia. *Literature: An Introduction to Fiction, Poetry, and Drama*. 8th ed. New York: Longman, 2002.

Michael Meyer. *The Bedford Introduction to Literature*. 8th ed. Bedford/St. Martin's, 2008.

Shao Jindi and Bai Jinpeng. *An Introduction to Literature*. Shanghai: Shanghai Foreign Languages Education Press, 2002.

Scholes, Robert E, ed. *Elements of Fiction: An Anthology*. New York: Oxford University Press, 1981.

Hills like White Elephants

Fletcher, Mary Dell. "Hemingway's 'Hills like White Elephants'". *Explicator* 38(1980):16—18.

Smith, Paul, ed. *New Essays on Hemingway's Short Fiction*. Beijing: Peking University Press; Cambridge University Press, 2006.

——. *A Reader's Guide to the Short Stories of Ernest Hemingway*. Boston: G. K. Hall & Co., 1989.

Weeks, Lewis E., Jr. "Hemingway's Hills: Symbolism in 'Hills like White Elephants'". *Studies in Short Fiction* 17.1 (Winter 1980): 75—77.

海明威著,董衡巽编选:《海明威谈创作》,北京:三联书店,1985年。

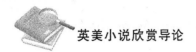

Part Two
Critical Approaches

You read a story which has so impressed and moved you and you have an idea about the story which you think is unique. However, when you make research in the library about the story you find some interpretations and comments of this story seemingly unrelated or similar to yours. "Young Goodman Brown" is a well-known story by Nathaniel Hawthorne. You read it for the first time and was absorbed in the setting, character, and plot, and just felt that you wanted to read it twice or more. Out of curiosity, you made a research in the library and found many articles about it. These articles are seemingly unrelated: The first explores the thematic significance of symbols of Faith's pink hair ribbons and the snake-like-staff, and images of dewdrops and "hanging twig" in the story; the second interprets the relation between Hawthorne's experience and the story; the third gives an analysis of Hawthorne's gender concerns; and the fourth examines Goodman Brown's subconscious guilt. When you were bewildered by the treatments of the novel which apparently you had never known and even thought of, you perhaps did not realize that these four articles were written from four different perspectives—formalist, autobiographical, feminist and psychological. These articles' varying approaches represent potentially ways of exploring the story that might otherwise have never occurred to you. There are many ways to approach a text and a useful step is to develop a sense of how a perspective shapes an understanding of a text. In other words, to master the critical approaches is your first step to widen and deepen the responses of your own reading.

You have developed skills to produce a literary analysis that describes how a character, plot, point of view, setting, or symbol supports a theme. These same skills are also useful for you to keep track of how the parts of a critical approach create a particular reading of a literary work. Each of critical perspectives is sensitive to point of view, symbol, tone, and other literary elements that you have been studying, but each also casts those elements in a special way. Therefore, your interpretation of a story involves the combination of a critical approach and a close examination on how its various elements relate to the whole. A work can be analyzed with the help of a wide variety of approaches, and your own critical thinking skills can help you determine the usefulness of a particular approach.

This part is intended to give an overview of critical approaches to literary works, which is concise in its presentation of the complexities inherent in them and shows emphasis on ways of thinking about literature rather than daunting lists of terms, names, and movements, and as well make comments on selected works with the guidance of some specific critical approaches. Therefore the aim here is modest and practical, and is to develop your appreciation of the intriguing possibilities that attend literary interpretation in a much easier way.

The approaches introduced here include those which have long been practiced by readers, such as autobiographical and historical approaches, and more recent approaches, such as gender, reader-response, and cultural studies. Each of these approaches raises its own questions and issues while seeking particular kinds of evidence to support itself. An awareness of the assumptions and methods that each approach inform you can help you make a better sense of a work, and therefore enhance your critical thinking.

Chapter Eight
Historical and Biographical Approaches

   Historical and biographical critics see a literary work chiefly as a reflection of the life and times of its author or the life and times of its characters. They believe that knowledge of an author's life can help readers understand his or her work more fully and deeply. Events in a work might follow actual events in a writer's life just as characters might be based on people known by the author. Stephen Crane's "The Open Boat" is a story about the hardships of four men shipwrecked at sea who must make their way to shore in a dinghy. This story is based on an actual incident from Stephen Crane's life in January of the same year when the story was published in 1897. While Crane traveled to Cuba to work as a newspaper correspondent during the Cuban insurrection against Spain, his ship sank off the coast of Florida. Crane and three other men were forced to navigate their way to shore in a small boat. One of the men, an oiler named Billy Higgins, drowned while trying to swim to shore. Crane wrote the story "The Open Boat" soon afterward. This kind of information can help deepen our understanding of how Crane achieves his grippingly realistic depiction of their life-threatening ordeal, the sensations and emotions of their suffering a close call with death, and Crane's philosophical speculations that human beings are at the mercy of natural forces, and can make clearer the source of Stephen's convictions and how his own experiences inform his major concerns as a storyteller although relevant facts about Stephen's life will not make "The Open Boat" a better written story than it is. Hence, many readers find biography useful for interpretation.

   Historical and biographical critics also believe it is necessary to know about the political, economical, and social context of the times of a work and its author in order to truly understand this work. In their views literature mirrors the history of its times. The historical context helps discover the beliefs of characters and thus serves to shed light on the subject of a literary work. Hawthorne's "Young Goodman Brown" is known for his criticism of the teachings of the Puritans. Without some knowledge of the historical context of the seventeenth-century Puritan England in which the story takes place and the Salem witch trials during which the story is set, we cannot gain a complete and deep understanding of what Hawthorne intends this story to expose—the hypocrisy in Puritan doctrine, and the theme of the story—the conflict between good and evil in human nature and, in particular, the problem of public goodness and private wickedness. Similarly Hawthorne's life is necessary for us to understand fully the characters. Hawthorne was born of a Puritan family and his great-great grandfather John Hathorne played a role as judge during the Salem witch trials. Hawthorne, for years plagued by guilt from his ancestor's role, vindicates his grandfather by featuring two fictional victims of the witch trials who really were witches and not merely innocent victims of the witch-hunt.

However, it is worth noting that sometimes historical and biographical, especially biographical, information might complicate our understanding a work. Kate Chopin's "The Story of an Hour" "presents a repressed wife's momentary discovery of what freedom from her husband might mean to her" (Meyer, p.2087). She has a sense of awakening immediately when she learns of her husband's death, and she dies of her heart attack suddenly when she sees that he comes home alive. Chopin's husband died twelve years before she wrote the story. Therefore readers might be inclined to interpret this story as Chopin's fictionalized commentary about her own marriage. Actually according to some biographers, Chopin's marriage is satisfying to her. And thus it might be a reasonable attitude that we take historical and biographical information as enriching our appreciation of a work.

Mark Twain (1835—1910)

Mark Twain is the pen name of Samuel Langhorne Clemens, born in Florida, Missouri, the fifth child of John Marshall Clemens and Jane Lampton Clemens. Twain spent most of his childhood in Hannibal, Missouri, which served as the inspiration for the fictional town of St. Petersburg in *The Adventures of Tom Sawyer* and *Adventures of Huckleberry Finn*, and gave him the unbridled freedom and the chances of being familiar with the institution of slavery, a theme he would later explore in his writing. After the death of his father when he was eleven, he worked at a series of jobs to support his family. A newspaper job made him travel east working for papers and exploring St. Louis, New York, and Philadelphia. Later he trained and worked as a steamboat pilot on the Mississippi until the outbreak of the Civil War. In 1863 Samuel assumed the pseudonym Mark Twain, from a boating term that means "two fathoms deep," and the name for the great American humorist was created. Twain gained his literary success in 1865 with his humorous tall tale "The Celebrated Jumping Frog of Calaveras County," which was published in the New York Saturday Press. He then continued to travel as a traveling correspondent, writing pieces on his visits of Europe and the Middle East. Following his return to the United States in 1870, he got married and moved to Connecticut. Twain was prolific during the years extending from 1869 until 1889. It was during this period of time that he produced *The Innocents Abroad* (1869), *Roughing It* (1872), *The Gilded Age* (1873), *The Adventures of Tom Sawyer* (1876), *A Tramp Abroad* (1880), *The Prince and the Pauper* (1881), *Life on the Mississippi* (1883), and *Adventures of Huckleberry Finn* (1884). Despite Twain's continuing success as a writer, his financial affairs were not stable. Twain's work is noted for the combination of rough humor and colloquial speech, which helped to create and popularize the distinctive American literature built on American themes and language. Twain, therefore, was called "the father of American literature" by William Faulkner.

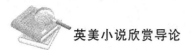

Adventures of Huckleberry Finn was one of Twain's major published works and an offshoot from Tom Sawyer. First published in England in December 1884, it solidified Twain as a noteworthy American writer. And some have called it the "first Great American Novel." The main premise behind Huckleberry Finn is the young boy's belief in the right thing to do even though the majority of society believe that it was wrong. And the following chapters are excerpted from a corrected version of the first American edition of 1885.

 *Text*

Adventures of Huckleberry Finn

(Tom Sawyer's Comrade)
Scene: The Mississippi Valley
Time: Forty to Fifty Years Ago[1]

NOTICE

Persons attempting to find a motive in this narrative will be prosecuted; persons attempting to find a moral in it will be banished; persons attempting to find a plot in it will be shot.

BY ORDER OF THE AUTHOR
Per G.G., CHIEF OF ORDNANCE.

Explanatory

In this book a number of dialects are used, to wit: the Missouri negro dialect; the extremest form of the backwoods South-Western dialect; the ordinary "Pike County"[2] dialect; and four modified varieties of this last. The shadings have not been done in a haphazard fashion, or by guesswork; but painstakingly, and with the trustworthy guidance and support of personal familiarity with these several forms of speech. I make this explanation for the reason that without it many readers would suppose that all these characters were trying to talk alike and not succeeding.

THE AUTHOR

I

You don't know about me, without you have read a book by the name of "The Adventures of Tom Sawyer"[3], but that ain't no matter. That book was made by Mr. Mark Twain, and he told the truth, mainly. There was things which he stretched, but mainly he told the truth. That is nothing. I never seen

---

1 指美国内战前的 1835 或 1845 年。
2 Pike County: 派克县,位于密苏里州。
3 The Adventures of Tom Sawyer:《汤姆·索亚历险记》是本文的姐妹篇,出版于 1876 年。

Chapter Eight Historical and Biographical Approaches

anybody but lied, one time or another, without it was Aunt Polly, or the widow, or maybe Mary. Aunt Polly—Tom's Aunt Polly, she is—and Mary, and the Widow Douglas is all told about in that book, which is mostly a true book; with some stretchers, as I said before.

Now the way that the book winds up[1], is this: Tom and me found the money that the robbers hid in the cave, and it made us rich. We got six thousand dollars apiece—all gold. It was an awful sight of money when it was piled up. Well, Judge Thatcher he took it and put it out at interest[2], and it fetched us a dollar a day apiece, all the year round—more than a body could tell what to do with. The Widow Douglas, she took me for her son, and allowed she would civilize me; but it was rough living in the house all the time, considering how dismal regular and decent the widow was in all her ways; and so when I couldn't stand it no longer I lit out[3]. I got into my old rags, and my sugar-hogshead again, and was free and satisfied. But Tom Sawyer he hunted me up[4] and said he was going to start a band of robbers, and I might join if I would go back to the widow and be respectable. So I went back.

The widow she cried over me, and called me a poor lost lamb[5], and she called me a lot of other names, too, but she never meant no harm by it. She put me in them new clothes again, and I couldn't do nothing but sweat and sweat, and feel all cramped up. Well, then, the old thing commenced again. The widow rung a bell for supper, and you had to come to time. When you got to the table you couldn't go right to eating, but you had to wait for the widow to tuck down her head and grumble a little over the victuals, though there warn't really anything the matter with them,—that is, nothing only everything was cooked by itself. In a barrel of odds and ends[6] it is different; things get mixed up, and the juice kind of swaps around, and the things go better.

After supper she got out her book and learned me about Moses and the Bulrushers;[7] and I was in a sweat to find out all about him; but by-and-by she let it out that Moses had been dead a considerable long time; so then I didn't care no more about him, because I don't take no stock in[8] dead people.

Pretty soon I wanted to smoke, and asked the widow to let me. But she wouldn't. She said it was a mean[9] practice and wasn't clean, and I must try to not do it any more. That is just the way with some people. They get down on[10] a thing when they don't know nothing about it. Here she was a bothering about Moses, which was no kin to her; and no use to anybody, being gone, you see, yet finding a power of fault with me for doing a thing that had some good in it. And she took snuff, too; of course that was all right, because she done it herself.

Her sister, Miss Watson, a tolerable slim old maid, with goggles on, had just come to live with her, and took a set at me now, with a spelling-book. She worked me middling hard for about an hour, and

---

1 wind up：结束
2 at interest：生利息
3 light out：匆匆离开，逃走
4 he hunted me up：他找到了我。
5 poor lost lamb：可怜的迷途羔羊
6 a barrel of odds and ends：一大桶杂七杂八的东西
7 Moses and the Bulrushers：摩西和"赶牛人"。这个故事出自圣经《出埃及记》。法老的女儿在尼罗河发现一只芦苇编的篮子，篮子里有个婴儿，她给他起名摩西。之后，她收养了摩西，把他带进了皇宫。寡妇道格拉斯收养哈克与此相像。
8 take no stock in：相信
9 mean：卑鄙的；卑劣的
10 get down on：不喜欢

then the widow made her ease up. I couldn't stood it much longer. Then for an hour it was deadly dull, and I was fidgety. Miss Watson would say, "Don't put your feet up there, Huckleberry;" and "Don't scrunch up like that, Huckleberry—set up straight;" and pretty soon she would say, "Don't gap and stretch like that, Huckleberry—why don't you try to behave?" Then she told me all about the bad place, and I said I wished I was there. She got mad then, but I didn't mean no harm. All I wanted was to go somewheres; all I wanted was a change, I warn't particular. She said it was wicked to say what I said; said she wouldn't say it for the whole world; she was going to live so as to go to the good place. Well, I couldn't see no advantage in going where she was going, so I made up my mind I wouldn't try for it. But I never said so, because it would only make trouble, and wouldn't do no good.

Now she had got a start, and she went on and told me all about the good place. She said all a body would have to do there was to go around all day long with a harp and sing, forever and ever. So I didn't think much of it. But I never said so. I asked her if she reckoned Tom Sawyer would go there, and she said not by a considerable sight. I was glad about that, because I wanted him and me to be together.

Miss Watson she kept pecking at me[1], and it got tiresome and lonesome. By and by they fetched the niggers[2] in and had prayers, and then everybody was off to bed. I went up to my room with a piece of candle, and put it on the table. Then I set down in a chair by the window and tried to think of something cheerful, but it warn't no use. I felt so lonesome I most wished I was dead. The stars were shining, and the leaves rustled in the woods ever so mournful; and I heard an owl, away off, who-whooing about somebody that was dead, and a whippowill and a dog crying about somebody that was going to die; and the wind was trying to whisper something to me, and I couldn't make out what it was, and so it made the cold shivers run over me. Then away out in the woods I heard that kind of a sound that a ghost makes when it wants to tell about something that's on its mind and can't make itself understood, and so can't rest easy in its grave, and has to go about that way every night grieving. I got so down-hearted and scared I did wish I had some company. Pretty soon a spider went crawling up my shoulder, and I flipped it off and it lit in the candle; and before I could budge it was all shriveled up. I didn't need anybody to tell me that that was an awful bad sign and would fetch me some bad luck, so I was scared and most shook the clothes off of me. I got up and turned around in my tracks three times and crossed my breast every time; and then I tied up a little lock of my hair with a thread to keep witches away. But I hadn't no confidence. You do that when you've lost a horseshoe that you've found, instead of nailing it up over the door, but I hadn't ever heard anybody say it was any way to keep off bad luck when you'd killed a spider.

I set down again, a shaking all over, and got out my pipe for a smoke; for the house was all as still as death, now, and so the widow wouldn't know. Well, after a long time I heard the clock away off in the town go boom—boom—boom—twelve licks—and all still again—stiller than ever. Pretty soon I heard a twig snap down in the dark amongst the trees—something was a stirring. I set still and listened. Directly I could just barely hear a "me-yow! me-yow!" down there. That was good! Says I, "me-yow! me-yow!" as soft as I could, and then I put out the light and scrambled out of the window on to the shed. Then I slipped down to the ground and crawled in among the trees, and sure enough there was Tom Sawyer waiting for me.

---

1 pecking at me: 找我麻烦
2 nigger: 黑鬼。此处哈克是用南方口语来描述黑奴, 并无嘲笑或蔑视之意。

Chapter Eight　Historical and Biographical Approaches

II

　　We went tiptoeing along a path amongst the trees back towards the end of the widow's garden, stooping down so as the branches wouldn't scrape our heads. When we was passing by the kitchen I fell over a root and made a noise. We scrouched down and laid still. Miss Watson's big nigger, named Jim, was setting in the kitchen door; we could see him pretty clear, because there was a light behind him. He got up and stretched his neck out about a minute, listening. Then he says:

　　"Who dah?"

　　He listened some more; then he come tiptoeing down and stood right between us; we could a touched him, nearly. Well, likely it was minutes and minutes that there warn't a sound, and we all there so close together. There was a place on my ankle that got to itching, but I dasn't scratch it; and then my ear begun to itch; and next my back, right between my shoulders. Seemed like I'd die if I couldn't scratch. Well, I've noticed that thing plenty times since. If you are with the quality, or at a funeral, or trying to go to sleep when you ain't sleepy—if you are anywheres where it won't do for you to scratch, why you will itch all over in upwards of a thousand places. Pretty soon Jim says:

　　"Say—who is you? Whar is you? Dog my cats ef I didn' hear sumf'n. Well, I knows what I's gwyne to do. I's gwyne to set down here and listen tell I hears it agin."

　　So he set down on the ground betwixt me and Tom. He leaned his back up against a tree, and stretched his legs out till one of them most touched one of mine. My nose begun to itch. It itched till the tears come into my eyes. But I dasn't scratch. Then it begun to itch on the inside. Next I got to itching underneath. I didn't know how I was going to set still. This miserableness went on as much as six or seven minutes; but it seemed a sight longer than that. I was itching in eleven different places now. I reckoned I couldn't stand it more'n a minute longer, but I set my teeth hard[1] and got ready to try. Just then Jim begun to breathe heavy; next he begun to snore—and then I was pretty soon comfortable again.

　　Tom he made a sign to me—kind of a little noise with his mouth—and we went creeping away on our hands and knees. When we was ten foot off Tom whispered to me, and wanted to tie Jim to the tree for fun. But I said no; he might wake and make a disturbance[2], and then they'd find out I warn't in. Then Tom said he hadn't got candles enough, and he would slip in the kitchen and get some more. I didn't want him to try. I said Jim might wake up and come. But Tom wanted to resk it; so we slid in there and got three candles, and Tom laid five cents on the table for pay. Then we got out, and I was in a sweat to get away; but nothing would do Tom but he must crawl to where Jim was, on his hands and knees, and play something on him. I waited, and it seemed a good while, everything was so still and lonesome.

　　As soon as Tom was back we cut along the path[3], around the garden fence, and by and by fetched up on the steep top of the hill the other side of the house. Tom said he slipped Jim's hat off of his head and hung it on a limb right over him, and Jim stirred a little, but he didn't wake. Afterwards Jim said the

---

1　I set my teeth hard: 我咬紧牙关。
2　make a disturbance: 闹事
3　cut along the path: 走捷径，抄近路

witches bewitched him and put him in a trance, and rode him all over the State, and then set him under the trees again, and hung his hat on a limb to show who done it. And next time Jim told it he said they rode him down to New Orleans[1]; and, after that, every time he told it he spread it more and more, till by-and-by he said they rode him all over the world, and tired him most to death, and his back was all over saddle-boils. Jim was monstrous proud about it, and he got so he wouldn't hardly notice the other niggers. Niggers would come miles to hear Jim tell about it, and he was more looked up to than any nigger in that country. Strange niggers would stand with their mouths open and look him all over, same as if he was a wonder. Niggers is always talking about witches in the dark by the kitchen fire; but whenever one was talking and letting on[2] to know all about such things, Jim would happen in and say, "Hm! What you know 'bout witches?" and that nigger was corked up and had to take a back seat. Jim always kept that five-center piece round his neck with a string, and said it was a charm the devil give to him with his own hands, and told him he could cure anybody with it and fetch witches whenever he wanted to just by saying something to it; but he never told what it was he said to it. Niggers would come from all around there and give Jim anything they had, just for a sight of that five-center piece; but they wouldn't touch it, because the devil had had his hands on it. Jim was most ruined for a servant, because he got stuck up[3] on account of having seen the devil and been rode by witches.

Well, when Tom and me got to the edge of the hill-top, we looked away down into the village[4] and could see three or four lights twinkling, where there was sick folks, maybe; and the stars over us was sparkling ever so fine; and down by the village was the river[5], a whole mile broad, and awful still and grand. We went down the hill and found Jo Harper and Ben Rogers, and two or three more of the boys, hid in the old tanyard. So we unhitched a skiff and pulled down the river two mile and a half, to the big scar on the hillside, and went ashore.

We went to a clump of bushes, and Tom made everybody swear to keep the secret, and then showed them a hole in the hill, right in the thickest part of the bushes. Then we lit the candles, and crawled in on our hands and knees. We went about two hundred yards, and then the cave opened up. Tom poked about amongst the passages and pretty soon ducked under a wall where you wouldn't a noticed that there was a hole. We went along a narrow place and got into a kind of room, all damp and sweaty and cold, and there we stopped. Tom says:

"Now we'll start this band of robbers and call it Tom Sawyer's Gang. Everybody that wants to join has got to take an oath, and write his name in blood."

Everybody was willing. So Tom got out a sheet of paper that he had wrote the oath on, and read it. It swore every boy to stick to the band, and never tell any of the secrets; and if anybody done anything to any boy in the band, whichever boy was ordered to kill that person and his family must do it, and he mustn't eat and he mustn't sleep till he had killed them and hacked a cross in their breasts, which was the sign of the band. And nobody that didn't belong to the band could use that mark, and if he did he

---

1 New Orleans: 新奥尔良, 美国南部港口城市, 位于路易斯安那州。
2 let on: 假装。
3 get stuck up: 翘尾巴, 得意洋洋。
4 the village: 在本书及《汤姆·索亚历险记》中指圣彼得堡(St. Petersburg), 密苏里州的汉尼巴尔(Hannibal)是其原型。
5 the river: 指密西西比河。

Chapter Eight Historical and Biographical Approaches

must be sued; and if he done it again he must be killed. And if anybody that belonged to the band told the secrets, he must have his throat cut, and then have his carcass burnt up and the ashes scattered all around, and his name blotted off of the list with blood and never mentioned again by the gang, but have a curse put on it and be forgot forever.

Everybody said it was a real beautiful oath, and asked Tom if he got it out of his own head. He said, some of it, but the rest was out of pirate-books, and robber-books, and every gang that was high-toned[1] had it.

Some thought it would be good to kill the *families* of boys that told the secrets. Tom said it was a good idea, so he took a pencil and wrote it in. Then Ben Rogers says:

"Here's Huck Finn[2], he hain't got no family—what you going to do 'bout him?"

"Well, hain't he got a father?" says Tom Sawyer.

"Yes, he's got a father, but you can't never find him, these days. He used to lay drunk with the hogs in the tanyard, but he hain't been seen in these parts for a year or more."

They talked it over, and they was going to rule me out[3], because they said every boy must have a family or somebody to kill, or else it wouldn't be fair and square[4] for the others. Well, nobody could think of anything to do—everybody was stumped, and set still. I was most ready to cry; but all at once I thought of a way, and so I offered them Miss Watson—they could kill her. Everybody said:

"Oh, she'll do, she'll do. That's all right. Huck can come in."

Then they all stuck a pin in their fingers to get blood to sign with, and I made my mark on the paper.

"Now," says Ben Rogers, "what's the line of business of this Gang?"

"Nothing only robbery and murder," Tom said.

"But who are we going to rob? houses—or cattle—or—"

"Stuff! stealing cattle and such things ain't robbery, it's burglary," says Tom Sawyer. "We ain't burglars. That ain't no sort of style. We are highwaymen. We stop stages and carriages on the road, with masks on, and kill the people and take their watches and money."

"Must we always kill the people?"

"Oh, certainly. It's best. Some authorities think different, but mostly it's considered best to kill them. Except some that you bring to the cave here, and keep them till they're ransomed."

"Ransomed? What's that?"

"I don't know. But that's what they do. I've seen it in books; and so of course that's what we've got to do."

"But how can we do it if we don't know what it is?"

"Why, blame it all, we've *got* to do it. Don't I tell you it's in the books? Do you want to go to doing different from what's in the books, and get things all muddled up?"

"Oh, that's all very fine to *say*, Tom Sawyer, but how in the nation are these fellows going to be

---

1 high-toned: 高贵的;高尚的
2 Huck Finn: Huckleberry Finn 的简称
3 rule me out: 把我排除在外
4 fair and square: 公平合理的

ransomed if we don't know how to do it to them?—that's the thing I want to get at. Now, what do you *reckon* it is?"

"Well, I don't know. But per'aps if we keep them till they're ransomed, it means that we keep them till they're dead."

"Now, that's something *like*. That'll answer. Why couldn't you said that before? We'll keep them till they're ransomed to death—and a bothersome lot they'll be, too, eating up everything, and always trying to get loose."

"How you talk, Ben Rogers. How can they get loose when there's a guard over them, ready to shoot them down if they move a peg[1]?"

"A guard! Well, that *is* good. So somebody's got to set up all night and never get any sleep, just so as to watch them. I think that's foolishness. Why can't a body take a club and ransom them as soon as they get here?"

"Because it ain't in the books so—that's why. Now, Ben Rogers, do you want to do things regular, or don't you?—that's the idea. Don't you reckon that the people that made the books knows what's the correct thing to do? Do you reckon *you* can learn 'em anything? Not by a good deal. No, sir, we'll just go on and ransom them in the regular way."

"All right. I don't mind; but I say it's a fool way, anyhow. Say—do we kill the women, too?"

"Well, Ben Rogers, if I was as ignorant as you I wouldn't let on. Kill the women? No—nobody ever saw anything in the books like that. You fetch them to the cave, and you're always as polite as pie[2] to them; and by-and-by they fall in love with you, and never want to go home any more."

"Well, if that's the way, I'm agreed, but I don't take no stock in it. Mighty soon we'll have the cave so cluttered up with women, and fellows waiting to be ransomed, that there won't be no place for the robbers. But go ahead, I ain't got nothing to say."

Little Tommy Barnes was asleep now, and when they waked him up he was scared, and cried, and said he wanted to go home to his ma, and didn't want to be a robber any more.

So they all made fun of him, and called him cry-baby, and that made him mad, and he said he would go straight and tell all the secrets. But Tom give him five cents to keep quiet, and said we would all go home and meet next week, and rob somebody and kill some people.

Ben Rogers said he couldn't get out much, only Sundays, and so he wanted to begin next Sunday; but all the boys said it would be wicked to do it on Sunday, and that settled the thing. They agreed to get together and fix a day as soon as they could, and then we elected Tom Sawyer first captain and Jo Harper second captain of the Gang, and so started home.

I clumb up the shed and crept into my window just before day was breaking. My new clothes was all greased up and clayey, and I was dog-tired[3].

---

1 move a peg: 跨出一条腿
2 as polite as pie: 相当于 as nice as pie, 意思是"很好的"
3 dog-tired: 疲倦极了, 筋疲力尽的

Chapter Eight Historical and Biographical Approaches

XVIII

Col.[1] Grangerford was a gentleman, you see. He was a gentleman all over; and so was his family. He was well born, as the saying is, and that's worth as much in a man as it is in a horse, so the Widow Douglas said, and nobody ever denied that she was of the first aristocracy in our town; and pap he always said it, too, though he warn't no more quality than a mudcat himself. Col. Grangerford was very tall and very slim, and had a darkish-paly complexion, not a sign of red in it anywheres; he was clean shaved every morning all over his thin face, and he had the thinnest kind of lips, and the thinnest kind of nostrils, and a high nose, and heavy eyebrows, and the blackest kind of eyes, sunk so deep back that they seemed like they was looking out of caverns at you, as you may say. His forehead was high, and his hair was black and straight and hung to his shoulders. His hands was long and thin, and every day of his life he put on a clean shirt and a full suit from head to foot made out of linen so white it hurt your eyes to look at it; and on Sundays he wore a blue tail-coat with brass buttons on it. He carried a mahogany cane with a silver head to it. There warn't no frivolishness about him, not a bit, and he warn't ever loud. He was as kind as he could be—you could feel that, you know, and so you had confidence. Sometimes he smiled, and it was good to see; but when he straightened himself up like a liberty-pole[2], and the lightning begun to flicker out from under his eyebrows, you wanted to climb a tree first, and find out what the matter was afterwards. He didn't ever have to tell anybody to mind their manners—everybody was always goodmannered where he was. Everybody loved to have him around, too; he was sunshine most always—I mean he made it seem like good weather. When he turned into a cloudbank it was awful dark for half a minute, and that was enough; there wouldn't nothing go wrong again for a week.

When him and the old lady come down in the morning, all the family got up out of their chairs and give them good-day, and didn't set down again till they had set down. Then Tom and Bob went to the sideboard where the decanter was, and mixed a glass of bitters and handed it to him, and he held it in his hand and waited till Tom's and Bob's was mixed, and then they bowed and said, "Our duty to you, sir, and madam;" and *they* bowed the least bit in the world and said thank you, and so they drank, all three, and Bob and Tom poured a spoonful of water on the sugar and the mite of whisky or apple brandy in the bottom of their tumblers, and give it to me and Buck, and we drank to the old people too.

Bob was the oldest, and Tom next. Tall, beautiful men with very broad shoulders and brown faces, and long black hair and black eyes. They dressed in white linen from head to foot, like the old gentleman, and wore broad Panama hats[3].

Then there was Miss Charlotte; she was twenty-five, and tall and proud and grand, but as good as she could be when she warn't stirred up; but when she was she had a look that would make you wilt in your tracks, like her father. She was beautiful.

So was her sister, Miss Sophia, but it was a different kind. She was gentle and sweet, like a dove, and she was only twenty.

---

1 Col.=colonel
2 liberty-pole：旗杆
3 Panama hat：巴拿马草帽

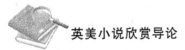

Each person had their own nigger to wait on them—Buck too. My nigger had a monstrous easy time, because I warn't used to having anybody do anything for me, but Buck's was on the jump[1] most of the time.

This was all there was of the family, now; but there used to be more—three sons; they got killed; and Emmeline that died.

The old gentleman owned a lot of farms, and over a hundred niggers. Sometimes a stack of people would come there, horseback, from ten or fifteen mile around, and stay five or six days, and have such junketings round about and on the river, and dances and picnics in the woods, day-times, and balls at the house, nights. These people was mostly kinfolks of the family. The men brought their guns with them. It was a handsome lot of quality, I tell you.

There was another clan of aristocracy around there—five or six families—mostly of the name of Shepherdson. They was as high-toned, and well born, and rich and grand, as the tribe of Grangerfords. The Shepherdsons and Grangerfords used the same steamboat landing, which was about two mile above our house; so sometimes when I went up there with a lot of our folks I used to see a lot of the Shepherdsons there, on their fine horses.

One day Buck and me was away out in the woods, hunting, and heard a horse coming. We was crossing the road. Buck says:

"Quick! Jump for the woods!"

We done it, and then peeped down the woods through the leaves. Pretty soon a splendid young man come galloping down the road, setting his horse easy and looking like a soldier. He had his gun across his pommel. I had seen him before. It was young Harney Shepherdson. I heard Buck's gun go off at my ear, and Harney's hat tumbled off from his head. He grabbed his gun and rode straight to the place where we was hid. But we didn't wait. We started through the woods on a run. The woods warn't thick, so I looked over my shoulder to dodge the bullet, and twice I seen Harney cover Buck with his gun; and then he rode away the way he come—to get his hat, I reckon, but I couldn't see. We never stopped running till we got home. The old gentleman's eyes blazed a minute—'twas pleasure, mainly, I judged—then his face sort of smoothed down[2], and he says, kind of gentle:

"I don't like that shooting from behind a bush. Why didn't you step into the road, my boy?"

"The Shepherdsons don't, father. They always take advantage."

Miss Charlotte she held her head up like a queen while Buck was telling his tale, and her nostrils spread and her eyes snapped. The two young men looked dark, but never said nothing. Miss Sophia she turned pale, but the color come back when she found the man warn't hurt.

Soon as I could get Buck down by the corn-cribs under the trees by ourselves, I says:

"Did you want to kill him, Buck?"

"Well, I bet I did."

"What did he do to you?"

"Him? He never done nothing to me."

---

1 on the jump：忙个不停

2 smoothed down：平静下来

"Well, then, what did you want to kill him for?"

"Why, nothing—only it's on account of the feud."

"What's a feud?"

"Why, where was you raised? Don't you know what a feud is?"

"Never heard of it before—tell me about it."

"Well," says Buck, "a feud is this way: A man has a quarrel with another man, and kills him; then that other man's brother kills HIM; then the other brothers, on both sides, goes for one another; then the *cousins* chip in[1]—and by-and-by everybody's killed off, and there ain't no more feud. But it's kind of slow, and takes a long time."

"Has this one been going on long, Buck?"

"Well, I should *reckon*! It started thirty year ago, or som'ers along there. There was trouble 'bout something, and then a lawsuit to settle it; and the suit went agin one of the men, and so he up and shot the man that won the suit—which he would naturally do, of course. Anybody would."

"What was the trouble about, Buck?—land?"

"I reckon maybe—I don't know."

"Well, who done the shooting?—Was it a Grangerford or a Shepherdson?"

"Laws, how do I know? It was so long ago."

"Don't anybody know?"

"Oh, yes, pa knows, I reckon, and some of the other old people; but they don't know, now, what the row[2] was about in the first place."

"Has there been many killed, Buck?"

"Yes—right smart chance of funerals. But they don't always kill. Pa's got a few buck-shot in him; but he don't mind it 'cuz he don't weigh much, anyway. Bob's been carved up some with a bowie, and Tom's been hurt once or twice."

"Has anybody been killed this year, Buck?"

"Yes, we got one and they got one. 'Bout three months ago, my cousin Bud, fourteen year old, was riding through the woods, on t'other side of the river, and didn't have no weapon with him, which was blame' foolishness, and in a lonesome place he hears a horse a-coming behind him, and sees old Baldy Shepherdson a-linkin' after him with his gun in his hand and his white hair a-flying in the wind; and 'stead of jumping off and taking to the brush, Bud 'lowed he could outrun him; so they had it, nip and tuck[3], for five mile or more, the old man a-gaining all the time; so at last Bud seen it warn't any use, so he stopped and faced around so as to have the bullet holes in front, you know, and the old man he rode up and shot him down. But he didn't git much chance to enjoy his luck, for inside of a week our folks laid *him* out[4]."

"I reckon that old man was a coward, Buck."

"I reckon he *warn't* a coward. Not by a blame' sight. There ain't a coward amongst them Shepherdsons—

---

1 chip in: 共同帮忙
2 row: 〈口〉吵架,口角
3 nip and tuck: 势均力敌
4 laid him out: 把他摆平了

not a one. And there ain't no cowards amongst the Grangerfords, either. Why, that old man kep' up his end in a fight one day, for half an hour, against three Grangerfords, and come out winner. They was all a-horseback; he lit off of his horse and got behind a little woodpile, and kep' his horse before him to stop the bullets; but the Grangerfords stayed on their horses and capered around the old man, and peppered away at him[1], and he peppered away at them. Him and his horse both went home pretty leaky and crippled, but the Grangerfords had to be *fetched* home—and one of 'em was dead, and another died the next day. No, sir; if a body's out hunting for cowards, he don't want to fool away[2] any time amongst them Shepherdsons, becuz they don't breed any of that *kind*."

Next Sunday we all went to church, about three mile, everybody a-horse-back. The men took their guns along, so did Buck, and kept them between their knees or stood them handy against the wall. The Shepherdsons done the same. It was pretty ornery preaching—all about brotherly love, and such-like tiresomeness; but everybody said it was a good sermon, and they all talked it over going home, and had such a powerful lot to say about faith, and good works, and free grace, and preforeordestination[3], and I don't know what all, that it did seem to me to be one of the roughest Sundays I had run across yet.

About an hour after dinner everybody was dozing around, some in their chairs and some in their rooms, and it got to be pretty dull. Buck and a dog was stretched out on the grass in the sun sound asleep. I went up to our room, and judged I would take a nap myself. I found that sweet Miss Sophia standing in her door, which was next to ours, and she took me in her room and shut the door very soft, and asked me if I liked her, and I said I did; and she asked me if I would do something for her and not tell anybody, and I said I would. Then she said she'd forgot her Testament[4], and left it in the seat at church between two other books, and would I slip out quiet and go there and fetch it to her, and not say nothing to nobody. I said I would. So I slid out and slipped off up the road, and there warn't anybody at the church, except maybe a hog or two, for there warn't any lock on the door, and hogs likes a puncheon floor in summer-time because it's cool. If you notice, most folks don't go to church only when they've got to; but a hog is different.

Says I to myself, something's up—it ain't natural for a girl to be in such a sweat about a Testament. So I give it a shake, and out drops a little piece of paper with *"Half-past two"* wrote on it with a pencil. I ransacked it, but couldn't find anything else. I couldn't make anything out of that, so I put the paper in the book again, and when I got home and upstairs there was Miss Sophia in her door waiting for me. She pulled me in and shut the door; then she looked in the Testament till she found the paper, and as soon as she read it she looked glad; and before a body could think she grabbed me and give me a squeeze, and said I was the best boy in the world, and not to tell anybody. She was mighty red in the face for a minute, and her eyes lighted up, and it made her powerful pretty. I was a good deal astonished, but when I got my breath I asked her what the paper was about, and she asked me if I had read it, and I said no, and she asked me if I could read writing, and I told her "no, only coarse-hand," and then she said the paper warn't anything but a book-mark to keep her place, and I might go and play now.

---

1 peppered away at him: 雨点般地向他扫射
2 fool away: 浪费
3 preforeordestination: 此词是哈克根据基督教长老会教义中的 predestination 和 foreordination 编造的。
4 Testament: 此处指《圣经旧约》

Chapter Eight Historical and Biographical Approaches

I went off down to the river, studying over this thing, and pretty soon I noticed that my nigger was following along behind. When we was out of sight of the house he looked back and around a second, and then comes a-running, and says:

"Mars Jawge, if you'll come down into de swamp, I'll show you a whole stack o' water-moccasins."

Thinks I, that's mighty curious; he said that yesterday. He oughter know a body don't love water-moccasins enough to go around hunting for them. What is he up to, anyway? So I says—

"All right, trot ahead."

I followed a half a mile, then he struck out over the swamp and waded ankle deep as much as another half mile. We come to a little flat piece of land which was dry and very thick with trees and bushes and vines, and he says—

"You shove right in dah, jist a few steps, Mars Jawge, dah's whah dey is. I's seed 'm befo'; I don't k'yer to see 'em no mo'."

Then he slopped right along and went away, and pretty soon the trees hid him. I poked into the place a-ways, and come to a little open patch as big as a bedroom, all hung around with vines, and found a man laying there asleep—and by jings it was my old Jim!

I waked him up, and I reckoned it was going to be a grand surprise to him to see me again, but it warn't. He nearly cried, he was so glad, but he warn't surprised. Said he swum along behind me, that night, and heard me yell every time, but dasn't answer, because he didn't want nobody to pick *him* up, and take him into slavery again. Says he—

"I got hurt a little, en couldn't swim fas', so I wuz a considable ways behine you, towards de las'; when you landed I reck'ned I could ketch up wid you on de lan' 'dout havin' to shout at you, but when I see dat house I begin to go slow. I 'uz off too fur to hear what dey say to you—I wuz 'fraid o' de dogs—but when it 'uz all quiet agin, I knowed you's in de house, so I struck out for de woods to wait for day. Early in de mawnin' some er de niggers come along, gwyne to de fields, en dey tuk me en showed me dis place, whah de dogs can't track me on accounts o' de water, en dey brings me truck to eat every night, en tells me how you's a-gitt'n along."

"Why didn't you tell my Jack to fetch me here sooner, Jim?"

"Well, 'twarn't no use to 'sturb you, Huck, tell we could do sumfn—but we's all right, now. I ben a-buyin' pots en pans en vittles, as I got a chanst, en a patchin' up de raf', nights, when— "

"*What* raft, Jim?"

"Our ole raf'."

"You mean to say our old raft warn't smashed all to flinders?"

"No, she warn't. She was tore up a good deal—one en' of her was—but dey warn't no great harm done, on'y our traps was mos' all los'. Ef we hadn' dive' so deep en swum so fur under water, en de night hadn' ben so dark, en we warn't so sk'yerd, en ben sich punkin-heads, as de sayin' is, we'd a seed de raf'. But it's jis' as well we didn't, 'kase now she's all fixed up agin mos' as good as new, en we's got a new lot o' stuff, too, in de place o' what 'uz los'."

"Why, how did you get hold of the raft again, Jim—did you catch her?"

"How I gwyne to ketch her, en I out in de woods? No, some er de niggers foun' her ketched on a snag, along heah in de ben', en dey hid her in a crick, 'mongst de willows, en dey wuz so much jawin'

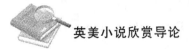

'bout which un 'um she b'long to de mos', dat I come to heah 'bout it pooty soon, so I ups en settles de trouble by tellin' 'um she don't b'long to none uv um, but to you en me; en I ast 'm if dey gwyne to grab a young white genlman's propaty, en git a hid'n for it? Den I gin 'm ten cents apiece, en dey 'uz mighty well satisfied, en wisht some mo' raf's 'ud come along en make 'm rich agin. Dey's mighty good to me, dese niggers is, en whatever I wants 'm to do fur me, I doan' have to ast 'm twice, honey. Dat Jack's a good nigger, en pooty smart."

"Yes, he is. He ain't ever told me you was here; told me to come, and he'd show me a lot of water-moccasins. If anything happens, *he* ain't mixed up in it. He can say he never seen us together, and it'll be the truth."

I don't want to talk much about the next day. I reckon I'll cut it pretty short. I waked up about dawn, and was agoing to turn over and go to sleep again, when I noticed how still it was—didn't seem to be anybody stirring. That warn't usual. Next I noticed that Buck was up and gone. Well, I gets up, a-wondering, and goes down stairs—nobody around; everything as still as a mouse[1]. Just the same outside; thinks I, what does it mean? Down by the wood-pile I comes across my Jack, and says:

"What's it all about?"

Says he:

"Don't you know, Mars Jawge?"

"No," says I, "I don't."

"Well, den, Miss Sophia's run off! 'deed she has. She run off in de night, sometime—nobody don't know jis' when—run off to git married to dat young Harney Shepherdson, you know—leastways, so dey 'spec. De fambly foun' it out, 'bout half an hour ago—maybe a little mo'—en' I *tell* you dey warn't no time los'. Sich another hurryin' up guns en hosses *you* never see! De women folks has gone for to stir up de relations, en ole Mars Saul en de boys tuck dey guns en rode up de river road for to try to ketch dat young man en kill him 'fo' he kin git acrost de river wid Miss Sophia. I reck'n dey's gwyne to be mighty rough times."

"Buck went off 'thout waking me up."

"Well, I reck'n he *did*! Dey warn't gwyne to mix you up in it. Mars Buck he loaded up his gun en 'lowed he's gwyne to fetch home a Shepherdson or bust. Well, dey'll be plenty un 'm dah, I reck'n, en you bet you he'll fetch one ef he gits a chanst."

I took up the river road as hard as I could put. By-and-by I begin to hear guns a good ways off. When I came in sight of the log store and the wood-pile where the steamboats lands, I worked along under the trees and brush till I got to a good place, and then I clumb up into the forks of a cotton-wood that was out of reach, and watched. There was a wood-rank four foot high, a little ways in front of the tree, and first I was going to hide behind that; but maybe it was luckier I didn't.

There was four or five men cavorting around on their horses in the open place before the log store, cussing and yelling, and trying to get at a couple of young chaps that was behind the wood-rank alongside of the steamboat landing—but they couldn't come it. Every time one of them showed himself on the river side of the wood-pile he got shot at. The two boys was squatting back to back behind the

---

1 as still as a mouse: 异常安静

Chapter Eight　Historical and Biographical Approaches

pile, so they could watch both ways.

　　By-and-by the men stopped cavorting around and yelling. They started riding towards the store; then up gets one of the boys, draws a steady bead over the wood-rank, and drops one of them out of his saddle. All the men jumped off of their horses and grabbed the hurt one and started to carry him to the store; and that minute the two boys started on the run. They got half-way to the tree I was in before the men noticed. Then the men see them, and jumped on their horses and took out after them. They gained on the boys, but it didn't do no good, the boys had too good a start; they got to the wood-pile that was in front of my tree, and slipped in behind it, and so they had the bulge[1] on the men again. One of the boys was Buck, and the other was a slim young chap about nineteen years old.

　　The men ripped around awhile, and then rode away. As soon as they was out of sight, I sung out to Buck and told him. He didn't know what to make of my voice coming out of the tree, at first. He was awful surprised. He told me to watch out sharp and let him know when the men come in sight again; said they was up to some devilment or other—wouldn't be gone long. I wished I was out of that tree, but I dasn't come down. Buck begun to cry and rip, and 'lowed that him and his cousin Joe (that was the other young chap) would make up for this day, yet. He said his father and his two brothers was killed, and two or three of the enemy. Said the Shepherdsons laid for them, in ambush[2]. Buck said his father and brothers ought to waited for their relations—the Shepherdsons was too strong for them. I asked him what was become of young Harney and Miss Sophia[3]. He said they'd got across the river and was safe. I was glad of that; but the way Buck did take on because he didn't manage to kill Harney that day he shot at him—I hain't ever heard anything like it.

　　All of a sudden, bang! bang! bang! goes three or four guns—the men had slipped around through the woods and come in from behind without their horses! The boys jumped for the river—both of them hurt—and as they swum down the current the men run along the bank shooting at them and singing out, "Kill them, kill them!" It made me so sick I most fell out of the tree. I ain't agoing to tell *all* that happened!—it would make me sick again if I was to do that. I wished I hadn't ever come ashore that night, to see such things. I ain't ever going to get shut of them—lots of times I dream about them.

　　I stayed in the tree till it begun to get dark, afraid to come down. Sometimes I heard guns away off in the woods; and twice I seen little gangs of men gallop past the log store with guns; so I reckoned the trouble was still agoing on. I was mighty downhearted; so I made up my mind I wouldn't ever go anear that house again, because I reckoned I was to blame, somehow. I judged that that piece of paper meant that Miss Sophia was to meet Harney somewheres at half-past two and run off; and I judged I ought to told her father about that paper and the curious way she acted, and then maybe he would a locked her up, and this awful mess wouldn't ever happened.

　　When I got down out of the tree, I crept along down the river bank a piece, and found the two bodies laying in the edge of the water, and tugged at them till I got them ashore; then I covered up their faces, and got away as quick as I could. I cried a little when I was covering up Buck's face, for he was mighty good to me.

1　had the bulge：占上风
2　laid for them, in ambush：给他们设下埋伏
3　what was become of young Harney and Miss Sophia：Harney 和 Miss Sophia 怎么样了

It was just dark, now. I never went near the house, but struck through the woods and made for the swamp. Jim warn't on his island, so I tramped off in a hurry for the crick, and crowded through the willows, red-hot to jump aboard and get out of that awful country—the raft was gone! My souls, but I was scared! I couldn't get my breath for most a minute. Then I raised a yell. A voice not twenty-five foot from me says—

"Good lan'! is dat you, honey? Doan' make no noise."

It was Jim's voice—nothing ever sounded so good before. I run along the bank a piece and got aboard, and Jim he grabbed me and hugged me, he was so glad to see me. He says—

"Laws bless you, chile, I 'uz right down sho' you's dead agin. Jack's been heah; he say he reck'n you's ben shot, kase you didn' come home no mo'; so I's jes' dis minute a startin' de raf' down towards de mouf er de crick, so's to be all ready for to shove out en leave soon as Jack comes agin en tells me for certain you *is* dead. Lawsy, I's mighty glad to git you back again, honey."

I says—

"All right—that's mighty good; they won't find me, and they'll think I've been killed, and floated down the river—there's something up there that 'll help them think so—so don't you lose no time, Jim, but just shove off¹ for the big water as fast as ever you can."

I never felt easy till the raft was two mile below there and out in the middle of the Mississippi. Then we hung up our signal lantern, and judged that we was free and safe once more. I hadn't had a bite to eat since yesterday, so Jim he got out some corn-dodgers and buttermilk, and pork and cabbage, and greens—there ain't nothing in the world so good, when it's cooked right—and whilst I eat my supper we talked, and had a good time. I was powerful glad to get away from the feuds, and so was Jim to get away from the swamp. We said there warn't no home like a raft, after all. Other places do seem so cramped up and smothery, but a raft don't. You feel mighty free and easy and comfortable on a raft.

XXXI

We dasn't stop again at any town, for days and days; kept right along down the river. We was down south in the warm weather, now, and a mighty long ways from home. We begun to come to trees with Spanish moss² on them, hanging down from the limbs like long, gray beards. It was the first I ever see it growing, and it made the woods look solemn and dismal. So now the frauds³ reckoned they was out of danger, and they begun to work the villages again⁴.

First they done a lecture on temperance; but they didn't make enough for them both to get drunk on. Then in another village they started a dancing-school; but they didn't know no more how to dance than a kangaroo does; so the first prance they made, the general public jumped in and pranced them out of town⁵. Another time they tried to go at yellocution⁶; but they didn't yellocute long till the audience got

---

1 shove off: 动身，离开

2 Spanish moss: 寄生藤

3 the frauds: 指书中冒充公爵和国王的两个骗子。

4 they begun to work the villages again: 他们又上那些村子去骗人了。

5 so the first prance they made, the general public jumped in and pranced them out of town: 所以他们刚蹦跶了几下，大伙就跑来了，把他们从镇子上撑走了。

6 tried to go at yellocution: 打算教演说。yellocution 和下文的 yellocute 是哈克自己编的字。

Chapter Eight　Historical and Biographical Approaches

up and give them a solid good cussing, and made them skip out[1]. They tackled missionarying, and mesmerizing, and doctoring, and telling fortunes[2], and a little of everything; but they couldn't seem to have no luck. So at last they got just about dead broke[3], and laid around the raft, as she floated along, thinking, and thinking, and never saying nothing, by the half a day at a time, and dreadful blue and desperate.

And at last they took a change, and begun to lay their heads together in the wigwam and talk low and confidential two or three hours at a time. Jim and me got uneasy. We didn't like the look of it. We judged they was studying up some kind of worse deviltry than ever. We turned it over and over[4], and at last we made up our minds they was going to break into somebody's house or store, or was going into the counterfeit-money business, or something. So then we was pretty scared, and made up an agreement that we wouldn't have nothing in the world to do with such actions, and if we ever got the least show we would give them the cold shake, and clear out[5] and leave them behind. Well, early one morning we hid the raft in a good, safe place about two mile below a little bit of a shabby village, named Pikesville, and the king he went ashore, and told us all to stay hid whilst he went up to town and smelt around to see if anybody had got any wind of the Royal Nonesuch[6] there yet. ("House to rob, you *mean*," says I to myself; "and when you get through robbing it you'll come back here and wonder what has become of me and Jim and the raft—and you'll have to take it out in wondering[7].") And he said if he warn't back by midday, the duke and me would know it was all right, and we was to come along.

So we stayed where we was. The duke he fretted and sweated around, and was in a mighty sour way. He scolded us for everything, and we couldn't seem to do nothing right; he found fault with[8] every little thing. Something was a-brewing, sure. I was good and glad when midday come and no king; we could have a change, anyway—and maybe a chance for *the* chance on top of it[9]. So me and the duke went up to the village, and hunted around there for the king, and by-and-by we found him in the back room of a little low doggery[10], very tight, and a lot of loafers bullyragging him for sport, and he a cussing and threatening[11] with all his might, and so tight he couldn't walk, and couldn't do nothing to them. The duke he begun to abuse him for an old fool, and the king begun to sass back, and the minute they was fairly at it, I lit out, and shook the reefs out of my hind legs[12], and spun down the river road like a deer—for I see our chance; and I made up my mind that it would be a long day before they ever see me and Jim again. I got down there all out of breath but loaded up with joy, and sung out—

---

1 skip out：偷偷溜走
2 telling fortunes：算命，占卜
3 dead broke：〈俚语〉身无分文
4 We turned it over and over：我们思来想去。
5 if we ever got the least show we would give them the cold shake, and clear out：只要有一点点机会，就会把他们悄悄甩掉，然后溜之大吉。
6 smelt around to see if anybody had got any wind of the Royal Nonesuch：去探听探听消息，看镇上是不是有人听到了"皇家奇物"的风声。
7 you'll have to take it out in wondering：那时候你就得抓瞎。
8 found fault with：挑剔，吹毛求疵，抱怨
9 maybe a chance for *the* chance on top of it：不光是活动的机会，说不定还能让我们碰上那个机会呢。it 指前文的 change
10 doggery：廉价的小酒吧
11 he a cussing and threatening= he was cussing and threatening
12 and the minute they was fairly at it, I lit out, and shook the reefs out of my hind legs：他们骂得正起劲，我就溜出来，撒腿拼命跑。shook the reefs out of：放开帆棚，(比喻)加快速度。

"Set her loose, Jim, we're all right, now!"

But there warn't no answer, and nobody come out of the wigwam. Jim was gone! I set up a shout—and then another—and then another one; and run this way and that in the woods, whooping and screeching; but it warn't no use—old Jim was gone. Then I set down and cried; I couldn't help it. But I couldn't set still long. Pretty soon I went out on the road, trying to think what I better do, and I run across a boy walking, and asked him if he'd seen a strange nigger, dressed so and so, and he says:

"Yes."

"Whereabouts?" says I.

"Down to Silas Phelps'[1] place, two mile below here. He's a runaway nigger, and they've got him. Was you looking for him?"

"You bet I ain't! I run across him in the woods about an hour or two ago, and he said if I hollered he'd cut my livers out—and told me to lay down and stay where I was; and I done it. Been there ever since; afeard to come out."

"Well," he says, "you needn't be afeard no more, becuz they've got him. He run off f'm down South, som'ers[2]."

"It's a good job they got him."

"Well, I *reckon*! There's two hunderd dollars reward on him. It's like picking up money out'n the road."

"Yes, it is—and I could a had it if I'd been big enough; I see him *first*. Who nailed him?"

"It was an old fellow—a stranger—and he sold out his chance in him for forty dollars, becuz he's got to go up the river and can't wait. Think o' that, now! You bet I'd wait, if it was seven year."

"That's me, every time[3]," says I. "But maybe his chance ain't worth no more than that, if he'll sell it so cheap. Maybe there's something ain't straight about it."

"But it *is*, though—straight as a string. I see the handbill[4] myself. It tells all about him, to a dot—paints him like a picture, and tells the plantation he's frum, below Newr*leans*[5]. No-sirree-*bob*[6], they ain't no trouble 'bout *that* speculation, you bet you. Say, gimme a chaw tobacker, won't ye[7]?"

I didn't have none, so he left. I went to the raft, and set down in the wigwam to think. But I couldn't come to nothing. I thought till I wore my head sore, but I couldn't see no way out of the trouble. After all this long journey, and after all we'd done for them scoundrels, here it was all come to nothing[8], everything all busted up[9] and ruined, because they could have the heart to serve Jim such a trick as that[10], and make him a slave again all his life, and amongst strangers, too, for forty dirty dollars.

Once I said to myself it would be a thousand times better for Jim to be a slave at home where his

---

1 Silas Phelps：赛拉斯·菲尔普斯，汤姆的姨夫，骗子把吉姆卖给了他。
2 He run off f'm down South, som'ers=He ran off from down South, somewhere
3 That's me, every time：当然，我也这么想。
4 handbill：指两个骗子事先准备好的传单
5 Newr*leans*=New Orleans
6 No-sirree-*bob*：相当于 No, sir. bob 是顺口带出的尾音，没有意义。
7 gimme a chaw tobacker, won't ye=give me a chew of tobacco, won't you?
8 after all we'd done for them scoundrels, here it was all come to nothing：我们对这两个骗子这么好，可到头来却落得一场空
9 busted up：破灭，失败
10 they could have the heart to serve Jim such a trick as that：他们的心肠这么黑，要这种卑鄙手段来害吉姆。

Chapter Eight Historical and Biographical Approaches

family was, as long as he'd *got* to be a slave, and so I'd better write a letter to Tom Sawyer and tell him to tell Miss Watson where he was. But I soon give up that notion, for two things: she'd be mad and disgusted at his rascality and ungratefulness for leaving her, and so she'd sell him straight down the river again; and if she didn't, everybody naturally despises an ungrateful nigger, and they'd make Jim feel it all the time, and so he'd feel ornery and disgraced[1]. And then think of *me*! It would get all around, that Huck Finn helped a nigger to get his freedom; and if I was ever to see anybody from that town again, I'd be ready to get down and lick his boots for shame[2]. That's just the way: a person does a low-down[3] thing, and then he don't want to take no consequences of it. Thinks as long as he can hide it, it ain't no disgrace. That was my fix exactly. The more I studied about this, the more my conscience went to grinding me, and the more wicked and low-down and ornery I got to feeling. And at last, when it hit me all of a sudden[4] that here was the plain hand of Providence[5] slapping me in the face and letting me know my wickedness was being watched all the time from up there in heaven, whilst I was stealing a poor old woman's nigger that hadn't ever done me no harm, and now was showing me there's One[6] that's always on the lookout, and ain't agoing to allow no such miserable doings to go only just so fur and no further, I most dropped in my tracks[7] I was so scared. Well, I tried the best I could to kinder[8] soften it up somehow for myself, by saying I was brung up wicked, and so I warn't so much to blame; but something inside of me kept saying, "There was the Sunday-school[9], you could a gone to it; and if you'd a done it they'd a learnt you[10], there, that people that acts as I'd been acting about that nigger goes to everlasting fire."

It made me shiver. And I about made up my mind to pray, and see if I couldn't try to quit being the kind of a boy I was, and be better. So I kneeled down. But the words wouldn't come. Why wouldn't they? It warn't no use to try and hide it from Him. Nor from *me*, neither. I knowed very well why they wouldn't come. It was because my heart warn't right; it was because I warn't square; it was because I was playing double[11]. I was letting *on* to give up sin, but away inside of me I was holding on to the biggest one of all[12]. I was trying to make my mouth *say* I would do the right thing and the clean thing, and go and write to that nigger's owner and tell where he was; but deep down in me I knowed it was a lie—and He knowed it. You can't pray a lie—I found that out.

So I was full of trouble, full as I could be; and didn't know what to do. At last I had an idea; and I says, I'll go and write the letter—and then see if I can pray. Why, it was astonishing, the way I felt as light as a feather, right straight off, and my troubles all gone. So I got a piece of paper and a pencil, all

---

1 He'd feel ornery and disgraced：他会感到丢脸，见不得人了。ornery=ordinary，这里的意思"understatement"。
2 I'd be ready to get down and lick his boots for shame：我会觉得自己丢了脸，下跪向其表示敬意。
3 low-down：〈口语〉下等的，卑劣的
4 it hit me all of a sudden：我突然想起
5 Providence：上帝
6 One：指上帝，与上文的 Providence 以及下文的 Him 和 He 同义。
7 I most dropped in my tracks：我差点倒在地上。
8 kinder=kind of
9 Sunday-school：主日学校，指星期日对儿童进行宗教教育的学校
10 they'd a learnt you：相当于 they would have taught you。learn 是俚语，意思是 teach。
11 playing double：要两面派；两面讨好
12 I was letting *on* to give up sin, but away inside of me I was holding on to the biggest one of all：我表面上假装要改邪归正，可内心深处还是紧紧抓着那桩最坏的事不肯撒手。one 这里指 sin。

glad and excited, and set down and wrote:

> Miss Watson, your runaway nigger Jim is down here two mile below Pikesville and Mr. Phelps has got him and he will give him up for the reward if you send.
>
> Huck Finn.

I felt good and all washed clean of sin for the first time I had ever felt so in my life, and I knowed I could pray now. But I didn't do it straight off, but laid the paper down and set there thinking—thinking how good it was all this happened so, and how near I come to being lost and going to hell. And went on thinking. And got to thinking over our trip down the river; and I see Jim before me, all the time: in the day, and in the night-time, sometimes moonlight, sometimes storms, and we a floating along, talking, and singing, and laughing. But somehow I couldn't seem to strike no places to harden me against him, but only the other kind[1]. I'd see him standing my watch on top of his'n, 'stead of calling me[2], so I could go on sleeping; and see him how glad he was when I come back out of the fog; and when I come to him again in the swamp, up there where the feud was; and such-like times; and would always call me honey, and pet me, and do everything he could think of for me, and how good he always was; and at last I struck the time I saved him by telling the men we had small-pox aboard[3], and he was so grateful, and said I was the best friend old Jim ever had in the world, and the *only* one he's got now; and then I happened to look around, and see that paper.

It was a close place[4]. I took it up, and held it in my hand. I was a trembling, because I'd got to decide, forever, betwixt two things, and I knowed it. I studied a minute, sort of holding my breath, and then says to myself:

"All right, then, I'll *go* to hell[5]"—and tore it up.

It was awful thoughts, and awful words, but they was said. And I let them stay said; and never thought no more about reforming. I shoved the whole thing out of my head; and said I would take up wickedness again, which was in my line[6], being brung up to it, and the other warn't. And for a starter, I would go to work and steal Jim out of slavery again; and if I could think up anything worse, I would do that, too; because as long as I was in, and in for good, I might as well go the whole hog[7].

Then I set to thinking over how to get at it, and turned over some considerable many ways in my mind; and at last fixed up a plan that suited me. So then I took the bearings of a woody island that was down the river a piece, and as soon as it was fairly dark I crept out with my raft and went for it, and hid it there, and then turned in. I slept the night through, and got up before it was light, and had my breakfast, and put on my store clothes[8], and tied up some others and one thing or another in a bundle, and took the

---

1 But somehow I couldn't seem to strike no places to harden me against him, but only the other kind: 我好像找不出在哪一点上可以叫我对他下狠心，想到的反倒是他对我的种种好处。

2 I'd see him standing my watch on top of his'n, 'stead of calling me: 我总是看见他站完自己的一班岗后却不叫醒我，替我值班。

3 at last I struck the time I saved him by telling the men we had small-pox aboard: 后来我想起那一回，我告诉那两个人说我们木筏上有人害了天花，结果就救了吉姆。

4 It was a close place: 这事儿真叫人为难。close 这里的意思是 "狭窄"。

5 All right, then, I'll *go* to hell: 那么，好吧，下地狱就下地狱吧。

6 in my line: 和我一致

7 go the whole hog: 干到底

8 store clothes: 现成的衣服

Chapter Eight   Historical and Biographical Approaches

canoe and cleared for shore. I landed below where I judged was Phelps's place, and hid my bundle in the woods, and then filled up the canoe with water, and loaded rocks into her and sunk her where I could find her again when I wanted her, about a quarter of a mile below a little steam sawmill that was on the bank.

Then I struck up the road[1], and when I passed the mill I see a sign on it, "Phelps's Sawmill," and when I come to the farm-houses, two or three hundred yards further along, I kept my eyes peeled[2], but didn't see nobody around, though it was good daylight, now. But I didn't mind, because I didn't want to see nobody just yet—I only wanted to get the lay of the land[3]. According to my plan, I was going to turn up there from the village, not from below. So I just took a look, and shoved along, straight for town. Well, the very first man I see, when I got there, was the duke. He was sticking up a bill for the Royal Nonesuch—three-night performance—like that other time. *They* had the cheek, them frauds! I was right on him, before I could shirk. He looked astonished, and says:

"Hel-*lo*! Where'd *you* come from?" Then he says, kind of glad and eager, "Where's the raft?—got her in a good place?"

I says:

"Why, that's just what I was going to ask your grace."

Then he didn't look so joyful—and says:

"What was your idea for asking *me*?" he says.

"Well," I says, "when I see the king in that doggery yesterday, I says to myself, we can't get him home for hours, till he's soberer; so I went a loafing around town to put in the time, and wait. A man up and offered me ten cents to help him pull a skiff over the river and back to fetch a sheep, and so I went along; but when we was dragging him to the boat, and the man left me aholt of[4] the rope and went behind him to shove him along, he was too strong for me, and jerked loose and run, and we after him. We didn't have no dog, and so we had to chase him all over the country till we tired him out. We never got him till dark; then we fetched him over, and I started down for the raft. When I got there and see it was gone, I says to myself, 'they've got into trouble and had to leave; and they've took my nigger, which is the only nigger I've got in the world, and now I'm in a strange country, and ain't got no property no more, nor nothing, and no way to make my living;' so I set down and cried. I slept in the woods all night. But what *did* become of the raft, then?—and Jim—poor Jim!"

"Blamed if I know—that is, what's become of the raft. That old fool had made a trade and got forty dollars, and when we found him in the doggery the loafers had matched half-dollars with him[5] and got every cent but what he'd spent for whisky; and when I got him home late last night and found the raft gone, we said, 'That little rascal has stole our raft and shook us, and run off down the river.'"

"I wouldn't shake my *nigger*, would I?—the only nigger I had in the world, and the only property."

"We never thought of that. Fact is, I reckon we'd come to consider him *our* nigger; yes, we did

---

1 I struck up the road: 我顺着大路走。
2 kept my eyes peeled=kept my eye open
3 get the lay of the land: 把这一带的地形了解清楚
4 aholt of: 〈俚语〉相当于 hold of
5 the loafers had matched half-dollars with him: 二流子们和他打半块钱的赌。

consider him so—goodness knows we had trouble enough for him. So when we see the raft was gone, and we flat broke[1], there warn't anything for it but to try the Royal Nonesuch another shake. And I've pegged along[2] ever since, dry as a powderhorn. Where's that ten cents? Give it here."

I had considerable money, so I give him ten cents, but begged him to spend it for something to eat, and give me some, because it was all the money I had, and I hadn't had nothing to eat since yesterday. He never said nothing. The next minute he whirls on me and says:

"Do you reckon that nigger would blow on[3] us? We'd skin him if he done that!"

"How can he blow? Hain't he run off?"

"No! That old fool sold him, and never divided with me, and the money's gone."

"*Sold* him?" I says, and begun to cry; "why, he was *my* nigger, and that was my money. Where is he?—I want my nigger."

"Well, you can't get your nigger, that's all—so dry up your blubbering[4]. Looky here—do you think *you'd* venture to blow on us? Blamed if I think I'd trust you. Why, if you was to blow on us —"

He stopped, but I never see the duke look so ugly out of his eyes before. I went on a-whimpering, and says:

"I don't want to blow on nobody; and I ain't got no time to blow, nohow. I got to turn out and find my nigger."

He looked kinder bothered, and stood there with his bills fluttering on his arm, thinking, and wrinkling up his forehead. At last he says:

"I'll tell you something. We got to be here three days. If you'll promise you won't blow, and won't let the nigger blow, I'll tell you where to find him."

So I promised, and he says:

"A farmer by the name of Silas Ph—" and then he stopped. You see, he started to tell me the truth; but when he stopped, that way, and begun to study and think again, I reckoned he was changing his mind. And so he was. He wouldn't trust me; he wanted to make sure of having me out of the way the whole three days. So pretty soon he says: "The man that bought him is named Abram Foster—Abram G. Foster—and he lives forty mile back here in the country, on the road to Lafayette."

"All right," I says, "I can walk it in three days. And I'll start this very afternoon."

"No you wont, you'll start *now*; and don't you lose any time about it, neither, nor do any gabbling by the way. Just keep a tight tongue in your head and move right along, and then you won't get into trouble with *us*, d'ye hear?"

That was the order I wanted, and that was the one I played for. I wanted to be left free to work my plans.

"So clear out," he says; "and you can tell Mr. Foster whatever you want to. Maybe you can get him to believe that Jim is your nigger—some idiots don't require documents—leastways I've heard there's such down South here. And when you tell him the handbill and the reward's bogus, maybe he'll believe

---

1 flat broke：身无分文的。flat 意思是"彻底地"。
2 pegged along：勤快地工作
3 blow on：告发
4 dry up your blubbering：别哭了

Chapter Eight Historical and Biographical Approaches

you when you explain to him what the idea was for getting 'em out[1]. Go 'long, now, and tell him anything you want to; but mind you don't work your jaw any *between* here and there[2]."

So I left, and struck for the back country. I didn't look around, but I kinder felt like he was watching me. But I knowed I could tire him out at that. I went straight out in the country as much as a mile before I stopped; then I doubled back[3] through the woods towards Phelps'. I reckoned I better start in on my plan straight off, without fooling around[4], because I wanted to stop Jim's mouth till these fellows could get away. I didn't want no trouble with their kind. I'd seen all I wanted to of them, and wanted to get entirely shut of them[5].

Understanding the Text

Adeventures of Huckleberry Finn appears something of a thriller at our first reading just because there are a string of sensational events in the story which may seem to make the story improbable. But when we have a close reading of the story and put it in its historical, social and cultural context, and associate the story with Mark Twain's personal experiences, we may get access to Twain's underlying purposes and convictions.

The historical and social context is what we should consider when we read *Adeventures of Huckleberry Finn*. *Adeventures of Huckleberry Finn* is set in frontier America of the 1840s and 1850s, a violent and bloody time. During that period of time, numerous stories about reckless adventurer like Jim Bowie and his famous "Bowie knife," gunslingers like Jack Slade, and Indian fighters like Davy Crockett and Sam Houston were well known. Black slaves attempted to escape and activists tried to help free the slaves while the planters and aristocrats tried to keep slaves. Just against such a background characters behave and take actions. Therefore we are not surprised about the sensational happenings in the story which are mostly based on actual events.

Mark Twain's biographical influences on the novel can be traced in many aspects. As a steamboat pilot for several years, he was familiar with every snag, sandbar, bend, or other landmarks on the Mississippi, as well as with the technical aspects of Navigation, which adds authenticity to the novel. He acquired vast knowledge of Negro superstitions from slaves in Hannibal, Missouri, and on the farm of his beloved uncle, John Quarles, prototype of Silas Phelps. Jim himself is modeled after Uncle Dan'l, a slave on the Quarters place. Mark Twain also got much knowledge of how black slaves obtained freedom from his friendship with abolitionists, socialists, and activists for women's rights and social equality, including Harriet Beecher Stowe, Frederick Douglass, and the writer and utopian socialist William Dean Howells. Therefore he set up the plot of Jim's escaping by heading south instead of crossing the Mississippi to Illinois right at St. Petersburg, his home. Although a free state, Illinois has a law requiring its citizens to return runaway slaves. Jim, therefore, wanted particularly to get to Cairo,

---

1 when you explain to him what the idea was for getting 'em out：给他解释一下，人家为什么要这些花招。
2 but mind you don't work your jaw any *between* here and there：可是，你千万要记住，从这儿到那儿，路上可不许瞎说。
3 doubled back：扭头往回跑
4 fooling around：闲逛
5 I'd seen all I wanted to of them, and wanted to get entirely shut of them：我看够了，再也不想知道有关他们的任何消息了。

Illinois, a junction of the underground railroad system where he could have been helped on his way north and east on the Ohio River by abolitionists so that he can attain the real freedom rather than just get to any free territory.

There are many other examples of sensational happenings and colorful characters in *Adeventures of Huckleberry Finn* based on actual events and persons Twain saw in Hannibal, Missouri, where he grew up, and in other towns up and down the Mississippi. Huck was based on Twain's boyhood friend Tom Blankenship who possessed most of the traits Twain gave him as a fictional character. Although young Blankenship's real life father was ornery enough, Twain modeled Huck's father on another Hannibal citizen, Jimmy Finn, the town drunk. The story in which Old Boggs is shot by Colonel Sherburn is drawn from the story in which one "Uncle Sam" Smarr was killed by William Owsley on the streets of Hannibal on January 24, 1845. Benson Blankenship, older brother of the prototype Huck, secretly aided a runaway slave during the summer of 1847 by taking food to him at his hideout on an island across the river from Hannibal and refused to betray the man for the reward offered for his capture. "This is undoubtedly the historical source of Huck's loyalty to Jim that finally resulted in his deciding to 'go to Hell' in defiance of law, society, and religion rather than turn in his friend." (Guerin, p.62)

Twain's personality helps us understand one of the themes in *Huckleberry Finn*: his hatred of aristocrats. And this is expressed in their notion of race superiority. With this notion, aristocrats could justify any kind of treatment of blacks. They could separate families, as in the case of Jim and the Wilks' slaves; they could load them with chains, hunt them like animals, curse and strike them, exploit their labor, even think of them as subhuman, and then justify the whole dirty history by claiming that the slaves ought to be grateful for any contact with civilization and Christianity. Colonel Sherburn represents some of the traditional aristocrats with contempt for the common man with "his cold-blooded shooting of Old Boggs, his cavalier gesture of tossing the pistol on the ground afterward, and his single-handedly facing down the lynch mob."(Guerin, p.62)

Not only aristocrats but every section of the society is subscribed to this novel. Pap Finn, filthy, impoverished, ignorant, disreputable, bigoted, thieving, pitifully makes sure of his superiority as a white man. Criminals like the robbers and cutthroats on the Walter Scott and those inimitable confidence men, the King and the Duke, show their cruelty and hypocrisy. The convincing slaves include not just stereotyped minstrel characters but interesting human beings, with the characteristics of being laughable, strong, honorable, superstitious, illiterate, loving, pathetic, loyal, and victimized.

The vivid depiction of the industrious, respectable, conforming bourgeoisie is also given who live in any size of towns. In this middle class are the Widow Douglas and her old-maid sister Miss Watson, the Peter Wilks family, Judge Thatcher, the Phelpses and Mrs. Judith Loftus. The host of anonymous but vivid minor characters reflects and improves upon the many eyewitness accounts. These minor characters, including the ferryboat owner, the raftsmen, and the Bible Belt poor white, are described with undeniable authenticity.

Our knowledge of Twain's biographical information, the historical and social situations in which Twain lived, and the relationship between the personal experiences and historical and social context deepens our understanding of the novel and its underlying purpose: exposing the real world in which cruel and dirty events happened now and then. And this goal is achieved in the story by Twain's employing dialect for comedy, burlesque, the tall tale, bombast, and humor, which is very much "in the tradition of such humorists of the Southwest as Thomas Bangs Thorpe and such professional comedians as Artemus Ward and Josh Billings." "*Huckleberry Finn*, of course, far transcends the examples of early American humor."(Guerin, pp.61—62)

Further Reading

Historical and Biographical Approaches

Eagleton, Terry. *Literary Theory: An Introduction*. Minneapolis: University of Minnesota Press, 1983.

Guerin, Wilfred L., et al. *A Handbook of Critical Approaches to Literature*. Beijing: Foreign Language Teaching and Research Press, 2004.

Adventures of Huckleberry Finn

Chadwick-Joshua, Jocelyn. *The Jim Dilemma: Reading Race in Huckleberry Finn*. Jackson: University Press of Mississippi, 1998.

Frederick Anderson, ed. *Mark Twain: The Critical Heritage*. London: Routledge, 1997.

Mark Twain. *The Adventures of Huckleberry Finn*. New York: Harcourt, 1961.

Messent, Peter. *The Cambridge Introduction to Mark Twain*. Shanghai: Shanghai Foreign Languages Education Press, 2008.

克劳迪娅·德斯特·约翰逊著:《<哈克贝利·费恩历险记>解读》(Understanding Adventures of Huckleberry Finn: A Student Casebook to Issues, Sources, and Historical),北京:中国人民大学出版社,2008年。

马克·吐温著,许汝祉译:《马克·吐温自传》,南京:江苏人民出版社,1981年。

Chapter Nine
The Formalist Approach

In contrast to the historical and biographical approaches which give more attention to the matters beyond a text in interpreting a literary work, the formalist approach in literary theory emphasizes a close reading of the text. The formalist approach is known as the New Criticism, which dominated American criticism from the 1940s through the 1960s, and shared some principles in methodology with the Russian formalists, who were the major voices of Russian criticism in the 1910s.

Formalist critics read a literary work as an independent work of art. They believe that all information essential to the interpretation of a work must be found within the work itself; and all the information that goes beyond the text, such as history and politics, is generally considered extrinsic matters, less important than what goes on within the autonomous text. Therefore, when formalist critics read a literary work they do not care about the name, the nationality, sex or the intentions of the author, or the era of composition, or whether the author took some similar real-life situation or incident that he or she then adapted and transformed into the work, or anything else outside the work. Instead, they focus on form and offer intense examinations of the relationship between form and meaning within a work, emphasizing the subtle complexity of how a work is arranged, and give special attention to intrinsic matters of a literary work, such as diction, irony, paradox, metaphor, and symbol, as well as larger elements, such as plot, characterization, and narrative technique. With all the formalist principles in our mind, our intensive reading of a literary work with this "the text and text alone" approach tends to begin with an analysis of individual words of the text and all their denotative and connotative meanings, and their etymological roots. Following this analysis, we search for any patterns developed through individual words, phrases, sentences, figures of speech, allusions and symbols. We also should be alert to the other elements, including point of view, tone, characters, dialogue, foreshadowing, parody, setting and plot, which directly relate to the work's dramatic situation. After ascertaining how all the above information interrelates and juxtaposes in the work, we can see what the internal logic of this work is, what this work means, and how the author achieves the dominant effect in this work. Thus the work's overall meaning or form, then, depends solely on the text in front of us. We do not need to make any literary research and any study of the author's life and times, for the work contains all the necessary information to discover its meaning.

Form is the key concept for the formalist approach. Formalist critics believe that form is the overall effect a literary work creates. And the overall effect of a work is achieved by the organic unity of the work. This means that all parts of a work are interrelated and interconnected, with each part reflecting and helping to support the work's central idea, and that harmonization of conflicting ideas, feelings, and attitudes results in the work's oneness, which is achieved through paradox, irony, and ambiguity. Since all the various parts of a work combine to create this effect, the form of each work is unique. When all the elements work together to form a single, unified effect—the work's form—formalist critics declare that the author has written a successful work, one that has organic unity. And because all good works have organic unity, it would be inconceivable to try to separate a work's form and its content.

Formalist strategies are useful for analyzing fiction although they were mainly employed in the analysis of poetry when they emerged. When we approach a formalist reading of Hawthorne's "Young Goodman Brown," we would trace the interplay of light and dark, and stress the pink ribbons in the story. The alternating light and dark of forest conclave and the mystery pink ribbons work together to assist us in seeing the ambiguity which creates the form of this story. When we make a formalist reading of *Huckleberry Finn*, we would give emphasis on how journeys occurring on land and in river set the repetitive form of this novel, how Huck's manner of telling his story controls our responses to this story and how his point of view assists us in perceiving the novel's form. And a formalist would start his analysis of Kate Chopin's "The Story of an Hour" with exploration of its ironic ending: a grieving wife "afflicted with a heart trouble" suddenly dies of a heart attack, not because she has learned that her kind and loving husband has been killed in a train accident but because she discovers that he is still much alive. Then he would have to look back over the story for signs of the ending in the imagery because Chopin's third-person narrator presents the story in "veiled hints that [reveal] in half concealing." Mrs. Mallard shows extreme grief immediately when she learns about her husband's death, but she soon begins to have a renewal emotion as she looks out the window at "the tops of trees...all quiver with the new spring life." A sudden "clear and exalted perception" occurs to her that she "would live for herself" instead of for and through her husband. However, it is ironic that Josephine interprets her ecstatic "self-assertion" as grief, and the doctors assume that she dies of joy for her realizing her husband is still alive. In the course of an hour, Mrs. Mallard's emotions stay between two extremes: from the ecstasy of her husband's assumed accidental death making her free to the shock of having to abandon her newly discovered self. "She does, indeed, die of a broken heart, but only Chopin's readers know the real ironic meaning of that exploration." (Meyer, p.2086)

Although this brief exposition of some of the formal elements of two stories and one novel does not describe all there is to say about how they produce an effect and create meaning in literary works, it does suggest the kinds of questions, issues, and evidence that a formalist approach might raise in providing a close reading of the text itself.

Virginia Woolf (1882—1941)

Virginia Woolf was born Adeline Virginia Stephen in London, the daughter of Julia Jackson Duckworth, a member of the Duckworth publishing family, and Sir Leslie Stephen, a literary critic and the first editor of the *Dictionary of National Biography*. In a comfortable upper middle class family, all her brothers and sisters received good education while Virginia received her education from private tutors and her extensive reading of literary classics in her father's library.

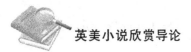

Woolf's youth was shadowed by series of emotional shocks: her half-brother, Gerald, sexually abused her; her mother died when she was in her early teens; her half-sister Stella, her brother Thoby, and her father died one after another. Following the death of her father, Woolf moved with her sister and two brothers to the house in Bloomsbury, which became central to activities of the Bloomsbury group whose other members included E. M. Forster, Lytton Strachey, Clive Bell, Duncan Grant, and Leonard Woolf. In 1912 she married the political theorist Leonard Woolf (1880—1969), who in 1917 set up a small hand press at Hogarth House, and worked as its director until his death. Virginia Woolf had a happy life with her husband, but her mental illness attacked her occasionally. After the final attack of mental illness, Woolf loaded her pockets with stones and drowned herself in the River Ouse near her Sussex home on March 28, 1941.

Virginia Woolf published in 1915 her first book *The Voyage Out*. In 1919 appeared *Night and Day*, a realistic novel about the lives of two friends, Katherine and Mary. *Jacob's Room* (1922) was based upon the life and death of her brother Thoby. *Mrs. Dalloway* (1925) explored thoughts of several groups of people during the course of a single day, when Clarissa Dalloway, the central figure, prepared for her evening party in London. In this story there is little action, but much movement in time from present to past and back again. *Orlando* (1928), a fantasy novel, traced the career of the androgynous protagonist, Orlando, which is based on writer Vita Sackville-West, with whom Woolf had a lesbian relationship. Woolf established herself as one of the leading writers of modernism with the publication of *To the Lighthouse* (1927), which presents the Victorian family life with Mrs. Ramsay, based on Woolf's mother, as the central figure, and *The Waves* (1931), which is Woolf's most difficult novel with the "poetic symbols of life." In these works Woolf developed innovative literary devices like stream of consciousness and interior monologue in order to reveal women's experience and find an alternative to the male-dominated views of reality.

A Room of One's Own (1929) reveals Virginia Woolf's concern with feminist thematics. In it she made her famous statement: "A woman must have money and a room of her own if she is to write fiction." And in *Three Guineas* (1938) she urged women to make a claim for their own history and literature.

As an essayist Woolf was prolific. She published some 500 essays in periodicals and collections, beginning 1905, of which dialogic style is characteristic and in which the reader is often directly addressed in a conversational tone.

"The Mark on the Wall," published in 1919, was Woolf's first successful stream-of-consciousness story. This story presents the narrator's speculations of the mark on the wall and concludes with the identification of the mark as a snail.

Chapter Nine   The Formalist Approach

 Text

The Mark on the Wall

Perhaps it was the middle of January in the present[1] that I first looked up and saw the mark on the wall. In order to fix a date it is necessary to remember what one saw. So now I think of the fire; the steady film of yellow light upon the page of my book[2]; the three chrysanthemums in the round glass bowl on the mantelpiece. Yes, it must have been the winter time, and we had just finished our tea, for I remember that I was smoking a cigarette when I looked up and saw the mark on the wall for the first time. I looked up through the smoke of my cigarette and my eye lodged for a moment upon the burning coals, and that old fancy of the crimson flag flapping from the castle tower came into my mind, and I thought of the cavalcade of red knights riding up the side of the black rock. Rather to my relief the sight of the mark interrupted the fancy, for it is an old fancy, an automatic fancy, made as a child perhaps[3]. The mark was a small round mark, black upon the white wall, about six or seven inches above the mantelpiece.

How readily our thoughts swarm upon a new object, lifting it a little way, as ants carry a blade of straw so feverishly, and then leave it... If that mark was made by a nail, it can't have been for a picture, it must have been for a miniature—the miniature of a lady with white powdered curls, powder-dusted cheeks, and lips like red carnations. A fraud of course[4], for the people who had this house before us would have chosen pictures in that way—an old picture for an old room. That is the sort of people they were—very interesting people, and I think of them so often, in such queer places, because one will never see them again, never know what happened next. They wanted to leave this house because they wanted to change their style of furniture, so he said, and he was in process of saying that in his opinion art should have ideas behind it when we were torn asunder[5], as one is torn from the old lady about to pour out tea and the young man about to hit the tennis ball in the back garden of the suburban villa as one rushes past in the train[6].

But as for that mark, I'm not sure about it; I don't believe it was made by a nail after all; it's too big, too round, for that. I might get up, but if I got up and looked at it, ten to one I shouldn't be able to say for certain; because once a thing's done, no one ever knows how it happened. Oh! dear me, the mystery of life; The inaccuracy of thought! The ignorance of humanity! To show how very little control of our possessions we have—what an accidental affair this living is after all our civilization—let me just

---

1 the middle of January in the present：今年元月中旬
2 the steady film of yellow light upon the page of my book：一片黄色的火光一动不动地照射在我的书页上
3 for it is an old fancy, an automatic fancy, made as a child perhaps：因为这是过去的幻觉，是一种无意识的幻觉，可能是在孩童时期产生的。
4 a fraud of course：当然是一件赝品
5 torn asunder：被分开
6 as one is torn from the old lady about to pour out tea and the young man about to hit the tennis ball in the back garden of the suburban villa as one rushes past in the train：这种情形就像坐火车一样，我们在火车上看见铁道旁的一个郊区别墅的后花园里，有个老太太正准备倒茶，有个年轻人正举起球拍打网球，火车一晃而过，老太太和年轻人被抛在后面，我们与他们就分开了。

count over a few of the things lost in one lifetime, beginning, for that seems always the most mysterious of losses—what cat would gnaw, what rat would nibble—three pale blue canisters of book-binding tools? Then there were the bird cages, the iron hoops, the steel skates, the Queen Anne coal-scuttle[1], the bagatelle board[2], the hand organ[3]—all gone, and jewels, too. Opals and emeralds, they lie about the roots of turnips[4]. What a scraping paring affair it is to be sure! The wonder is that I've any clothes on my back, that I sit surrounded by solid furniture at this moment. Why, if one wants to compare life to anything, one must liken it to being blown through the Tube at fifty miles an hour—landing at the other end without a single hairpin in one's hair[5]! Shot out at the feet of God entirely naked! Tumbling head over heels in the asphodel meadows like brown paper parcels pitched down a shoot in the post office! With one's hair flying back like the tail of a race-horse. Yes, that seems to express the rapidity of life, the perpetual waste and repair; all so casual, all so haphazard...

But after life[6]. The slow pulling down of thick green stalks so that the cup of the flower, as it turns over, deluges one with purple and red light. Why, after all, should one not be born there as one is born here, helpless, speechless, unable to focus one's eyesight, groping at the roots of the grass, at the toes of the Giants[7]? As for saying which are trees, and which are men and women, or whether there are such things, that one won't be in a condition to do for fifty years or so. There will be nothing but spaces of light and dark, intersected by thick stalks, and rather higher up perhaps, rose-shaped blots of an indistinct colour—dim pinks and blues—which will, as time goes on, become more definite, become—I don't know what...

And yet that mark on the wall is not a hole at all. It may even be caused by some round black substance, such as a small rose leaf, left over from the summer, and I, not being a very vigilant housekeeper—look at the dust on the mantelpiece, for example, the dust which, so they say, buried Troy three times over, only fragments of pots utterly refusing annihilation, as one can believe[8].

The tree outside the window taps very gently on the pane... I want to think quietly, calmly, spaciously, never to be interrupted, never to have to rise from my chair, to slip easily from one thing to another, without any sense of hostility, or obstacle. I want to sink deeper and deeper, away from the surface, with its hard separate facts. To steady myself, let me catch hold of the first idea that passes... Shakespeare... Well, he will do as well as another. A man who sat himself solidly in an arm-chair, and looked into the fire, so—A shower of ideas fell perpetually from some very high Heaven down through his mind. He leant his forehead on his hand, and people, looking in through the open door,—for this scene is supposed to take place on a summer's evening—But how dull this is, this historical fiction! It

---

1 the Queen Anne coal-scuttle:安妮女王时代的煤斗子
2 the bagatelle board:弹子球台
3 the hand organ:手风琴
4 Opals and emeralds, they lie about the roots of turnips:还有欧珀和祖母绿,它们都散落在芜菁的根部四周。
5 one must liken it to being blown through the Tube at fifty miles an hour—landing at the other end without a single hairpin in one's hair:就应该把生活与一个人被时速五十英里的风从地铁吹出来的情形相比,当他从地铁的另一出口出来的时候头发上一根发夹也不剩。
6 after life:来世
7 the Giants:希腊神话中的一个巨人族,在与天上诸神作战中,他们总是能够取胜。后来雅典娜和宙斯在海格力斯的帮助下,最终将他们打败。
8 look at the dust on the mantelpiece, for example, the dust which, so they say, buried Troy three times over, only fragments of pots utterly refusing annihilation, as one can believe:比如说,只要看看壁炉上的尘土就知道了,据说就是这样的尘土把特洛伊城严严地埋了三层,只有一些罐子的碎片是它们没法毁灭的,这一点完全能叫人相信。

doesn't interest me at all. I wish I could hit upon a pleasant track of thought, a track indirectly reflecting credit upon myself, for those are the pleasantest thoughts, and very frequent even in the minds of modest mouse-coloured people, who believe genuinely that they dislike to hear their own praises. They are not thoughts directly praising oneself; that is the beauty of them; they are thoughts like this:

"And then I came into the room. They were discussing botany. I said how I'd seen a flower growing on a dust heap on the site of an old house in Kingsway[1]. The seed, I said, must have been sown in the reign of Charles the First[2]. "What flowers grew in the reign of Charles the First?" I asked—(but, I don't remember the answer). Tall flowers with purple tassels to them perhaps. And so it goes on. All the time I'm dressing up the figure of myself in my own mind, lovingly, stealthily, not openly adoring it, for if I did that, I should catch myself out, and stretch my hand at once for a book in self-protection. Indeed, it is curious how instinctively one protects the image of oneself from idolatry or any other handling that could make it ridiculous, or too unlike the original to be believed in any longer. Or is it not so very curious after all? It is a matter of great importance. Suppose the looking glass smashes, the image disappears, and the romantic figure with the green of forest depths all about it is there no longer, but only that shell of a person which is seen by other people—what an airless, shallow, bald, prominent world it becomes! A world not to be lived in. As we face each other in omnibuses and underground railways we are looking into the mirror that accounts for the vagueness, the gleam of glassiness, in our eyes. And the novelists in future will realize more and more the importance of these reflections, for of course there is not one reflection but an almost infinite number; those are the depths they will explore, those the phantoms they will pursue, leaving the description of reality more and more out of their stories, taking a knowledge of it for granted, as the Greeks did and Shakespeare perhaps[3]—but these generalizations are very worthless. The military sound of the word is enough. It recalls leading articles, cabinet ministers—a whole class of things indeed which as a child one thought the thing itself, the standard thing, the real thing, from which one could not depart save at the risk of nameless damnation[4]. Generalizations bring back somehow Sunday in London, Sunday afternoon walks, Sunday luncheons, and also ways of speaking of the dead, clothes, and habits—like the habit of sitting all together in one room until a certain hour, although nobody liked it. There was a rule for everything. The rule for tablecloths at that particular period was that they should be made of tapestry with little yellow compartments marked upon them, such as you may see in photographs of the carpets in the corridors of the royal palaces. Tablecloths of a different kind were not real tablecloths. How shocking, and yet how wonderful it was to discover that these real things, Sunday luncheons, Sunday walks, country houses, and tablecloths were not entirely real, were indeed half phantoms, and the damnation which visited the disbeliever in them was only a sense of illegitimate freedom[5]. What now takes the place of those things I wonder, those real standard

---

1 Kingsway: 金斯威, 位于伦敦
2 Charles the First: 查理一世 (1600年11月19日—1649年1月30日), 英格兰、苏格兰与爱尔兰国王, 英国历史上唯一一位被公开处死的国王
3 leaving the description of reality more and more out of their stories, taking a knowledge of it for granted, as the Greeks did and Shakespeare perhaps: 越来越把现实的描绘排除在他们的故事之外, 认为人们生来就了解现实, 希腊人就是这样想的, 或许莎士比亚也是这样想的。it 此处指 reality。
4 from which one could not depart save at the risk of nameless damnation: 人人都必须遵循, 否则就得冒着被打下地狱的危险。
5 and the damnation which visited the disbeliever in them was only a sense of illegitimate freedom: 而不相信它们的人所得到的处罚只不过是一种非法的自由感。

things? Men perhaps, should you be a woman; the masculine point of view which governs our lives, which sets the standard, which establishes Whitaker's Table of Precedency[1], which has become, I suppose, since the war half a phantom to many men and women, which soon—one may hope, will be laughed into the dustbin where the phantoms go, the mahogany sideboards and the Landseer prints[2], Gods and Devils, Hell and so forth, leaving us all with an intoxicating sense of illegitimate freedom—if freedom exists...

In certain lights that mark on the wall seems actually to project from the wall. Nor is it entirely circular. I cannot be sure, but it seems to cast a perceptible shadow, suggesting that if I ran my finger down that strip of the wall it would, at a certain point, mount and descend a small tumulus, a smooth tumulus like those barrows on the South Downs[3] which are, they say, either tombs or camps. Of the two I should prefer them to be tombs, desiring melancholy like most English people, and finding it natural at the end of a walk to think of the bones stretched beneath the turf[4]... There must be some book about it. Some antiquary must have dug up those bones and given them a name... What sort of a man is an antiquary, I wonder? Retired Colonels for the most part, I dare say, leading parties of aged labourers to the top here, examining clods of earth and stone, and getting into correspondence with the neighbouring clergy, which, being opened at breakfast time, gives them a feeling of importance, and the comparison of arrow-heads necessitates cross-country journeys to the county towns, an agreeable necessity both to them and to their elderly wives, who wish to make plum jam or to clean out the study, and have every reason for keeping that great question of the camp or the tomb in perpetual suspension, while the Colonel himself feels agreeably philosophic in accumulating evidence on both sides of the question. It is true that he does finally incline to believe in the camp; and, being opposed, indites a pamphlet which he is about to read at the quarterly meeting of the local society when a stroke lays him low, and his last conscious thoughts are not of wife or child, but of the camp and that arrowhead there, which is now in the case at the local museum, together with the foot of a Chinese murderess, a handful of Elizabethan nails, a great many Tudor[5] clay pipes, a piece of Roman pottery, and the wine-glass that Nelson drank out of—proving I really don't know what.

No, no, nothing is proved, nothing is known. And if I were to get up at this very moment and ascertain that the mark on the wall is really—what shall we say?—the head of a gigantic old nail, driven in two hundred years ago, which has now, owing to the patient attrition of many generations of housemaids, revealed its head above the coat of paint, and is taking its first view of modern life in the sight of a white-walled fire-lit room, what should I gain?—Knowledge? Matter for further speculation? I can think sitting still as well as standing up. And what is knowledge? What are our learned men save the descendants of witches and hermits who crouched in caves and in woods brewing herbs, interrogating shrew-mice and writing down the language of the stars? And the less we honour them as our superstitions

---

1 Whitaker's Table of Precedency:《惠特克的尊卑序列表》,这本书将英国的贵族身份进行了尊卑排列。惠特克为英国出版商,创办过《书商》杂志。
2 the Landseer prints:兰德西尔版画。Sir Edwin Henry Landseer(1802—1873),绘画天才,维多利亚时期最著名的动物画家。
3 the South Downs:英国南部丘陵草原地带
4 the bones stretched beneath the turf:草地下埋着的白骨
5 Tudor:(英国)都铎王朝(1485—1603)

Chapter Nine　The Formalist Approach

dwindle and our respect for beauty and health of mind increases... Yes, one could imagine a very pleasant world. A quiet, spacious world, with the flowers so red and blue in the open fields. A world without professors or specialists or house-keepers with the profiles of policemen, a world which one could slice with one's thought as a fish slices the water with his fin, grazing the stems of the water-lilies, hanging suspended over nests of white sea eggs... How peaceful it is drown here, rooted in the centre of the world and gazing up through the grey waters, with their sudden gleams of light, and their reflections—if it were not for Whitaker's Almanack[1]—if it were not for the Table of Precedency!

　　I must jump up and see for myself what that mark on the wall really is—a nail, a rose-leaf, a crack in the wood?

　　Here is nature once more at her old game of self-preservation. This train of thought, she perceives, is threatening mere waste of energy, even some collision with reality, for who will ever be able to lift a finger against Whitaker's Table of Precedency? The Archbishop of Canterbury[2] is followed by the Lord High Chancellor[3]; the Lord High Chancellor is followed by the Archbishop of York[4]. Everybody follows somebody, such is the philosophy of Whitaker; and the great thing is to know who follows whom. Whitaker knows, and let that, so Nature counsels, comfort you, instead of enraging you; and if you can't be comforted, if you must shatter this hour of peace, think of the mark on the wall.

　　I understand Nature's game—her prompting to take action as a way of ending any thought that threatens to excite or to pain. Hence, I suppose, comes our slight contempt for men of action—men, we assume, who don't think. Still, there's no harm in putting a full stop to one's disagreeable thoughts by looking at a mark on the wall.

　　Indeed, now that I have fixed my eyes upon it, I feel that I have grasped a plank in the sea; I feel a satisfying sense of reality which at once turns the two Archbishops and the Lord High Chancellor to the shadows of shades. Here is something definite, something real. Thus, waking from a midnight dream of horror, one hastily turns on the light and lies quiescent, worshipping the chest of drawers, worshipping solidity, worshipping reality, worshipping the impersonal world which is a proof of some existence other than ours. That is what one wants to be sure of... Wood is a pleasant thing to think about. It comes from a tree; and trees grow, and we don't know how they grow. For years and years they grow, without paying any attention to us, in meadows, in forests, and by the side of rivers—all things one likes to think about. The cows swish their tails beneath them on hot afternoons; they paint rivers so green that when a moorhen dives one expects to see its feathers all green when it comes up again. I like to think of the fish balanced against the stream like flags blown out; and of water-beetles slowly raiding domes of mud upon the bed of the river. I like to think of the tree itself:—first the close dry sensation of being wood; then the grinding of the storm; then the slow, delicious ooze of sap[5]. I like to think of it, too, on winter's nights

---

1　Whitaker's Almanack：惠特克年鉴。惠特克于1868年开始编纂惠特克年鉴。
2　the Archbishop of Canterbury：坎特伯雷大主教。英国国教的两大主教分别为：坎特伯雷大主教和约克大主教。坎特伯雷大主教是英国国教的教主。
3　the Lord High Chancellor：(英国上议院的)大法官
4　the Archbishop of York：约克大主教
5　I like to think of the tree itself—first the close dry sensation of being wood; then the grinding of the storm; then the slow, delicious ooze of sap：我喜欢想象那棵树本身的情景：首先是它的木质细密干燥的感觉，然后是它遭受暴风雨摧残的情景，接下去是树液缓慢地、顺畅地一滴滴流出来的情景。

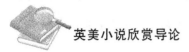

standing in the empty field with all leaves close-furled, nothing tender exposed to the iron bullets of the moon, a naked mast upon an earth that goes tumbling, tumbling, all night long. The song of birds must sound very loud and strange in June; and how cold the feet of insects must feel upon it, as they make laborious progresses up the creases of the bark, or sun themselves upon the thin green awning of the leaves, and look straight in front of them with diamond-cut red eyes... One by one the fibres snap beneath the immense cold pressure of the earth, then the last storm comes and, falling, the highest branches drive deep into the ground again. Even so, life isn't done with; there are a million patient, watchful lives still for a tree, all over the world, in bedrooms, in ships, on the pavement, lining rooms, where men and women sit after tea, smoking cigarettes. It is full of peaceful thoughts, happy thoughts, this tree. I should like to take each one separately—but something is getting in the way...Where was I? What has it all been about? A tree? A river? The Downs? Whitaker's Almanack? The fields of asphodel? I can't remember a thing. Everything's moving, falling, slipping, vanishing...There is a vast upheaval of matter. Someone is standing over me and saying—

"I'm going out to buy a newspaper."

"Yes?"

"Though it's no good buying newspapers... Nothing ever happens. Curse this war; God damn this war!... All the same, I don't see why we should have a snail on our wall."

Ah, the mark on the wall! It was a snail.

Understanding the Text

"The Mark on the Wall," renowned for its stream-of-consciousness technique, appears a reminiscence of what occurred long months before the moment of writing when we read it for the first time. However, a second reading indicates that it is not a reminiscence, except for perhaps the very beginning and the very end in which objective reality is presented in past tense because the main part of the story is the narrator's consciousness flowing which is presented in present tense—several pages of digressions or reveries on history, reality, society, art, writing, and life itself. This story tells us the narrator's six speculations about the mark on the wall, which the story centers on, and concludes with the identification of that mark on the wall as a snail by her companion. Far away from the traditional story, it appears that the story, with no coherence and logic, is in lack of plot structure, and thematic significance. Is it really so? A detailed analysis of the six speculations might show us a completely different view of its structure, thematic significance and doubtful closure.

The mark on the wall is just a symbolic image from which the reader is led into the story. The six speculations come from and are knotted by the mark. Unlike some critics who think that the six speculations are just the narrator's fancy about the mark and are not interrelated, we, after a close reading of the text, can see that the story has a rigorous structure below its chaotic surface.

The narrator "I" first notices the mark on the wall in the middle of January. "The mark was a small round mark, black upon the white wall." The sight of the mark interrupts her fancy and she is relieved to be interrupted. And why? It is perhaps because she wants to get out of conventional fairy tales of "flag flapping" and "knights riding" and get her imagination onto something new.

The narrator then turns her thoughts to the new object: the mark on the wall. She is speculating on where the mark comes from: it is made by a nail for a miniature of a lady. This takes her mind to previous residents whom one will never see again and never know what happened next. These residents "wanted to leave this house because they wanted to change their style of furniture," and wanted a different style of life—just as she wants to think about something different rather than old fantasy of knights. Then her mind rushes past the memory of home owners as if she was on a train watching "the old lady about to pour out tea and the young man about to hit the tennis ball in the back garden of the suburban villa." Old residents and the train images are actually her speculation on life—how much our life depends on chance.

The narrator's third speculation on the mark comes up when she refuses to believe that the mark is a nail hole because it is "too big, too round, for that." What follows is the narrator's meditation on life mystery, the ignorance of man, things lost—cats, rats, birdcages and steel skates—fleeing time, wasted life, and after life. It is virtually the narrator's speculation on the mystery of life and how fast life passes.

The narrator refuses to believe that the mark on the wall is a hole at all. She thinks that it is a spot left from a rose leaf. She speculates on dust covering Troy, Shakespeare, Charles the First, Sunday in London, and Whitaker's Table of Precedency. While Shakespeare and Charles the First act as the representatives of past standard and "real things," Sunday in London, and Whitaker's Table of Precedency present us with a vivid description of "the masculine point of view which governs our lives, which sets the standard." Although nobody likes the rule or standard, "there was a rule for everything" that we follow as a child. How shocking it is that these rules that we believe are "real things" turn out not to be "entirely real," and "indeed half phantoms, and the damnation which visited the disbeliever in them was only a sense of illegitimate freedom."

The narrator imagines that the mark may be projecting from the wall. This reminds her of tombs or camps, retired Colonels, learned men that proves that history cannot prove anything, and human beings are ridiculous and ignorant when they are inclined to impose standards on their illegitimate freedom. Without professors or specialists or house-keepers with the profiles of policemen and without these standards, human beings can live freely in "a very pleasant world. A quiet, spacious world, with the flowers so red and blue in the open fields." This speculation is actually preparation for the last speculation.

The sixth speculation on the mark is an imaged life of the narrator, an ideal existence: "The cows swish their tails beneath them on hot afternoons; they paint rivers so green that when a moorhen dives one expects to see its feathers all green when it comes up again"; the fish balances "against the stream like flags blown out"; and water-beetles are "slowly raiding domes of mud upon the bed of the river." In contrast to hierarchies and boundaries, the world of nature is peaceful where things flow and change. The narrator's reflection is interrupted at this time by a new voice who says it's going to get a newspaper, cursing the war and defining the mark as a snail. Till now the narrator puts her meditations to stop.

The narrator's six speculations go from reality to meditation, then back to reality. Her first speculation on the red flag and knights seem associated with the war, the First World War, which broke out in 1919 when the story was published. This is confirmed at the end of the story "'Though it's no good buying newspapers... Curse this war; God damn this war!... All the same, I don't see why we should have a snail on our wall.'" This is the reality at that time which all the speculations center on and disappear from. The second and the third speculations are the narrator's mediations on life, which is mysterious, fast and accidental. And the fourth and fifth speculations reveal that past actions of human beings cannot help us understand the nature of life and therefore cannot prove anything. And the sixth speculation comes to a conclusion that we should go back to nature where we can enjoy freedom so that we can understand life and enjoy life. We have no doubt that this is the thematic significance of these speculations. The reality, however, prevents us from enjoying the freedom, which is definitely revealed in the closure of this story.

Throughout this story, while the narrator is not specifically identified as female and her companion as male, "gender coding" strongly suggests that the narrator is a woman, and her companion a man. The narrator acting as the speaker for Woolf attacks any standard in life or art which "masculine point of view" imposes on, and when her companion identifies the mark on the wall as a snail, the narrator, without rising from her chair, simply accepts his version of the truth. To some degree the "masculine point of view" has not yet been "laughed into the dustbin."

Just as the narrator tells us "the great thing" about Whitaker's Table of Precedency "is to know who follows whom" and it is a "comfort," in fiction, it is a traditional comfort to know that closure will follow at the story's end.

Although the narrator confirms her companion's identification in the final line of the story ("Ah, the mark on the wall! It was a snail"), the greatest "proof" that the mark is a snail is that the narrator's companion identifies it as such. The "Ah" of the last line may be read as an exhalation of relief as well as an expression of surprise because it is very comforting, not only for the reader but for the narrator. Just as the narrator says, we and she want the comfort of "something definite, something real," and the snail at the end of the story is just such "a plank in the sea," offering closure at least, though individual readers may find it more a sliver than a plank. That the mark is a snail is the "real thing" or the truth the "masculine point of view" imposes on the narrator and us.

And so it may not matter what the mark actually is, but what it is not (or may not be) could matter a lot. Woolf gives us such a closure not because it is a proper closure, but because we expect a closure. As a result, the conclusion of this story offers not closure, but opening. And just in the opening closure we perceive the implication Woolf intends the story to suggest.

Further Reading

The Formalist Approach

Bressler, Charles E. *Literary Criticism: An Introduction to Theory and Practice*. 2nd ed. Upper Saddle River, N. J: Prentice-Hall, Inc., 1999.

Guerin, Wilfred L., et al. *A Handbook of Critical Approaches to Literature*. Beijing: Foreign Language Teaching and Research Press, 2004.

Lentricchia, Frank. *After the New Criticism*. Chicago: University of Chicago Press, 1980.

Ransom, John Crowe. *The New Criticism*. New York: New Directions, 1972.

Wellek, Rene, and Austin Warren. *Theory of Literature*. San Diego: Harcourt Brace Jovanovich, 1977.

The Mark on the Wall

Cyr, Marc D. "A Conflict of Closure in Virginia Woolf's 'The Mark on the Wall'". *Studies in Short Fiction* 33.2 (Spring 1996):197-205.

Hanson, Clare. *Virginia Woolf*. Basingstoke: Macmillan, 1994.

Narey, Wayne. "Virginia Woolf's 'The Mark on the Wall': An Einsteinian View of Art". *Studies in Short Fiction* 29.1 (Winter 1992): 35—42.

Poole, Roger. *The Unknown Virginia Woolf*. 3rd ed. Atlantic Highlands, N.J: Humanities Press International, 1990.

Roe, Sue, and Susan Sellers, eds. *The Cambridge Companion to Virginia Woolf*. Cambridge: Cambridge University Press, 2000.

Rosenthal, Michael. *Virginia Woolf*. London: Routledge & Kegan Paul, 1979.

Smith, Anna. *Virginia Woolf: Public and Private Negotiations*. Basingstoke and London: Palgrave, 2000.

Woolf, Virginia. *The Complete Shorter Fiction of Virginia Woolf*. Ed. Susan Dick. London: Hogarth Press, 1985.

Chapter Ten
The Psychoanalytic Approach

First introduced to literary studies in the 1920s and 1930s, psychoanalytic criticism, drawing on Sigmund Freud's theories and other psychoanalytic theories, such as Carl G. Jung's, is based heavily on the idea of the existence of a human unconscious. As an approach to literature, psychoanalytic criticism pays great attention to psychological motivations of authors, readers, as well as characters.

Freud is the intellectual founding father of psychoanalytic criticism. He provides the foundation for all forms of psychoanalytic criticism. Although it is not feasible to explain psychoanalytic terms and concepts in so brief space as this, it is possible to give a brief description of major concepts about psychoanalytic approach.

The foundation of Freud's contribution to modern psychology is his emphasis on the unconscious aspects of the human psyche. He asserts that our minds are a dichotomy consisting of the conscious (the rational) and the unconscious (the irrational): the conscious perceives and records external reality and is the reasoning part of the mind, and the unconscious receives and stores our hidden desires, ambitions, fears, passions, and irrational thoughts; it is the unconscious, not the conscious, that governs a large part of our actions. Freud has three major premises concerning the unconscious. His first major premise is that most of the individual's mental processes are unconscious; the second is that all human behaviour is motivated ultimately by sexual energy, the prime psyche force called as libido by Freud; and the third is that because of the powerful social taboos attached to certain sexual impulses, many of our desires and memories are repressed. Based on these three premises, Freud developed his most famous model of the human psyche, the tripartite model, which divides the psyche into three parts: the id, the ego, and the superego. The id is the reservoir of libido, the source of all our psychosexual desires and all our psychic energy. As the irrational, instinctual, and unconscious part of the psyche, the id contains our secret desires, darkest wishes, and most intense fears. Its function is to satisfy our instincts for pleasure without regard for social conventions, legal ethics, or moral restraint. The ego is the rational part of the psyche although its large portion is unconscious. The ego lacks the strong vitality of the id, but it regulates the instinctual desires of the id so that they may be released in some nondestructive way. Consequently, the ego serves as intermediary between the world inside and the world outside. Whereas the id is dominated by the pleasure principle, the ego is dominated by the reality principle. The superego acts as a censoring agency, causing us to make moral judgments in light of social pressures. In contrast to the id, the superego is dominated by the morality principle and functions primarily to protect the society and us from the id. Acting either directly or through the ego, the superego serves to suppress the desires and instincts forbidden by the society, such as aggression, sexual passions, and the Oedipal instinct, and thrust them back into the unconscious. Freud attributes the development of the superego to the parental influence that manifests itself through punishment for what society considers good behaviour. And an overactive superego often creates an unconscious sense of guilt and fear. If allowed to operate at its own discretion, the superego will create an unconscious sense of guilt. Consequently the id would make us devils, the superego have us behave as angels, and the ego would keep us healthy human beings by maintaining a balance between these two opposing forces. And this balance is what Freud advocated.

In "Young Goodman Brown," Brown's journey from the village of Salem into the forest is actually a psychological journey, which reveals his predicament of being unable to reconcile the two forces: his id and his superego. Goodman Brown, who, the cradle on, has been indoctrinated with admonitions against tasting the forbidden fruit, and obsessed with the nature of sin and with the psychological results of violating the taboos imposed by this system, has developed a morbid compulsion to taste of them. However, the "naturalness" of sex as a part of humankind's physical and mental constitution which the society has shut its eyes to is inevitable. Then, Brown, impelled by unmistakably libidinal force, moves from the village into the forest. In the story, "the village is a place of light and order, both social and moral order," and the forest is "a place of darkness and unknown terrors."(Guerin, p.170) The village, as a place of social and moral order, may be equated with Freud's superego, the morally inhibiting agent of the psyche, whereas, the forest, as a place of wild, untamed passions and terrors, is analogous to the Freudian id. "As mediator between these opposing forces, Brown himself resembles the poor ego, which tries to effect a healthy balance and is shattered because it is unable to do so" (Guerin, p.170) because he has not been properly educated to confront the realities of the external world or of the inner world. This is why after his night in the forest he becomes a walking guilt complex, burdened with anxiety and doubt.

Freud also applied his sexual theories to the symbolic interpretation of literature. The most controversial facet of psychoanalytic criticism is its tendency to interpret imagery in terms of sexuality. In *The Interpretation of Dreams* (1900), Freud asserts that in the process of becoming a man or a woman, a child has stored many painful memories of repressed sexual desires, anger, rage, and guilt in his or her unconscious. The unconscious redirects and reshapes these concealed wishes into acceptable social activities, presenting them in the form of images or symbols in our dreams or writings. By so doing, the psyche creates a window to the id by allowing these socially acceptable desires to seep into the conscious state. According to Freud, all human bebaviour, including dreams, is fundamentally sexual, being driven by one's sexual energy or libido. Interpreting dreams almost exclusively in sexual terms, Freud linked most dreams to the Oedipus or Electra complexes.

Following Freud's example in his interpretation of dreams, psychoanalytic critics tend to see all concave images, such as ponds, flowers, cups or vases, caves, and hollows, as female or yonic symbols, and all images whose length exceeds their diameter, such as towers, mountains, peaks, snakes, knives, lances, and swords, as male or phallic symbols. They even see activities, such as dancing, riding, and flying, as symbols of sexual pleasure.

The concept of the Oedipus complex is one of Freud's most significant contributions not only to psychoanalytic criticism but also to all literary criticism in general. Freud borrowed the term from the tragedy *Oedipus the King*, written by Greek playwright Sophocles. Oedipus, raised away from his parents, accidently kills his father and marries his mother. Freud suggested that all boys go through a stage where they want to take their father's place with his mother. According to Freud, the essence of Oedipus' story becomes universal human experience. In "The Rocking-Horse Winner," Paul's desire to take care of the family's needs is Oedipal. And the main way of his earning money—the rocking horse—seems a sexual image that Lawrence intentionally creates in characterizing Paul.

The female version of the psychological conflict is called the Electra complex, a term used to describe a girl's unconscious rivalry with her mother for her father. The term comes from a Greek legend about Electra who avenged the death of her father, Agamemnon, by plotting the death of her mother.

Freud developed both a body of theory and a practical methodology for his science of the mind. Although we are reluctant to accept all his theories and psychoanalytic approaches to literature, his theories and approaches which have been challenged, revised, and supplemented definitely offer a completely different perspective of authors, readers, and characters.

Charles Dickens (1812—1870)

Charles Dickens was born in Portsmouth, England, but he spent most of his childhood in London and Kent on which he based many of his novels. He grew up in poverty and had little formal education, yet became the most prominent and revered of all English Victorian writers, as well as a political reporter and journalist.

Dickens started his writing career with the pen name Boz, and his first publication was the short story collection *Sketches By Boz* (1836). He is well known for creating characters such as orphans and urchins, rogues, shopkeepers, widows, and other colorful characters pulled from the sooty streets of London, and telling about the bad conditions under which the working classes and poor people had to live. Among his major works are *Oliver Twist* (1839), *The Old Curiosity Shop* (1841), *David Copperfield* (1850), the historical drama *A Tale of Two Cities* (1859), and *Great Expectations* (1861). His novels were often published first in serial form—as chapter-by-chapter monthly installments in magazines of the day.

Dickens is probably most remembered at Christmas time because of his novel *A Christmas Carol* (1843) which tells the story of a selfish, grouchy miser called Ebenezer Scrooge. He is visited by three ghosts: the first took him back to his past to let him know that as a young man he had been kind and happy; the second showed him life as it was now and how mean he was being especially to his clerk; and the third showed him what the future would be like if he did not change. Being guilty and frightened, he said he would from that day change and he would celebrate Christmas properly when he was given a second chance. He ordered a turkey for his clerk and raised his wages and did what he could to help the poor, and became a good man.

David Copperfield, always considered the most autobiographical of all his works and his "favorite child," is the story of a young man's adventures on his journey from an unhappy and impoverished childhood to the discovery of his vocation as a successful novelist. Among the gloriously vivid cast of characters he encounters are his tyrannical stepfather, Mr. Murdstone; his formidable aunt, Betsey Trotwood; the eternally humble yet treacherous Uriah Heep; frivolous, enchanting Dora; and the magnificently impecunious Micawber, one of literature's great comic creations.

 **Text**

David Copperfield

XV

I Make Another Beginning

Mr. Dick[1] and I soon became the best of friends, and very often, when his day's work was done, went out together to fly the great kite. Every day of his life he had a long sitting at the Memorial, which never made the least progress, however hard he laboured, for King Charles the First always strayed into it, sooner or later, and then it was thrown aside, and another one begun. The patience and hope with which he bore these perpetual disappointments, the mild perception he had that there was something wrong about King Charles the First, the feeble efforts he made to keep him out, and the certainty with which he came in, and tumbled the Memorial out of all shape[2], made a deep impression on me. What Mr. Dick supposed would come of the Memorial, if it were completed; where he thought it was to go, or what he thought it was to do; he knew no more than anybody else, I believe. Nor was it at all necessary that he should trouble himself with such questions, for if anything were certain under the sun, it was certain that the Memorial never would be finished. It was quite an affecting sight, I used to think, to see him with the kite when it was up a great height in the air. What he had told me, in his room, about his belief in its disseminating the statements pasted on it, which were nothing but old leaves of abortive Memorials, might have been a fancy with him sometimes; but not when he was out, looking up at the kite in the sky, and feeling it pull and tug at his hand. He never looked so serene as he did then. I used to fancy, as I sat by him of an evening, on a green slope, and saw him watch the kite high in the quiet air, that it lifted his mind out of its confusion, and bore it (such was my boyish thought) into the skies. As he wound the string in and it came lower and lower down out of the beautiful light, until it fluttered to the ground, and lay there like a dead thing, he seemed to wake gradually out of a dream; and I remember to have seen him take it up, and look about him in a lost way[3], as if they had both come down together, so that I pitied him with all my heart.

---

1 Mr. Dick: 一位孩子气、神经有点问题,但非常和蔼可亲的人,与 Betsey Trotwood 一起生活。
2 tumbled the Memorial out of all shape: 把呈文搞成一团糟
3 in a lost way: 失落地,若有所失地

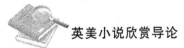

While I advanced in friendship and intimacy with Mr. Dick, I did not go backward in the favour of his staunch friend, my aunt. She took so kindly to me, that, in the course of a few weeks, she shortened my adopted name of Trotwood into Trot; and even encouraged me to hope, that if I went on as I had begun, I might take equal rank in her affections with my sister Betsey Trotwood.

"Trot," said my aunt one evening, when the backgammon-board[1] was placed as usual for herself and Mr. Dick, "we must not forget your education."

This was my only subject of anxiety, and I felt quite delighted by her referring to it.

"Should you like to go to school at Canterbury[2]?" said my aunt.

I replied that I should like it very much, as it was so near her.

"Good," said my aunt. "Should you like to go tomorrow?"

Being already no stranger to the general rapidity of my aunt's evolutions, I was not surprised by the suddenness of the proposal, and said: "Yes."

"Good," said my aunt again. "Janet, hire the grey pony and chaise tomorrow morning at ten o'clock, and pack up Master Trotwood's clothes tonight."

I was greatly elated by these orders; but my heart smote me for my selfishness, when I witnessed their effect on Mr. Dick, who was so low-spirited at the prospect of our separation, and played so ill in consequence, that my aunt, after giving him several admonitory raps on the knuckles with her dice-box, shut up the board, and declined to play with him any more. But, on hearing from my aunt that I should sometimes come over on a Saturday, and that he could sometimes come and see me on a Wednesday, he revived; and vowed to make another kite for those occasions, of proportions greatly surpassing the present one. In the morning he was downhearted again, and would have sustained himself by giving me all the money he had in his possession, gold and silver too, if my aunt had not interposed, and limited the gift to five shillings, which, at his earnest petition, were afterwards increased to ten. We parted at the garden-gate in a most affectionate manner, and Mr. Dick did not go into the house until my aunt had driven me out of sight of it.

My aunt, who was perfectly indifferent to public opinion, drove the grey pony through Dover[3] in a masterly manner; sitting high and stiff like a state coachman, keeping a steady eye upon him wherever he went, and making a point of not letting him have his own way in any respect. When we came into the country road, she permitted him to relax a little, however; and looking at me down in a valley of cushion by her side, asked me whether I was happy?

"Very happy indeed, thank you, aunt," I said.

She was much gratified; and both her hands being occupied, patted me on the head with her whip.

"Is it a large school, aunt?" I asked.

"Why, I don't know," said my aunt. "We are going to Mr. Wickfield's first."

"Does he keep a school?" I asked.

---

1 backgammon-board：西洋双陆棋盘。双陆棋是一种游戏，双方各有 15 枚棋子，掷骰子决定行棋格数。
2 Canterbury：坎特伯雷，位于英国东南部，属于有"英格兰花园"之称的肯特郡
3 Dover：多佛，英国东南部港口城市

Chapter Ten   The Psychoanalytic Approach

"No, Trot," said my aunt. "He keeps an office."

I asked for no more information about Mr. Wickfield, as she offered none, and we conversed on other subjects until we came to Canterbury, where, as it was market-day, my aunt had a great opportunity of insinuating the grey pony among carts, baskets, vegetables, and huckster's goods. The hair-breadth turns and twists we made, drew down upon us a variety of speeches from the people standing about, which were not always complimentary; but my aunt drove on with perfect indifference, and I dare say would have taken her own way with as much coolness through an enemy's country.

At length we stopped before a very old house bulging out over the road; a house with long low lattice-windows bulging out still farther, and beams with carved heads on the ends bulging out too, so that I fancied the whole house was leaning forward, trying to see who was passing on the narrow pavement below. It was quite spotless in its cleanliness. The old-fashioned brass knocker on the low arched door, ornamented with carved garlands of fruit and flowers, twinkled like a star; the two stone steps descending to the door were as white as if they had been covered with fair linen; and all the angles and corners, and carvings and mouldings, and quaint little panes of glass, and quainter little windows, though as old as the hills, were as pure as any snow that ever fell upon the hills.

When the pony-chaise stopped at the door, and my eyes were intent upon the house, I saw a cadaverous face appear at a small window on the ground floor (in a little round tower that formed one side of the house), and quickly disappear. The low arched door then opened, and the face came out. It was quite as cadaverous as it had looked in the window, though in the grain of it there was that tinge of red which is sometimes to be observed in the skins of red-haired people. It belonged to a red-haired person—a youth of fifteen, as I take it now, but looking much older—whose hair was cropped as close as the closest stubble; who had hardly any eyebrows, and no eyelashes, and eyes of a red-brown, so unsheltered and unshaded, that I remember wondering how he went to sleep. He was high-shouldered and bony; dressed in decent black, with a white wisp of a neckcloth; buttoned up to the throat; and had a long, lank, skeleton hand, which particularly attracted my attention, as he stood at the pony's head, rubbing his chin with it, and looking up at us in the chaise.

"Is Mr. Wickfield at home, Uriah Heep[1]?" said my aunt.

"Mr. Wickfield's at home, ma'am," said Uriah Heep, "if you'll please to walk in there"—pointing with his long hand to the room he meant.

We got out; and leaving him to hold the pony, went into a long low parlour looking towards the street, from the window of which I caught a glimpse, as I went in, of Uriah Heep breathing into the pony's nostrils, and immediately covering them with his hand, as if he were putting some spell upon him. Opposite to the tall old chimney-piece were two portraits: one of a gentleman with grey hair (though not by any means an old man) and black eyebrows, who was looking over some papers tied together with red tape; the other, of a lady, with a very placid and sweet expression of face, who was looking at me.

I believe I was turning about in search of Uriah's picture, when, a door at the farther end of the room opening, a gentleman entered, at sight of whom I turned to the first-mentioned portrait again, to make quite sure that it had not come out of its frame. But it was stationary; and as the gentleman

---

1 Uriah Heep:Mr. Wickfield 的职员,奸诈,善用欺骗伎俩

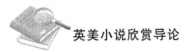

advanced into the light, I saw that he was some years older than when he had had his picture painted.

"Miss Betsey Trotwood," said the gentleman, "pray[1] walk in. I was engaged for a moment, but you'll excuse my being busy. You know my motive. I have but one in life."

Miss Betsey thanked him, and we went into his room, which was furnished as an office, with books, papers, tin boxes, and so forth. It looked into a garden, and had an iron safe let into the wall; so immediately over the mantelshelf, that I wondered, as I sat down, how the sweeps got round it when they swept the chimney.

"Well, Miss Trotwood," said Mr. Wickfield; for I soon found that it was he, and that he was a lawyer, and steward of the estates of a rich gentleman of the county; "what wind blows you here? Not an ill wind, I hope?"

"No," replied my aunt. "I have not come for any law."

"That's right, ma'am," said Mr. Wickfield. "You had better come for anything else." His hair was quite white now, though his eyebrows were still black. He had a very agreeable face, and, I thought, was handsome. There was a certain richness in his complexion, which I had been long accustomed, under Peggotty's tuition, to connect with port wine; and I fancied it was in his voice too, and referred his growing corpulency to the same cause. He was very cleanly dressed, in a blue coat, striped waist coat, and nankeen trousers; and his fine frilled shirt and cambric neckcloth looked unusually soft and white, reminding my strolling fancy (I call to mind) of the plumage on the breast of a swan.

"This is my nephew," said my aunt.

"Wasn't aware you had one, Miss Trotwood," said Mr. Wickfield.

"My grand-nephew, that is to say," observed my aunt.

"Wasn't aware you had a grand-nephew, I give you my word[2]," said Mr. Wickfield.

"I have adopted him," said my aunt, with a wave of her hand, importing that his knowledge and his ignorance were all one to her, "and I have brought him here, to put to a school where he may be thoroughly well taught, and well treated. Now tell me where that school is, and what it is, and all about it."

"Before I can advise you properly," said Mr. Wickfield—"the old question, you know. What's your motive in this?"

"Deuce take the man[3]!" exclaimed my aunt. "Always fishing for motives, when they're on the surface! Why, to make the child happy and useful."

"It must be a mixed motive, I think," said Mr. Wickfield, shaking his head and smiling incredulously.

"A mixed fiddlestick," returned my aunt. "You claim to have one plain motive in all you do yourself. You don't suppose, I hope, that you are the only plain dealer in the world?"

"Ay, but I have only one motive in life, Miss Trotwood," he rejoined, smiling. "Other people have dozens, scores, hundreds. I have only one. There's the difference. However, that's beside the question. The best school? Whatever the motive, you want the best?"

My aunt nodded assent.

---

1 pray: 请

2 I give you my word: 我向你保证。

3 Deuce take the man: 真见鬼!

Chapter Ten The Psychoanalytic Approach

"At the best we have," said Mr. Wickfield, considering, "your nephew couldn't board just now."

"But he could board somewhere else, I suppose?" suggested my aunt.

Mr. Wickfield thought I could. After a little discussion, he proposed to take my aunt to the school, that she might see it and judge for herself; also, to take her, with the same object, to two or three houses where he thought I could be boarded. My aunt embracing the proposal, we were all three going out together, when he stopped and said:

"Our little friend here might have some motive, perhaps, for objecting to the arrangements. I think we had better leave him behind?"

My aunt seemed disposed to contest the point; but to facilitate matters I said I would gladly remain behind, if they pleased; and returned into Mr. Wickfield's office, where I sat down again, in the chair I had first occupied, to await their return.

It so happened that this chair was opposite a narrow passage, which ended in the little circular room where I had seen Uriah Heep's pale face looking out of the window. Uriah, having taken the pony to a neighbouring stable, was at work at a desk in this room, which had a brass frame on the top to hang paper upon, and on which the writing he was making a copy of was then hanging. Though his face was towards me, I thought, for some time, the writing being between us, that he could not see me; but looking that way more attentively, it made me uncomfortable to observe that, every now and then, his sleepless eyes would come below the writing, like two red suns, and stealthily stare at me for I dare say a whole minute at a time, during which his pen went, or pretended to go, as cleverly as ever. I made several attempts to get out of their way—such as standing on a chair to look at a map on the other side of the room, and poring over the columns of a Kentish newspaper—but they always attracted me back again; and whenever I looked towards those two red suns, I was sure to find them, either just rising or just setting.

At length, much to my relief, my aunt and Mr. Wickfield came back, after a pretty long absence. They were not so successful as I could have wished; for though the advantages of the school were undeniable, my aunt had not approved of any of the boarding-houses proposed for me.

"It's very unfortunate," said my aunt. "I don't know what to do, Trot."

"It does happen unfortunately," said Mr. Wickfield. "But I'll tell you what you can do, Miss Trotwood."

"What's that?" inquired my aunt.

"Leave your nephew here, for the present. He's a quiet fellow. He won't disturb me at all. It's a capital[1] house for study. As quiet as a monastery, and almost as roomy. Leave him here."

My aunt evidently liked the offer, though she was delicate of accepting it. So did I. "Come, Miss Trotwood," said Mr. Wickfield. "This is the way out of the difficulty. It's only a temporary arrangement, you know. If it don't act well, or don't quite accord with our mutual convenience, he can easily go to the right-about. There will be time to find some better place for him in the meanwhile. You had better determine to leave him here for the present!"

"I am very much obliged to you," said my aunt; "and so is he, I see; but—"

---

1 capital: 极好的

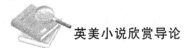
英美小说欣赏导论

"Come! I know what you mean," cried Mr. Wickfield. "You shall not be oppressed by the receipt of favours, Miss Trotwood. You may pay for him, if you like. We won't be hard about terms[1], but you shall pay if you will."

"On that understanding," said my aunt, "though it doesn't lessen the real obligation, I shall be very glad to leave him."

"Then come and see my little housekeeper," said Mr. Wickfield.

We accordingly went up a wonderful old staircase; with a balustrade[2] so broad that we might have gone up that, almost as easily; and into a shady old drawing-room, lighted by some three or four of the quaint windows I had looked up at from the street: which had old oak seats in them, that seemed to have come of the same trees as the shining oak floor, and the great beams in the ceiling. It was a prettily furnished room, with a piano and some lively furniture in red and green, and some flowers. It seemed to be all old nooks and corners; and in every nook and corner there was some queer little table, or cupboard, or bookcase, or seat, or something or other, that made me think there was not such another good corner in the room; until I looked at the next one, and found it equal to it, if not better. On everything there was the same air of retirement and cleanliness that marked the house outside.

Mr. Wickfield tapped at a door in a corner of the panelled wall, and a girl of about my own age came quickly out and kissed him. On her face, I saw immediately the placid and sweet expression of the lady whose picture had looked at me downstairs. It seemed to my imagination as if the portrait had grown womanly, and the original remained a child. Although her face was quite bright and happy, there was a tranquillity about it, and about her—a quiet, good, calm spirit—that I never have forgotten; that I shall never forget. This was his little housekeeper, his daughter Agnes[3], Mr. Wickfield said. When I heard how he said it, and saw how he held her hand, I guessed what the one motive of his life was.

She had a little basket-trifle hanging at her side, with keys in it; and she looked as staid and as discreet a housekeeper as the old house could have. She listened to her father as he told her about me, with a pleasant face; and when he had concluded, proposed to my aunt that we should go upstairs and see my room. We all went together, she before us: and a glorious old room it was, with more oak beams, and diamond panes; and the broad balustrade going all the way up to it.

I cannot call to mind where or when, in my childhood, I had seen a stained glass[4] window in a church. Nor do I recollect its subject. But I know that when I saw her turn round, in the grave light of the old staircase, and wait for us, above, I thought of that window; and I associated something of its tranquil brightness with Agnes Wickfield ever afterwards.

My aunt was as happy as I was, in the arrangement made for me; and we went down to the drawing-room again, well pleased and gratified. As she would not hear of staying to dinner, lest she should by any chance fail to arrive at home with the grey pony before dark; and as I apprehend Mr. Wickfield knew her too well to argue any point with her; some lunch was provided for her there, and Agnes went back to her governess, and Mr. Wickfield to his office. So we were left to take leave of one

---

1 We won't be hard about terms: 我们的条件不会太苛刻。
2 balustrade: 栏杆
3 Agnes: David 的第二任妻子
4 stained glass: 彩绘玻璃, 中世纪盛行, 绘画内容多为宗教故事, 在教堂中常见。

Chapter Ten The Psychoanalytic Approach

another without any restraint.

She told me that everything would be arranged for me by Mr. Wickfield, and that I should want for nothing[1], and gave me the kindest words and the best advice.

"Trot," said my aunt in conclusion, "be a credit to[2] yourself, to me, and Mr. Dick, and Heaven be with you!"

I was greatly overcome, and could only thank her, again and again, and send my love to Mr. Dick.

"Never," said my aunt, "be mean in anything; never be false; never be cruel. Avoid those three vices, Trot, and I can always be hopeful of you."

I promised, as well as I could, that I would not abuse her kindness or forget her admonition.

"The pony's at the door," said my aunt, "and I am off! Stay here." With these words she embraced me hastily, and went out of the room, shutting the door after her. At first I was startled by so abrupt a departure, and almost feared I had displeased her; but when I looked into the street, and saw how dejectedly she got into the chaise, and drove away without looking up, I understood her better and did not do her that injustice.

By five o'clock, which was Mr. Wickfield's dinner-hour, I had mustered up my spirits again, and was ready for my knife and fork. The cloth was only laid for us two; but Agnes was waiting in the drawing-room before dinner, went down with her father, and sat opposite to him at table. I doubted whether he could have dined without her.

We did not stay there, after dinner, but came upstairs into the drawing-room again: in one snug corner of which, Agnes set glasses for her father, and a decanter of port wine. I thought he would have missed its usual flavour, if it had been put there for him by any other hands.

There he sat, taking his wine, and taking a good deal of it, for two hours; while Agnes played on the piano, worked, and talked to him and me. He was, for the most part, gay and cheerful with us; but sometimes his eyes rested on her, and he fell into a brooding state, and was silent. She always observed this quickly, I thought, and always roused him with a question or caress. Then he came out of his meditation, and drank more wine.

Agnes made the tea, and presided over it[3]; and the time passed away after it, as after dinner, until she went to bed; when her father took her in his arms and kissed her, and, she being gone, ordered candles in his office. Then I went to bed too.

But in the course of the evening I had rambled down to the door, and a little way along the street, that I might have another peep at the old houses, and the grey Cathedral[4]; and might think of my coming through that old city on my journey, and of my passing the very house I lived in, without knowing it. As I came back, I saw Uriah Heep shutting up the office; and feeling friendly towards everybody, went in and spoke to him, and at parting, gave him my hand. But oh, what a clammy hand his was! as ghostly to the touch as to the sight! I rubbed mine afterwards, to warm it, and to rub his off.

It was such an uncomfortable hand, that, when I went to my room, it was still cold and wet upon my

---

1 want for nothing：什么都不缺
2 be a credit to：为……争光
3 and presided over it：并为大家斟上
4 the grey Cathedral：此处指坎特伯雷大教堂

memory. Leaning out of the window, and seeing one of the faces on the beam-ends looking at me sideways, I fancied it was Uriah Heep got up there somehow, and shut him out in a hurry.

XVI

I Am a New Boy in More Senses Than One

Next morning, after breakfast, I entered on school life again. I went, accompanied by Mr. Wickfield, to the Nscene of my future studies—a grave building in a courtyard, with a learned air about it that seemed very well suited to the stray rooks and jackdaws who came down from the Cathedral towers to walk with a clerkly bearing on the grass-plot—and was introduced to my new master, Doctor Strong.

Doctor Strong looked almost as rusty, to my thinking, as the tall iron rails and gates outside the house; and almost as stiff and heavy as the great stone urns that flanked them, and were set up, on the top of the red-brick wall, at regular distances all round the court, like sublimated skittles, for Time to play at. He was in his library (I mean Doctor Strong was), with his clothes not particularly well brushed, and his hair not particularly well combed; his knee-smalls unbraced; his long black gaiters unbuttoned; and his shoes yawning like two caverns on the hearth-rug. Turning upon me a lustreless eye, that reminded me of a long-forgotten blind old horse who once used to crop the grass, and tumble over the graves, in Blunderstone churchyard, he said he was glad to see me: and then he gave me his hand; which I didn't know what to do with, as it did nothing for itself.

But, sitting at work, not far from Doctor Strong, was a very pretty young lady—whom he called Annie, and who was his daughter, I supposed—who got me out of my difficulty by kneeling down to put Doctor Strong's shoes on, and button his gaiters, which she did with great cheerfulness and quickness. When she had finished, and we were going out to the schoolroom, I was much surprised to hear Mr. Wickfield, in bidding her good morning, address her as "Mrs. Strong"; and I was wondering could she be Doctor Strong's son's wife, or could she be Mrs. Doctor Strong, when Doctor Strong himself unconsciously enlightened me.

"By the by, Wickfield," he said, stopping in a passage with his hand on my shoulder; "you have not found any suitable provision for my wife's cousin yet?"

"No," said Mr. Wickfield. "No. Not yet."

"I could wish it done as soon as it can be done, Wickfield," said Doctor Strong, "for Jack Maldon is needy, and idle; and of those two bad things, worse things sometimes come. What does Doctor Watts[1] say," he added, looking at me, and moving his head to the time of his quotation, "'Satan finds some mischief still, for idlen hands to do.'"

"Egad[2], Doctor," returned Mr. Wickfield, "if Doctor Watts knew mankind, he might have written, with as much truth, 'Satan finds some mischief still, for busy hands to do.' The busy people achieve their full share of mischief in the world, you may rely upon it. What have the people been about, who

---

1 Doctor Watts：沃兹博士(1674—1748)，诗人，诗作多为宗教题材，后面所引诗句来源于其1714年所作《不要懒惰做坏事》。该诗句大意为"撒旦总是为懒惰者找些坏事做"。

2 Egad：天哪！

Chapter Ten The Psychoanalytic Approach

have been the busiest in getting money, and in getting power, this century or two? No mischief?"

"Jack Maldon will never be very busy in getting either, I expect," said Doctor Strong, rubbing his chin thoughtfully.

"Perhaps not," said Mr. Wickfield; "and you bring me back to the question, with an apology for digressing. No, I have not been able to dispose of Mr. Jack Maldon yet. I believe," he said this with some hesitation, "I penetrate your motive, and it makes the thing more difficult."

"My motive," returned Doctor Strong, "is to make some suitable provision for a cousin, and an old playfellow, of Annie's."

"Yes, I know," said Mr. Wickfield; "at home or abroad."

"Aye!" replied the Doctor, apparently wondering why he emphasized those words so much. "At home or abroad."

"Your own expression, you know," said Mr. Wickfield. "Or abroad."

"Surely," the Doctor answered. "Surely. One or other."

"One or other? Have you no choice?" asked Mr. Wickfield.

"No," returned the Doctor.

"No?" with astonishment.

"Not the least."

"No motive," said Mr. Wickfield, "for meaning abroad, and not at home?"

"No," returned the Doctor.

"I am bound to believe you, and of course I do believe you," said Mr. Wickfield. "It might have simplified my office very much, if I had known it before. But I confess I entertained another impression."

Doctor Strong regarded him with a puzzled and doubting look, which almost immediately subsided into a smile that gave me great encouragement; for it was full of amiability and sweetness, and there was a simplicity in it, and indeed in his whole manner, when the studious, pondering frost upon it was got through, very attractive and hopeful to a young scholar like me. Repeating "no," and "not the least," and other short assurances to the same purport, Doctor Strong jogged on before us, at a queer, uneven pace; and we followed: Mr. Wickfield, looking grave, I observed, and shaking his head to himself, without knowing that I saw him.

The schoolroom was a pretty large hall, on the quietest side of the house, confronted by the stately stare of some half-dozen of the great urns, and commanding a peep of an old secluded garden belonging to the Doctor, where the peaches were ripening on the sunny south wall. There were two great aloes, in tubs, on the turf outside the windows; the broad hard leaves of which plant (looking as if they were made of painted tin) have ever since, by association, been symbolical to me of silence and retirement. About five-and-twenty boys were studiously engaged at their books when we went in, but they rose to give the Doctor good morning, and remained standing when they saw Mr. Wickfield and me.

"A new boy, young gentlemen," said the Doctor; "Trotwood Copperfield."

One Adams, who was the head-boy, then stepped out of his place and welcomed me. He looked like a young clergyman, in his white cravat, but he was very affable and good-humoured; and he showed me my place, and presented me to the masters, in a gentlemanly way that would have put me at my ease, if

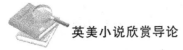

anything could.

It seemed to me so long, however, since I had been among such boys, or among any companions of my own age, except Mick Walker and Mealy Potatoes, that I felt as strange as ever I have done in my life. I was so conscious of having passed through scenes of which they could have no knowledge, and of having acquired experiences foreign to my age, appearance, and condition as one of them, that I half believed it was an imposture to come there as an ordinary little schoolboy. I had become, in the Murdstone[1] and Grinby time, however short or long it may have been, so unused to the sports and games of boys, that I knew I was awkward and inexperienced in the commonest things belonging to them. Whatever I had learnt, had so slipped away from me in the sordid cares of my life from day to night, that now, when I was examined about what I knew, I knew nothing, and was put into the lowest form of the school. But, troubled as I was, by my want of boyish skill, and of book-learning too, I was made infinitely more uncomfortable by the consideration, that, in what I did know, I was much farther removed from my companions than in what I did not[2]. My mind ran upon what they would think, if they knew of my familiar acquaintance with the King's Bench Prison[3]? Was there anything about me which would reveal my proceedings in connexion with the Micawber family—all those pawnings, and sellings, and suppers—in spite of myself? Suppose some of the boys had seen me coming through Canterbury, wayworn and ragged, and should find me out? What would they say, who made so light of money, if they could know how I had scraped my halfpence together, for the purchase of my daily saveloy and beer, or my slices of pudding? How would it affect them, who were so innocent of London life, and London streets, to discover how knowing I was (and was ashamed to be) in some of the meanest phases of both? All this ran in my head so much, on that first day at Doctor Strong's, that I felt distrustful of my slightest look and gesture; shrunk within myself whensoever I was approached by one of my new schoolfellows; and hurried off the minute school was over, afraid of committing myself in my response to any friendly notice or advance.

But there was such an influence in Mr. Wickfield's old house, that when I knocked at it, with my new school-books under my arm, I began to feel my uneasiness softening away. As I went up to my airy old room, the grave shadow of the staircase seemed to fall upon my doubts and fears, and to make the past more indistinct. I sat there, sturdily conning my books, until dinner-time (we were out of school for good at three); and went down, hopeful of becoming a passable sort of boy yet.

Agnes was in the drawing-room, waiting for her father, who was detained by someone in his office. She met me with her pleasant smile, and asked me how I liked the school. I told her I should like it very much, I hoped; but I was a little strange to it at first.

"You have never been to school," I said, "have you?"

"Oh yes! Every day."

"Ah, but you mean here, at your own home?"

---

1 Murdstone：Edward Murdstone，David 的继父，David 小时候经常因学习落后而挨他打。

2 But, troubled as I was, by my want of boyish skill, and of book-learning too, I was made infinitely more uncomfortable by the consideration, that, in what I did know, I was much farther removed from my companions than in what I did not：但是，我所烦恼的不只是不会玩男孩子玩的那一套，缺乏书本知识，一想到我所知道的比我不知道的更能使我和我的同学们疏远，我就更加痛苦。

3 King's Bench Prison：高等法院

Chapter Ten The Psychoanalytic Approach

"Papa couldn't spare me to go anywhere else," she answered, smiling and shaking her head. "His housekeeper must be in his house, you know."

"He is very fond of you, I am sure," I said.

She nodded "Yes," and went to the door to listen for his coming up, that she might meet him on the stairs. But, as he was not there, she came back again.

"Mama has been dead ever since I was born," she said, in her quiet way. "I only know her picture, downstairs. I saw you looking at it yesterday. Did you think whose it was?"

I told her yes, because it was so like herself.

"Papa says so, too," said Agnes, pleased. "Hark[1]! That's papa now!"

Her bright calm face lighted up with pleasure as she went to meet him, and as they came in, hand in hand. He greeted me cordially; and told me I should certainly be happy under Doctor Strong, who was one of the gentlest of men.

"There may be some, perhaps—I don't know that there are—who abuse his kindness," said Mr. Wickfield. "Never be one of those, Trotwood, in anything. He is the least suspicious of mankind; and whether that's a merit, or whether it's a blemish, it deserves consideration in all dealings with the Doctor, great or small."

He spoke, I thought, as if he were weary, or dissatisfied with something; but I did not pursue the question in my mind, for dinner was just then announced, and we went down and took the same seats as before.

We had scarcely done so, when Uriah Heep put in his red head and his lank hand at the door, and said:

"Here's Mr. Maldon begs the favour of a word, sir."

"I am but this moment quit of Mr. Maldon," said his master.

"Yes, sir," returned Uriah, "but Mr. Maldon has come back, and he begs the favour of a word." As he held the door open with his hand, Uriah looked at me, and looked at Agnes, and looked at the dishes, and looked at the plates, and looked at every object in the room, I thought—yet seemed to look at nothing; he made such an appearance all the while of keeping his red eyes dutifully on his master. "I beg your pardon. It's only to say, on reflection," observed a voice behind Uriah, as Uriah's head was pushed away, and the speaker's substituted—"pray excuse me for this intrusion—that as it seems I have no choice in the matter, the sooner I go abroad the better. My cousin Annie did say, when we talked of it, that she liked to have her friends within reach rather than to have them banished, and the old Doctor—"

"Doctor Strong, was that?" Mr. Wickfield interposed, gravely.

"Doctor Strong, of course," returned the other. "I call him the old Doctor; it's all the same, you know."

"I don't know," returned Mr. Wickfield.

"Well, Doctor Strong," said the other—"Doctor Strong was of the same mind, I believed. But as it appears from the course you take with me he has changed his mind, why there's no more to be said, except that the sooner I am off, the better. Therefore, I thought I'd come back and say, that the sooner I

---

1 hark: 听

am off the better. When a plunge is to be made into the water, it's of no use lingering on the bank."

"There shall be as little lingering as possible, in your case, Mr. Maldon, you may depend upon it," said Mr. Wickfield.

"Thank'ee," said the other. "Much obliged. I don't want to look a gift-horse in the mouth[1], which is not a gracious thing to do; otherwise, I dare say, my cousin Annie could easily arrange it in her own way. I suppose Annie would only have to say to the old Doctor—"

"Meaning that Mrs. Strong would only have to say to her husband—do I follow you?" said Mr. Wickfield.

"Quite so," returned the other, "—would only have to say, that she wanted such and such a thing to be so and so; and it would be so and so, as a matter of course."

"And why as a matter of course, Mr. Maldon?" asked Mr. Wickfield, sedately eating his dinner.

"Why, because Annie's a charming young girl, and the old Doctor—Doctor Strong, I mean—is not quite a charming young boy," said Mr. Jack Maldon, laughing. "No offence to anybody, Mr. Wickfield. I only mean that I suppose some compensation is fair and reasonable in that sort of marriage."

"Compensation to the lady, sir?" asked Mr. Wickfield gravely.

"To the lady, sir," Mr. Jack Maldon answered, laughing. But appearing to remark that Mr. Wickfield went on with his dinner in the same sedate, immovable manner, and that there was no hope of making him relax a muscle of his face, he added: "However, I have said what I came to say, and, with another apology for this intrusion, I may take myself off. Of course I shall observe your directions, in considering the matter as one to be arranged between you and me solely, and not to be referred to, up at the Doctor's."

"Have you dined?" asked Mr. Wickfield, with a motion of his hand towards the table.

"Thank'ee. I am going to dine," said Mr. Maldon, "with my cousin Annie. Good-bye!"

Mr. Wickfield, without rising, looked after him thoughtfully as he went out. He was rather a shallow sort of young gentleman, I thought, with a handsome face, a rapid utterance, and a confident, bold air. And this was the first I ever saw of Mr. Jack Maldon; whom I had not expected to see so soon, when I heard the Doctor speak of him that morning.

When we had dined, we went upstairs again, where everything went on exactly as on the previous day. Agnes set the glasses and decanters in the same corner, and Mr. Wickfield sat down to drink, and drank a good deal. Agnes played the piano to him, sat by him, and worked and talked, and played some games at dominoes with me. In good time she made tea; and afterwards, when I brought down my books, looked into them, and showed me what she knew of them (which was no slight matter, though she said it was), and what was the best way to learn and understand them. I see her, with her modest, orderly, placid manner, and I hear her beautiful calm voice, as I write these words. The influence for all good, which she came to exercise over me at a later time, begins already to descend upon my breast. I love little Em'ly[2], and I don't love Agnes—no, not at all in that way—but I feel that there are goodness, peace, and truth, wherever Agnes is; and that the soft light of the coloured window in the church, seen long ago, falls on

---

1 look a gift-horse in the mouth: 白送的马还看牙口，比喻对礼物吹毛求疵。
2 Em'ly: Daniel Peggotty 的侄女，David 小时候喜欢她。被 Steerforth 诱奸后抛弃，后与 Peggotty 一同去了澳大利亚。

her always, and on me when I am near her, and on everything around.

The time having come for her withdrawal for the night, and she having left us, I gave Mr. Wickfield my hand, preparatory to going away myself. But he checked me and said: "Should you like to stay with us, Trotwood, or to go elsewhere?"

"To stay," I answered, quickly.

"You are sure?"

"If you please. If I may!"

"Why, it's but a dull life that we lead here, boy, I am afraid," he said.

"Not more dull for me than Agnes, sir. Not dull at all!"

"Than Agnes," he repeated, walking slowly to the great chimney-piece, and leaning against it. "Than Agnes!"

He had drank wine that evening (or I fancied it), until his eyes were bloodshot. Not that I could see them now, for they were cast down, and shaded by his hand; but I had noticed them a little while before.

"Now I wonder," he muttered, "whether my Agnes tires of me. When should I ever tire of her! But that's different, that's quite different."

He was musing, not speaking to me; so I remained quiet.

"A dull old house," he said, "and a monotonous life; but I must have her near me. I must keep her near me. If the thought that I may die and leave my darling, or that my darling may die and leave me, comes like a spectre, to distress my happiest hours, and is only to be drowned in—"

He did not supply the word; but pacing slowly to the place where he had sat, and mechanically going through the action of pouring wine from the empty decanter, set it down and paced back again.

"If it is miserable to bear, when she is here," he said, "what would it be, and she away? No, no, no. I cannot try that."

He leaned against the chimney-piece, brooding so long that I could not decide whether to run the risk of disturbing him by going, or to remain quietly where I was, until he should come out of his reverie. At length he aroused himself, and looked about the room until his eyes encountered mine.

"Stay with us, Trotwood, eh?" he said in his usual manner, and as if he were answering something I had just said. "I am glad of it. You are company to us both. It is wholesome to have you here. Wholesome for me, wholesome for Agnes, wholesome perhaps for all of us."

"I am sure it is for me, sir," I said. "I am so glad to be here."

"That's a fine fellow!" said Mr. Wickfield. "As long as you are glad to be here, you shall stay here." He shook hands with me upon it, and clapped me on the back; and told me that when I had anything to do at night after Agnes had left us, or when I wished to read for my own pleasure, I was free to come down to his room, if he were there and if I desired it for company's sake, and to sit with him. I thanked him for his consideration; and, as he went down soon afterwards, and I was not tired, went down too, with a book in my hand, to avail myself, for half-an-hour, of his permission.

But, seeing a light in the little round office, and immediately feeling myself attracted towards Uriah Heep, who had a sort of fascination for me, I went in there instead. I found Uriah reading a great fat book, with such demonstrative attention, that his lank forefinger followed up every line as he read, and made clammy tracks along the page (or so I fully believed) like a snail.

"You are working late tonight, Uriah," says I.

"Yes, Master Copperfield," says Uriah.

As I was getting on the stool opposite, to talk to him more conveniently, I observed that he had not such a thing as a smile about him, and that he could only widen his mouth and make two hard creases down his cheeks, one on each side, to stand for one.

"I am not doing office-work, Master Copperfield," said Uriah.

"What work, then?" I asked.

"I am improving my legal knowledge, Master Copperfield," said Uriah. "I am going through Tidd's Practice[1]. Oh, what a writer Mr. Tidd is, Master Copperfield!"

My stool was such a tower of observation, that as I watched him reading on again, after this rapturous exclamation, and following up the lines with his forefinger, I observed that his nostrils, which were thin and pointed, with sharp dints in them, had a singular and most uncomfortable way of expanding and contracting themselves—that they seemed to twinkle instead of his eyes, which hardly ever twinkled at all.

"I suppose you are quite a great lawyer?" I said, after looking at him for some time.

"Me, Master Copperfield?" said Uriah. "Oh, no! I'm a very 'umble person."

It was no fancy of mine about his hands, I observed; for he frequently ground the palms against each other as if to squeeze them dry and warm, besides often wiping them, in a stealthy way, on his pocket-handkerchief.

"I am well aware that I am the umblest person going," said Uriah Heep, modestly; "let the other be where he may. My mother is likewise a very umble person. We live in a numble abode[2], Master Copperfield, but have much to be thankful for. My father's former calling[3] was umble. He was a sexton[4]."

"What is he now?" I asked.

"He is a partaker of glory at present, Master Copperfield," said Uriah Heep. "But we have much to be thankful for. How much have I to be thankful for in living with Mr. Wickfield!"

I asked Uriah if he had been with Mr. Wickfield long?

"I have been with him, going on four year, Master Copperfield," said Uriah; shutting up his book, after carefully marking the place where he had left off. "Since a year after my father's death. How much have I to be thankful for, in that! How much have I to be thankful for, in Mr. Wickfield's kind intention to give me my articles, which would otherwise not lay within the 'umble means of mother and self!"

"Then, when your articled time[5] is over, you'll be a regular lawyer, I suppose?" said I.

"With the blessing of Providence, Master Copperfield," returned Uriah.

"Perhaps you'll be a partner in Mr. Wickfield's business, one of these days," I said, to make myself agreeable; "and it will be Wickfield and Heep, or Heep late[6] Wickfield."

---

1 Tidd's Practice：威廉·提得（William Tidd）于 1790—1794 年之间撰写的《皇家法席审理规程》(Practice of the Court of King's Bench)

2 a numble abode：一个简陋的住所。尤利亚·希普在此将"humble"念成"numble"，在多处还念成"'umble"。

3 calling：职业

4 Sexton：教堂执事，担任教堂内外管理、敲钟、墓地等工作

5 articled time：见习期

6 late：已故的

Chapter Ten The Psychoanalytic Approach

"Oh no, Master Copperfield," returned Uriah, shaking his head, "I am much too umble for that!"

He certainly did look uncommonly like the carved face on the beam outside my window, as he sat, in his humility, eyeing me sideways, with his mouth widened, and the creases in his cheeks.

"Mr. Wickfield is a most excellent man, Master Copperfield," said Uriah. "If you have known him long, you know it, I am sure, much better than I can inform you."

I replied that I was certain he was; but that I had not known him long myself, though he was a friend of my aunt's.

"Oh, indeed, Master Copperfield," said Uriah. "Your aunt is a sweet lady, Master Copperfield!"

He had a way of writhing when he wanted to express enthusiasm, which was very ugly; and which diverted my attention from the compliment he had paid my relation, to the snaky twistings of his throat and body.

"A sweet lady, Master Copperfield!" said Uriah Heep. "She has a great admiration for Miss Agnes, Master Copperfield, I believe?"

I said, "Yes," boldly; not that I knew anything about it, Heaven forgive me!

"I hope you have, too, Master Copperfield," said Uriah. "But I am sure you must have."

"Everybody must have," I returned.

"Oh, thank you, Master Copperfield," said Uriah Heep, "for that remark! It is so true! Umble as I am, I know it is so true! Oh, thank you, Master Copperfield!" He writhed himself quite off his stool in the excitement of his feelings, and, being off, began to make arrangements for going home.

"Mother will be expecting me," he said, referring to a pale, inexpressive-faced watch in his pocket, "and getting uneasy; for though we are very umble, Master Copperfield, we are much attached to one another. If you would come and see us, any afternoon, and take a cup of tea at our lowly dwelling, mother would be as proud of your company as I should be."

I said I should be glad to come.

"Thank you, Master Copperfield," returned Uriah, putting his book away upon the shelf—"I suppose you stop here, some time, Master Copperfield?"

I said I was going to be brought up there, I believed, as long as I remained at school.

"Oh, indeed!" exclaimed Uriah. "I should think you would come into the business at last, Master Copperfield!"

I protested that I had no views of that sort, and that no such scheme was entertained in my behalf by anybody; but Uriah insisted on blandly replying to all my assurances, "Oh, yes, Master Copperfield, I should think you would, indeed!" and, "Oh, indeed, Master Copperfield, I should think you would, certainly!" over and over again. Being, at last, ready to leave the office for the night, he asked me if it would suit my convenience to have the light put out; and on my answering "Yes," instantly extinguished it. After shaking hands with me-his hand felt like a fish, in the dark-he opened the door into the street a very little, and crept out, and shut it, leaving me to grope my way back into the house: which cost me some trouble and a fall over his stool. This was the proximate cause, I suppose, of my dreaming about him, for what appeared to me to be half the night; and dreaming, among other things, that he had launched Mr. Peggotty's house on a piratical expedition, with a black flag at the masthead, bearing the inscription "Tidd's Practice," under which diabolical ensign he was carrying me and little Em'ly to the

Spanish Main[1], to be drowned.

  I got a little the better of my uneasiness when I went to school next day, and a good deal the better next day, and so shook it off by degrees, that in less than a fortnight I was quite at home, and happy, among my new companions. I was awkward enough in their games, and backward enough in their studies; but custom would improve me in the first respect, I hoped, and hard work in the second. Accordingly, I went to work very hard, both in play and in earnest, and gained great commendation. And, in a very little while, the Murdstone and Grinby life became so strange to me that I hardly believed in it, while my present life grew so familiar, that I seemed to have been leading it a long time.

  Doctor Strong's was an excellent school; as different from Mr. Creakle[2]'s as good is from evil. It was very gravely and decorously ordered, and on a sound system; with an appeal, in everything, to the honour and good faith of the boys, and an avowed intention to rely on their possession of those qualities unless they proved themselves unworthy of it, which worked wonders. We all felt that we had a part in the management of the place, and in sustaining its character and dignity. Hence, we soon became warmly attached to it—I am sure I did for one, and I never knew, in all my time, of any other boy being otherwise—and learnt with a good will, desiring to do it credit. We had noble games out of hours, and plenty of liberty; but even then, as I remember, we were well spoken of in the town, and rarely did any disgrace, by our appearance or manner, to the reputation of Doctor Strong and Doctor Strong's boys.

  Some of the higher scholars boarded in the Doctor's house, and through them I learned, at second hand, some particulars of the Doctor's history—as, how he had not yet been married twelve months to the beautiful young lady I had seen in the study, whom he had married for love; for she had not a sixpence, and had a world of poor relations (so our fellows said) ready to swarm the Doctor out of house and home. Also, how the Doctor's cogitating manner was attributable to his being always engaged in looking out for Greek roots[3]; which, in my innocence and ignorance, I supposed to be a botanical furor on the Doctor's part, especially as he always looked at the ground when he walked about, until I understood that they were roots of words, with a view to a new Dictionary which he had in contemplation. Adams, our head-boy, who had a turn for mathematics, had made a calculation, I was informed, of the time this Dictionary would take in completing, on the Doctor's plan, and at the Doctor's rate of going. He considered that it might be done in one thousand six hundred and forty-nine years, counting from the Doctor's last, or sixty-second, birthday.

  But the Doctor himself was the idol of the whole school: and it must have been a badly composed school if he had been anything else, for he was the kindest of men; with a simple faith in him that might have touched the stone hearts of the very urns upon the wall. As he walked up and down that part of the courtyard which was at the side of the house, with the stray rooks and jackdaws looking after him with their heads cocked slyly, as if they knew how much more knowing they were in worldly affairs than he, if any sort of vagabond could only get near enough to his creaking shoes to attract his attention to one sentence of a tale of distress, that vagabond was made for the next two days. It was so notorious in the

---

 1 Spanish Main：包括中美洲和南美洲北部海岸，这些地方在16至18世纪曾是西班牙的殖民地。
 2 Mr. Creakle：David 寄宿学校(Salem House)的校长，Murdstone 的朋友。此人冷酷残忍。
 3 Greek roots：希腊词根。这里博士要编写一本词典，研究词源。

house, that the masters and head-boys took pains to cut these marauders off at angles, and to get out of windows, and turn them out of the courtyard, before they could make the Doctor aware of their presence; which was sometimes happily effected within a few yards of him, without his knowing anything of the matter, as he jogged to and fro. Outside his own domain, and unprotected, he was a very sheep for the shearers. He would have taken his gaiters off his legs, to give away. In fact, there was a story current among us (I have no idea, and never had, on what authority, but I have believed it for so many years that I feel quite certain it is true), that on a frosty day, one winter-time, he actually did bestow his gaiters on a beggar-woman, who occasioned some scandal in the neighbourhood by exhibiting a fine infant from door to door, wrapped in those garments, which were universally recognized, being as well known in the vicinity as the Cathedral. The legend added that the only person who did not identify them was the Doctor himself, who, when they were shortly afterwards displayed at the door of a little second-hand shop of no very good repute, where such things were taken in exchange for gin, was more than once observed to handle them approvingly, as if admiring some curious novelty in the pattern, and considering them an improvement on his own.

It was very pleasant to see the Doctor with his pretty young wife. He had a fatherly, benignant way of showing his fondness for her, which seemed in itself to express a good man. I often saw them walking in the garden where the peaches were, and I sometimes had a nearer observation of them in the study or the parlour. She appeared to me to take great care of the Doctor, and to like him very much, though I never thought her vitally interested in the Dictionary: some cumbrous fragments of which work the Doctor always carried in his pockets, and in the lining of his hat, and generally seemed to be expounding to her as they walked about.

I saw a good deal of Mrs. Strong, both because she had taken a liking for me on the morning of my introduction to the Doctor, and was always afterwards kind to me, and interested in me; and because she was very fond of Agnes, and was often backwards and forwards at our house. There was a curious constraint between her and Mr. Wickfield, I thought (of whom she seemed to be afraid), that never wore off. When she came there of an evening, she always shrunk from accepting his escort home, and ran away with me instead. And sometimes, as we were running gaily across the Cathedral yard together, expecting to meet nobody, we would meet Mr. Jack Maldon, who was always surprised to see us.

Mrs. Strong's mama was a lady I took great delight in. Her name was Mrs. Markleham; but our boys used to call her the Old Soldier, on account of her generalship, and the skill with which she marshalled great forces of relations against the Doctor. She was a little, sharp-eyed woman, who used to wear, when she was dressed, one unchangeable cap, ornamented with some artificial flowers, and two artificial butterflies supposed to be hovering above the flowers. There was a superstition among us that this cap had come from France, and could only originate in the workmanship of that ingenious nation: but all I certainly know about it, is, that it always made its appearance of an evening, wheresoever Mrs. Markleham made her appearance; that it was carried about to friendly meetings in a Hindoo basket; that the butterflies had the gift of trembling constantly; and that they improved the shining hours at Doctor Strong's expense, like busy bees.

I observed the Old Soldier—not to adopt the name disrespectfully—to pretty good advantage, on a night which is made memorable to me by something else I shall relate. It was the night of a little party at the Doctor's, which was given on the occasion of Mr. Jack Maldon's departure for India, whither he was going as a cadet, or something of that kind: Mr. Wickfield having at length arranged the business. It happened to be the Doctor's birthday, too. We had had a holiday, had made presents to him in the morning, had made a speech to him through the head-boy, and had cheered him until we were hoarse, and until he had shed tears. And now, in the evening, Mr. Wickfield, Agnes, and I, went to have tea with him in his private capacity.

Mr. Jack Maldon was there, before us. Mrs. Strong, dressed in white, with cherry-coloured ribbons, was playing the piano, when we went in; and he was leaning over her to turn the leaves. The clear red and white of her complexion was not so blooming and flower-like as usual, I thought, when she turned round; but she looked very pretty, Wonderfully pretty.

"I have forgotten, Doctor," said Mrs. Strong's mama, when we were seated, "to pay you the compliments of the day—though they are, as you may suppose, very far from being mere compliments in my case. Allow me to wish you many happy returns[1]."

"I thank you, ma'am," replied the Doctor.

"Many, many, many, happy returns," said the Old Soldier. "Not only for your own sake, but for Annie's, and John Maldon's, and many other people's. It seems but yesterday to me, John, when you were a little creature, a head shorter than Master Copperfield, making baby love to Annie behind the gooseberry bushes in the back-garden."

"My dear mama," said Mrs. Strong, "never mind that now."

"Annie, don't be absurd," returned her mother. "If you are to blush to hear of such things now you are an old married woman, when are you not to blush to hear of them?"

"Old?" exclaimed Mr. Jack Maldon. "Annie? Come!"

"Yes, John," returned the Soldier. "Virtually, an old married woman. Although not old by years—for when did you ever hear me say, or who has ever heard me say, that a girl of twenty was old by years! —your cousin is the wife of the Doctor, and, as such, what I have described her. It is well for you, John, that your cousin is the wife of the Doctor. You have found in him an influential and kind friend, who will be kinder yet, I venture to predict, if you deserve it. I have no false pride. I never hesitate to admit, frankly, that there are some members of our family who want a friend. You were one yourself, before your cousin's influence raised up one for you."

The Doctor, in the goodness of his heart, waved his hand as if to make light of it, and save Mr. Jack Maldon from any further reminder. But Mrs. Markleham changed her chair for one next the Doctor's, and putting her fan on his coat-sleeve, said:

"No, really, my dear Doctor, you must excuse me if I appear to dwell on this rather, because I feel so very strongly. I call it quite my monomania[2], it is such a subject of mine. You are a blessing to us. You really are a Boon[3], you know."

---

1 many happy returns: 福寿无疆, 长命百岁

2 monomania: 偏执狂

3 Boon: 恩惠, 赐福

Chapter Ten　The Psychoanalytic Approach

"Nonsense, nonsense," said the Doctor.

"No, no, I beg your pardon," retorted the Old Soldier. "With nobody present, but our dear and confidential friend Mr. Wickfield, I cannot consent to be put down. I shall begin to assert the privileges of a mother-in-law, if you go on like that, and scold you. I am perfectly honest and outspoken. What I am saying, is what I said when you first overpowered me with surprise—you remember how surprised I was?—by proposing for Annie. Not that there was anything so very much out of the way, in the mere fact of the proposal—it would be ridiculous to say that!—but because, you having known her poor father, and having known her from a baby six months old, I hadn't thought of you in such a light at all, or indeed as a marrying man in any way—simply that, you know."

"Aye, aye," returned the Doctor, good-humouredly. "Never mind."

"But I do mind," said the Old Soldier, laying her fan upon his lips. "I mind very much. I recall these things that I may be contradicted if I am wrong. Well! Then I spoke to Annie, and I told her what had happened. I said, 'My dear, here's Doctor Strong has positively been and made you the subject of a handsome declaration and an offer[1].' Did I press it in the least? No. I said, 'Now, Annie, tell me the truth this moment; is your heart free?' 'Mama,' she said crying, 'I am extremely young'—which was perfectly true—'and I hardly know if I have a heart at all.' 'Then, my dear,' I said, 'you may rely upon it, it's free. At all events, my love,' said I, 'Doctor Strong is in an agitated state of mind, and must be answered. He cannot be kept in his present state of suspense.' 'Mama,' said Annie, still crying, 'would he be unhappy without me? If he would, I honour and respect him so much, that I think I will have him.' So it was settled. And then, and not till then, I said to Annie, 'Annie, Doctor Strong will not only be your husband, but he will represent your late father: he will represent the head of our family, he will represent the wisdom and station, and I may say the means, of our family; and will be, in short, a Boon to it.' I used the word at the time, and I have used it again, today. If I have any merit it is consistency."

The daughter had sat quite silent and still during this speech, with her eyes fixed on the ground; her cousin standing near her, and looking on the ground too. She now said very softly, in a trembling voice:

"Mama, I hope you have finished?"

"No, my dear Annie," returned the Old Soldier, "I have not quite finished. Since you ask me, my love, I reply that I have not. I complain that you really are a little unnatural towards your own family; and, as it is of no use complaining to you. I mean to complain to your husband. Now, my dear Doctor, do look at that silly wife of yours."

As the Doctor turned his kind face, with its smile of simplicity and gentleness, towards her, she drooped her head more. I noticed that Mr. Wickfield looked at her steadily.

"When I happened to say to that naughty thing, the other day," pursued her mother, shaking her head and her fan at her, playfully, "that there was a family circumstance she might mention to you—indeed, I think, was bound to mention—she said, that to mention it was to ask a favour; and that, as you were too generous, and as for her to ask was always to have, she wouldn't."

"Annie, my dear," said the Doctor. "That was wrong. It robbed me of a pleasure."

---

1 here's Doctor Strong has positively been and made you the subject of a handsome declaration and an offer: 斯特朗博士一片诚心，把你赞扬了一番，还向你求婚了。

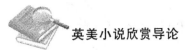

"Almost the very words I said to her!" exclaimed her mother. "Now really, another time, when I know what she would tell you but for this reason, and won't, I have a great mind, my dear Doctor, to tell you myself."

"I shall be glad if you will," returned the Doctor.

"Shall I?"

"Certainly."

"Well, then, I will!" said the Old Soldier. "That's a bargain." And having, I suppose, carried her point, she tapped the Doctor's hand several times with her fan (which she kissed first), and returned triumphantly to her former station.

Some more company coming in, among whom were the two masters and Adams, the talk became general; and it naturally turned on Mr. Jack Maldon, and his voyage, and the country he was going to, and his various plans and prospects. He was to leave that night, after supper, in a post-chaise, for Gravesend[1]; where the ship, in which he was to make the voyage, lay; and was to be gone—unless he came home on leave, or for his health—I don't know how many years. I recollect it was settled by general consent that India was quite a misrepresented country, and had nothing objectionable in it, but a tiger or two, and a little heat in the warm part of the day. For my own part, I looked on Mr. Jack Maldon as a modern Sindbad[2], and pictured him the bosom friend of all the Rajahs[3] in the East, sitting under canopies, smoking curly golden pipes—a mile long, if they could be straightened out. Mrs. Strong was a very pretty singer: as I knew, who often heard her singing by herself. But, whether she was afraid of singing before people, or was out of voice that evening, it was certain that she couldn't sing at all. She tried a duet, once, with her cousin Maldon, but could not so much as begin; and afterwards, when she tried to sing by herself, although she began sweetly, her voice died away on a sudden, and left her quite distressed, with her head hanging down over the keys. The good Doctor said she was nervous, and, to relieve her, proposed a round game at cards; of which he knew as much as of the art of playing the trombone. But I remarked that the Old Soldier took him into custody directly, for her partner; and instructed him, as the first preliminary of initiation, to give her all the silver he had in his pocket.

We had a merry game, not made the less merry by the Doctor's mistakes, of which he committed an innumerable quantity, in spite of the watchfulness of the butterflies, and to their great aggravation. Mrs. Strong had declined to play, on the ground of not feeling very well; and her cousin Maldon had excused himself because he had some packing to do. When he had done it, however, he returned, and they sat together, talking, on the sofa. From time to time she came and looked over the Doctor's hand, and told him what to play. She was very pale, as she bent over him, and I thought her finger trembled as she pointed out the cards; but the Doctor was quite happy in her attention, and took no notice of this, if it were so.

At supper, we were hardly so gay. Everyone appeared to feel that a parting of that sort was an awkward thing, and that the nearer it approached, the more awkward it was. Mr. Jack Maldon tried to be

---

1 Gravesend: 地名,格雷夫森德

2 Sindbad: 辛巴德,《天方夜谭》中的人物,一个了不起的探险家,《天方夜谭》中有七个关于他在海上航行的故事。

3 Rajahs: (印度的)邦主,王公

Chapter Ten The Psychoanalytic Approach

very talkative, but was not at his ease, and made matters worse. And they were not improved, as it appeared to me, by the Old Soldier: who continually recalled passages of Mr. Jack Maldon's youth. The Doctor, however, who felt, I am sure, that he was making everybody happy, was well pleased, and had no suspicion but that we were all at the utmost height of enjoyment.

"Annie, my dear," said he, looking at his watch, and filling his glass, "it is past your cousin Jack's time, and we must not detain him, since time and tide—both concerned in this case—wait for no man. Mr. Jack Maldon, you have a long voyage, and a strange country, before you; but many men have had both, and many men will have both, to the end of time. The winds you are going to tempt, have wafted thousands upon thousands to fortune, and brought thousands upon thousands happily back."

"It's an affecting thing," said Mrs. Markleham—"however it's viewed, it's affecting, to see a fine young man one has known from an infant, going away to the other end of the world, leaving all he knows behind, and not knowing what's before him. A young man really well deserves constant support and patronage," looking at the Doctor, "who makes such sacrifices."

"Time will go fast with you, Mr. Jack Maldon," pursued the Doctor, "and fast with all of us. Some of us can hardly expect, perhaps, in the natural course of things, to greet you on your return. The next best thing is to hope to do it, and that's my case. I shall not weary you with good advice. You have long had a good model before you, in your cousin Annie. Imitate her virtues as nearly as you can."

Mrs. Markleham fanned herself, and shook her head.

"Farewell, Mr. Jack," said the Doctor, standing up; on which we all stood up. "A prosperous voyage out, a thriving career abroad, and a happy return home!"

We all drank the toast, and all shook hands with Mr. Jack Maldon; after which he hastily took leave of the ladies who were there, and hurried to the door, where he was received, as he got into the chaise, with a tremendous broadside of cheers discharged by our boys, who had assembled on the lawn for the purpose. Running in among them to swell the ranks, I was very near the chaise when it rolled away; and I had a lively impression made upon me, in the midst of the noise and dust, of having seen Mr. Jack Maldon rattle past with an agitated face, and something cherry-coloured in his hand.

After another broadside for the Doctor, and another for the Doctor's wife, the boys dispersed, and I went back into the house, where I found the guests all standing in a group about the Doctor, discussing how Mr. Jack Maldon had gone away, and how he had borne it, and how he had felt it, and all the rest of it. In the midst of these remarks, Mrs. Markleham cried: "Where's Annie?"

No Annie was there; and when they called to her, no Annie replied. But all pressing out of the room, in a crowd, to see what was the matter, we found her lying on the hall floor. There was great alarm at first, until it was found that she was in a swoon[1], and that the swoon was yielding to the usual means of recovery; when the Doctor, who had lifted her head upon his knee, put her curls aside with his hand, and said, looking around:

"Poor Annie! She's so faithful and tender-hearted! It's the parting from her old playfellow and friend—her favourite cousin—that has done this. Ah! It's a pity! I am very sorry!"

When she opened her eyes, and saw where she was, and that we were all standing about her, she

---

1 in a swoon: 昏厥

arose with assistance: turning her head, as she did so, to lay it on the Doctor's shoulder—or to hide it, I don't know which. We went into the drawing-room, to leave her with the Doctor and her mother; but she said, it seemed, that she was better than she had been since morning, and that she would rather be brought among us; so they brought her in, looking very white and weak, I thought, and sat her on a sofa.

"Annie, my dear," said her mother, doing something to her dress. "See here! You have lost a bow. Will anybody be so good as find a ribbon; a cherry-coloured ribbon?"

It was the one she had worn at her bosom. We all looked for it; I myself looked everywhere, I am certain—but nobody could find it.

"Do you recollect where you had it last, Annie?" said her mother.

I wondered how I could have thought she looked white, or anything but burning red, when she answered that she had had it safe, a little while ago, she thought, but it was not worth looking for.

Nevertheless, it was looked for again, and still not found. She entreated that there might be no more searching; but it was still sought for, in a desultory way, until she was quite well, and the company took their departure.

We walked very slowly home, Mr. Wickfield, Agnes, and I—Agnes and I admiring the moonlight, and Mr. Wickfield scarcely raising his eyes from the ground. When we, at last, reached our own door, Agnes discovered that she had left her little reticule behind. Delighted to be of any service to her, I ran back to fetch it.

I went into the supper-room where it had been left, which was deserted and dark. But a door of communication between that and the Doctor's study, where there was a light, being open, I passed on there, to say what I wanted, and to get a candle.

The Doctor was sitting in his easy-chair by the fireside, and his young wife was on a stool at his feet. The Doctor, with a complacent smile, was reading aloud some manuscript explanation or statement of a theory out of that interminable Dictionary, and she was looking up at him. But with such a face as I never saw. It was so beautiful in its form, it was so ashy pale, it was so fixed in its abstraction, it was so full of a wild, sleep-walking, dreamy horror of I don't know what. The eyes were wide open, and her brown hair fell in two rich clusters on her shoulders, and on her white dress, disordered by the want of the lost ribbon. Distinctly as I recollect her look, I cannot say of what it was expressive, I cannot even say of what it is expressive to me now, rising again before my older judgment. Penitence, humiliation, shame, pride, love, and trustfulness—I see them all; and in them all, I see that horror of I don't know what.

My entrance, and my saying what I wanted, roused her. It disturbed the Doctor too, for when I went back to replace the candle I had taken from the table, he was patting her head, in his fatherly way, and saying he was a merciless drone to let her tempt him into reading on; and he would have her go to bed.

But she asked him, in a rapid, urgent manner, to let her stay—to let her feel assured (I heard her murmur some broken words to this effect) that she was in his confidence that night. And, as she turned again towards him, after glancing at me as I left the room and went out at the door, I saw her cross her hands upon his knee, and look up at him with the same face, something quieted, as he resumed his reading.

It made a great impression on me, and I remembered it a long time afterwards; as I shall have occasion to narrate when the time comes.

Chapter Ten   The Psychoanalytic Approach

Understanding the Text

Sigmund Freud developed the psychoanalytic theories based on his tripartite model of the human mind, which represents the unconscious part of the human psyche. According to Freud, the unconscious part of the human psyche houses three parts: the id, the ego, and the superego. The id is the reservoir of the primal instincts of sexuality and aggression. Being dominated by the "pleasure principle" that strives to satisfy the dark desires it houses, the id can result in a person's self-destruction if left unchecked. To counter-balance this dangerous part of the unconscious, the mind possesses two regulating agencies: the ego and the superego. The superego is the exact opposite of the id. Dominated by "the morality principle," the superego asks a person to abide by certain moral restrictions and make moral judgments in light of social pressures, which frequently leads to an unconscious and often overwhelming sense of guilt. And the ego that is dominated by the reality principle and regulates between these two psychic forces (the id and superego) acts as the rational governing agency of the mind and intermediary between the world inside and the world outside. It is the ego that frequently succeeds in directing the potentially dangerous desires housed in the unconscious mind into non-destructive activities. Freud argues that in the process of becoming a man or a woman, a child has stored many painful memories of repressed sexual desires, anger, rage, and guilt in his or her unconscious, which are frequently presented in the form of images or symbols in our dreams. And dreams are fundamentally sexual.

In *David Copperfield,* "more than twenty of David's dreams are recounted." (Bressler, p.170) These dreams mirror David's psychological life which is closely linked to two characters in the novel—Uriah Heep and James Steerforth. Uriah, David and Steerforth are actually triply splits of David's psyche according to Freud's tripartite model of the human mind. Uriah is equated to the id, Steerforth is analogous to the superego, and David is the ego. More specifically, Uriah represents the dark and sexual desires of David's psyche while Steerforth represents his sense of guilt resulted from the morality principle for Steerforth is aristocratic in manner if not in fact (David fails to notice his abundantly obvious faults). And David, dominated by the reality principle, acts as the intermediary between his other two splits—the world inside and the world outside. Considering we have only two chapters of *David Copperfield* in this book, we will focus our interpretation only on one of David's dreams in these two chapters and David's association with Uriah Heep.

On the night of David's first meeting with Uriah Heep, his sleep is troubled by dreams. In his odd circular office at Canterbury, Uriah has suggested more than once his fear that David has the ambition to usurp his place in Wickfield's firm although David denies such a scheme. Uriah turns off the light when he leaves the office by an outside door. As David gropes his way in the dark back to Wickfield's house by a connecting passage, he falls over Uriah's stool, which serves as the catalyst that precipitates the dream:

> *This was the proximate cause, I suppose, of my dreaming about him, for what appeared to me to be half the night; and dreaming, among other things, that he [Uriah] had launched Mr. Peggotty's house on a piratical expedition, with a black flag at the masthead, bearing the*

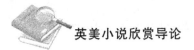

inscription "Tidd's Practice," under which diabolical ensign he was carrying me and little Em'ly to the Spanish Main, to be drowned.

This dream of drowning unconsciously reflects David's desires from childhood to now. It is firstly an unconscious flashback to childish fantasies from David's reading of picaresque adventure. "Sometime in daylight and sometime in dreams, David longs to be a great seagoing heroic figure..., and the Spanish Main is one of the demesnes of great men." But David is bound to the land (This is identified by the second components of his surname "copper" and "field") and "comes no closer to the sea than to study nautical law at Doctors' Commons. Even in the dream, he does not command the ship. David is a passenger; Heep is the captain." (Bressler, p.170)

This dream is also unconsciously a reflection of David's desire for Em'ly. When he was a child, David wished to marry Em'ly; now he is old and wise enough to know clearly from the society that a gentleman does not marry a fisherman's niece. However, his latent desire for Em'ly still exists in his unconscious. Traditionally, water is associated with sexuality. Drowning does not only mean dying, but refers to the plunge into the sea of sexual passion, dangerous and destructive. Little Em'ly is first seen running "along a jagged timber" which protrudes over the water, as if "spring forward to her destruction." David is "afraid of her falling over"(III), "but in the dream, exercising the prerogative of the unconscious, he falls with her" (Bressler, p.171) and fantasizes for himself the role that Steerforth enacts, who carries off little Em'ly and drowns.

"The medium of the dream is water; the primary subject is Uriah Heep, who is a sexual, an economic, and a moral threat to David." (Bressler, p.171) Firstly, Uriah is a rival of David for possession of Agnes although Uriah is more loathsome as a partner for Agnes. In the novel, a male character's hand occasionally symbolizes his phallus. Old Dr. Strong's hand "did nothing for itself" and David bites Murdstone on the hand when the Oedipal struggle between them comes to a crisis. "Heep's hands are long, dangly, and wet, and he manipulates them constantly." (Bressler, p.171)

It was not fancy of mine about his hands, I observed; for he frequently ground the palms against each other as if to squeeze them dry and warm, besides often wiping them, in a stealthy way, on his pocket-handkerchief.

Heep's writhing and snaky appearance obviously bears something indecent and flaccidity. His Christian name and surname, no less than his appearance, associate him with dirty things like micturition and excrement, thus being associated with "a kind of immature or diseased or perverted sexuality which David finds sometimes attractive—'[he] had a sort of fascination for me'—but more often despicable." (Bressler, p.172) When David dreams that Uriah launches him, the latent meaning is that he is pulled into a world of dangerous and potentially destructive sexuality, where David would be willing to be launched. However, his rational mind tells him that he can only achieve his desires when he scapegoats them onto Uriah. Therefore Uriah "is not scapegoat only, but the id within David, projected outward." (Bressler, p.172)

Heep also excites David's distress of a social order, for David unconsciously acknowledges his kinship with Uriah who represents the unpropertied with social pretensions. David lives in fear that he might lose gentlemanly status that accompanies financial well-being and fall again into the proletariat who have nothing but horrible manual labor, for he clearly knows that "his path through life would have been the same as Heep's" (Bressler, p.170) if his Aunt had not transformed him into a gentleman in a magic way. David dreams that Uriah "had launched Mr. Peggotty's house on a piratical expedition, with a black flag at the mast-head, bearing the inscription, 'Tidd's Practice.'" The "piratical expedition" symbolizes the means by which Heep attempts to clamber upward while "Tidd's Practice" is a symbol for his ambition. And David is obviously unwilling to follow Heep. And the ship foreshadows the disastrous consequences ("shipwrecks") of the Wickfield and Peggotty families. Each family is initially free of sexual passion, but in the course of the novel each of them is invaded, one by Steerforth, at David's invitation; the other by Heep, who exclaims to David:"To think that you should be the first to kindle the sparks of ambition in my, 'umble breast!"(XXV)

Heep is also, as the dream reveals, cruel and evil. He enjoys villainy for its own sake, and his hatred for David is intense and obscure. And the stool that excites the dream represents Heep's evil and hatred for David:

Being, at last, ready to leave the office for the night, he asked me if it would suit my convenience to have the light put out; and on my answering, "Yes," instantly extinguished it. after shaking hands with me—his hand felt like a fish, in the dark he opened the door into the street a very little, and crept out, and shut it, leaving me to grope my way back into the house: which cost me some trouble and a fall over his stool. This was the proximate cause, I suppose, of my dreaming about him, for what appeared half the night, and dreaming.

This description has its deep reference: Heep, under the guise of serving David's convenience, inconveniences him severely; Heep, locking himself up in a circular room as a snake creeping about, acts as an odious sexual creature, waiting until the light is extinguished to shake hands; the symbolic fall over the high stool is associated with Heep's ambitions and David seems to carry a sexual reference. However, what makes Heep terrifying is his connection with death. He is "cadaverous" and has long "skeleton" hands. He usually wears "decent black," and his ship has "a black flag at the masthead," and his father was a sexton. This association explains why Heep appears in the dream as an Angel of death.

Therefore, Uriah is for David a nightmare of a special kind. He is ostentatiously immoral, sexually diseased and socially unacceptable.

The dream of drowning, then, contains David and the two men, Uriah and Steerforth, who stand for alternative moral paths, and in the world of dreams, symbolize parts of the self. Uriah Heep represents what David fears he is or might become; Steerforth, briefly, stands for what David wishes to be, but can neither achieve nor reject. (Bressler, p.170)

Dickens is an extraordinarily subtle novelist. He creates the rich and complex relationship between David and Heep with exercise of dream of drowning, which is a path into the central structural pattern of the novel and has made this novel a "favourite child."

Further Reading

The Psychoanalytic Approach

Bressler, Charles E. *Literary Criticism: An Introduction to Theory and Practice*. 2nd ed. Upper Saddle River, N. J: Prentice-Hall, Inc., 1999.

Felman, Shoshana. *Jacques Lacan and the Adventure of Insight: Psychoanalysis in Contemporary Culture*. Cambridge, Mass.: Harvard University Press, 1987.

Freud, Sigmund. *The Interpretation of Dreams*. Trans. A. A. Brill. Beijing: China Social Sciences Publishing House, 1999.

——. *Writings on art and literature*. Stanford: Stanford University Press, 1997.

——. *Introductory Lectures on Psycho-Analysis*. Trans. Joan Riviere. London: Allen, 1922.

——. *Group Psychology and the Analysis of the Ego*. Trans. James Strachey. New York: Norton, 1990.

Guerin, Wilfred L., et al. *A Handbook of Critical Approaches to Literature*. Beijing: Foreign Language Teaching and Research Press, 2004.

Hoffman, Frederick J. *Freudianism and the Literary Mind*. Westport: Greenwood Press, 1977.

David Copperfield

Jordan, John O., ed. *The Cambridge Companion to Charles Dickens*. New York: Cambridge University Press, 2001.

Manheim, Leonard F. "The Personal History of David Copperfield: A Study in Psychoanalytic Criticism". *American Imago* 9.1 (Spring 1952): 21—43.

Pearlman, E. "David Copperfield Dreams of Drowning". *American Imago* 28.4 (Winter 1971): 391—403.

Smith, Grahame. *Charles Dickens: A Literary Life*. Basingstoke: Macmillan, 1996.

Chapter Eleven
The Mythological Approach

The task of the myth critic is a special one. Unlike the historical and autobiographical critic who relies heavily on history and the biography of the writer, the myth critic shows more interest in prehistory and biographies of the gods. Unlike the formalist critic who focuses on the structure and form of the work itself, the myth critic is inclined to explore the inner spirit which gives that form its vitality and its enduring appeal. And unlike the psychoanalytical critic who looks on the literary work as the product of the personal sexual unconsciousness, the myth critic sees the work as the manifestation of integrative forces arising from the depths of humankind's collective psyche, and attempts to interpret the hopes, fears, values, aspirations, and expectations of entire culture.

Mythological criticism appeared in 1950s with Northrop Frye as its primary advocate. Myth critics state that there is a collection of literary archetypes, which fall into three categories: archetypal images, archetypal motifs or patterns, and archetypal genres.

Archetypal images usually include good mother, trees, wise old man, as well as rising suns suggesting reawakening and setting suns foreshadowing death, colors such as green indicating growth and fertility, or black suggesting chaos, evil, and death, and bodies of water symbolizing the unconscious or eternity or rebirth. The great Mississippi River in *Huckleberry Finn* is an archetypal symbol of the mystery of life and creation—birth, the flowing of time into eternity, and rebirth.

Archetypal motifs are generally associated with creation, immortality, quest and initiation, scapegoats, and the death and rebirth theme that relates the human life cycle of the seasons. Huck's idealistic search of one more substantial than that embraced by the hypocritical, materialistic society he has rejected shows us a quest archetype. And Huck, after a series of painful experiences, grows from ignorance and innocence into spiritual maturity and decides to go to hell rather than turn Jim in to the authorities. This story indicates an initiation archetype.

Archetypal genres or types of literature may conform with the major phases of the seasonal cycle. Northrop Frye, in his *Anatomy of Criticism* (1957), explores the four genres which correspond to the four seasons and to peculiar cycles of human experiences: comedy, romance, tragedy and irony. According to him, romance is our summer story, in which all our wishes are fulfilled and our total happiness is achieved; and irony or anti-romance is our winter story which presents our bondage, imprisonment, frustration, and fear. Spring and fall separately correspond to comedy and tragedy. Comedy relates our spring story in which we rise from irony and frustration to freedom and happiness. And tragedy narrates our fall from romance phase and from happiness and freedom to disaster. Frye asserts that all stories can be placed in one of these four phases. Frye's contribution leads us directly into the mythological approach to literary analysis and allows us to compare stories on the basis of their

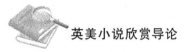

relationship among themselves.

Despite the special importance of the myth critic's contribution, we cannot forget what Sir James G. Frazer and C. G. Jung, two major influences on the growth of mythological criticism, contributed to the mythological approach in making its proper interpretive tools become available.

Frazer has exerted an enormous influence on twentieth-century literary critics. His monumental *The Golden Bough* (1890), "a comparative study of the primitive origins of religion in magic, ritual, and myth," indicates that man's chief wants are essentially similar everywhere and at all times "particularly as these wants were reflected throughout ancient mythologies." (Guerin, p.192) Frazer deals with the archetype of crucifixion and resurrection, specifically the myths describing the "killing of the divine king." According to Frazer, among some peoples the kings were killed at regular intervals to ensure the welfare of the tribe; later, however, substitute figures or sacred animals were killed symbolically rather than literally. Then there was the scapegoat archetype. Sophocles' *Oedipus the King*, a well-known mythic narrative long before Sophocles made it a tragic drama, is an excellent example of fusion of myth and literature. A mythological reading of *Oedipus* might focus on Oedipus's role as a scapegoat. The welfare of his state, both human and natural (plague and drought are threatening to destroy Thebes), is directly linked to the well-being of the ruler. If he was sick or corrupt, he had to be replaced in order to guarantee the health of the community. Therefore, only after Oedipus has offered himself up as a scapegoat is the land saved and the fertility of its fields restored. And following his sacrificial punishment, Thebes is restored to health and abundance. The story of Oedipus also contains the quest motif. In this motif, Oedipus, on his journey to Thebes, encounters the Sphinx, a supernatural monster with the body of a lion and the head of a woman; by solving her bridle, he delivers the kingdom and marries the queen.

The second major influence on mythological criticism is C. G. Jung. "His primary contribution to myth criticism is his theory of racial memory and archetypes," (Guerin, p.202) which Jung developed by expanding Freud's theories of the personal unconscious. Jung asserts that beneath the personal unconscious is "a primeval, collective unconscious shared in the psychic inheritance of all members of the human family." (Guerin, p.202) He stresses that archetypes are not inherited ideas or patterns of thought, but "inherited forms," which "are inherited genetically, making up an identical collective unconsciousness for all humankind." (Bressler, p.155) These forms, ever present in the unconscious psyche, are passed down from one generation to the next through the structure of the psyche itself. Occurring in literature in the form of recurrent images, character types, motifs or plot patterns, "these archetypes stir profound emotions in the reader because they awaken images stored in the collective unconscious and thereby produce feelings or emotions over which the reader initially has little control." (Bressler, p.155)

Jung's another major contribution is his theory of individuation which is related to such special archetypes as the shadow, the persona, and the anima. Individuation is a psychological process of "discovering those aspects of one's self that make one an individual different from other members of the species." "The shadow, the persona, and the anima are structural components of the psyche that human beings have inherited."(Guerin, p.205) The shadow is the darker side of our unconscious self—the less pleasing aspects of the personality, which we wish to repress. The anima refers to the feminine image in the male psyche, which a man usually carries in both his personal and his collective unconscious (in the female psyche this archetype is called the animus). The persona is the "mask that we show to the world—it is our social personality, a personality that is sometimes quite different from our true self." (Guerin, p.205) It mediates between our ego and the external world. To achieve psychological maturity, the individual must have a flexible, viable persona that can produce harmonious relationship with the other components of his or her psyche. When his or her persona is too artificial or rigid he or she is inclined to have such symptoms of neurotic disturbance as irritability and melancholy. We encounter the symbolic projections of these archetypes throughout the myths and the literatures of humankind.

A close reading of Hawthorne's "Young Goodman Brown" indicates the relevance of Jung's theory of individuation to young Goodman Brown. Brown's individuation has proved to be a failure. In the first place, "Brown's persona is both false and inflexible." (Guerin, p.207) He shows as much respect and fear for God as any self-righteous Puritan, thus considering himself the good Christian and the good husband who gets married to a "blessed angel on earth." In truth, however, he, from start to finish, behaves more like a bad boy than a good man. He leaves his wife for the forest just for one last fling motivated by his juvenile compulsion; he cannot recognize his own base motives when he confronts Satan—his shadow. These indicate his spiritual immaturity.

Just as Brown's persona is incompetent at mediating between his ego and the external world, his anima fails in conforming to his inner world. His anima or soul-image should fittingly be named Faith; he, however, sees Faith not as a true wifely companion but as a mother, which is indicated by his willingness to "cling to her skirts and follow her to heaven." "If a young man's Faith has the qualities of the Good Mother, he might expect to be occasionally indulged in his juvenile escapades." (Guerin, p.207) But marriage must be guaranteed by mature faith of both parties. Either party's unfaithfulness will lead to the unpleasant consequences: separation at worst, and suspicion and loss of harmony, trust, and peace of mind at best. And it is the latter consequences that Brown has to face. Even then, he still behaves like a child without being aware of his error and working maturely for a reconciliation.

What Young Goodman Brown suffers from is a failure of individuation in his psychological growth. His psychological immaturity makes him unable to create a harmonious relationship among the components of his psyche and achieve his personality integration. He ultimately sees the whole world as one of the shadow, or gloom.

Kate Chopin (1851—1904)

Kate Chopin was born Kate O'Flaherty in St. Louis, Missouri, the daughter of Eliza, a French-American, and Thomas O'Flaherty, a prosperous Irish merchant. She was the third of five children, but her sisters and brothers died when they were very young. In 1855, her father died suddenly and she lived at home with her mother, grandmother, and great-grandmother, all of them smart and independent widows. And she could learn music and literature from her grandmother. Until Kate was sixteen, no married couples lived in her home. This

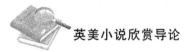

developed her awareness of female roles in society and shaped her views on women's role in society in her writing, and also made her a well-known and well-liked belle of St. Louis.

In 1870, Kate married Oscar Chopin of New Orleans, the son of a wealthy cotton-growing family in Louisiana. He adored his wife, admired her independence and intelligence, and allowed her enormous freedom. After their marriage they lived in New Orleans where she had five boys and two girls. Oscar died a sudden death in Louisiana in 1883, and Kate sold up and moved back to St. Louis to live with her mother. Sadly, her mother died the next year, leaving Kate alone with her children again. To support herself and her family, and relieve her tremendous grief for the loss of her husband, she was encouraged by his family doctor to pursue her passion of writing. The success of her first novel, *At Fault* (1890), stimulated her to write two collections of short stories, *Bayou Folk* (1894) and *A Night in Acadia* (1897) about people in Louisiana, and female roles and love. As *The Awakening* was published in 1899, she had been well known as both a local colorist and a woman writer, and had published over one hundred stories, essays, and sketches in literary magazines. However, *The Awakening,* a rebellious novel, which gave focus on roles of women, was harshly received by critics, her contemporaries, and readers. She was terribly hurt by the reaction to the book and in the remaining five years of her life she wrote only a few short stories, and only a small number of those were published.

Kate put much concentration on women's lives and their continual struggles to create an identity of their own within the patriarchy. Her writings produced two quite different views: some saw them as a new feminist voice while others saw them as the voice of an individual who happens to be a woman.

"The Story of an Hour" was written on April 19, 1894, and first published in *Vogue* on December 6, 1894, under the title "The Dream of an Hour." It is one of Kate's most popular stories and was called "one of feminism's sacred texts" in 1975 by Susan Cahill. In this story Kate displayed her often-celebrated yearning for freedom through Mrs. Mallard.

 *Text*

The Story of an Hour

Knowing that Mrs. Mallard was afflicted with a heart trouble, great care was taken to break to her as gently as possible the news of her husband's death.

It was her sister Josephine who told her, in broken sentences; veiled hints that revealed in half concealing[1]. Her husband's friend Richards was there, too, near her. It was he who had been in the newspaper office when intelligence[2] of the railroad disaster was received, with Brently Mallard's name leading the list of "killed[3]." He had only taken the time to assure himself of its truth by a second

---

1 veiled hints that revealed in half concealing: 半遮半掩地做了一些暗示
2 intelligence: 消息
3 leading the list of "killed": 排在"遇难者"名单的第一位

Chapter Eleven The Mythological Approach

telegram, and had hastened to forestall any less careful, less tender friend in bearing the sad message[1].

She did not hear the story as many women have heard the same, with a paralyzed inability to accept its significance[2]. She wept at once, with sudden, wild abandonment[3], in her sister's arms. When the storm of grief had spent itself she went away to her room alone. She would have no one follow her.

There stood, facing the open window, a comfortable, roomy armchair. Into this she sank, pressed down by a physical exhaustion that haunted her body and seemed to reach into her soul.

She could see in the open square before her house the tops of trees that were all aquiver with the new spring life. The delicious breath of rain was in the air. In the street below a peddler was crying his wares. The notes of a distant song which some one was singing reached her faintly, and countless sparrows were twittering in the eaves[4].

There were patches of blue sky showing here and there through the clouds that had met and piled one above the other in the west facing her window.

She sat with her head thrown back upon the cushion of the chair, quite motionless, except when a sob came up into her throat and shook her, as a child who has cried itself to sleep continues to sob in its dreams.

She was young, with a fair, calm face, whose lines bespoke repression and even a certain strength[5]. But now there was a dull stare in her eyes[6], whose gaze was fixed away off yonder on one of those patches of blue sky. It was not a glance of reflection, but rather indicated a suspension of intelligent thought[7].

There was something coming to her and she was waiting for it, fearfully. What was it? She did not know; it was too subtle and elusive to name. But she felt it, creeping out of the sky, reaching toward her through the sounds, the scents, the color that filled the air.

Now her bosom rose and fell tumultuously[8]. She was beginning to recognize this thing that was approaching to possess her, and she was striving to beat it back with her will—as powerless as her two white slender hands would have been.

When she abandoned herself a little whispered word escaped her slightly parted lips[9]. She said it over and over under her breath: "free, free, free!" The vacant stare[10] and the look of terror that had followed it went from her eyes. They stayed keen and bright. Her pulses beat fast, and the coursing blood[11] warmed and relaxed every inch of her body.

---

1 and had hastened to forestall any less careful, less tender friend in bearing the sad message：并急忙赶在那些不够细心与体恤的友人之前把这个不幸的消息带了回来。
2 with a paralyzed inability to accept its significance：全身瘫软，神情麻木，无法接受这种事。
3 wild abandonment：毫无顾忌地
4 countless sparrows were twittering in the eaves：无数的麻雀在屋檐下叽叽喳喳叫个不停。
5 whose lines bespoke repression and even a certain strength：她脸上的表情显示出一种压抑甚或说是一种力量
6 there was a dull stare in her eyes：她目光呆滞
7 It was not a glance of reflection, but rather indicated a suspension of intelligent thought：这不是匆匆一闪念，而是智性的思考，只是尚未有结果。
8 Now her bosom rose and fell tumultuously：此刻，她的内心在骚动。
9 When she abandoned herself a little whispered word escaped her slightly parted lips：当她的精神稍稍放松下来的时候，她微微张开的双唇喃喃地说出了一个词。
10 vacant stare：茫然的目光
11 the coursing blood：沸腾的血液

She did not stop to ask if it were or were not a monstrous joy that held her. A clear and exalted perception enabled her to dismiss the suggestion as trivial.

She knew that she would weep again when she saw the kind, tender hands folded in death; the face that had never looked save with love upon her, fixed and gray and dead[1]. But she saw beyond that bitter moment a long procession of years to come that would belong to her absolutely. And she opened and spread her arms out to them[2] in welcome.

There would be no one to live for during those coming years; she would live for herself. There would be no powerful will bending hers in that blind persistence with which men and women believe they have a right to impose a private will upon a fellow creature. A kind intention or a cruel intention made the act seem no less a crime as she looked upon it in that brief moment of illumination[3].

And yet she had loved him—sometimes. Often she had not. What did it matter! What could love, the unsolved mystery, count for in face of this possession of self-assertion which she suddenly recognized as the strongest impulse of her being!

"Free! Body and soul free!" she kept whispering.

Josephine was kneeling before the closed door with her lips to the keyhole, imploring for admission[4]. "Louise, open the door! I beg; open the door—you will make yourself ill. What are you doing, Louise? For heaven's sake open the door."

"Go away. I am not making myself ill." No; she was drinking in a very elixir of life[5] through that open window.

Her fancy was running riot[6] along those days ahead of her. Spring days, and summer days, and all sorts of days that would be her own. She breathed a quick prayer that life might be long. It was only yesterday she had thought with a shudder that life might be long.

She arose at length and opened the door to her sister's importunities. There was a feverish triumph in her eyes, and she carried herself unwittingly like a goddess of Victory. She clasped her sister's waist, and together they descended the stairs. Richards stood waiting for them at the bottom.

Someone was opening the front door with a latchkey. It was Brently Mallard who entered, a little travel-stained, composedly carrying his gripsack and umbrella[7]. He had been far from the scene of accident, and did not even know there had been one. He stood amazed at Josephine's piercing cry; at Richards' quick motion to screen him from the view of his wife.

But Richards was too late.

When the doctors came they said she had died of heart disease—of joy that kills.

---

1 the face that had never looked save with love upon her, fixed and gray and dead: 那张从来都不吝啬向她表达爱意的脸变得毫无表情, 面如死灰。

2 them: 此处指上文的 "a long procession of years to come"。

3 A kind intention or a cruel intention made the act seem no less a crime as she looked upon it in that brief moment of illumination: 在她觉醒的那一刻, 她清楚地认识到, 促成这种行为的动机无论是出于善意还是出于恶意, 这种行为本身都是有罪的。

4 imploring for admission: 恳求让她进来

5 She was drinking in a very elixir of life: 她正陶醉在不息的生命里

6 Her fancy was running riot: 她的想象在纵情驰骋。

7 a little travel-stained, composedly carrying his gripsack and umbrella: 略显旅途劳顿, 但泰然自若地提着他的大旅行包和伞。

Chapter Eleven   The Mythological Approach

Understanding the Text

Chopin's "The Story of an Hour" is the story of an hour in the life of Mrs. Louise Mallard, who goes within an hour from shock of knowing her husband's death in a railroad disaster to wild joy of being free from her husband to her dying of happiness. While many critics and scholars give interpretations of this story from feminist or psychological perspectives, we may understand it by resorting to the mythological approach.

A careful reading of the story makes us identify the archetypal pattern which exists in it: Mrs. Mallard's life parallels the end of winter and the earth's renewal in spring. This story occurs at the end of winter and the beginning of spring. Before the day when the story happens, Mrs. Mallard did not have a clear idea of her life and her desire. She lived just as all the other women. But her look betrayed her: she was repressed. As the news suddenly comes to her that her husband was killed in a railroad accident, she feels a surge of new life after grieving over her husband's death. Her powerful unconscious desires for freedom that were long suppressed are released. She senses the life outside her window. She sits facing the open window and is completely taken with the outside world which is buzzing and alive in spring: the trees "were all aquiver with the new spring life." Mrs. Mallard realizes with sudden and intense clarity what is troubling and begins to whisper the words, "free, free, free" as she sees that her life can be her own now. And at this moment, "she saw beyond that bitter moment a long procession of years to come that would belong to her absolutely. And she opened and spread her arms out to them in welcome" as it becomes clear that her husband, who she only loved "sometimes," is gone and now she would be "Free! Body and soul free!" She initially tries to suppress the thought by "beat[ing] it back with her will," but she cannot repress the life force that surges within her and all around her. When she finally gives herself to the energy and life she experiences, she feels like a "goddess of Victory." But this victory is short lived when she suddenly sees her husband walking in the door as she comes downstairs.

Mrs. Mallard dies abruptly, as the narrator says, "of joy that kills." "Her death is an ironic version of a rebirth ritual." (Meyer, p.2098) When spring comes after winter, Mrs. Mallard rises from imprisonment and frustration to happiness and freedom. She awakens and has a new discovery of her life and marriage: She has lived a repressed, imprisoned, and frustrated life with her husband for long, and being with her husband means all the obligations that made her marriage feel like a wasteland; her husband's death stimulates her desperate desire for the autonomy and fulfillment she was unable to admit. Her husband's being back home means that the old, corrupt social order which her husband represents will force her back to a repressed, circumscribed life and make her lose personal freedom. And sense of this leads to her sudden death. Death turns out to be preferable to the living death that her marriage means to her. Therefore Mrs. Mallard's death is a cruel irony: Death helps her achieve her freedom.

Further Reading

The Mythological Approach

Bressler, Charles E. *Literary Criticism: An Introduction to Theory and Practice.* 2nd ed. Upper Saddle River, N. J: Prentice-Hall, Inc., 1999.

Eagleton, Terry. *Literary Theory: An Introduction.* Minneapolis: University of Minnesota Press, 1983.

Frye, Northrop. *Anatomy of Criticism.* Princeton, NJ: Princeton University Press, 1979.

Guerin, Wilfred L., et al. *A Handbook of Critical Approaches to Literature.* Beijing: Foreign Language Teaching and Research Press, 2004.

Jung, Carl Gustav. *The Archetypes and the Collective Unconscious.* Trans. R.F.C. Hull. Beijing: China Social Sciences Publishing. House, 1999.

The Story of an Hour

Green, Suzanne D., et. al. *Kate Chopin: An Annotated Bibliography of Critical Works.* Westport: Greenwood, 1999.

Koloski, Bernard. *Kate Chopin: A Study of the Short Fiction.* New York: Twayne Publishers, 1996.

Stein, Allen F. *Women and Autonomy in Kate Chopin's Short Fiction.* New York: Peter Lang, 2005.

Skaggs, Peggy. *Kate Chopin.* Boston: Twayne Publishers, 1985.

Chapter Twelve
Gender Studies

Gender critics examine how ideas about men and women—what is masculine and feminine—can be more socially constructed by particular cultures than by nature. Some gender critics claim that sex is biologically determined by categories of male or female, and gender is culturally constructed. Thus, ideas about gender and what constitutes masculine and feminine behaviour are completely constructed by cultural expectations, norms and institutions in response to the political aims of the society's dominant class, which are transmitted and enhanced through the "technologies of gender," the forces in modern technological society that create sex roles in response to ideology and marketplace needs, specifically, the product of various social technologies, such as television, movies, songs, and literature. Consciously or unconsciously women and men conform to the cultural ideas established for them by society. Little boys, for example, must be aggressive, self-assertive, and domineering, whereas little girls must be passive, meek, and humble. Gender criticism has been expanding, gone far beyond the definitions and categories of what is masculine or feminine, heterosexual or homosexual, and come to include gay and lesbian criticism as well as feminist criticism.

Feminist Criticism

The major roots of feminist criticism began to grow in the early 1900s when women gained the right to vote and became active in the social issues of the day, such as education, politics, and literature. Until now, however, no one critical theory dominates feminist criticism. Feminist criticism houses "more internal disagreements than unity among its adherents that are found in perhaps any other approach to literary analysis." (Bressler, p.189) Furthermore, feminist theories have been growing more and more diverse as they engage with a broad range of disciplines, including history, sociology, psychology, linguistics, cultural studies, as well as ethnic and race studies. Behind all these seemingly contradictory theories, however, is a set of principles that unites this criticism.

Although feminist critics vary in their ideas of the directions of their criticism, "feminists possess a collective identity: They are struggling to discover who women are, how women have arrived at their present situation, and where women are going" (Bressler, p.188); they have the same aim of changing the world in which they live. Feminist critics believe that the world where we live is a male-dominated world. In this world it is man, not woman, who defines what it means to be female and who controls the political, economic, social, and literary structures. Men's voices articulate and determine the social role and cultural and personal significance of women. The direct result of the society's opinion of women is that they are intellectually inferior to men by nature and the woman is subordinate in the male/female relationship. Once our culture consciously and unconsciously assimilates this belief into its social structures and allows it to permeate all levels of its society, females become the oppressed people, inferiors who must be suppressed. Thus, women in traditional literary canon are often fictionalized and stereotyped as angels, barmaids, bitches, whores, brainless housewives, or old maids.

To free themselves from such oppression, assert feminist critics, women must analyze the established literary canon that has helped shape the images of female inferiority and oppression ingrained in our culture, identify the stereotypes of women (angels or demons, saints or whores, or brainless housewives or eccentric spinsters) found throughout the literary canon, and expose the ways men have consciously or unconsciously demeaned, devalued, and demoralized women, and change their prejudice and false assumptions about women. In this way feminists can achieve their purpose of changing Western culture's assumption that males are superior to females and therefore are better thinkers, more rational, more serious, and more reflective than women. Besides, characters in the literary canon are heralded who reject the societal construct that men are the subject or the absolute and that women are the other and establish their own identity.

Having identified the antifeminist characterization that occurs in many texts, feminist critics then turn to discover works written by women in the literary canon. They maintain that these female authors must be "rediscovered" and their works must be republished and reevaluated so that a valuable body of female authors who share common themes, histories, and often writing styles can be revealed.

Some feminist critics also suggest that we reread the canonized works of male authors from a woman's point of view. More exactly, when we analyze the canonized work, we should give more concerns with our uniquely female consciousness resulted from female experience rather than the traditional male theories of reading, writing, and critiquing. Known as gynocriticism, this model of literary study centers on four areas of investigation: (1) Images of the female body presented in a text—how various parts of the female body such as the uterus and breast become significant images in women's works; (2) Female language—how grammatical constructions, recurring themes, and other linguistic elements in women's works differ from those in men's works when they both live in patriarchal societies; (3) The female psyche and its relationship to the writing process—how the physical and psychological development of women evidence itself in the writing process; and (4) Culture—how society shapes a woman's understanding of herself, her society, and her world. (Bressler, pp.190—91)

Whatever method of feminist criticism we choose to apply to a text, we can begin textual analysis by asking some general questions like these: Is the author male or female? Is the text narrated by a male or a female? Do any stereotypical characterizations of women appear? What is the author's attitude toward women in society?

A feminist reading of "Young Goodman Brown" might explore Hawthorne's sympathy with the women, which is frequently demonstrated in his other works. Unlike such heroic characters as Hester in *The Scarlet Letter*, Miriam in *The Marble Faun*, and Georgiana in "The Birthmark," Faith Brown in "Young Goodman Brown" is not even a three-dimensional character. Her allegorical name and small role in the action of the story often make readers overlook her significance. But Hawthorne's sympathy with her cannot be overlooked when we read the following descriptions. Brown, Faith's husband, rejects her sexuality for "some unstated but sexually appalling ritual in the forest" (Guerin, p. 258) and then returns home to rebuke his wife. At the end of his life, Brown's "hoary corpse" is carried to the grave followed by his wife, children, and grandchildren. Instead of shuddering at his gloomy death, we tend to have a picture of Faith and her children who "have had to live all those empty years with his blighted self, a failed husband, father, and human being." (Guerin, p. 258)

A feminist analysis of Chopin's "The Story of an Hour" might center on the psychological stress created by the expectations that marriage imposes on Mrs. Mallard, expectations that literally and figuratively kill her. In Chopin's view, marriage is a social institution that creates men's expectations of women in favour of men. Therefore Mrs Mallard's death does not result from her being married to Brently but her being married at all. Surely a feminist critic might note that the protagonist is introduced as Mrs Mallard although we are told later that her first name is Louise, and discern that Mrs. Mallard's emotions and cause of death are interpreted in male terms by the doctors.

Gay and Lesbian Criticism

Gay and lesbian criticism, coming to be focused on in the 1970s and 1980s after the famous Stonewall riots in New York, "explores a variety of issues, including how homosexuals are represented and distorted in literature, how they read literature, and whether sexuality and gender are culturally constructed or innate" (Meyer, p. 2095). Gay and lesbian critics have discovered homosexual concerns in the works of writers such as Herman Melville and Henry James, and Willa Cather and Toni Morrison while they study problematic attitude toward homosexuality of some authors like Walt Whitman. Increasingly in recent few years, gay characters and themes have become the subjects of literary works. And currently "Queer Theory" is used as a common term for the studies of gays and lesbians.

Critics have also paid more attention to the homosexual motifs and characters in works considered classics of literature, and even the homosexual vision of the classic authors. One of the familiar examples is Leslie Fiedler's bold look at the homosexual relationship of Huck Finn and Nigger Jim in his *Love and Death in the American Novel* (p. 571).

A careful reading of Willa Cather's story "Paul's Case" will show how some classic writers deal with the homosexual nature of characters. In "Paul's Case" there are indeed some hints of Paul's homosexuality which help us put together the pieces of the puzzle presented by the main character, Paul, and understand the full depth of his alienation from the "normal" American society in which he feels so hideously trapped and hence the full pathos of his situation.

Paul's physical appearance gives some suggestions of his deviation from what the culture of his day would consider the sexual "norm." He has "narrow chest" and "high cramped shoulders"; aside from his love of the clothing of the dandy, the most prominent feature is "a certain hysterical brilliancy in his eyes" as he confronts his bewildered teachers; "he continually used them in a conscious, theatrical sort of way, peculiarly offensive in a boy." His drawing instructor, the only one of all his teachers who shows any compassion for his differentness, says: "I don't really believe that smile of his comes altogether from insolence; there's something sort of haunted about it. The boy is not strong, for one thing. There is something wrong about the fellow." His love of use of violet water seems to reinforce the reader's impression of the feminine side of his nature—especially when judged within the framework of the standards set by the Middle America of his time. Paul's relationship with the Yale freshman has an unshakable sense of innuendo. Paul and the Yale freshman spend a night on the town while both of them are registered at the Waldorf in New York. Although they start out on friendly terms, "their parting in the elevator was singularly cool." This ending conveys a curious note. Here one interpretation might explain the problem between them. The "wild San Francisco boy" has come into the city for "'a little flyer' over Sunday." He just wants to relieve his sexual drive through the customary channels. And so he offers to "show Paul the night side of the town," but it seems quite possible to conjecture that Paul wants something from his companion that the latter is unprepared to give.

"Paul's Case" was published in 1905, at the height of the period of Victorian repressiveness, during which a writer's direct confrontation with the topic of homosexuality was avoided. Thus, Willa Cather dealt with her protagonist's sexual nature by dropping a number of broad hints that, taken cumulatively, point strongly in this direction. It was just Willa Cather's superb craftsmanship that made her able to convey a sense of this previously unmentionable dimension of her protagonist's inner being without violating any of the literary taboos of her time.

Washington Irving (1783—1859)

Washington Irving, the famed essayist, biographer, historian, writer and politician, is the first American to achieve an international literary reputation, and often referred to as "The Father of American Literature." Washington Irving was born in New York City at the end of the Revolutionary War. He was named after General George Washington because both his Scottish-born father and his English-born mother were his great admirers.

Irving's interests covered a wide range of reading, writing, architecture and landscape design, traveling, and diplomacy. As an avid reader, he usually "immersed himself in romance and adventure tales, in Burns, Addison, Goldsmith, Columbus, the conquest of Mexico, and in everything English and European." (Cracroft, p.7)

Irving enjoyed visiting different places and a large part of his life was spent in Europe, particularly England, France, Germany, and Spain. He often wrote about the places he visited. For example, *Bracebridge Hall* (1822) is a view of life in England, *The Life and Voyages of Christopher Columbus* (1828), considered the greatest of his historical and biographical works and establishing Irving in these new genres, is about the Italian explorer who sailed under the Spanish flag, and *Alhambra* (1832) is a Spanish sketchbook.

Irving's imagination, however, frequently drew upon his childhood memories of New York State. These memories are reflected in letters that he wrote to his family and friends from Europe, as well as in the stories from his most famous work, *The Sketch Book of Geoffrey Crayon, Gent.* His series of letters titled *The Letters of Jonathan Oldstyle, Gent.* which mock New York society, were published under the pseudonym Johnathan Oldstyle in *The Morning Chronicle* and earned him the first recognition as a writer in 1802. In 1809, Irving wrote, under the pen name "Diedrich Knickerbocker," *A History of New-York,* which describes and pokes fun at the lives of the early Dutch settlers of Manhattan. *The*

Chapter Twelve   Gender Studies

History of New York from the Beginning of the World to the End of the Dutch Dynasty (1809) was a humorous "tale about Dutch colonization in which Irving gave a deliberately inaccurate account of New York's past from the perspective of the fictional Diedrich Knickerbocker." (Bylington, p. 217) *The Sketch Book,* which was published serially throughout 1819 and 1820, includes Irving's two best-known short stories "The Legend of Sleepy Hollow" and "Rip Van Winkle." Stories from this collection present a fine example of Irving's craft and serves as models for the modern American short story.

By the late 1820s, Irving had gained a reputation throughout Europe and America as a great writer. His popularity earned him many important honors. In 1830, Irving received a gold medal in history from the Royal Society of Literature in London, and also received honorary degrees from Oxford, Columbia, and Harvard. In 1842, American President Tyler appointed him Minister to Spain and he traveled throughout Europe as a diplomatic representative of the United States.

Feeling a desire to be among fellow Americans and his family, in 1832, Irving returned from Europe to New York, and chose to settle in Tarrytown and purchased an estate called Sunnyside where he lived with two of his brothers and several of his nieces.

On November 28, 1859, Washington Irving died at Sunnyside surrounded by his family. He was buried in the Sleepy Hollow Cemetery at the Old Dutch Church in Sleepy Hollow, New York.

"Rip Van Winkle," first published in 1819 in *The Sketch Book,* was written while Irving was living in Birmingham, England. It is based on German folk tales that Irving learned about through his reading and travel in Europe. In a humorous context, it gives the United States, a new country, some of the same feeling of tradition that older nations had because of their traditional lore. The issues "Rip Van Winkle" deals with include issues of politics, as it shows how the American Revolution changed one small village, and gender issues, as he shows the comical relationship between a lazy husband and a bad-tempered wife.

"Rip Van Winkle" has been adapted for other media for the last two centuries, from stage plays to an operetta to cartoons to films. And Rip Van Winkle has become one of the best-known characters in American popular culture, widely recognized through his many appearances and references in books, movies, cartoons, and advertisements.

 **Text**

Rip Van Winkle

[The following Tale was found among the papers of the late Diedrich Knickerbocker, an old gentleman of New York, who was very curious in the Dutch history of the province, and the manners of the descendants from its primitive settlers. His historical researches, however, did not lie so much among books as among men; for the former are lamentably scanty on his favorite topics; whereas he found the old burghers, and still more, their wives, rich in that legendary lore, so invaluable to true history. Whenever, therefore, he happened upon a genuine Dutch family, snugly shut up in its low-roofed farmhouse, under a spreading sycamore, he looked upon it as a little clasped volume of black-letter[1], and studied it with the zeal of a book-worm.

The result of all these researches was a history of the province, during the reign of the Dutch governors, which he published some years since. There have been various opinions as to the literary character of his work, and, to tell the truth, it is not a whit[2] better than it should be. Its chief merit is its scrupulous accuracy, which, indeed, was a little questioned, on its first appearance, but has since been completely established; and it is now admitted into all historical collections, as a book of unquestionable authority.

The old gentleman died shortly after the publication of his work, and now, that he is dead and gone, it cannot do much harm to his memory, to say, that his time might have been better employed in weightier labors. He, however, was apt to ride his hobby his own way; and though it did now and then kick up[3] the dust a little in the eyes of his neighbors, and grieve the spirit of some friends, for whom he felt the truest deference and affection; yet his errors and follies are remembered "more in sorrow than in anger," and it begins to be suspected, that he never intended to injure or offend. But however his memory may be appreciated by critics, it is still held dear by many folks, whose good opinion is well worth having; particularly by certain biscuit bakers, who have gone so far as to imprint his likeness on their new year cakes, and have thus given him a chance for immortality, almost equal to being stamped on a Waterloo Medal, or a Queen Anne's Farthing[4].]

Rip Van Winkle

A Posthumous Writing of Diedrich Knickerbocker

By Woden[5], God of Saxons,
From whence comes Wensday, that is Wodensday,
Truth is a thing that ever I will keep
Unto thylke day in which I creep into
My sepulchre—

—*Cartwright[6]*

Whoever has made a voyage up the Hudson[7] must remember the Kaatskill mountains. They are a dismembered branch of the great Appalachian family[8], and are seen away to the west of the river, swelling up to a noble height, and lording it over the surrounding country. Every change of season, every

---

1 clasped volume of black-letter:用夹子锁起来的一本古黑体的书。早期书的字体很像中世纪的手抄本,因为这些书具有很高的价值,一般书上都有夹子,可以把书锁起来。
2 not a whit:一点也不
3 kick up:引起,激起
4 a Waterloo Medal, or a Queen Anne's Farthing:此处欧文使用反讽。Waterloo Medal:滑铁卢奖章,自1815年拿破仑战败后就公开铸造。Queen Anne's Farthing:指安妮女王在位(1710—1714)时所发行的铜币,被认为很稀有。有种说法说只铸造了三枚。
5 Woden:沃登,挪威神话中的战神
6 Cartwright (William Cartwright):威廉·卡特怀特(1611—1643),英国剧作家。这首诗选自其剧作"The Ordinary"。
7 the Hudson:哈德逊河
8 Appalachian family:阿巴拉契亚山脉

change of weather, indeed, every hour of the day, produces some change in the magical hues and shapes of these mountains, and they are regarded by all the good wives, far and near, as perfect barometers. When the weather is fair and settled, they are clothed in blue and purple, and print their bold outlines on the clear evening sky, but some times, when the rest of the landscape is cloudless, they will gather a hood of gray vapors about their summits, which, in the last rays of the setting sun, will glow and light up like a crown of glory.

At the foot of these fairy mountains, the voyager may have descried the light smoke curling up from a village, whose shingle-roofs gleam among the trees, just where the blue tints of the upland melt away into the fresh green of the nearer landscape. It is a little village of great antiquity, having been founded by some of the Dutch colonists, in the early times of the province, just about the beginning of the government of the good Peter Stuyvesant[1], (may he rest in peace!) and there were some of the houses of the original settlers standing within a few years, with lattice windows, gable fronts surmounted with weather-cocks, and built of small yellow bricks brought from Holland.

In that same village, and in one of these very houses, (which, to tell the precise truth, was sadly time worn and weather beaten,) there lived many years since, while the country was yet a province of Great Britain, a simple good natured fellow, of the name of Rip Van Winkle. He was a descendant of the Van Winkles who figured so gallantly in the chivalrous days of Peter Stuyvesant, and accompanied him to the siege of Fort Christina[2]. He inherited, however, but little of the martial character of his ancestors. I have observed that he was a simple good-natured man; he was moreover a kind neighbor, and an obedient, henpecked[3] husband. Indeed, to the latter circumstance might be owing that meekness of spirit which gained him such universal popularity; for those men are most apt to be obsequious and conciliating abroad, who are under the discipline of shrews at home. Their tempers, doubtless, are rendered pliant and malleable in the fiery furnace of domestic tribulation, and a curtain lecture[4] is worth all the sermons in the world for teaching the virtues of patience and long suffering. A termagant wife may, therefore, in some respects, be considered a tolerable blessing; and if so, Rip Van Winkle was thrice blessed.

Certain it is, that he was a great favorite among all the good wives of the village, who, as usual with the amiable sex, took his part in all family squabbles; and never failed, whenever they talked those matters over in their evening gossippings, to lay all the blame on[5] Dame Van Winkle[6]. The children of the village, too, would shout with joy whenever he approached. He assisted at their sports, made their playthings, taught them to fly kites and shoot marbles, and told them long stories of ghosts, witches, and Indians. Whenever he went dodging about the village, he was surrounded by a troop of them, hanging on his skirts, clambering on his back, and playing a thousand tricks on him with impunity; and not a dog would bark at him throughout the neighborhood.

The great error in Rip's composition was an insuperable aversion to all kinds of profitable labor. It

---

1 Peter Stuyvesant: 彼得·史岱文森 (1592—1672), 荷兰新荷兰省的最后一任长官, 1655 年在克里斯蒂纳要塞打败了瑞典殖民者。
2 Fort Christina: 克里斯蒂纳要塞。现为特拉华州的威尔明顿市, 是瑞典人在北美的第一个殖民地。
3 henpecked: 惧内的, 怕老婆的
4 curtain lecture: 枕边劝诫, 妻子私下对丈夫的训话
5 lay all the blame on: 把所有的责任归咎于
6 Dame Van Winkle: Van Winkle 夫人

could not be from the want of assiduity or perseverance; for he would sit on a wet rock, with a rod as long and heavy as a Tartar's lance, and fish all day without a murmur, even though he should not be encouraged by a single nibble. He would carry a fowling-piece on his shoulder, for hours together, trudging through woods and swamps, and up hill and down dale, to shoot a few squirrels or wild pigeons. He would never refuse to assist a neighbor even in the roughest toil, and was a foremost man at all country frolics for husking Indian corn, or building stone fences; the women of the village, too, used to employ him to run their errands, and to do such little odd jobs as their less obliging husbands would not do for them;—in a word, Rip was ready to attend to anybody's business but his own; but as to doing family duty, and keeping his farm in order, it was impossible.

In fact, he declared it was of no use to work on his farm; it was the most pestilent little piece of ground in the whole country; every thing about it went wrong, and would go wrong, in spite of him. His fences were continually falling to pieces; his cow would either go astray, or get among the cabbages; weeds were sure to grow quicker in his fields than any where else; the rain always made a point of setting in just as he had some out-door work to do; so that though his patrimonial estate had dwindled away under his management, acre by acre, until there was little more left than a mere patch of Indian corn and potatoes, yet it was the worst conditioned farm in the neighborhood.

His children, too, were as ragged and wild as if they belonged to nobody. His son Rip, an urchin begotten in his own likeness, promised to inherit the habits, with the old clothes of his father. He was generally seen trooping like a colt at his mother's heels, equipped in a pair of his father's cast-off galligaskins[1], which he had much ado to hold up with one hand, as a fine lady does her train[2] in bad weather.

Rip Van Winkle, however, was one of those happy mortals, of foolish, well-oiled dispositions, who take the world easy, eat white bread or brown, whichever can be got with least thought or trouble, and would rather starve on a penny than work for a pound. If left to himself, he would have whistled life away in perfect contentment; but his wife kept continually dinning[3] in his ears about his idleness, his carelessness, and the ruin he was bringing on his family. Morning, noon, and night, her tongue was incessantly going, and everything he said or did was sure to produce a torrent of household eloquence. Rip had but one way of replying to all lectures of the kind, and that, by frequent use, had grown into a habit. He shrugged his shoulders, shook his head, cast up his eyes, but said nothing. This, however, always provoked a fresh volley from his wife, so that he was fain to draw off his forces, and take to the outside of the house—the only side which, in truth, belongs to a henpecked husband.

Rip's sole domestic adherent was his dog Wolf, who was as much henpecked as his master; for Dame Van Winkle regarded them as companions in idleness, and even looked upon Wolf with an evil eye, as the cause of his master's so often going astray. True it is, in all points of spirit befitting an honorable dog, he was as courageous an animal as ever scoured the woods—but what courage can withstand the ever-during and all-besetting terrors of a woman's tongue? The moment Wolf entered the

---

1 cast-off galligaskins：丢弃的灯笼裤
2 train：长袍(裙)拖地的部分
3 dinning：絮聒不休地说，唠叨

Chapter Twelve   Gender Studies

house his crest fell, his tail drooped to the ground, or curled between his legs, he sneaked about with a gallows air, casting many a sidelong glance at Dame Van Winkle, and at the least flourish of a broomstick or ladle, would fly to the door with yelping precipitation.

Times grew worse and worse with Rip Van Winkle as years of matrimony rolled on; a tart temper never mellows with age, and a sharp tongue is the only edged tool that grows keener with constant use. For a long while he used to console himself, when driven from home, by frequenting a kind of perpetual club of the sages, philosophers, and other idle personages of the village; which held its sessions on a bench before a small inn, designated by a rubicund portrait of His Majesty George the Third.[1] Here they used to sit in the shade, of a long lazy summer's day, talk listlessly over village gossip, or telling endless sleepy stories about nothing. But it would have been worth any statesman's money to have heard the profound discussions that sometimes took place, when by chance an old newspaper fell into their hands from some passing traveler. How solemnly they would listen to the contents, as drawled out by Derrick Van Bummel, the schoolmaster, a dapper learned little man, who was not to be daunted by the most gigantic word in the dictionary; and how sagely they would deliberate upon public events some months after they had taken place.

The opinions of this junto[2] were completely controlled by Nicholas Vedder, a patriarch of the village, and landlord of the inn, at the door of which he took his seat from morning till night, just moving sufficiently to avoid the sun, and keep in the shade of a large tree; so that the neighbors could tell the hour by his movements as accurately as by a sun dial[3]. It is true, he was rarely heard to speak, but smoked his pipe incessantly. His adherents, however, (for every great man has his adherents,) perfectly understood him, and knew how to gather his opinions. When any thing that was read or related displeased him, he was observed to smoke his pipe vehemently, and send forth short, frequent, and angry puffs; but when pleased, he would inhale the smoke slowly and tranquilly, and emit it in light and placid clouds, and sometimes, taking the pipe from his mouth, and letting the fragrant vapor curl about his nose, would gravely nod his head in token of perfect approbation[4].

From even this stronghold the unlucky Rip was at length routed by his termagant wife, who would suddenly break in upon the tranquillity of the assemblage and call the members all to naught; nor was that august personage, Nicholas Vedder himself, sacred from the daring tongue of this terrible virago, who charged him outright with encouraging her husband in habits of idleness.

Poor Rip was at last reduced almost to despair; and his only alternative, to escape from the labor of the farm and clamor of his wife, was to take gun in hand, and stroll away into the woods. Here he would sometimes seat himself at the foot of a tree, and share the contents of his wallet[5] with Wolf, with whom he sympathized as a fellow-sufferer in persecution. "Poor Wolf," he would say, "thy mistress leads thee a dog's life of it; but never mind, my lad, whilst I live thou shalt never want a friend to stand by thee!"

---

1 His Majesty George the Third：乔治三世国王陛下。乔治·威廉·腓特烈（George William Frederick）(1738—1820)，1760 年至 1810 年同时为大不列颠国王和爱尔兰国王。1801 年，这两个国家合并，他任大不列颠及爱尔兰联合王国的国王，直至去世。

2 junto：团体，派别

3 sun dial：日晷仪

4 in token of perfect approbation：表示完全赞同

5 wallet：(士兵或徒步旅行者用的)背包

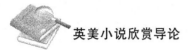

Wolf would wag his tail, look wistfully in his master's face, and if dogs can feel pity, I verily believe he reciprocated the sentiment with all his heart.

In a long ramble of the kind on a fine autumnal day, Rip had unconsciously scrambled to one of the highest parts of the Kaatskill mountains. He was after his favorite sport of squirrel shooting, and the still solitudes had echoed and re-echoed with the reports of his gun. Panting and fatigued, he threw himself, late in the afternoon, on a green knoll, covered with mountain herbage, that crowned the brow of a precipice. From an opening between the trees, he could overlook all the lower country for many a mile of rich woodland. He saw at a distance the lordly Hudson, far, far below him, moving on its silent but majestic course, with the reflection of a purple cloud, or the sail of a lagging bark, here and there sleeping on its glassy bosom, and at last losing itself in the blue highlands.

On the other side he looked down into a deep mountain glen, wild, lonely, and shagged, the bottom filled with fragments from the impending cliffs, and scarcely lighted by the reflected rays of the setting sun. For some time Rip lay musing on this scene; evening was gradually advancing, the mountains began to throw their long blue shadows over the valleys; he saw that it would be dark long before he could reach the village, and he heaved a heavy sigh[1] when he thought of encountering the terrors of Dame Van Winkle.

As he was about to descend, he heard a voice from a distance, hallooing, "Rip Van Winkle! Rip Van Winkle!" He looked round, but could see nothing but a crow winging its solitary flight across the mountain. He thought his fancy must have deceived him, and turned again to descend, when he heard the same cry ring through the still evening air; "Rip Van Winkle! Rip Van Winkle!"—at the same time Wolf bristled up his back[2], and giving a low growl, skulked to his master's side, looking fearfully down into the glen. Rip now felt a vague apprehension stealing over him[3]; he looked anxiously in the same direction, and perceived a strange figure slowly toiling up the rocks, and bending under the weight of something he carried on his back. He was surprised to see any human being in this lonely and unfrequented place, but supposing it to be some one of the neighborhood in need of his assistance, he hastened down to yield it.

On nearer approach, he was still more surprised at the singularity[4] of the stranger's appearance. He was a short square built old fellow, with thick bushy hair, and a grizzled beard. His dress was of the antique Dutch fashion—a cloth jerkin[5] strapped round the waist—several pair of breeches, the outer one of ample volume, decorated with rows of buttons down the sides, and bunches at the knees. He bore on his shoulder a stout keg, that seemed full of liquor, and made signs for Rip to approach and assist him with the load. Though rather shy and distrustful of this new acquaintance, Rip complied with his usual alacrity, and mutually relieving one another, they clambered up a narrow gully, apparently the dry bed of a mountain torrent. As they ascended, Rip every now and then heard long rolling peals, like distant thunder, that seemed to issue out of a deep ravine, or rather cleft between lofty rocks, toward which their

---

1 heaved a heavy sigh：长长地叹了一口气
2 bristled up his back：背上的汗毛都竖起来了
3 Rip now felt a vague apprehension stealing over him：瑞普突然感到一种莫名的害怕。
4 singularity：奇怪，奇特
5 jerkin：(16、17 世纪时)男用无袖紧身短上衣

Chapter Twelve Gender Studies

rugged path conducted. He paused for an instant, but supposing it to be the muttering of one of those transient thunder-showers which often take place in mountain heights, he proceeded. Passing through the ravine, they came to a hollow, like a small amphitheatre, surrounded by perpendicular precipices[1], over the brinks of which impending trees shot their branches, so that you only caught glimpses of the azure sky, and the bright evening cloud. During the whole time, Rip and his companion had labored on in silence; for though the former marvelled greatly what could be the object of carrying a keg of liquor up this wild mountain, yet there was something strange and incomprehensible about the unknown, that inspired awe, and checked familiarity.

On entering the amphitheatre, new objects of wonder presented themselves. On a level spot in the centre was a company of odd-looking personages playing at nine-pins[2]. They were dressed in a quaint, outlandish fashion: some wore short doublets[3], others jerkins, with long knives in their belts, and most of them had enormous breeches, of similar style with that of the guide's. Their visages, too, were peculiar: one had a large beard, broad face, and small piggish eyes: the face of another seemed to consist entirely of nose, and was surmounted by a white sugarloaf hat[4], set off[5] with a little red cock's tail. They all had beards, of various shapes and colors. There was one who seemed to be the commander. He was a stout old gentleman, with a weather-beaten countenance; he wore a laced doublet, broad belt and hanger[6], high crowned hat and feather, red stockings, and high heeled shoes, with roses in them. The whole group reminded Rip of the figures in an old Flemish painting, in the parlor of Dominie[7] Van Shaick, the village parson, and which had been brought over from Holland at the time of the settlement.

What seemed particularly odd to Rip was, that though these folks were evidently amusing themselves, yet they maintained the gravest faces, the most mysterious silence, and were, withal, the most melancholy party of pleasure he had ever witnessed. Nothing interrupted the stillness of the scene, but the noise of the balls, which, whenever they were rolled, echoed along the mountains like rumbling peals of thunder.

As Rip and his companion approached them, they suddenly desisted from their play, and stared at him with such fixed statue-like gaze, and such strange, uncouth, lack lustre countenances, that his heart turned within him, and his knees smote together. His companion now emptied the contents of the keg into large flagons, and made signs to him to wait upon the company. He obeyed with fear and trembling; they quaffed the liquor in profound silence, and then returned to their game.

By degrees, Rip's awe and apprehension subsided[8]. He even ventured, when no eye was fixed upon him, to taste the beverage, which he found had much of the flavor of excellent Hollands[9]. He was naturally a thirsty soul, and was soon tempted to repeat the draught. One taste provoked another, and he

---

1 a small amphitheatre, surrounded by perpendicular precipices:一个被垂直的峭壁包围着的小型露天竞技场
2 a company of odd-looking personages playing at nine-pins:一帮相貌古怪的人在玩九柱戏
3 doublets:男紧身上衣,从颈部长至大腿
4 sugarloaf hat:圆锥形的帽子
5 set off:装饰
6 hanger:短弯剑
7 Dominie:牧师
8 By degrees, Rip's awe and apprehension subsided:渐渐地,瑞普的惊惧和忧虑消失了。
9 Hollands:荷兰造杜松子酒

reiterated his visits to the flagon so often, that at length his senses were overpowered, his eyes swam in his head, his head gradually declined, and he fell into a deep sleep.

On waking, he found himself on the green knoll whence he had first seen the old man of the glen. He rubbed his eyes—it was a bright sunny morning. The birds were hopping and twittering among the bushes, and the eagle was wheeling aloft, and breasting the pure mountain breeze. "Surely," thought Rip, "I have not slept here all night." He recalled the occurrences before he fell asleep. The strange man with a keg of liquor—the mountain ravine—the wild retreat among the rocks—the wo-begone[1] party at nine-pins—the flagon—"Oh! that flagon! that wicked flagon!" thought Rip—"what excuse shall I make to Dame Van Winkle!"

He looked round for his gun, but in place of the clean well-oiled fowling-piece, he found an old firelock lying by him, the barrel incrusted with rust, the lock falling off, and the stock worm-eaten. He now suspected that the grave roysters[2] of the mountain had put a trick upon him, and having dosed him with liquor, had robbed him of his gun. Wolf, too, had disappeared, but he might have strayed away after a squirrel or partridge. He whistled after him, shouted his name, but all in vain; the echoes repeated his whistle and shout, but no dog was to be seen.

He determined to revisit the scene of the last evening's gambol, and if he met with any of the party, to demand his dog and gun. As he rose to walk, he found himself stiff in the joints, and wanting in his usual activity[3]. "These mountain beds do not agree with me," thought Rip; "and if this frolic should lay me up[4] with a fit of the rheumatism[5], I shall have a blessed time with Dame Van Winkle." With some difficulty he got down into the glen: he found the gully up which he and his companion had ascended the preceding evening; but to his astonishment a mountain stream was now foaming down it, leaping from rock to rock, and filling the glen with babbling murmurs. He, however, made shift to scramble up its sides, working his toilsome way through thickets of birch, sassafras, and witch hazel, and sometimes tripped up or entangled by the wild grape vines that twisted their coils or tendrils from tree to tree, and spread a kind of network in his path.

At length he reached to where the ravine had opened through the cliffs, to the amphitheatre; but no traces of such opening remained. The rocks presented a high impenetrable wall, over which the torrent came tumbling in a sheet of feathery foam, and fell into a broad deep basin, black from the shadows of the surrounding forest. Here, then, poor Rip was brought to a stand. He again called and whistled after his dog; he was only answered by the cawing of a flock of idle crows, sporting high in air about a dry tree that overhung a sunny precipice; and who, secure in their elevation, seemed to look down and scoff at the poor man's perplexities. What was to be done? the morning was passing away, and Rip felt famished for his breakfast[6]. He grieved to give up his dog and gun; he dreaded to meet his wife; but it would not do to starve among the mountains. He shook his head, shouldered the rusty firelock, and, with

---

1 wo-begone：悲哀的，忧愁的
2 roysters：相当于 roisters，喧闹作乐者。这里指玩九柱戏的那些人。
3 he found himself stiff in the joints, and wanting in his usual activity：他发现自己关节僵硬，不能像平常一样自如活动。
4 lay me up：让我卧床不起
5 rheumatism：风湿病
6 felt famished for his breakfast：感到很饿，想吃早饭。

Chapter Twelve Gender Studies

a heart full of trouble and anxiety, turned his steps homeward.

As he approached the village, he met a number of people, but none whom he knew, which somewhat surprised him, for he had thought himself acquainted with every one in the country round. Their dress, too, was of a different fashion from that to which he was accustomed. They all stared at him with equal marks of surprise, and whenever they cast their eyes upon him, invariably stroked their chins[1]. The constant recurrence of this gesture, induced Rip, involuntarily, to do the same, when, to his astonishment, he found his beard had grown a foot long!

He had now entered the skirts[2] of the village. A troop of strange children ran at his heels, hooting after him, and pointing at his gray beard. The dogs, too, not one of which he recognized for an old acquaintance, barked at him as he passed. The very village was altered: it was larger and more populous. There were rows of houses which he had never seen before, and those which had been his familiar haunts had disappeared. Strange names were over the doors—strange faces at the windows—every thing was strange. His mind now began to misgive him; that both he and the world around him were not bewitched. Surely this was his native village, which he had left but the day before. There stood the Kaatskill mountains—there ran the silver Hudson at a distance—there was every hill and dale precisely as it had always been—Rip was sorely perplexed—"That flagon last night," thought he, "has addled my poor head sadly!"

It was with some difficulty that he found the way to his own house, which he approached with silent awe, expecting every moment to hear the shrill voice of Dame Van Winkle. He found the house gone to decay—the roof fallen in, the windows shattered, and the doors off the hinges. A half starved dog, that looked like Wolf was skulking about it. Rip called him by name, but the cur snarled, showed his teeth, and passed on. This was an unkind cut indeed—"My very dog," sighed poor Rip, "has forgotten me!"

He entered the house, which, to tell the truth, Dame Van Winkle had always kept in neat order. It was empty, forlorn, and apparently abandoned. This desolateness overcame all his connubial fears—he called loudly for his wife and children—the lonely chambers rang for a moment with his voice, and then all again was silence.

He now hurried forth, and hastened to his old resort[3], the village inn—but it too was gone. A large rickety wooden building stood in its place, with great gaping windows, some of them broken, and mended with old hats and petticoats, and over the door was painted, "The Union Hotel, by Jonathan Doolittle." Instead of the great tree that used to shelter the quiet little Dutch inn of yore, there now was reared a tall naked pole, with something on the top that looked like a red night cap[4], and from it was fluttering a flag, on which was a singular assemblage of stars and stripes—all this was strange and incomprehensible. He recognized on the sign, however, the ruby face of King George, under which he had smoked so many a peaceful pipe, but even this was singularly metamorphosed. The red coat was changed for one of blue and buff[5], a sword was held in the hand instead of a sceptre, the head was

---

1 invariably stroked their chins: 总是抚摸他们的下巴
2 skirts: 边缘, 外围
3 resort: 常去的地方
4 night cap: 指法国大革命时期所用的"自由帽"（一种松软贴身的帽子），是自由的象征，而前面提到的旗杆也指"自由之杆"。
5 blue and buff: 蓝色和浅黄色是独立革命时期军装的颜色。欧文这里戏谑新房主是个小气的北方佬，只是把颜色换了一下，并没有真正用华盛顿的画像。

decorated with a cocked hat, and underneath was painted in large characters, GENERAL WASHINGTON.

There was, as usual, a crowd of folk about the door, but none that Rip recollected. The very character of the people seemed changed. There was a busy, bustling, disputatious tone about it, instead of the accustomed phlegm and drowsy tranquility. He looked in vain for the sage Nicholas Vedder, with his broad face, double chin, and fair long pipe, uttering clouds of tobacco smoke instead of idle speeches; or Van Bummel, the schoolmaster, doling forth the contents of an ancient newspaper. In place of these, a lean, bilious looking fellow, with his pockets full of handbills, was haranguing vehemently about rights of citizens—elections—members of congress—liberty—Bunker's hill—heroes of seventy-six—and other words, which were a perfect Babylonish jargon[1] to the bewildered Van Winkle.

The appearance of Rip, with his long grizzled beard, his rusty fowling piece, his uncouth dress, and an army of women and children at his heels, soon attracted the attention of the tavern politicians. They crowded round him, eyeing him from head to foot with great curiosity. The orator bustled up to him, and, drawing him partly aside, inquired "on which side he voted?" Rip stared in vacant stupidity. Another short but busy little fellow pulled him by the arm, and, rising on tiptoe, inquired in his ear, "Whether he was Federal or Democrat?[2]" Rip was equally at a loss to comprehend the question; when a knowing, self-important old gentleman, in a sharp cocked hat, made his way through the crowd, putting them to the right and left with his elbows as he passed, and planting himself before Van Winkle, with one arm akimbo[3], the other resting on his cane, his keen eyes and sharp hat penetrating, as it were, into his very soul, demanded, in an austere tone, "what brought him to the election with a gun on his shoulder, and a mob at his heels, and whether he meant to breed a riot in the village?" "Alas! gentlemen," cried Rip, somewhat dismayed, "I am a poor quiet man, a native of the place, and a loyal subject of the king, God bless him!"

Here a general shout burst from the bystanders—"A tory[4]! a tory! a spy! a refugee! hustle him! away with him!" It was with great difficulty that the self-important man in the cocked hat restored order; and having assumed a tenfold austerity of brow, demanded again of the unknown culprit, what he came there for, and whom he was seeking. The poor man humbly assured him that he meant no harm; but merely came there in search of some of his neighbors, who used to keep about the tavern.

"Well—who are they?—name them."

Rip bethought himself a moment, and inquired, "Where's Nicholas Vedder?"

There was a silence for a little while, when an old man replied, in a thin piping voice, "Nicholas Vedder! why he is dead and gone these eighteen years! There was a wooden tombstone in the church-yard that used to tell all about him, but that's rotten and gone too."

"Where's Brom Dutcher?"

"Oh he went off to the army in the beginning of the war[5]; some say he was killed at the storming of

---

1 Babylonish jargon:让人不能理解的话
2 Federal or Democrat:指乔治·华盛顿在任时的两个政治派别,以亚历山大·汉密尔顿为首的联邦党和托马斯·杰斐逊领导的民主党
3 with one arm akimbo:一手叉腰
4 tory:指美国独立战争时期支持英国的美国人
5 the war:指美国独立战争

Stony-Point[1]—others say he was drowned in a squall, at the foot of Antony's Nose[2]. I don't know—he never came back again."

"Where's Van Bummel, the schoolmaster?"

"He went off to the wars too, was a great militia general, and is now in Congress."

Rip's heart died away, at hearing of these sad changes in his home and friends, and finding himself thus alone in the world. Every answer puzzled him, too, by treating of such enormous lapses of time, and of matters which he could not understand: war—congress—Stony-Point;—he had no courage to ask after any more friends, but cried out in despair, "Does nobody here know Rip Van Winkle?"

"Oh, Rip Van Winkle!" exclaimed two or three, "Oh, to be sure! that's Rip Van Winkle yonder, leaning against the tree."

Rip looked, and beheld a precise counterpart of himself, as he went up the mountain: apparently as lazy, and certainly as ragged. The poor fellow was now completely confounded. He doubted his own identity, and whether he was himself or another man. In the midst of his bewilderment, the man in the cocked hat demanded who he was, and what was his name?

"God knows," exclaimed he, at his wit's end[3]; "I'm not myself—I'm somebody else—that's me yonder—no—that's somebody else, got into my shoes—I was myself last night, but I fell asleep on the mountain, and they've changed my gun, and every thing's changed, and I'm changed, and I can't tell what's my name, or who I am!"

The bystanders began now to look at each other, nod, wink significantly, and tap their fingers against their foreheads. There was a whisper, also, about securing the gun, and keeping the old fellow from doing mischief. At the very suggestion of which, the self-important man in the cocked hat retired with some precipitation. At this critical moment a fresh comely woman pressed through the throng[4] to get a peep at the graybearded man. She had a chubby child in her arms, which, frightened at his looks, began to cry. "Hush, Rip," cried she, "hush, you little fool; the old man wont hurt you." The name of the child, the air of the mother, the tone of her voice, all awakened a train of recollections in his mind.

"What is your name, my good woman?" asked he.

"Judith Gardenier."

"And your father's name?"

"Ah, poor man, his name was Rip Van Winkle; but it's twenty years since he went away from home with his gun, and never has been heard of since—his dog came home without him; but whether he shot himself, or was carried away by the Indians, nobody can tell. I was then but a little girl."

Rip had but one question more to ask; but he put it with a faltering voice:

"Where's your mother?"

"Oh, she too had died but a short time since; she broke a blood-vessel in a fit of passion at a New-England peddler."

---

1 Stony-Point：位于西点以南的哈德逊河西岸，在独立战争时期被安东尼·韦恩(1745—1796)将军占领
2 Antony's Nose：西点附近的山
3 at his wit's end：全然不知所措
4 pressed through the throng：从人群中挤过来

There was a drop of comfort, at least, in this intelligence[1]. The honest man could contain himself no longer[2].—He caught his daughter and her child in his arms.—"I am your father!" cried he—"Young Rip Van Winkle once—old Rip Van Winkle now!—Does nobody know poor Rip Van Winkle!"

All stood amazed, until an old woman, tottering out from among the crowd, put her hand to her brow, and peering under it in his face for a moment, exclaimed, "Sure enough! it is Rip Van Winkle—it is himself! Welcome home again, old neighbor—Why, where have you been these twenty long years?"

Rip's story was soon told, for the whole twenty years had been to him but as one night. The neighbors stared when they heard it; some were seen to wink at each other, and put their tongues in their cheeks: and the self-important man in the cocked hat, who, when the alarm was over, had returned to the field, screwed down the corners of his mouth, and shook his head—upon which there was a general shaking of the head throughout the assemblage.

It was determined, however, to take the opinion of old Peter Vanderdonk, who was seen slowly advancing up the road. He was a descendant of the historian of that name[3], who wrote one of the earliest accounts of the province. Peter was the most ancient inhabitant of the village, and well versed in[4] all the wonderful events and traditions of the neighborhood. He recollected Rip at once, and corroborated his story in the most satisfactory manner. He assured the company that it was a fact, handed down from his ancestor the historian, that the Kaatskill mountains had always been haunted by strange beings. That it was affirmed that the great Hendrick Hudson[5], the first discoverer of the river and country, kept a kind of vigil there every twenty years, with his crew of the Half-moon; being permitted in this way to revisit the scenes of his enterprise, and keep a guardian eye upon the river, and the great city[6] called by his name. That his father had once seen them in their old Dutch dresses playing at nine pins in a hollow of the mountain; and that he himself had heard, one summer afternoon, the sound of their balls, like distant peals of thunder.

To make a long story short, the company broke up, and returned to the more important concerns of the election. Rip's daughter took him home to live with her; she had a snug, well-furnished house, and a stout cheery farmer for a husband, whom Rip recollected for one of the urchins that used to climb upon his back. As to Rip's son and heir, who was the ditto[7] of himself, seen leaning against the tree, he was employed to work on the farm; but evinced a hereditary disposition to attend to anything else but his business.

Rip now resumed his old walks and habits; he soon found many of his former cronies, though all rather the worse for the wear and tear[8] of time; and preferred making friends among the rising generation, with whom he soon grew into great favor.

---

1 intelligence：消息

2 The honest man could contain himself no longer：这个老实人再也无法控制自己。

3 that name：指 Adriaen Van der Donck(1620—1655?)，他曾写过新荷兰史。

4 versed in：熟悉，精通

5 Hendrick Hudson：亨利·哈德逊(Henry Hudson)，效忠荷兰的英国探险家与航海家，以搜寻西北航道而闻名。

6 the great city：此处称这座城市为"大都市"是反话。以哈德逊命名的这座城市位于哈德逊河东岸，当时很繁荣，但算不上是大都市。

7 ditto：很相似的东西

8 wear and tear：消耗，消磨

Chapter Twelve Gender Studies

Having nothing to do at home, and being arrived at that happy age when a man can be idle with impunity, he took his place once more on the bench, at the inn door, and was reverenced as one of the patriarchs of the village, and a chronicle of the old times "before the war." It was some time before he could get into the regular track of gossip, or could be made to comprehend the strange events that had taken place during his torpor. How that there had been a revolutionary war—that the country had thrown off the yoke of old England—and that, instead of being a subject of his Majesty George the Third, he was now a free citizen of the United States. Rip, in fact, was no politician; the changes of states and empires made but little impression on him; but there was one species of despotism under which he had long groaned, and that was—petticoat government. Happily, that was at an end; he had got his neck out of the yoke of matrimony, and could go in and out whenever he pleased, without dreading the tyranny of Dame Van Winkle. Whenever her name was mentioned, however, he shook his head, shrugged his shoulders, and cast up his eyes; which might pass either for an expression of resignation to his fate[1], or joy at his deliverance[2].

He used to tell his story to every stranger that arrived at Mr. Doolittle's hotel. He was observed, at first, to vary on some points every time he told it, which was, doubtless, owing to his having so recently awaked. It at last settled down precisely to the tale I have related, and not a man, woman, or child in the neighborhood, but knew it by heart. Some always pretended to doubt the reality of it, and insisted that Rip had been out of his head, and that this was one point on which he always remained flighty. The old Dutch inhabitants, however, almost universally gave it full credit[3]. Even to this day they never hear a thunderstorm of a summer afternoon, about the Kaatskill, but they say Hendrick Hudson and his crew are at their game of nine pins; and it is a common wish of all henpecked husbands in the neighborhood, when life hangs heavy on their hands[4], that they might have a quieting draught out of Rip Van Winkle's flagon.

NOTE

The foregoing tale, one would suspect, had been suggested to Mr. Knickerbocker by a little German superstition about CharlesV. and the Kypphauser mountain; the subjoined note, however, which he had appended to the tale, shows that it is an absolute fact, narrated with his usual fidelity:

"The story of Rip Van Winkle may seem incredible to many, but nevertheless I give it my full belief, for I know the vicinity of our old Dutch settlements to have been very subject to marvellous events and appearances. Indeed, I have heard many stranger stories than this, in the villages along the Hudson; all of which were too well authenticated to admit of a doubt. I have even talked with Rip Van Winkle myself, who, when last I saw him, was a very venerable old man, and so perfectly rational and consistent on every other point, that I think no conscientious person could refuse to take this into the bargain; nay, I have seen a certificate on the subject taken before a country justice, and signed with a

---

1 resignation to his fate: 听从命运的安排
2 deliverance: 解脱
3 gave it full credit: 完全相信这是真的
4 life hangs heavy on their hands: 他们感到生活很沉重

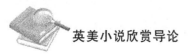

cross, in the justice's own handwriting. The story, therefore, is beyond the possibility of doubt.

D. K."

1819

Understanding the Text

"Rip Van Winkle" has received broad criticism since it was published in 1819. Its criticism has predominantly explored its domestication and the relationship between his personal identity and the burgeoning national identity. Now a feminist interpretation of this story might reveal how the women of that age were suppressed and help the reader comprehend the story and its author from a quite different perspective.

The story of Rip Van Winkle, which is set in the years immediately before and after the American Revolutionary War, tells of a good-natured fellow who lives in a quiet hamlet inhabited by Dutch settlers at the foot of New York's Kaatskill mountains. The fellow named Rip Van Winkle is an impotent provider for his family whose home and farm suffer from his lazy neglect, and therefore is always being scolded by his wife, Dame Van Winkle, who is a nagging, broom-wielding shrew.

One autumn day, Rip and his dog wander up the mountains to seek some relief from the tongue-lashings of this "virago." In a ravine leading up to a natural amphitheatre, Rip encounters strangely dressed men, who are rumored to be the ghosts of Henry Hudson's crew, and are solemnly playing nine-pins. And after drinking some of their liquor, he settles down under a shady tree and falls asleep.

On awakening and returning to the village twenty years later, he is amazed to find that everything has changed. His wife is dead, all his friends are either gone or dead, and his country has won a revolution against the motherland. It seems that he has been asleep for twenty years and has come back an old man. At the moment of his uncertainty of his own identity, an old woman recognizes him. Vanderdonk Peter, "the most ancient inhabitant of the village, and well versed in all the wonderful events and traditions of the neighborhood," recollects Rip and confirms Rip's story "in the most satisfactory manner." Rip sees his son, Rip II, now a grown man, who acts just like him. His daughter, now grown and married, holding an infant—Rip III, takes him home to live with her. The story ends on a happy note, for Rip has finally found the peace and contentment he sought, and certain henpecked husbands especially wish they shared Rip's luck. When feminist readers come to the end of the story they are not comfortable with the ending, and are sure to go over the whole story and find hints making them uncomfortable.

In the first place, the story and its main characters' fates do not go in the direction they have expected. In the story, Rip Van Winkle, who idles all the day and childishly rejects his responsibility for the family, is depicted as "a simple good-natured man," "a kind neighbor," and "an obedient, henpecked husband." He always understands how to help other men's wives with "those little odd jobs their less obliging husbands would not do for them." He always takes pleasure in helping his neighbors "in the roughest toil." He assists the children of the village with their sports and tells them stories. His meekness gains him universal popularity, and a dog would not bark at him throughout the neighborhood.

In contrast, Dame Van Winkle who works hard for the family is characterized as "a terrible virago" or a "termagent wife" with the bitter acid of hatred and "a tart temper." Her tongue is "the only edged tool that grows keener with constant use" and a butcher dreams of. Constantly nagging Rip about his idleness, his carelessness, and the ruin he was bringing on his family, she heaps verbal abuse on him until he can hardly bear it. Rip's dog, "as courageous an animal as ever scoured the woods," grows as henpecked as his master with the spectre of the woman. Thus Irving gives us a searing picture of a phallic woman, set in sharp contrast to the gentle sensitive portrait of Rip.

It appears that Rip Van Winkle is rendered impotent as a provider by Dame Van Winkle's oppression and her tyranny. Rip acts as a victim of his marriage. Rip's newfound happiness at the end of the story is no less a product of his marital release than it is of his "being arrived at that happy age when a man can be idle with impunity." Rip's experience of marital deliverance is to achieve his masculinity. Therefore, Rip at the end of the story looks more like a hero than a henpecked husband.

At this time the feminist readers have grown indignant when they have a much clearer idea of how much Dame Van Winkle suffered from Rip's continual avoidance of his masculine responsibility which leaves Dame Van Winkle little choice but to dominate the world outside Rip's "personal universe." However, if they take Irving's life and the times when the story was published into consideration they may find the reasons: Dame Van Winkle is actually the product of the male-dominated society of that age as well as the author of the story.

Early nineteenth century was a more male-dominated age than that of today. At that time the male who have the privilege of acting as they like and taking control of women's fate established a multitude of standards and conventions the women must follow, and tenderness, submission to the men, and staying at home to take care of their families without their own voice and identity are some qualities "good" women should have. Those who comply with them are regarded as "angels" while those who disobey them and even fight against them are treated as "bitches" deserving to be despised, devalued, and demoralized. Washington Irving who lived at that time naturally accepted the established views of women and applied them to the characterization. In the story although she took on the responsibilities, working hard both on farm and at home to support the family and raise the children, which should have undertaken by Rip Van Winkle, Dame Van Winkle was awarded nothing for this instead of her "disgraceful death"—"she broke a blood-vessel in a fit of passion at a New-England peddler"—because she gave out her voice against the male-dominated society instead of keeping her mouth shut. In other words, Dame Van Winkle, who overtly acts against the conventions, is doomed as the scapegoat and enemy of the male-dominated society and died in the disgraceful manner. Thus, it is not surprising that Dame Van Winkle did not have her own name which indicated her independent identity, that she was sarcastically depicted as a "virago" who dies in the ridiculous way, and that her fellow villagers, including her female villagers, lay all the blame on her instead of making any complaint about Rip's laziness and irresponsibility. It is not surprising as well that Washington Irving demonstrates deep-hearted sympathy with Rip Van Winkle throughout the story and even assures him of the social happiness and the village patriarch at the end of the story. And surely it is not surprising that the new independent American government is called "petticoat government" by Rip Van Winkle, who hates politicians and new government.

Undoubtedly, Rip survives his wife to become the undisputed victor of the war of the Van Winkles. This means not only husband's victory over wife but the male's victory over the female to a large degree. Surely if we remember that writing the Rip Van Winkle story was intended as a kind of economic catalyst for its author, we might take it as "Irving's wish to be carefree again, even as Rips Van Winkle" "since he had decided to devote himself seriously to writing 'for bread and cheese.'"(Heiman)

Further Reading

Gender Studies

Beauvoir, Simone de. *The Second Sex*. Ed. and Trans. H. M. Parshley. New York: Modern Library, 1952.

Bressler, Charles E. *Literary Criticism: An Introduction to Theory and Practice*. 2nd ed. Upper Saddle River, N. J: Prentice-Hall, Inc., 1999.

Eagleton, Terry. *Literary Theory: An Introduction*. Minneapolis: University of Minnesota Press, 1983.

Gilbert, Sandra M. and Susan Gubar. *The Madwoman in the Attic: The Woman Writer and the Nineteenth-Century Literary Imagination*. New Haven: Yale University Press, 1979.

Guerin, Wilfred L., et al. *A Handbook of Critical Approaches to Literature*. Beijing: Foreign Language Teaching and Research Press, 2004.

Jacobus, Mary. *Reading Woman: Essays in Feminist Criticism*. New York: Columbia University Press, 1986.

Millett, Kate. *Sexual Politics*. New York: Doubleday, 1970.

Munt, Sally, ed. *New Lesbian Criticism: Library and Cultural Readings*. Brighton: Harvester Press, 1987.

Nicholson, Linda J. *Feminism/Postmodernism*. New York: Routledge, 1990.

Showalter, Elaine. *A Literature of Their Own: British Women Novelists from Bronte to Lessing*. Princeton: Princeton University Press, 1977.

Spivak, Gayatri Chakravorty. *In Other Worlds: Essays in Cultural Politics*. New York: Methuen, 1987.

Wyatt, Jean. *Reconstructing Desire: The Role of the Unconscious in Women's Reading and Writing*. Chapel Hill: University of North Carolina Press, 1990.

Rip Van Winkle

Catalano, Susan M. "Henpecked to Heroism: Placing Rip Van Winkle and Francis Macomber in the American Literary Tradition". *Hemingway Review* 17.2 (Spring 1998): 111—17.

Ferguson, Robert A. "Rip Van Winkle and the Generational Divide in American Culture". *Early American Literature* 40 (2005):529—44.

Heiman, Mareel. "Rip Van Winkle: A Psychoanalytic Note on the Story and Its Author". *American*

Imago 16.1 (Spring 1959): 3—47.

Scanlan, Tom. "The Domestication of Rip Van Winkle". *Virginia Quarterly Review* 50.1 (Winter 1974): 51—62.

Schachel, Robert C. "Textual Projections: The Emergence of a Postcolonial American Gothic". Dissertation. University of Florida, 2006.

Chapter Thirteen
Reader-response Criticism

Reader-response theory arose to a degree as a reaction against the formalist approach, which dominated literary criticism for roughly half a century. Unlike formalism which focuses on the text and regards it as an art object independent of its author, its readers, the historical time it depicts, and the historical period in which it was written, reader-response criticism holds to the assumption that readers should be the central concern in the process of reading and production of meaning of a literary work. According to reader-response critics, in literary interpretation, the text is not the most important component; and the reader is. In fact, there is no text unless there is a reader. A literary work does not even exist, in a sense, until it is read by some reader; the meaning of a text can emerge only when a reader is actively involved in a text. They argue, therefore, that just as writing is a creative act, reading is, since it creates the text.

Like any other critical theory, reader-response theory is by no means a monolithic critical position. It does not provide us with a unified body of theory or a single methodological approach for textual analysis. Those who give emphasis on readers and their responses in interpreting a literary work come from a number of different critical camps, not excluding formalism.

The first group of reader-response critics, usually called structuralists, maintains that, instead of a finished product, a literary work is an evolving creation of the reader as he or she investigates characters, plots, images, and other elements while reading. According to them, the act of creative reading is, to a degree, more controlled by the text than by the reader. During the reading process all the various linguistic elements, such as words, phrases and images in a text, may trigger in the reader's mind a specific interpretation which is closely associated with the reader's worldview, background, purpose for reading, knowledge of words, and other such factors. Thus many different interpretations of the same text are produced by readers. They stress that a reader brings to the text a predetermined system of signs or codes like sirens and the red light and applies this sign system directly to the text. The text becomes important because it contains signs or signals to the reader that have established and acceptable interpretations. Therefore, they are more concerned about interpreting any sign in the context of acceptable societal standards and try to look for specific codes or signs in the text that allow meaning to occur.

The second group of reader-response critics, often regarded as phenomenologists, gives the important place to the reader's experience in interpretation of a literary work. These critics declare that both the reader and the text play roughly equal parts in interpreting a text. For them, reading is an event that culminates in the creation of the work, and a literary work and its meaning exist only in the consciousness of the reader. Thus, reading and the textual analysis are an aesthetic experience whereby both the reader and the text combine in the consciousness of the reader to create the work. Naturally, the critic should not explain the text as an object but its effect on the reader. They maintain that a text does not tell readers everything; there are gaps or blanks, which readers with very different backgrounds must fill in and thereby assemble the meanings, thus becoming coauthors in a sense. Readers' experiences in a sense will govern the effects the text produces on them. And meanings of a text may "go far beyond the single 'best' meaning of the formalist because they are the products of such varied reader backgrounds." (Guerin, p.355)

The third group of reader-response critics, generally called psychological or subjective critics, places the greatest emphasis on the reader in the interpretive process. They assert that the reader's thoughts, beliefs, and experiences play a greater part than the actual text in shaping a work's meaning because the reader shapes and finds his self-identities in the reading process. For them, the act of interpretation is a subjective experience, and so there are as many valid interpretations for a literary work as there are readers. There is no such a thing as a correct interpretation.

To summarize, two distinguishing features characterize reader-response criticism. First, reader-response critics analyze the effect of the text on the reader, and the analysis often resembles formalist criticism or rhetorical criticism or psychological criticism. The major distinction is the emphasis on the reader's response in the analysis by answering such questions as "how does the work affect the reader" and "what strategies or devices have come into play in the production of these effects"? The second feature is the relegation of the text to secondary importance: the reader is of primary importance. Thus, reader-response criticism attacks the authority of the text, which results in subjectivism. (Guerin, pp.359—360)

Willa Cather's "Paul's Case" illustrates how we read and what influences our readings. This is a tragic story with Paul's death ending the story. To the ending of this story readers may respond differently. For a reader in the early 20th century, he might not comprehend why Paul ends his life since he has such a rich family and can enjoy so many fine things. In contrast, a reader in our times would probably argue that Paul may have other alternatives than killing himself: he can just tell his father about his feelings and try to get his understanding and support. And a reader, perhaps someone who has recently lost a son, might be worried about Paul's father while he wishes that he could have more understanding of Paul. Although Cather might intend to reveal the alienation of a boy with special sexual tendency from the people in his society, she could not get the readers' responses under her control.

Although responses to a text cover a wide range, it does not mean that any interpretation is valid, for the text does establish some limits that allow us to reject certain readings as erroneous.

Ring Lardner(1885—1933)

Ring Lardner, the shortened name for Ringgold Wilmer Lardner, was an American sports columnist and short story writer best known for his satires on the sports world, marriage, and the theatre.

Ring Lardner, born in Niles, Michigan, was the son of wealthy parents Henry and Lena Phillips Lardner. He was married to Ellis Abbott of Goshen, Indiana, in 1911. They had four sons, John, James, Ring Jr., and David. Among them, John, James and David were newspapermen, and Ring Jr. was a screenwriter.

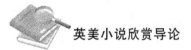

Lardner's first successful book, *You Know Me Al* (1916), was written in the form of letters by "Jack Keefe," a bush league baseball player, to a friend back home. It had initially been published as six separate, but inter-related short stories in *The Saturday Evening Post*. It employed satire to show the stupidity and avarice of a certain type of athlete and earned the appreciation of Virginia Woolf and other very serious, unfunny people when it was published.

Lardner is considered by many to be one of America's best writers of the short story. His well-known stories include "Haircut," "Some Like Them Cold," "The Golden Honeymoon," "Alibi Ike," and "A Day in the Life of Conrad Green."

Lardner also had a lifelong fascination with the theatre. Although he wrote a series of brief plays which poked fun at the conventions of the theatre, his only success was *June Moon,* a comedy co-written with Broadway veteran George S. Kaufman.

Lardner was also a well-known sports columnist, and began his career as a teenager with the *South Bend Tribune*. Then he joined the *South Bend Times*, the *Inter-Ocean* in Chicago, the *Chicago Examiner*, the *Tribune* and then the *Boston American* one after another.

Lardner was a close friend of F. Scott Fitzgerald and other writers of the Jazz Age. He was in some respects the model for the tragic character Abe North in Fitzgerald's last completed novel, *Tender Is the Night*.

Lardner influenced Ernest Hemingway, who sometimes wrote articles for his high school newspaper under the pseudonym Ring Lardner. Ring Lardner died at age 48 in East Hampton, New York, of complications from tuberculosis.

"Haircut," generally considered Lardner's masterpiece, is one of Lardner's darkest satires. Set in a fictitious town in Michigan in the early 1920s, the story is told by the town barber, who insists to the end that Jim Kendall was basically a good man who was just a little wild. It reflects the moral blindness of the towners in this small town.

Haircut

I got another barber that comes over from Carterville and helps me out[1] Saturdays, but the rest of the time I can get along all right alone. You can see for yourself that this ain't no New York City and besides that, the most of the boys works all day and don't have no leisure to drop in here and get themselves prettied up[2].

---

1 helps me out: 给我帮忙
2 prettied up: 使……漂亮

You're a newcomer, ain't you? I thought I hadn't seen you round before. I hope you like it good enough to stay. As I say, we ain't no New York City or Chicago, but we have pretty good times. Not as good, though, since Jim Kendall got killed. When he was alive, him and Hod Meyers used to keep this town in an uproar. I bet they was more laughin' done here than any town its size in America[1].

Jim was comical, and Hod was pretty near a match for him[2]. Since Jim's gone, Hod tries to hold his end up just the same as ever[3], but it's tough goin' when you ain't got nobody to kind of work with.

They used to be plenty fun in here Saturdays. This place is jampacked Saturdays, from four o'clock on. Jim and Hod would show up right after their supper round six o'clock. Jim would set himself down in that big chair, nearest the blue spittoon. Whoever had been settin' in that chair, why they'd get up when Jim come in and at" it to him.

You'd of thought it was a reserved seat like they have sometimes in a theatre. Hod would generally always stand or walk up and down or some Saturdays, of course, he'd be settin' in this chair part of the time, gettin' a haircut.

Well, Jim would set there a w'ile without opening his mouth only to spit, and then finally he'd say to me, "Whitey,"—my right name, that is, my right first name, is Dick, but everybody round here calls me Whitey—Jim would say, "Whitey, your nose looks like a rosebud tonight. You must of been drinkin' some of your aw de cologne."

So I'd say, "No, Jim, but you look like you'd been drinkin' something of that kind or somethin' worse."

Jim would have to laugh at that, but then he'd speak up and say, "No, I ain't had nothin' to drink, but that ain't sayin' I wouldn't like somethin'. I wouldn't even mind if it was wood alcohol."

Then Hod Meyers would say, "Neither would your wife." That would set everybody to laughin' because Jim and his wife wasn't on very good terms[4]. She'd of divorced him only they wasn't no chance to get alimony and she didn't have no way to take care of herself and the kids. She couldn't never understand Jim. He was kind of rough, but a good fella[5] at heart.

Jim and Hod had all kinds of sport with[6] Milt Sheppard. I don't suppose you've seen Milt. Well, he's got an Adam's apple[7] that looks more like a mush-melon. So I'd be shavin' Milt and when I'd start to shave down here on his neck, Hod would holler, "Hey, Whitey, wait a minute! Before you cut into it, let's make up a pool and see who can guess closest to the number of seeds."

And Jim would say, "If Milt hadn't of been so hoggish, he'd of ordered a half a cantaloupe instead of a whole one and it might not of stuck in his throat."

All the boys would roar at this and Milt himself would force a smile, though the joke was on him. Jim certainly was a card!

---

1 they was more laughin' done here than any town its size in America: 他们给这座城市带来了比美国任何一座与之规模相同的城市更多的笑声。
2 a match for him: 可与之相匹敌；跟他差不多
3 hold his end up just the same as ever: 想跟以前那样兴头不减
4 on very good terms: 关系很好
5 fella: (俚语)小伙子
6 all kinds of sport with: 跟……开各种玩笑
7 Adam's apple: 喉结

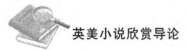

There's his shavin' mug, setting on the shelf, right next to Charley Vail's. "Charles M. Vail." That's the druggist. He comes in regular for his shave, three times a week. And Jim's is the cup next to Charley's. "dames H. Kendall." Jim won't need no shavin' mug no more, but I'll leave it there just the same for old time's sake. Jim certainly was a character[1]!

Years ago, Jim used to travel for a canned goods concern over in Carterville. They sold canned goods. Jim had the whole northern half of the State and was on the road five days out of every week. He'd drop in here Saturdays and tell his experiences for that week. It was rich.

I guess he paid more attention to playin' jokes than makin' sales. Finally the concern[2] let him out and he come right home here and told everybody he'd been fired instead of sayin' he'd resigned like most fellas would of.

It was a Saturday and the shop was full and Jim got up out of that chair and says, "Gentlemen, I got an important announcement to make. I been fired from my job."

Well, they asked him if he was in earnest[3] and he said he was and nobody could think of nothin' to say till Jim finally broke the ice[4] himself. He says, "I been sellin' canned goods and now I'm canned goods myself.

You see, the concern he'd been workin' for was a factory that made canned goods. Over in Carterville. And now Jim said he was canned himself. He was certainly a card!

Jim had a great trick that he used to play w'ile he was travelin'. For instance, he'd be ridin' on a train and they'd come to some little town like, well, like, well, like, we'll say, like Benton. Jim would look out the train window and read the signs of the stores.

For instance, they'd be a sign, "Henry Smith, Dry Goods." Well, Jim would write down the name and the name of the town and when he got to wherever he was goin' he'd mail back a postal card to Henry Smith at Benton and not sign no name to it, but he'd write on the card, well somethin' like "Ask your wife about that book agent that spent the afternoon last week," or "Ask your Missus[5] who kept her from gettin' lonesome the last time you was in Carterville." And he'd sign the card, "A Friend."

Of course, he never knew what really come of none of these jokes, but he could picture what probably happened and that was enough.

Jim didn't work very steady after he lost his position with the Carterville people. What he did earn, coin' odd jobs round town why he spent pretty near all of it on gin, and his family might of starved if the stores hadn't of carried them along. Jim's wife tried her hand at dressmakin', but they ain't nobody goin' to get rich makin' dresses in this town.

As I say, she'd of divorced Jim, only she seen that she couldn't support herself and the kids and she was always hopin' that some day Jim would cut out his habits and give her more than two or three dollars a week.

They was a time when she would go to whoever he was workin' for and ask them to give her his

---

1 character: 怪人,与众不同的人
2 concern: 公司,企业
3 in earnest: 认真地
4 broke the ice: 打破僵局,打破沉默
5 Missus: (已婚的)……夫人

wages, but after she done this once or twice, he beat her to it by borrowin' most of his pay in advance. He told it all round town, how he had outfoxed[1] his Missus. He certainly was a caution[2]!

But he wasn't satisfied with just outwittin' her. He was sore the way she had acted, tryin' to grab off[3] his pay. And he made up his mind he'd get even[4]. Well, he waited till Evans's Circus was advertised to come to town. Then he told his wife and two kiddies that he was goin' to take them to the circus. The day of the circus, he told them he would get the tickets and meet them outside the entrance to the tent.

Well, he didn't have no intentions of bein' there or buyin' tickets or nothin'. He got full of gin and laid round Wright's poolroom all day. His wife and the kids waited and waited and of course he didn't show up. His wife didn't have a dime[5] with her, or nowhere else, I guess. So she finally had to tell the kids it was all off and they cried like they wasn't never goin' to stop.

Well, it seems, w'ile they was cryin', Doc Stair come along and he asked what was the matter, but Mrs. Kendall was stubborn and wouldn't tell him, but the kids told him and he insisted on takin' them and their mother in the show. Jim found this out afterwards and it was one reason why he had it in for Doc Stair.

Doc Stair come here about a year and a half ago. He's a mighty handsome young fella and his clothes always look like he has them made to order. He goes to Detroit two or three times a year and w'ile he's there must have a tailor take his measure and then make him a suit to order. They cost pretty near twice as much, but they fit a whole lot better than if you just bought them in a store.

For a w'ile everybody was wonderin' why a young doctor like Doc Stair should come to a town like this where we already got old Doc Gamble and Doc Foote that's both been here for years and all the practice in town was always divided between the two of them.

Then they was a story got round[6] that Doc Stair's gal had thronged him over, a gal up in the Northern Peninsula somewhere, and the reason he come here was to hide himself away and forget it. He said himself that he thought they wasn't nothin' like general practice in a place like ours to fit a man to be a good all round doctor. And that's why he'd came.

Anyways, it wasn't long before he was makin' enough to live on, though they tell me that he never dunned nobody for[7] what they owed him, and the folks here certainly has got the owin' habit, even in my business. If I had all that was comin' to me for just shaves alone, I could go to Carterville[8] and put up at[9] the Mercer[10] for a week and see a different picture every night. For instance, they's old George Purdy— but I guess I shouldn't ought to be gossipin'.

Well, last year, our coroner died, died of the flu. Ken Beatty, that was his name. He was the

---

1 outfox: 以机智胜过
2 caution: 令人好笑的人
3 grab off: 抢先获得, 捷足先登; 预支
4 get even: 报复
5 dime: (美国、加拿大的)一角硬币
6 got round: (消息)传开
7 dun ... for: 追讨, 向……催要
8 Carterville: 卡特维尔, 美国城市名
9 put up at: 投宿
10 the Mercer: the Mercer Hotel

coroner. So they had to choose another man to be coroner in his place and they picked Doc Stair. He laughed at first and said he didn't want it, but they made him take it. It ain't no job that anybody would fight for and what a man makes out of it in a year would just about buy seeds for their garden. Doc's the kind, though, that can't say no to nothin' if you keep at him long enough.

But I was goin' to tell you about a poor boy we got here in town-Paul Dickson. He fell out of a tree when he was about ten years old. Lit on his head and it done somethin' to him and he ain't never been right. No harm in him, but just silly. Jim Kendall used to call him cuckoo; that's a name Jim had for anybody that was off their head¹, only he called people's head their bean. That was another of his gags, callin' head bean and callin' crazy people cuckoo. Only poor Paul ain't crazy, but just silly.

You can imagine that Jim used to have all kinds of fun with Paul. He'd send him to the White Front Garage for a left-handed monkey wrench. Of course they ain't no such thing as a left-handed monkey wrench.

And once we had a kind of a fair here and they was a baseball game between the fats and the leans and before the game started Jim called Paul over and sent him way down to Schrader's hardware store to get a key for the pitcher's box.

They wasn't nothin' in the way of gags that Jim couldn't think up, when he put his mind to it.²

Poor Paul was always kind of suspicious of people, maybe on account of how Jim had kept foolin' him. Paul wouldn't have much to do with anybody only his own mother and Doc Stair and a girl here in town named Julie Gregg. That is, she ain't a girl no more, but pretty near thirty or over.

When Doc first come to town, Paul seemed to feel like here was a real friend and he hung round³ Doc's office most of the w'ile; the only time he wasn't there was when he'd go home to eat or sleep or when he seen Julie Gregg coin' her shoppin'.

When he looked out Doc's window and seen her, he'd run downstairs and join her and tag along with⁴ her to the different stores. The poor boy was crazy about Julie and she always treated him mighty nice and made him feel like he was welcome, though of course it wasn't nothin' but pity on her side.

Doc done all he could to improve Paul's mind and he told me once that he really thought the boy was getting better, that they was times when he was as bright and sensible as anybody else.

But I was goin' to tell you about Julie Gregg. Old man Gregg was in the lumber business, but got to drinkin' and lost the most of his money and when he died, he didn't leave nothin' but the house and just enough insurance for the girl to skimp along on.

Her mother was a kind of a half invalid and didn't hardly ever leave the house. Julie wanted to sell the place and move somewhere else after the old man died, but the mother said she was born here and would die here. It was tough on Julie as the young people round this town—well, she's too good for them.

She'd been away to school and Chicago and New York and different places and they ain't no subject she can't talk on, where you take the rest of the young folks here and you mention anything to

---

1 off their head：神经错乱的，发疯的
2 he put his mind to it：把他的心思全用在这上。
3 hung round：徘徊在……附近，在……闲呆着
4 tag along with：跟随

them outside of Gloria Swanson or Tommy Meighan and they think you're delirious. Did you see Gloria in Wages of Virtue? You missed somethin'!

Well, Doc Stair hadn't been here more than a week when he came in one day to get shaved and I recognized who he was, as he had been pointed out to me, so I told him about my old lady. She's been ailin' for a couple years and either Doc Gamble or Doc Foote, neither one, seemed to be helpin' her. So he said he would come out and see her, but if she was able to get out herself, it would be better to bring her to his office where he could make a completer examination.

So I took her to his office and w'ile I was waitin' for her in the reception room, in come Julie Gregg. When somebody comes in Doc Stair's office, they's a bell that rings in his inside office so he can tell they's somebody to see him.

So he left my old lady inside and come out to the front office and that's the first time him and Julie met and I guess it was what they call love at first sight. But it wasn't fifty-fifty. This young fella was the slickest lookin' fella she'd ever seen in this town and she went wild over him. To him she was just a young lady that wanted to see the doctor.

She'd came on about the same business I had. Her mother had been doctorin' for years with Doc Gamble and Doc Foote and with out no results. So she'd heard they was a new doc in town and decided to give him a try. He promised to call and see her mother that same day.

I said a minute ago that it was love at first sight on her part. I'm not only judgin' by how she acted afterwards but how she looked at him that first day in his office. I ain't no mind reader[1], but it was wrote all over her face that she was gone.

Now Jim Kendall, besides bein' a jokesmith[2] and a pretty good drinker, well Jim was quite a lady-killer[3]. I guess he run pretty wild durin' the time he was on the road for them Carterville people, and besides that, he'd had a couple little affairs of the heart right here in town. As I say, his wife would have divorced him, only she couldn't.

But Jim was like the majority of men, and women, too, I guess. He wanted what he couldn't get. He wanted Julie Gregg and worked his head off tryin' to land her[4]. Only he'd of said bean instead of head.

Well, Jim's habits and his jokes didn't appeal to Julie and of course he was a married man, so he didn't have no more chance than, well, than a rabbit. That's an expression of Jim's himself. When somebody didn't have no chance to get elected or somethin', Jim would always say they didn't have no more chance than a rabbit.

He didn't make no bones about[5] how he felt. Right in here, more than once, in front of the whole crowd, he said he was stuck on[6] Julie and anybody that could get her for him was welcome to his house and his wife and kids included. But she wouldn't have nothin' to do with him; wouldn't even speak to

---

1 mind reader:能看透别人心思的人
2 jokesmith:爱说笑话者
3 lady-killer:(俚语)专门勾引女子的男人,使女人倾心的男人
4 worked his head off tryin' to land her:绞尽脑汁想把她弄到手
5 make no bones about:对……毫不犹豫,对……直言不讳
6 was stuck on:迷恋于

him on the street. He finally seen he wasn't gettin' nowheres with his usual line[1] so he decided to try the rough stuff[2]. He went right up to her house one evenin' and when she opened the door he forced his way in and grabbed her. But she broke loose and before he could stop her, she run in the next room and locked the door and phoned to Joe Barnes. Joe's the marshal. Jim could hear who she was phonin' to and he beat it[3] before Joe got there.

Joe was an old friend of Julie's pa. Joe went to Jim the next day and told him what would happen if he ever done it again.

I don't know how the news of this little affair leaked out. Chances is that Joe Barnes told his wife and she told somebody else's wife and they told their husband. Anyways, it did leak out and Hod Meyers had the nerve[4] to kid Jim about it, right here in this shop. Jim didn't deny nothin' and kind of laughed it off[5] and said for us all to wait; that lots of people had tried to make a monkey out of[6] him, but he always got even.

Meanw'ile everybody in town was wise to Julie's bein' wild mad over the Doc. I don't suppose she had any idea how her face changed when him and her was together; of course she couldn't of, or she'd of kept away from him. And she didn't know that we was all noticin' how many times she made excuses to go up to his office or pass it on the other side of the street and look up in his window to see if he was there. I felt sorry for her and so did most other people.

Hod Meyers kept rubbin' it into[7] Jim about how the Doc had cut him out[8]. Jim didn't pay no attention to the kiddie' and you could see he was plannin' one of his jokes.

One trick Jim had was the knack of changin' his voice. He could make you think he was a girl talkie' and he could mimic any man's voice. To show you how good he was along this line[9], I'll tell you the joke he played on me once.

You know, in most towns of any size, when a man is dead and needs a shave, why the barber that shaves him soaks him five dollars for the job; that is, he don't soak him, but whoever ordered the shave. I just charge three dollars because personally I don't mind much shavin' a dead person. They lay a whole lot stiller than live customers. The only thing is that you don't feel like talkie' to them and you get kind of lonesome.

Well, about the coldest day we ever had here, two years ago last winter, the phone rung at the house w'ile I was home to dinner and I answered the phone and it was a woman's voice and she said she was Mrs. John Scott and her husband was dead and would I come out and shave him.

Old John had always been a good customer of mine. But they live seven miles out in the country, on the Streeter road. Still I didn't see how I could say no.

---

1 line:方式,方法
2 rough stuff:(俚语)暴力行为
3 beat it:跑掉
4 nerve:勇气,胆量
5 laughed it off:对此一笑了之
6 make a monkey out of:愚弄;戏弄
7 rubbin' it into:反复地讲
8 cut him out:击败他,比他捷足先登
9 how good he was along this line:他多么擅长于这行

So I said I would be there, but would have to come in a jitney and it might cost three or four dollars besides the price of the shave. So she, or the voice, it said that was all right, so I got Frank Abbott to drive me out to the place and when I got there, who should open the door but old John himself! He wasn't no more dead than, well, than a rabbit.

It didn't take no private detective to figure out who had played me this little joke. Nobody could of thought it up but Jim Kendall. He certainly was a card!

I tell you this incident just to show you how he could disguise his voice and make you believe it was somebody else talkie'. I'd of swore it was Mrs. Scott had called me. Anyways, some woman.

Well, Jim waited till he had Doc Stair's voice down pat[1]; then he went after revenge.

He called Julie up on a night when he knew Doc was over in Carterville. She never questioned but what it was Doc's voice. Jim said he must see her that night; he couldn't wait no longer to tell her somethin'. She was all excited and told him to come to the house. But he said he was expectin' an important long distance call and wouldn't she please forget her manners for once and come to his office. He said they couldn't nothin' hurt her and nobody would see her and he just must talk to her a little w'ile. Well, poor Julie fell for it[2].

Doc always keeps a night light in his office, so it looked to Julie like they was somebody there.

Meanw'ile Jim Kendall had went to Wright's poolroom, where they was a whole gang amusin' themselves. The most of them had drank plenty of gin, and they was a rough bunch even when sober. They was always strong for Jim's jokes and when he told them to come with him and see some fun they give up their card games and pool games[3] and followed along.

Doc's office is on the second floor. Right outside his door they's a flight of stairs leadin' to the floor above. Jim and his gang hid in the dark behind these stairs.

Well, Julie come up to Doc's door and rung the bell and they was nothin' coin'. She rung it again and she rung it seven or eight times. Then she tried the door and found it locked. Then Jim made some kind of a noise and she heard it and waited a minute, and then she says, "Is that you, Ralph?" Ralph is Doc's first name.

They was no answer and it must of came to her all of a sudden that she'd been bunked. She pretty near fell downstairs and the whole gang after her. They chased her all the way home, hollerin', "Is that you, Ralph?" and "Oh, Ralphie, dear, is that you?" Jim says he couldn't holler it himself, as he was laughin' too hard.

Poor Julie! She didn't show up here on Main Street for a long, long time afterward.

And of course Jim and his gang told everybody in town, everybody but Doc Stair. They was scared to tell him, and he might of never knowed only for Paul Dickson. The poor cuckoo, as Jim called him, he was here in the shop one night when Jim was still gloatin' yet over what he'd done to Julie. And Paul took in as much of it as he could understand and he run to Doc with the story.

It's a cinch Doc went up in the air[4] and swore he'd make Jim suffer. But it was a kind of a delicate

---

1 he had Doc Stair's voice down pat：他能模仿 Stair 医生的声音。
2 fell for it：受骗，上当
3 pool games：台球游戏
4 Doc went up in the air：医生暴跳如雷，火冒三丈

thing, because if it got out that he had beat Jim up[1], Julie was bound to hear of it and then she'd know that Doc knew and of course knowin' that he knew would make it worse for her than ever. He was goin' to do somethin', but it took a lot of figurin'.

Well, it was a couple days later when Jim was here in the shop again, and so was the cuckoo. Jim was goin' duck-shootin' the next day and had come in lookin' for Hod Meyers to go with him. I happened to know that Hod had went over to Carterville and wouldn't be home till the end of the week. So Jim said he hated to go alone and he guessed he would call it off. Then poor Paul spoke up and said if Jim would take him he would go along. Jim thought a w'ile and then he said, well, he guessed a half-wit[2] was better than nothin'.

I suppose he was plottin' to get Paul out in the boat and play some joke on him, like pushin' him in the water. Anyways, he said Paul could go. He asked him had he ever shot a duck and Paul said no, he'd never even had a gun in his hands. So Jim said he could set in the boat and watch him and if he behaved himself, he might lend him his gun for a couple of shots. They made a date to meet in the mornin' and that's the last I seen of Jim alive.

Next mornin', I hadn't been open more than ten minutes when Doc Stair come in. He looked kind of nervous. He asked me had I seen Paul Dickson. I said no, but I knew where he was, out duckshootin' with Jim Kendall. So Doc says that's what he had heard, and he couldn't understand it because Paul had told him he wouldn't never have no more to do with Jim as long as he lived.

He said Paul had told him about the joke Jim had played on Julie. He said Paul had asked him what he thought of the joke and the Doc told him that anybody that would do a thing like that ought not to be let live. I said it had been a kind of a raw thing, but Jim just couldn't resist no kind of a joke, no matter how raw. I said I thought he was all right at heart, but just bubblin' over with mischief. Doc turned and walked out.

At noon he got a phone call from old John Scott. The lake where Jim and Paul had went shootin' is on John's place. Paul had came runnin' up to the house a few minutes before and said they'd been an accident. Jim had shot a few ducks and then give the gun to Paul and told him to try his luck. Paul hadn't never handled a gun and he was nervous. He was shakin' so hard that he couldn't control the gun. He let fire and Jim sunk back in the boat, dead.

Doc Stair, bein' the coroner, jumped in Frank Abbott's flivver and rushed out to Scott's farm. Paul and old John was down on the shore of the lake. Paul had rowed the boat to shore, but they'd left the body in it, waiting for Doc to come.

Doc examined the body and said they might as well fetch it back to town. They was no use leavin' it there or callin' a jury, as it was a plain case of accidental shootin'.

Personally I wouldn't never leave a person shoot a gun in the same boat I was in unless I was sure they knew somethin' about guns. Jim was a sucker[3] to leave a new beginner have his gun, let alone a half-wit. It probably served Jim right[4], what he got. But still we miss him round here. He certainly was a card! Comb it wet or dry?

---

1 beat up: 狠揍

2 half-wit: 傻瓜，笨蛋

3 sucker: 笨蛋

4 served Jim right: Jim 是活该

Chapter Thirteen Reader-response Criticism

Understanding the Text

    Few readers may miss Lardner's irony in "Haircut": "they perceive the invitation to seek darker meanings below the innocuous surface." (Cowlishaw) In other words, few readers can overlook their activity in Lardner's achieving his rhetoric effect for readers assist the author in the completion of the text and operation of the irony.

    Readers are never passive; as Walter J. Ong has asserted, "all readers of all texts actively collate and decipher textual clues regarding the role of 'implied reader,' and decide the degree to which they will accept that proffered role."(Cowlishaw) And readers of ironic stories such as Ring Lardner's must work particularly hard.

    When readers read the story "Haircut," especially when they come to its end, they tend to feel that, just as Brooks and Warren suggest in *Understanding Fiction*, "We have the moral satisfaction of seeing the biter bit, the joker caught in the destructive consequences of a joke whose destructive nature for other people he could never have understood or cared about" and they have "a sense that brutality and evil thrive by a kind of connivance on the part of those who do not directly participate in it, a sense of the spreading ripples of complicity always around the evil act." (p.145) This response indicates readers' notion that Mendall "richly deserves his fate" and their moral involvement in approval of the extreme penalty for Jim for his practical jokes. However, if a reader's reading just stops here it may ignore the important act in the story which is more evil than Jim's jokes—Jim's "accidental death," with which Lardner attempts to fulfill a purpose of satire: social correction; and it may ignore the reader's more significant role in the fulfillment of this purpose.

    "Haircut" is told by the first-person barber-narrator Whitey. In this story, the author, more exactly the implied author, never assumes the role of the narrator, and is a separate entity from the narrator. The implied author "teaches" the reader, and for that reason occupies the highest position. The reader is invited to share the implied author's views of characters and dramatized narrator, and therefore share the implied author's values. In "Haircut," the implied author-reader coalition is at its most disdain toward the narrator and characters. Whitey, the narrator, is too stupid to see that Kendall's "jokes" aren't funny, and that Kendall's anonymous nasty postcards, cruelty to wife and children, and attempted rape of Julie Gregg are exactly evils. Whitey is also too stupid to understand what a reader understands clearly: Paul Dickson intentionally shot Kendall, and in revenge against Kendall, Doc Stair used his coroner's position to cover Paul's guilt.

    However, readers do more than share the implied author's views about the narrator and characters: They have to actively participate in the interpretation of the text by finding evidence to support alternative explanations and proving the presence of irony in this story.

    Many clues in the story suggest that the townspeople are not so delighted with Jim's jokes as the barber implies, thus rejecting the surface meaning that Kendall truly was a "card" and accept the alternate meaning that Kendall was cruel. For example, Jim has his own special chair in the barber shop, and if anyone was sitting in it, "why they'd get up when Jim came in and give it to him"; when he is

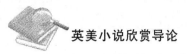

making fun of Milt Sheppard's Adam's apple, Milt would have to "force a smile"—"all this should be sufficient to indicate that Jim is not so much admired as he is feared." (May)

At the end of the story, the barber narrates that the doctor told Paul that "anybody that would do a thing like that ought not be let live." Such a clue, along with the barber's final comment "It probably served Jim right, what he got," surely indicates that the barber is not so stupid that he believes Jim's death was "a plain case of accidental shootin'." He knows that "Poor Paul" is nothing more than a pawn, who was made use of by the doctor and the town to rid themselves of a troublemaker that they hated and feared.

While readers are exploring the alternatives of interpretation, the irony of "spreading ripples of complicity always around the evil act" is produced. And thus stands out a reader "who is bright, literate, and psychologically adept, who would join the implied author in despising this narrator and this character for being so inferior by these standards."(May) Therefore, the reader becomes as morally involved in the death as the barber and the townspeople by accepting the fact that Jim was accidentally killed by the half-wit Paul.

The barber says at the end that "Jim was a sucker to leave a new beginner have his gun..." But the biggest sucker of all is the reader who, by allowing himself to be taken in by Lardner's control of the story and feeling so morally superior to the barber, becomes an accomplice to the most evil act of all. (May)

Such coalition between the implied author and the reader brings on satirical mitigation. Although characters are stupid, they become merely humorous, for the reader shares his views of them. Moreover, readers see that the implied author is a discerning, humane person attempting to kid society into improving itself. Accepting the role of the implied reader, readers assist the implied author in accomplishing this important task.

Further Reading

Reader-response Criticism

Bleich, David. *Readings and Feelings: An Introduction to Subjective Criticism.* New York: Harper, 1977.

Fish, Stanley E. "Literature in the Reader: Affective Stylistics". *New Literary History* 2(1970): 123—61.

Iser, Wolfgang. *The Act of Reading: A Theory of Aesthetic Response.* Baltimore: Johns Hopkins University Press, 1978.

——. *Prospecting: From Reader Response to Literary Anthropology.* Baltimore: Johns Hopkins University Press, 1989.

Haircut

Cowlishaw, Brian T. "The Reader's Role in Ring Lardner's Rhetoric". *Studies in Short Fiction* 31.2 (Spring 1994): 207—16.

Kasten, Margaret Cotton. "The Satire of Ring Lardner". *The English Journal* 36.4 (Apr., 1947): 192—95.

May, Charles E. "Lardner's 'Haircut'". *Explicator* 31.9 (May 1973): Item #69.

Webb, Howard W. Jr. "The Meaning of Ring Lardner's Fiction: A Re-Evaluation". *American Literature* 31.4 (Jan., 1960):434—45.

Chapter Fourteen
Cultural Studies

Cultural studies, appearing as an alternative approach to the literary interpretation in the 1960s, is widely influenced by anthropology, sociology, psychology, postmodernism, and feminism, and contains the elements of Marxism, structuralism and poststructuralism, gender studies, race and ethnic studies, film theory, urban studies, public policy, and popular culture studies. Cultural studies, therefore, is not so much a discrete approach as a set of practices. As Patrick Brantlinger has pointed out, cultural studies is not "a tightly coherent, unified movement with a fixed agenda," but a "loosely coherent group of tendencies, issues, and questions." (ix) However, cultural studies approaches generally share four goals: (1) Cultural studies goes beyond the borders of a particular discipline such as literary criticism or history. A cultural studies scholar often examines the cultural phenomenon of a text and draws conclusions about the changes in the textual phenomenon over time. (2) Cultural studies is politically involved. Cultural critics tend to question inequalities within social power structures and seek to discover models for restructuring relationships among dominant and "minority" discourses. (3) Cultural studies refuses the separation of "high" and "low" or elite and popular culture. Instead of "determining which are the 'best' works produced, cultural critics describe what is produced and how various productions relate to one another" and "aim to reveal the political and economic reasons why a certain cultural product is more valued at certain times than others." (4) "Cultural studies analyzes not only the cultural work, but also the means of production." "These studies help us recognize that literature does not occur in a space separate from other concerns of our lives." (Guerin, pp. 277—280)

Marxism, the new historicism, multiculturalism, postmodernism, popular culture, and postcolonialism are connected with cultural studies. Here we just introduce two branches of cultural studies: new historicism and postcolonialism.

New Historicism

New historicism appeared as a historical approach to textual interpretation in the 1970s and early 1980s in America. By challenging the long-held belief of the old historicism "that historians can articulate a unified and internally consistent worldview of any given people, country, or time period and can reconstruct an accurate and objective description of any historical event," new historicists declare that "all history is subjective, written by people whose personal biases affect their interpretation of the past," and that history "can never provide us with the truth or give us a totally accurate description of past events or the worldview of a group of people."(Bressler, p. 238) Disclaiming the assumption of the old historicism that history is autonomous, new historicists assert that history is only one of many equally important discourses such as sociology, economics, and politics. Rejecting the old historical assumption that a text simply reflects its historical context and that history serves as useful background information for literary analysis, new historicists redefine the definition of a text and of history, and the relationship between a text and history, and assert that a text—a work of art—is like any other social discourse that interacts with its culture to produce meaning, and any interpretation of a text is invalid if we do not consider its relationship to the various discourses that helped shape it: political, economic, social and aesthetic discourses.

New historicists declare that an aesthetic work is a social production, and a text's meaning lies in the cultural system composed of the interlocking discourses of the author, text, and reader. To unlock textual meaning, critics must investigate three areas of concern: the life of the author, the social rules and codes found within a text, and a reflection of a work's historical situation in the text. (Bressler, p.246) Certainly, during this process of textual analysis critics must not forget to question their own assumptions and methods, for they too are shaped by the culture where they live.

What is unique of new historicism is that in their interpretive process, new historicists avoid making generalizations and often focus on the seemingly insignificant details and happenings, and manifestations of culture usually ignored by most historians and literary critics. In this way new historicists would demonstrate the intricate relationship "that exists among all discourses and show how narrative discourses such as history, literature, and other social productions interact, define, and are in turn shaped by their culture." (Bressler, p.246) Thus, "there is not one single voice but many to be heard in interpreting texts and culture: our own voices, those of others, and those of the past, the present and the future." (Bressler, p. 247)

When we apply the principles of new historicism to the interpretation of the pressures that destroy Mrs. Mallard in "The Story of an Hour," we might first examine the public attitudes towards women contemporary to this story as well as documents of medical diagnoses to explore "how the same forces—expectations about how women are supposed to feel, think, and behave—shape different kinds of texts and how these texts influence each other." (Meyer, p. 2092) Besides, we may consider both readers of Mrs. Mallard's contemporaries and readers in the twenty-first century who might differ much in their attitude towards her: the former might not be aware of how selfish and self-destructive she is, and the latter might miss the pervasive pressures embedded in her marriage and social surroundings. This awareness makes it more understandable when the doctors make the diagnosis that she died of her joy for her husband's not being dead.

Postcolonalism

Postcolonialism refers to an approach to literary analysis that concerns itself particularly with literature written in English by writers from countries and cultures that at one time were controlled by colonizing powers—such as Indian writers during or after British colonial rule. It usually concentrates on writings from colonized cultures in Australia, New Zealand, Africa, South America, and other places and societies that were once dominated by male European cultural, political, and philosophical tradition. And the term also refers to the analysis of literary works written about colonial cultures by writers from the colonizing countries. Postcolonial literature and theoretical concerns can date back to the 1950s. The

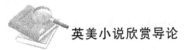

terms post-colonial and postcolonialism, however, first appeared in the late 1980s in many scholarly journal articles. By the mid-1990s, the terms had become firmly established in scholarly writing. Postcolonial theory came into being in the cultural clashes between the colonized and the colonizer.

Post-colonial theory critics are a heterogeneous group of critics with different backgrounds: the first group of critics come from a European and American cultural, literary, and scholarly background, the second group were raised in the Third World cultures but reside, study and write in the West, and the third group live and work in the Third World. So at the center of this theory exists an inherent tension. (Bressler, p. 267)

Like the postcolonial critics with diverse backgrounds, the issues and subjects postcolonialism concerns itself with are diverse, including "universality, ethnicity, feminism, language, education, history, place, and production." (Bressler, p. 266) Although these topics appear diverse, all of them point at one of postcolonialism's major concerns: highlighting the struggle that occurs when one culture is dominated by another. For this postcolonialist critics emphatically state "that European colonialism did occur, that the British Empire was at the center of this colonialism, that the conquerors not only dominated the physical land but also the hegemony or ideology of the colonized people, and that the effects of these colonizations are many and are still being felt today."(Bressler, pp.266—267) Then they point out that for the colonized, to be colonized is to be removed from history because in its interaction with the conquering culture, the colonized or indigenous culture is forced to go underground or to be obliterated. Therefore, a post-colonial author always asks of himself or herself three questions: "Who am I? How did I develop into the person that I am? To what country or countries or to what cultures am I forever linked?" (Bressler, p. 267) By asking these questions the author is actually revealing the fact that he or she is both an individual and a social construct created and shaped by the dominant culture, a new culture which was imposed upon the writer by the conquerors and made him or her lose his or her historical roots and therefore lose his or her identity. Therefore, the reading and writing of postcolonial literature in which the colonized's frustrations, their direct and personal cultural clashes with the conquering culture, their responses to the changes in language and culture, and their fears, hopes, and dreams about the future and their own identities may be political and ideological, and painful, disturbing, and enlightening as well. Thus, a message will be sent to the conquerors, telling them what they did wrong and how their hegemony damaged and suppressed the ideologies of those who were conquered, and voices can be heard that suggest the colonized's challenge of the conquerors' hegemony and misrepresentation of colonized cultures.

Joseph Conrad (1857—1924)

Joseph Conrad was born in Poland to an aristocratic family. His father, an aristocrat without lands, just devoted himself to literary and political activities, wrote a variety of plays and social satires, and translated Shakespeare into Polish. As a boy, the young Joseph read Polish and French versions of English novels with his father. In 1862 his family was sent to exile in Russia because his father worked for the Polish independence. By 1869 Conrad's both parents had died of tuberculosis, and he was sent to

Switzerland to live with his maternal uncle Tadeusz Bobrowski, who was to be a continuing influence on his life. In the mid-1870s he joined the French merchant marine as an apprentice, and made between 1875 and 1878 three voyages to the West Indies. It was at the age of twenty that he left the Continent and continued his career at the seas in the British merchant navy for 16 years. This was a turning point in his life. Conrad rose through the ranks from common seaman to first mate, and by 1886 he obtained his master mariner's certificate, commanding his own ship, *Otago*. In the same year he was given British citizenship.

Conrad sailed to many parts of the world, including Australia, various ports of the Indian Ocean, Borneo, the Malay states, South America, and the South Pacific Island. In 1890 he made a voyage up the Congo River, which provided the material for his novella *Heart of Darkness*. He then began writing seriously in the English language. In 1895 his first novel *Almayer's Folly* was published and he ended his sea life and devoted himself entirely to literature. His course was set for fame.

The major productive phase of Conrad's career spanned from 1897 to 1911, during which period of time he wrote *The Nigger of the Narcissus* (1897), *Youth* (1902), *Heart of Darkness* (1902), *Lord Jim* (1900), *Nostromo* (1904), *The Secret Agent* (1907), and *Under Western Eyes* (1911), among other works. Although Conrad was prolific, his financial situation wasn't secure until the publication of *Chance* in 1914. *The Nigger of the Narcissus* was a complex story of a storm off the Cape of Good Hope and of an enigmatic black sailor. *Youth* recorded Conrad's experiences on the sailing-ship *Palestine*. *Lord Jim,* narrated by Charlie Marlow, told about the fall of a young sailor and his redemption. *Nostromo* was an imaginative novel which again explored man's vulnerability and corruptibility. *The Secret Agent,* dedicated to H.G. Wells, took a bleak view of prophets of destruction and utopians.

In the last years of his life, Conrad suffered from rheumatism. He died of a heart attack on August 3, 1924, and was buried in Canterbury. Conrad's literary work influenced a long list of writers, including T. S. Eliot, Graham Greene, Virginia Woolf, Thomas Mann, Andre Gide, Ernest Hemingway, F. Scott Fitzgerald, William Faulkner, Marcel Proust, André Malraux, Louis-Ferdiand Céline and Jean-Paul Sartre.

Heart of Darkness, widely regarded as a significant work of English literature, was partly based on Conrad's experience of working as a captain of a steamboat on the Congo River. The novella was written in 1899 and published in 1902 in *Youth: A Narrative with Two Other Stories.* It is actually a story within a story, or frame narrative, one in which an unnamed narrator recounts Charles Marlow's depiction of his trip into Africa, and exposes the myth behind colonization.

Text

Heart of Darkness

I

The *Nellie*[1], a cruising yawl, swung to her anchor without a flutter of the sails, and was at rest. The flood had made, the wind was nearly calm, and being bound down the river[2], the only thing for it was to come to and wait for the turn of the tide.

The sea-reach[3] of the Thames[4] stretched before us like the beginning of an interminable waterway. In the offing[5] the sea and the sky were welded together without a joint, and in the luminous space the tanned sails of the barges drifting up with the tide seemed to stand still in red clusters of canvas sharply peaked, with gleams of varnished sprits. A haze rested on the low shores that ran out to sea in vanishing flatness[6]. The air was dark above Gravesend[7], and farther back still seemed condensed into a mournful gloom, brooding motionless over the biggest, and the greatest, town on earth.

The Director of Companies[8] was our captain and our host. We four affectionately watched his back as he stood in the bows looking to seaward. On the whole river there was nothing that looked half so nautical. He resembled a pilot, which to a seaman is trustworthiness personified. It was difficult to realize his work was not out there in the luminous estuary, but behind him, within the brooding gloom.

Between us there was, as I have already said somewhere, the bond of the sea. Besides holding our hearts together through long periods of separation, it had the effect of making us tolerant of each other's yarns—and even convictions. The Lawyer—the best of old fellows—had, because of his many years and many virtues, the only cushion on deck, and was lying on the only rug. The Accountant had brought out already a box of dominoes[9], and was toying architecturally with the bones. Marlow sat cross-legged right aft, leaning against the mizzen-mast[10]. He had sunken cheeks, a yellow complexion, a straight back, an ascetic aspect[11], and, with his arms dropped, the palms of hands outwards, resembled an idol. The Director, satisfied the anchor had good hold, made his way aft and sat down amongst us. We exchanged a few words lazily. Afterwards there was silence on board the yacht. For some reason or other we did not begin that game of dominoes. We felt meditative, and fit for nothing but placid staring. The day was

---

1 The *Nellie*:"奈利号"船
2 being bound down the river:正沿江而下
3 sea-reach:入海口
4 the Thames:泰晤士河
5 In the offing:在远处
6 in vanishing flatness:在一望无际的河岸低地
7 Gravesend:格雷夫森德,英国肯特西南,泰晤士河南岸的一个城镇、港口
8 Director of Companies:公司经理
9 a box of dominoes:一副多米诺骨牌
10 mizzen-mast:后桅
11 an ascetic aspect:样子显得很严肃

ending in a serenity of still and exquisite brilliance[1]. The water shone pacifically; the sky, without a speck, was a benign immensity of unstained light[2]; the very mist on the Essex[3] marsh was like a gauzy and radiant fabric[4], hung from the wooded rises inland, and draping the low shores in diaphanous folds. Only the gloom to the west, brooding over the upper reaches, became more sombre every minute, as if angered by the approach of the sun.

And at last, in its curved and imperceptible fall, the sun sank low, and from glowing white changed to a dull red without rays and without heat, as if about to go out suddenly, stricken to death by the touch of that gloom brooding over a crowd of men.

Forthwith[5] a change came over the waters, and the serenity became less brilliant but more profound. The old river in its broad reach[6] rested unruffled at the decline of day[7], after ages of good service done to the race that peopled its banks, spread out in the tranquil dignity of a waterway leading to the uttermost ends of the earth. We looked at the venerable stream not in the vivid flush of a short day that comes and departs for ever, but in the august light of abiding memories[8]. And indeed nothing is easier for a man who has, as the phrase goes, "followed the sea" with reverence and affection, than to evoke the great spirit of the past upon the lower reaches of the Thames. The tidal current runs to and fro in its unceasing service, crowded with memories of men and ships it had borne to the rest of home or to the battles of the sea. It had known and served all the men of whom the nation is proud, from Sir Francis Drake[9] to Sir John Franklin[10], knights all, titled and untitled—the great knights-errant of the sea. It had borne all the ships whose names are like jewels flashing in the night of time, from the *Golden Hind*[11] returning with her rotund flanks full of treasure, to be visited by the Queen's Highness[12] and thus pass out of the gigantic tale, to the *Erebus*[13] and *Terror*[14], bound on other conquests—and that never returned. It had known the ships and the men. They had sailed from Deptford[15], from Greenwich[16], from Erith[17]—the adventurers and the settlers; kings' ships and the ships of men on "Change"; captains, admirals, the dark

---

1 The day was ending in a serenity of still and exquisite brilliance：这一天即将在宁静、祥和、瑰丽中结束。
2 a benign immensity of unstained light：纤尘不染，亮丽炫目
3 the Essex：艾塞克斯，英格兰东南部的一个郡
4 like a gauzy and radiant fabric：像一缕光芒四射的薄纱
5 forthwith：霎时间，立刻
6 in its broad reach：在宽阔的河道里
7 at the decline of day：一天行将结束时
8 in the august light of abiding memories：永久记忆中庄严的光辉
9 Sir Francis Drake：弗朗西斯·德雷克爵士。16 世纪英国著名探险家和航海家，据知他是在麦哲伦之后第二位完成环球航海的探险家，并于 1587 年指挥"金鹿号"攻击加的斯，挫败了西班牙的无敌舰队。
10 Sir John Franklin：约翰·富兰克林爵士。19 世纪英国船长及北极探险家，在搜寻西北航道之旅中失踪，他和其他队员的下落在其后十多年间成谜。
11 the *Golden Hind*：金鹿号，英国著名的大型帆船，曾周游世界，船长为弗朗西斯·德雷克爵士。
12 the Queen's Highness：女王陛下
13 *Erebus*："瑞巴斯号"船
14 *Terror*："恐怖号"船
15 Deptford：德普特福特，英国南部地区泰晤士河南岸的一小镇
16 Greenwich：格林威治，位于英国伦敦东南部，为本初子午线所经之地，原设有英国皇家格林威治天文台。
17 Erith：艾瑞斯，位于伦敦东南部泰晤士河畔

"interlopers"[1] of the Eastern trade[2], and the commissioned "generals" of East India[3] fleets. Hunters for gold or pursuers of fame, they all had gone out on that stream, bearing the sword, and often the torch, messengers of the might within the land, bearers of a spark from the sacred fire. What greatness had not floated on the ebb of that river into the mystery of an unknown earth! The dreams of men, the seed of commonwealths, the germs of empires.

The sun set; the dusk fell on the stream, and lights began to appear along the shore. The Chapman light-house, a three-legged thing erect on a mud-flat, shone strongly. Lights of ships moved in the fairway—a great stir of lights[4] going up and going down. And farther west on the upper reaches the place of the monstrous town was still marked ominously on the sky, a brooding gloom in sunshine, a lurid glare under the stars.

"And this also," said Marlow suddenly, "has been one of the dark places of the earth."

He was the only man of us who still "followed the sea." The worst that could be said of him was that he did not represent his class. He was a seaman, but he was a wanderer, too, while most seamen lead, if one may so express it, a sedentary life. Their minds are of the stay-at-home order, and their home is always with them—the ship; and so is their country—the sea. One ship is very much like another, and the sea is always the same. In the immutability of their surroundings[5] the foreign shores, the foreign faces, the changing immensity of life, glide past, veiled not by a sense of mystery but by a slightly disdainful ignorance; for there is nothing mysterious to a seaman unless it be the sea itself, which is the mistress of his existence and as inscrutable as Destiny[6]. For the rest, after his hours of work, a casual stroll or a casual spree on shore suffices to unfold for him the secret of a whole continent, and generally he finds the secret not worth knowing. The yarns of seamen have a direct simplicity, the whole meaning of which lies within the shell of a cracked nut[7]. But Marlow was not typical (if his propensity to spin yarns[8] be excepted), and to him the meaning of an episode was not inside like a kernel but outside, enveloping the tale which brought it out only as a glow brings out a haze, in the likeness of one of these misty halos that sometimes are made visible by the spectral illumination of moonshine.

His remark did not seem at all surprising. It was just like Marlow. It was accepted in silence. No one took the trouble to grunt even; and presently he said, very slow:

"I was thinking of very old times, when the Romans[9] first came here, nineteen hundred years ago—the other day... Light came out of this river since—you say Knights[10]? Yes; but it is like a running blaze on a plain, like a flash of lightning in the clouds. We live in the flicker—may it last as long as the old earth keeps rolling! But darkness was here yesterday. Imagine the feelings of a commander of a fine—

---

1 the dark "interlopers":浑水摸鱼的神秘"黑手"
2 the Eastern trade:东方贸易公司
3 East India:东印度公司
4 a great stir of lights:一大片闪烁的灯光
5 In the immutability of their surroundings:在他们永久不变的环境中
6 Destiny:命运之神
7 the shell of a cracked nut:被砸开的坚果壳,意指"直截了当"
8 his propensity to spin yarns:讲故事的习惯
9 the Romans:古罗马人
10 Knights:(欧洲中世纪的)骑士,武士

what d'ye call 'em?¹—trireme in the Mediterranean², ordered suddenly to the north; run overland across the Gauls³ in a hurry; put in charge of one of these craft the legionaries—a wonderful lot of handy men they must have been, too—used to build, apparently by the hundred, in a month or two, if we may believe what we read. Imagine him here—the very end of the world, a sea the colour of lead, a sky the colour of smoke, a kind of ship about as rigid as a concertina—and going up this river with stores, or orders, or what you like. Sand-banks, marshes, forests, savages,—precious little to eat fit for a civilized man, nothing but Thames water to drink. No Falernian wine⁴ here, no going ashore. Here and there a military camp lost in a wilderness, like a needle in a bundle of hay—cold, fog, tempests, disease, exile, and death—death skulking in the air, in the water, in the bush. They must have been dying like flies⁵ here. Oh, yes—he did it. Did it very well, too, no doubt, and without thinking much about it either, except afterwards to brag of what he had gone through in his time, perhaps. They were men enough to face the darkness. And perhaps he was cheered by keeping his eye on a chance of promotion to the fleet at Ravenna⁶ by and by, if he had good friends in Rome and survived the awful climate. Or think of a decent young citizen in a toga—perhaps too much dice, you know—coming out here in the train of⁷ some prefect, or tax-gatherer, or trader even, to mend his fortunes. Land in a swamp, march through the woods, and in some inland post feel the savagery, the utter savagery, had closed round him—all that mysterious life of the wilderness that stirs in the forest, in the jungles, in the hearts of wild men. There's no initiation either into such mysteries. He has to live in the midst of the incomprehensible, which is also detestable. And it has a fascination, too, that goes to work upon him. The fascination of the abomination—you know, imagine the growing regrets, the longing to escape, the powerless disgust, the surrender, the hate."

He paused.

"Mind," he began again, lifting one arm from the elbow, the palm of the hand outwards, so that, with his legs folded before him, he had the pose of a Buddha preaching in European clothes and without a lotus-flower—"Mind, none of us would feel exactly like this. What saves us is efficiency—the devotion to efficiency. But these chaps were not much account, really. They were no colonists; their administration was merely a squeeze, and nothing more, I suspect. They were conquerors, and for that you want only brute force—nothing to boast of, when you have it, since your strength is just an accident arising from the weakness of others. They grabbed what they could get for the sake of what was to be got. It was just robbery with violence, aggravated murder on a great scale, and men going at it blind—as is very proper for those who tackle a darkness. The conquest of the earth, which mostly means the taking it away from those who have a different complexion or slightly flatter noses than ourselves, is not a pretty thing when you look into it too much. What redeems it is the idea only. An idea at the back of it; not a sentimental pretence but an idea; and an unselfish belief in the idea—something you can set up, and bow down before, and offer a sacrifice to..."

---

1 what d'ye call 'em?: What would you call them? 你们叫他们什么来着？
2 the Mediterranean: 地中海
3 Gauls: 高卢, 欧洲西部一地区, 指现今西欧的法国、比利时、意大利北部、荷兰南部、瑞士西部和德国莱茵河西岸的一带。
4 Falernian wine: 法勒里酒, 罗马帝国时代坎伯尼亚所产的一种白葡萄酒
5 die like flies: 大批死亡
6 Ravenna: 拉文纳, 意大利东北部港市
7 in the train of: 跟着

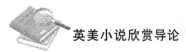

He broke off. Flames glided in the river, small green flames, red flames, white flames, pursuing, overtaking, joining, crossing each other—then separating slowly or hastily. The traffic of the great city went on in the deepening night upon the sleepless river. We looked on, waiting patiently—there was nothing else to do till the end of the flood; but it was only after a long silence, when he said, in a hesitating voice, "I suppose you fellows remember I did once turn fresh-water sailor for a bit," that we knew we were fated, before the ebb began to run, to hear about one of Marlow's inconclusive experiences.

"I don't want to bother you much with what happened to me personally," he began, showing in this remark the weakness of many tellers of tales who seem so often unaware of what their audience would like best to hear; "yet to understand the effect of it on me you ought to know how I got out there, what I saw, how I went up that river to the place where I first met the poor chap. It was the farthest point of navigation and the culminating point of my experience. It seemed somehow to throw a kind of light on everything about me—and into my thoughts. It was sombre enough, too—and pitiful—not extraordinary in any way—not very clear either. No, not very clear. And yet it seemed to throw a kind of light.

"I had then, as you remember, just returned to London after a lot of Indian Ocean, Pacific, China Seas—a regular dose of the East[1]—six years or so, and I was loafing about, hindering you fellows in your work and invading your homes, just as though I had got a heavenly mission to civilize you. It was very fine for a time, but after a bit I did get tired of resting. Then I began to look for a ship—I should think the hardest work on earth. But the ships wouldn't even look at me. And I got tired of that game, too.

"Now when I was a little chap I had a passion for maps. I would look for hours at South America, or Africa, or Australia, and lose myself in all the glories of exploration. At that time there were many blank spaces on the earth, and when I saw one that looked particularly inviting[2] on a map (but they all look that) I would put my finger on it and say, 'When I grow up I will go there.' The North Pole was one of these places, I remember. Well, I haven't been there yet, and shall not try now. The glamour's off. Other places were scattered about the hemispheres. I have been in some of them, and... well, we won't talk about that. But there was one yet—the biggest, the most blank, so to speak—that I had a hankering after.

"True, by this time it was not a blank space any more. It had got filled since my boyhood with rivers and lakes and names. It had ceased to be a blank space of delightful mystery—a white patch for a boy to dream gloriously over. It had become a place of darkness. But there was in it one river especially, a mighty big river, that you could see on the map, resembling an immense snake uncoiled, with its head in the sea, its body at rest curving afar over a vast country, and its tail lost in the depths of the land. And as I looked at the map of it in a shop-window, it fascinated me as a snake would a bird—a silly little bird. Then I remembered there was a big concern, a Company for trade on that river. Dash it all[3]! I thought to myself, they can't trade without using some kind of craft on that lot of fresh water—steamboats! Why shouldn't I try to get charge of one? I went on along Fleet Street[4], but could not shake off the idea. The snake had charmed me.

---

1 a regular dose of the East: 一次去东方一带的旅行
2 inviting: 引人动心的, 诱人的
3 Dash it all: (俚语)他妈的!
4 Fleet Street: 舰队街, 伦敦中部的一条街, 为英国新闻和出版业中心。

"You understand it was a continental[1] concern, that trading society; but I have a lot of relations living on the continent, because it's cheap and not so nasty as it looks, they say.

"I am sorry to own I began to worry them. This was already a fresh departure[2] for me. I was not used to get things that way, you know. I always went my own road and on my own legs where I had a mind to go. I wouldn't have believed it of myself; but, then—you see—I felt somehow I must get there by hook or by crook[3]. So I worried them. The men said 'My dear fellow,' and did nothing. Then—would you believe it?—I tried the women. I, Charlie Marlow, set the women to work—to get a job. Heavens! Well, you see, the notion drove me. I had an aunt, a dear enthusiastic soul. She wrote: 'It will be delightful. I am ready to do anything, anything for you. It is a glorious idea. I know the wife of a very high personage in the administration, and also a man who has lots of influence with,' etc., etc. She was determined to make no end of fuss to get me appointed skipper of a river steamboat, if such was my fancy.

"I got my appointment—of course; and I got it very quick. It appears the company had received news that one of their captains had been killed in a scuffle with the natives. This was my chance, and it made me the more anxious to go. It was only months and months afterwards, when I made the attempt to recover what was left of the body, that I heard the original quarrel arose from a misunderstanding about some hens. Yes, two black hens. Fresleven[4]—that was the fellow's name, a Dane[5]—thought himself wronged somehow in the bargain, so he went ashore and started to hammer the chief of the village with a stick. Oh, it didn't surprise me in the least to hear this, and at the same time to be told that Fresleven was the gentlest, quietest creature that ever walked on two legs. No doubt he was; but he had been a couple of years already out there engaged in the noble cause, you know, and he probably felt the need at last of asserting his self-respect in some way. Therefore he whacked the old nigger mercilessly, while a big crowd of his people watched him, thunderstruck[6], till some man—I was told the chief's son—in desperation at hearing the old chap yell, made a tentative jab with a spear at the white man—and of course it went quite easy between the shoulder-blades. Then the whole population cleared into the forest, expecting all kinds of calamities to happen, while, on the other hand, the steamer Fresleven commanded left also in a bad panic, in charge of the engineer, I believe. Afterwards nobody seemed to trouble much about Fresleven's remains[7], till I got out and stepped into his shoes[8]. I couldn't let it rest, though; but when an opportunity offered at last to meet my predecessor, the grass growing through his ribs was tall enough to hide his bones. They were all there. The supernatural being had not been touched after he fell. And the village was deserted, the huts gaped black, rotting, all askew[9] within the fallen enclosures. A calamity had come to it, sure enough. The people had vanished. Mad terror had scattered them, men,

---

1 continental：欧洲大陆的
2 a fresh departure：一次新的转变
3 by hook or by crook：不择手段地，千方百计地
4 Fresleven：弗莱斯列文，马洛的前任
5 Dane：丹麦人
6 thunderstruck：大吃一惊；惊呆了
7 remains：尸体
8 stepped into his shoes：接替他的职位
9 all askew：全部东倒西歪

women, and children, through the bush, and they had never returned. What became of the hens I don't know either. I should think the cause of progress got them, anyhow. However, through this glorious affair I got my appointment, before I had fairly begun to hope for it.

"I flew around like mad to get ready, and before forty-eight hours I was crossing the Channel[1] to show myself to my employers, and sign the contract. In a very few hours I arrived in a city[2] that always makes me think of a whited sepulchre[3]. Prejudice no doubt. I had no difficulty in finding the Company's offices. It was the biggest thing in the town, and everybody I met was full of it. They were going to run an over-sea empire, and make no end of coin[4] by trade.

"A narrow and deserted street in deep shadow, high houses, innumerable windows with venetian blinds[5], a dead silence, grass sprouting right and left, immense double doors standing ponderously ajar[6]. I slipped through one of these cracks, went up a swept and ungarnished staircase, as arid as a desert, and opened the first door I came to. Two women, one fat and the other slim, sat on straw-bottomed chairs, knitting black wool. The slim one got up and walked straight at me—still knitting with downcast eyes—and only just as I began to think of getting out of her way, as you would for a somnambulist[7], stood still, and looked up. Her dress was as plain as an umbrella-cover, and she turned round without a word and preceded me into a waiting-room. I gave my name, and looked about. Deal table in the middle, plain chairs all round the walls, on one end a large shining map, marked with all the colours of a rainbow. There was a vast amount of red—good to see at any time, because one knows that some real work is done in there, a deuce of a lot of blue, a little green, smears of orange, and, on the East Coast, a purple patch, to show where the jolly pioneers of progress drink the jolly lager-beer. However, I wasn't going into any of these. I was going into the yellow[8]. Dead in the centre[9]. And the river was there—fascinating deadly—like a snake. Ough! A door opened, a white-haired secretarial head, but wearing a compassionate expression, appeared, and a skinny forefinger beckoned me into the sanctuary. Its light was dim, and a heavy writing-desk squatted in the middle. From behind that structure came out an impression of pale plumpness in a frock-coat. The great man himself. He was five feet six, I should judge, and had his grip on the handle-end of[10] ever so many millions. He shook hands, I fancy, murmured vaguely, was satisfied with my French. *Bon voyage*[11].

"In about forty-five seconds I found myself again in the waiting-room with the compassionate secretary, who, full of desolation and sympathy, made me sign some document. I believe I undertook amongst other things not to disclose any trade secrets. Well, I am not going to.

---

1 the Channel：此处指英吉利海峡
2 city：此处指比利时的布鲁塞尔
3 a whited sepulchre：语出《圣经·马太福音》，意为"伪君子"，"伪善者"或"假道学"
4 make no end of coin：赚数不清的钱
5 venetian blinds：软百叶窗
6 standing ponderously ajar：死气沉沉地半开着
7 somnambulist：梦游者
8 the yellow：不同的颜色代表不同国家的殖民地。黄色代表比利时，红色代表英国，蓝色代表法国，绿色代表葡萄牙，橙色代表荷兰，紫色代表德国。
9 Dead in the centre：位于正中心
10 had his grip on the handle-end of：手里捏着
11 *Bon voyage*：〈法语〉一路平安，再见

"I began to feel slightly uneasy. You know I am not used to such ceremonies, and there was something ominous in the atmosphere. It was just as though I had been let into some conspiracy—I don't know—something not quite right; and I was glad to get out. In the outer room the two women knitted black wool feverishly. People were arriving, and the younger one was walking back and forth[1] introducing them. The old one sat on her chair. Her flat cloth slippers were propped up on a foot-warmer[2], and a cat reposed on her lap. She wore a starched white affair on her head, had a wart on one cheek, and silver-rimmed spectacles hung on the tip of her nose. She glanced at me above the glasses. The swift and indifferent placidity of that look troubled me. Two youths with foolish and cheery countenances were being piloted over, and she threw at them the same quick glance of unconcerned wisdom. She seemed to know all about them and about me, too. An eerie feeling came over me. She seemed uncanny and fateful. Often far away there I thought of these two, guarding the door of Darkness, knitting black wool as for a warm pall, one introducing, introducing continuously to the unknown, the other scrutinizing the cheery and foolish faces with unconcerned old eyes. *Ave!* [3] Old knitter of black wool. *Morituri te salutant.*[4] Not many of those she looked at ever saw her again—not half, by a long way.

"There was yet a visit to the doctor. 'A simple formality,' assured me the secretary, with an air of taking an immense part in all my sorrows. Accordingly a young chap wearing his hat over the left eyebrow, some clerk I suppose—there must have been clerks in the business, though the house was as still as a house in a city of the dead—came from somewhere up-stairs, and led me forth. He was shabby and careless, with ink stains on the sleeves of his jacket, and his cravat was large and billowy, under a chin shaped like the toe of an old boot. It was a little too early for the doctor, so I proposed a drink, and thereupon he developed a vein of joviality[5]. As we sat over our vermouths[6] he glorified the Company's business, and by and by I expressed casually my surprise at him not going out there. He became very cool and collected all at once. 'I am not such a fool as I look, quoth Plato to his disciples[7],' he said sententiously, emptied his glass with great resolution, and we rose.

"The old doctor felt my pulse, evidently thinking of something else the while. 'Good, good for there,' he mumbled, and then with a certain eagerness asked me whether I would let him measure my head. Rather surprised, I said 'Yes,' when he produced a thing like calipers and got the dimensions back and front and every way, taking notes carefully. He was an unshaven little man in a threadbare[8] coat like a gaberdine, with his feet in slippers, and I thought him a harmless fool. 'I always ask leave, in the interests of science[9], to measure the crania of those going out there,' he said. 'And when they come back, too?' I asked. 'Oh, I never see them,' he remarked; 'and, moreover, the changes take place inside, you know.' He smiled, as if at some quiet joke. 'So you are going out there. Famous. Interesting, too.' He gave me a

---

1 back and forth：来来往往地，来回地
2 a foot-warmer：脚炉
3 *Ave*：〈拉丁语〉万福，是对圣母玛利亚的专用欢呼语。
4 *Morituri te salutant*：〈拉丁语〉死神向你致敬。古罗马公开表演的格斗者向观众致意时的用语。
5 developed a vein of joviality：现出高兴的样子
6 vermouth：味美斯酒，苦艾酒
7 I am not such a fool as I look, quoth Plato to his disciples：柏拉图告诫他的弟子说："不可以吾貌丑遽以吾为笑。"quoth：〈古〉说（用于第一与第三人称的过去式）
8 threadbare：衣服破旧的
9 in the interests of science：为了促进科学的发展

searching glance, and made another note. 'Ever any madness in your family?' he asked, in a matter-of-fact tone[1]. I felt very annoyed. 'Is that question in the interests of science, too?' 'It would be,' he said, without taking notice of my irritation, 'interesting for science to watch the mental changes of individuals, on the spot, but...' 'Are you an alienist[2]?' I interrupted. 'Every doctor should be—a little,' answered that original, imperturbably. 'I have a little theory which you messieurs[3] who go out there must help me to prove. This is my share in the advantages my country shall reap from the possession of such a magnificent dependency. The mere wealth I leave to others. Pardon my questions, but you are the first Englishman coming under my observation ...' I hastened to assure him I was not in the least typical[4]. 'If I were,' said I, 'I wouldn't be talking like this with you.' 'What you say is rather profound, and probably erroneous,' he said, with a laugh. 'Avoid irritation more than exposure to the sun. Adieu[5]. How do you English say, eh? Good-bye. Ah! Good-bye. Adieu. In the tropics one must before everything keep calm.' ... He lifted a warning forefinger...'*Du calme*[6], *du calme. Adieu.*'

"One thing more remained to do—say good-bye to my excellent aunt. I found her triumphant. I had a cup of tea—the last decent cup of tea for many days—and in a room that most soothingly looked just as you would expect a lady's drawing-room to look, we had a long quiet chat by the fireside. In the course of these confidences it became quite plain to me I had been represented to the wife of the high dignitary, and goodness knows to how many more people besides, as an exceptional and gifted creature—a piece of good fortune for the Company—a man you don't get hold of every day. Good heavens! and I was going to take charge of a two-penny-half-penny river-steamboat with a penny whistle attached! It appeared, however, I was also one of the Workers, with a capital—you know. Something like an emissary of light[7], something like a lower sort of apostle[8]. There had been a lot of such rot let loose in print[9] and talk just about that time, and the excellent woman, living right in the rush of all that humbug, got carried off her feet[10]. She talked about 'weaning those ignorant millions from their horrid ways,' till, upon my word[11], she made me quite uncomfortable. I ventured to hint that the Company was run for profit.

"'You forget, dear Charlie, that the labourer is worthy of his hire,' she said, brightly. It's queer how out of touch with truth women are. They live in a world of their own, and there has never been anything like it, and never can be. It is too beautiful altogether, and if they were to set it up it would go to pieces before the first sunset. Some confounded fact we men have been living contentedly with ever since the day of creation would start up and knock the whole thing over.

"After this I got embraced, told to wear flannel, be sure to write often, and so on—and I left. In the

---

1 in a matter-of-fact tone:以一种十分严肃的口气
2 alienist:psychiatrist,精神病学家
3 messieurs:〈法语〉先生
4 not in the least typical:绝非典型
5 *adieu*:〈法语〉再见,再会
6 *du calme*:〈法语〉冷静些
7 an emissary of light:光明使者
8 apostle:使徒(指耶稣十二使徒),传道者
9 such rot let loose in print:陈词滥调
10 got carried off her feet:被弄得晕头转向,站不住脚
11 upon my word:说实在话,的确

street—I don't know why—a queer feeling came to me that I was an imposter. Odd thing that I, who used to clear out for any part of the world at twenty-four hours' notice, with less thought than most men give to the crossing of a street, had a moment—I won't say of hesitation, but of startled pause, before this commonplace affair. The best way I can explain it to you is by saying that, for a second or two, I felt as though, instead of going to the centre of a continent, I were about to set off for the centre of the earth.

"I left in a French steamer, and she called in every blamed port[1] they have out there, for, as far as I could see, the sole purpose of landing soldiers and custom-house officers. I watched the coast. Watching a coast as it slips by the ship is like thinking about an enigma. There it[2] is before you—smiling, frowning, inviting, grand, mean, insipid, or savage, and always mute with an air of whispering[3], 'Come and find out.' This one was almost featureless, as if still in the making, with an aspect of monotonous grimness. The edge of a colossal jungle, so dark-green as to be almost black, fringed with white surf, ran straight, like a ruled line, far, far away along a blue sea whose glitter was blurred by a creeping mist. The sun was fierce, the land seemed to glisten and drip with steam. Here and there greyish-whitish specks showed up clustered inside the white surf, with a flag flying above them perhaps. Settlements some centuries old, and still no bigger than pinheads on the untouched expanse of their background. We pounded along, stopped, landed soldiers; went on, landed custom-house[4] clerks to levy toll in what looked like a God-forsaken[5] wilderness, with a tin shed and a flag-pole lost in it; landed more soldiers—to take care of the custom-house clerks, presumably. Some, I heard, got drowned in the surf; but whether they did or not, nobody seemed particularly to care. They were just flung out there, and on we went. Every day the coast looked the same, as though we had not moved; but we passed various places—trading places—with names like Gran' Bassam, Little Popo[6]; names that seemed to belong to some sordid farce acted in front of a sinister back-cloth[7]. The idleness of a passenger, my isolation amongst all these men with whom I had no point of contact, the oily and languid sea, the uniform sombreness of the coast, seemed to keep me away from the truth of things, within the toil of a mournful and senseless delusion. The voice of the surf heard now and then was a positive pleasure, like the speech of a brother[8]. It was something natural, that had its reason, that had a meaning. Now and then a boat from the shore gave one a momentary contact with reality. It was paddled by black fellows. You could see from afar the white of their eyeballs glistening. They shouted, sang; their bodies streamed with perspiration; they had faces like grotesque masks—these chaps; but they had bone, muscle, a wild vitality, an intense energy of movement, that was as natural and true as the surf along their coast. They wanted no excuse for being there. They were a great comfort to look at. For a time I would feel I belonged still to a world of straightforward facts; but the feeling would not last long. Something would turn up to scare it away. Once, I remember, we came

---

1 call in every blamed port: 在每一个该死的港口都停
2 it: 指海岸
3 an air of whispering: 一副耳语的神态
4 custom-house: 海关
5 God-forsaken: 被上帝抛弃的,凄凉的
6 Gran' Bassam, Little Popo: 大巴萨姆或小波波
7 in front of a sinister back-cloth: 在一个险恶的背景前
8 brother: 教友

upon a man-of-war anchored off the coast[1]. There wasn't even a shed there, and she was shelling the bush. It appears the French had one of their wars going on thereabouts. Her ensign dropped limp like a rag; the muzzles of the long six-inch guns stuck out all over the low hull[2]; the greasy, slimy swell swung her up lazily and let her down, swaying her thin masts. In the empty immensity of earth, sky, and water, there she was, incomprehensible, firing into a continent. Pop, would go one of the six-inch guns; a small flame would dart and vanish, a little white smoke would disappear, a tiny projectile would give a feeble screech—and nothing happened. Nothing could happen. There was a touch of insanity in the proceeding[3], a sense of lugubrious drollery[4] in the sight; and it was not dissipated by somebody on board assuring me earnestly there was a camp of natives—he called them enemies!—hidden out of sight somewhere.

"We gave her[5] her letters (I heard the men in that lonely ship were dying of fever at the rate of three a day) and went on. We called at some more places with farcical names, where the merry dance of death and trade goes on in a still and earthy atmosphere as of an overheated catacomb; all along the formless coast bordered by dangerous surf, as if Nature herself had tried to ward off intruders; in and out of rivers, streams of death in life, whose banks were rotting into mud, whose waters, thickened into slime, invaded the contorted mangroves[6], that seemed to writhe at us in the extremity of an impotent despair. Nowhere did we stop long enough to get a particularized impression, but the general sense of vague and oppressive wonder grew upon me. It was like a weary pilgrimage amongst hints for nightmares.

"It was upward of thirty days before I saw the mouth of the big river. We anchored off the seat of the government. But my work would not begin till some two hundred miles farther on. So as soon as I could I made a start for a place thirty miles higher up.

"I had my passage on a little sea-going steamer. Her captain was a Swede, and knowing me for a seaman, invited me on the bridge[7]. He was a young man, lean, fair, and morose, with lanky hair and a shuffling gait[8]. As we left the miserable little wharf, he tossed his head contemptuously at the shore. 'Been living there?' he asked. I said, 'Yes'. 'Fine lot these government chaps—are they not?' he went on, speaking English with great precision and considerable bitterness. 'It is funny what some people will do for a few francs a month. I wonder what becomes of that kind when it goes up country[9]?' I said to him I expected to see that soon. 'So-o-o!' he exclaimed. He shuffled athwart, keeping one eye ahead[10] vigilantly. 'Don't be too sure,' he continued. 'The other day I took up a man who hanged himself on the road. He was a Swede, too.' 'Hanged himself! Why, in God's name[11]?' I cried. He kept on looking out watchfully. 'Who knows? The sun too much for him, or the country perhaps.'

---

1 a man-of-war anchored off the coast：一艘停靠在岸边的军舰
2 stuck out all over the low hull：从低低的船体上方突伸出来
3 in the proceeding：在行动中
4 lugubrious drollery：让人啼笑皆非的滑稽剧
5 her：指上文提到的 man-of-war
6 the contorted mangroves：一些弯曲的红树
7 the bridge：文中指驾驶台
8 shuffling gait：步态缓慢
9 country：指旷野
10 keeping one eye ahead：一只眼睛注视前方
11 in God's name：(表示惊奇)天啊

Chapter Fourteen   Cultural Studies

"At last we opened a reach. A rocky cliff appeared, mounds of turned-up earth by the shore, houses on a hill, others with iron roofs, amongst a waste of excavations, or hanging to the declivity[1]. A continuous noise of the rapids above hovered over this scene of inhabited devastation. A lot of people, mostly black and naked, moved about like ants. A jetty projected into the river. A blinding sunlight drowned all this at times in a sudden recrudescence of glare. 'There's your Company's station,' said the Swede, pointing to three wooden barrack-like structures on the rocky slope. 'I will send your things up. Four boxes did you say? So. Farewell.'

"I came upon a boiler wallowing in the grass, then found a path leading up the hill. It turned aside for the boulders, and also for an undersized railway-truck lying there on its back with its wheels in the air. One was off. The thing looked as dead as the carcass of some animal. I came upon more pieces of decaying machinery, a stack of[2] rusty rails. To the left a clump of trees made a shady spot, where dark things seemed to stir feebly. I blinked, the path was steep. A horn tooted to the right, and I saw the black people run. A heavy and dull detonation[3] shook the ground, a puff of smoke came out of the cliff, and that was all. No change appeared on the face of the rock. They were building a railway. The cliff was not in the way or anything; but this objectless blasting was all the work going on.

"A slight clinking behind me made me turn my head. Six black men advanced in a file, toiling up the path. They walked erect and slow, balancing small baskets full of earth on their heads, and the clink kept time with their footsteps. Black rags were wound round their loins, and the short ends[4] behind waggled to and fro like tails. I could see every rib, the joints of their limbs were like knots in a rope; each had an iron collar on his neck, and all were connected together with a chain whose bights swung between them, rhythmically clinking. Another report from the cliff made me think suddenly of that ship of war I had seen firing into a continent. It was the same kind of ominous voice; but these men could by no stretch of imagination[5] be called enemies. They were called criminals, and the outraged law, like the bursting shells, had come to them, an insoluble mystery from the sea. All their meagre breasts panted together, the violently dilated nostrils quivered, the eyes stared stonily uphill. They passed me within six inches, without a glance, with that complete, deathlike indifference of unhappy savages. Behind this raw matter[6] one of the reclaimed, the product of the new forces at work, strolled despondently, carrying a rifle by its middle. He had a uniform jacket with one button off, and seeing a white man on the path, hoisted his weapon to his shoulder with alacrity. This was simple prudence, white men being so much alike at a distance that he could not tell who I might be. He was speedily reassured, and with a large, white, rascally grin, and a glance at his charge[7], seemed to take me into partnership in his exalted trust. After all, I also was a part of the great cause of these high and just proceedings.

"Instead of going up, I turned and descended to the left. My idea was to let that chain-gang[8] get out of

---

1 hanging to the declivity：悬挂在半山坡上
2 a stack of：一堆
3 a heavy and dull detonation：一声沉闷的爆炸声
4 the short ends：破布头
5 by no stretch of imagination：不论你的想象力有多丰富都不能
6 raw matter：生藩
7 charge：押管的人
8 chain-gang：被铁链锁住的一帮人

sight before I climbed the hill. You know I am not particularly tender; I've had to strike and to fend off[1]. I've had to resist and to attack sometimes—that's only one way of resisting—without counting the exact cost, according to the demands of such sort of life as I had blundered into. I've seen the devil of violence, and the devil of greed, and the devil of hot desire[2]; but, by all the stars[3]! these were strong, lusty, red-eyed devils, that swayed and drove men—men, I tell you. But as I stood on this hillside, I foresaw that in the blinding sunshine of that land I would become acquainted with a flabby, pretending, weak-eyed devil of a rapacious and pitiless folly. How insidious he could be, too, I was only to find out several months later and a thousand miles farther. For a moment I stood appalled, as though by a warning. Finally I descended the hill, obliquely, towards the trees I had seen.

"I avoided a vast artificial hole somebody had been digging on the slope, the purpose of which I found it impossible to divine. It wasn't a quarry or a sandpit, anyhow. It was just a hole. It might have been connected with the philanthropic desire[4] of giving the criminals something to do. I don't know. Then I nearly fell into a very narrow ravine, almost no more than a scar in the hillside. I discovered that a lot of imported drainage-pipes for the settlement had been tumbled in there. There wasn't one that was not broken. It was a wanton smash-up[5]. At last I got under the trees. My purpose was to stroll into the shade for a moment; but no sooner within than it seemed to me I had stepped into the gloomy circle of some Inferno[6]. The rapids were near, and an uninterrupted, uniform, headlong, rushing noise filled the mournful stillness of the grove, where not a breath stirred, not a leaf moved, with a mysterious sound—as though the tearing pace of the launched earth[7] had suddenly become audible.

"Black shapes crouched, lay, sat between the trees leaning against the trunks, clinging to the earth, half coming out, half effaced within the dim light, in all the attitudes of[8] pain, abandonment, and despair. Another mine on the cliff went off[9], followed by a slight shudder of the soil under my feet. The work was going on. The work! And this was the place where some of the helpers had withdrawn to die.

"They were dying slowly—it was very clear. They were not enemies, they were not criminals, they were nothing earthly now—nothing but black shadows of disease and starvation, lying confusedly in the greenish gloom. Brought from all the recesses of the coast in all the legality of time contracts, lost in uncongenial surroundings, fed on unfamiliar food, they sickened, became inefficient, and were then allowed to crawl away and rest. These moribund shapes[10] were free as air—and nearly as thin. I began to distinguish the gleam of the eyes under the trees. Then, glancing down, I saw a face near my hand. The black bones reclined at full length[11] with one shoulder against the tree, and slowly the eyelids rose and the sunken eyes looked up at me, enormous and vacant, a kind of blind, white flicker in the depths of the orbs, which died out slowly. The man seemed young—almost a boy—but you know with them it's hard

---

1 fend off：抵挡
2 the devil of hot desire：欲壑难填的魔鬼
3 by all the stars：老天作证
4 philanthropic desire：慈善之心
5 a wanton smash-up：恶意砸碎
6 Inferno：地狱
7 the tearing pace of the launched earth：地球匆忙奔跑的脚步声
8 in all the attitudes of：以各种不同的姿态
9 went off：爆炸
10 moribund shapes：垂死的物体，指那些因生病失去工作能力的人
11 at full length：完全伸展开

Chapter Fourteen Cultural Studies

to tell. I found nothing else to do but to offer him one of my good Swede's ship's biscuits I had in my pocket. The fingers closed slowly on it[1] and held—there was no other movement and no other glance. He had tied a bit of white worsted round his neck—Why? Where did he get it? Was it a badge—an ornament—a charm—a propitiatory act? Was there any idea at all connected with it? It looked startling round his black neck, this bit of white thread from beyond the seas.

"Near the same tree two more bundles of acute angles[2] sat with their legs drawn up. One, with his chin propped on his knees, stared at nothing, in an intolerable and appalling manner: his brother phantom[3] rested its forehead, as if overcome with a great weariness; and all about others were scattered in every pose of contorted collapse, as in some picture of a massacre or a pestilence. While I stood horror-struck, one of these creatures rose to his hands and knees, and went off on all-fours[4] towards the river to drink. He lapped out of his hand, then sat up in the sunlight, crossing his shins in front of him, and after a time let his woolly head fall on his breastbone.

"I didn't want any more loitering in the shade, and I made haste towards[5] the station. When near the buildings I met a white man, in such an unexpected elegance of get-up that in the first moment I took him for a sort of vision[6]. I saw a high starched collar, white cuffs, a light alpaca jacket, snowy trousers, a clean necktie, and varnished boots. No hat. Hair parted, brushed, oiled, under a green-lined parasol held in a big white hand. He was amazing, and had a penholder behind his ear.

"I shook hands with this miracle, and I learned he was the Company's chief accountant, and that all the book-keeping was done at this station. He had come out for a moment, he said, 'to get a breath of fresh air.' The expression sounded wonderfully odd, with its suggestion of sedentary desk-life[7]. I wouldn't have mentioned the fellow to you at all, only it was from his lips that I first heard the name of the man who is so indissolubly connected with the memories of that time. Moreover, I respected the fellow. Yes; I respected his collars, his vast cuffs, his brushed hair[8]. His appearance was certainly that of a hairdresser's dummy; but in the great demoralization of the land he kept up his appearance. That's backbone[9]. His starched collars and got-up shirt-fronts were achievements of character[10]. He had been out nearly three years; and, later, I could not help asking him how he managed to sport[11] such linen. He had just the faintest blush, and said modestly, 'I've been teaching one of the native women about the station. It was difficult. She had a distaste for the work.' Thus this man had verily accomplished something. And he was devoted to his books, which were in apple-pie order[12].

"Everything else in the station was in a muddle[13]—heads, things, buildings. Strings of dusty niggers

---

1 The fingers closed slowly on it：手指慢慢收拢伸向饼干。
2 acute angles：指瘦骨嶙峋的黑人
3 phantom：指上文中的黑人
4 on all-fours：爬着
5 made haste towards：匆忙向……赶去
6 took him for a sort of vision：以为是鬼魂显灵了
7 with its suggestion of sedentary desk-life：具有长期伏案工作的痕迹
8 brushed hair：油光闪亮的头发
9 That's backbone：那叫有骨气。
10 achievements of character：性格的伟大体现
11 sport：使……引人注目
12 in apple-pie order：整整齐齐
13 in a muddle：杂乱无章，一塌糊涂

with splay feet[1] arrived and departed; a stream of manufactured goods, rubbishy cottons, beads, and brass-wire set into the depths of darkness, and in return came a precious trickle of ivory.

"I had to wait in the station for ten days—an eternity. I lived in a hut in the yard, but to be out of the chaos I would sometimes get into the accountant's office. It was built of horizontal planks, and so badly put together that, as he bent over his high desk, he was barred from neck to heels with narrow strips of sunlight. There was no need to open the big shutter to see. It was hot there, too; big flies buzzed fiendishly, and did not sting, but stabbed. I sat generally on the floor, while, of faultless appearance[2] (and even slightly scented), perching on a high stool, he wrote, he wrote. Sometimes he stood up for exercise. When a truckle-bed[3] with a sick man (some invalid agent from upcountry) was put in there, he exhibited a gentle annoyance. 'The groans of this sick person,' he said, 'distract my attention. And without that it is extremely difficult to guard against clerical errors in this climate.'

"One day he remarked, without lifting his head, 'In the interior you will no doubt meet Mr. Kurtz.' On my asking who Mr. Kurtz was, he said he was a first-class agent; and seeing my disappointment at this information, he added slowly, laying down his pen, 'He is a very remarkable person.' Further questions elicited from him that Mr. Kurtz was at present in charge of a trading-post, a very important one, in the true ivory-country, at 'the very bottom of there. Sends in as much ivory as all the others put together ...' He began to write again. The sick man was too ill to groan. The flies buzzed in a great peace.

"Suddenly there was a growing murmur of voices and a great tramping of feet. A caravan[4] had come in. A violent babble of uncouth sounds burst out on the other side of the planks. All the carriers were speaking together, and in the midst of the uproar the lamentable voice of the chief agent was heard 'giving it up' tearfully for the twentieth time that day... He rose slowly. 'What a frightful row,' he said. He crossed the room gently to look at the sick man, and returning, said to me, 'He does not hear.' 'What! Dead?' I asked, startled. 'No, not yet,' he answered, with great composure. Then, alluding with a toss of the head to the tumult in the station-yard[5], 'When one has got to make correct entries, one comes to hate those savages—hate them to the death.' He remained thoughtful for a moment. 'When you see Mr. Kurtz,' he went on, 'tell him from me that everything here'—he glanced at the deck—'is very satisfactory. I don't like to write to him—with those messengers of ours you never know who may get hold of your letter—at that Central Station.' He stared at me for a moment with his mild, bulging eyes. 'Oh, he will go far, very far[6],' he began again. 'He will be a somebody in the Administration before long. They, above—the Council in Europe[7], you know—mean him to be[8].'

"He turned to his work. The noise outside had ceased, and presently in going out I stopped at the

---

1 splay feet：八字脚
2 faultless appearance：一尘不染
3 truckle-bed：(不用时可推到床下的)装有小轮的矮床
4 caravan：沙漠商队，文中指运输队
5 alluding with a toss of the head to the tumult in the station-yard：摇了摇头意指贸易站大院里的嘈杂声
6 he will go far, very far：他将前程似锦。
7 the Council in Europe：欧洲的董事会
8 mean him to be：有意提拔他

door. In the steady buzz of flies the homeward-bound agent[1] was lying finished and insensible; the other, bent over his books, was making correct entries of perfectly correct transactions; and fifty feet below the doorstep I could see the still tree-tops of the grove of death.

"Next day I left that station at last, with a caravan of sixty men, for a two-hundred-mile tramp.

"No use telling you much about that. Paths, paths, everywhere; a stamped-in network of paths[2] spreading over the empty land, through the long grass, through burnt grass, through thickets, down and up chilly ravines, up and down stony hills ablaze with heat; and a solitude, a solitude, nobody, not a hut. The population had cleared out a long time ago. Well, if a lot of mysterious niggers armed with all kinds of fearful weapons suddenly took to travelling on the road between Deal[3] and Gravesend, catching the yokels right and left[4] to carry heavy loads for them, I fancy every farm and cottage thereabouts would get empty very soon. Only here the dwellings were gone, too. Still I passed through several abandoned villages. There's something pathetically childish in the ruins of grass walls. Day after day, with the stamp and shuffle of sixty pair of bare feet behind me, each pair under a 60-lb. load. Camp, cook, sleep, strike camp, march. Now and then a carrier dead in harness, at rest in the long grass near the path, with an empty water-gourd and his long staff lying by his side. A great silence around and above. Perhaps on some quiet night the tremor of far-off drums, sinking, swelling, a tremor vast, faint; a sound weird, appealing, suggestive, and wild—and perhaps with as profound a meaning as the sound of bells in a Christian country. Once a white man in an unbuttoned uniform, camping on the path with an armed escort of lank Zanzibaris[5], very hospitable and festive—not to say drunk. Was looking after the upkeep of the road[6], he declared. Can't say I saw any road or any upkeep, unless the body of a middle-aged negro, with a bullet-hole in the forehead, upon which I absolutely stumbled three miles farther on, may be considered as a permanent improvement. I had a white companion, too, not a bad chap, but rather too fleshy and with the exasperating habit of fainting on the hot hillsides, miles away from the least bit of shade and water. Annoying, you know, to hold your own coat like a parasol over a man's head while he is coming to. I couldn't help asking him once what he meant by coming there at all. 'To make money, of course. What do you think?' he said, scornfully. Then he got fever, and had to be carried in a hammock[7] slung under a pole. As he weighed sixteen stone I had no end of rows[8] with the carriers. They jibbed, ran away, sneaked off with their loads in the night—quite a mutiny. So, one evening, I made a speech in English with gestures, not one of which was lost to the sixty pairs of eyes before me, and the next morning I started the hammock off in front all right. An hour afterwards I came upon the whole concern wrecked in a bush—man, hammock, groans, blankets, horrors. The heavy pole had skinned his poor nose. He was very anxious for me to kill somebody, but there wasn't the shadow of a carrier near. I remembered the old doctor, 'It would be interesting for science to watch the mental changes of individuals, on the spot.'

---

[1] homeward-bound agent：送回家的代理人，指上文中内地患病的公司代理人
[2] a stamped-in network of paths：人踩出来的崎岖的道路网
[3] Deal：迪尔，英国多佛尔海边的一个小镇
[4] yokels right and left：大路两旁的乡巴佬们
[5] Zanzibaris：桑给巴尔的，桑给巴尔人的
[6] upkeep of the road：道路的维护情况
[7] hammock：吊床
[8] no end of rows：没完没了的争吵

I felt I was becoming scientifically interesting. However, all that is to no purpose[1]. On the fifteenth day I came in sight of the big river again, and hobbled into the Central Station. It was on a back water surrounded by scrub and forest[2], with a pretty border of smelly mud on one side, and on the three others enclosed by a crazy fence of rushes. A neglected gap was all the gate it had, and the first glance at the place was enough to let you see the flabby devil[3] was running that show. White men with long staves in their hands appeared languidly from amongst the buildings, strolling up to take a look at me, and then retired out of sight somewhere. One of them, a stout, excitable chap with black moustaches, informed me with great volubility and many digressions[4], as soon as I told him who I was, that my steamer was at the bottom of the river. I was thunderstruck. What, how, why? Oh, it was 'all right.' The 'manager himself' was there. All quite correct. 'Everybody had behaved splendidly! splendidly!'—'you must,' he said in agitation, 'go and see the general manager at once. He is waiting!'

"I did not see the real significance of that wreck at once. I fancy I see it now, but I am not sure—not at all. Certainly the affair was too stupid—when I think of it—to be altogether natural. Still ... But at the moment it presented itself simply as a confounded nuisance[5]. The steamer was sunk. They had started two days before in a sudden hurry up the river with the manager on board, in charge of some volunteer skipper, and before they had been out three hours they tore the bottom out of her on stones, and she sank near the south bank. I asked myself what I was to do there, now my boat was lost. As a matter of fact, I had plenty to do in fishing my command out of the river. I had to set about it the very next day. That, and the repairs when I brought the pieces to the station, took some months.

"My first interview with the manager was curious. He did not ask me to sit down after my twenty-mile walk that morning. He was commonplace in complexion, in features, in manners, and in voice. He was of middle size and of ordinary build[6]. His eyes, of the usual blue, were perhaps remarkably cold, and he certainly could make his glance fall on one as trenchant and heavy as an axe. But even at these times the rest of his person seemed to disclaim the intention. Otherwise there was only an indefinable, faint expression of his lips, something stealthy—a smile—not a smile—I remember it, but I can't explain. It was unconscious, this smile was, though just after he had said something it got intensified for an instant. It came at the end of his speeches like a seal applied on the words to make the meaning of the commonest phrase appear absolutely inscrutable. He was a common trader, from his youth up employed in these parts—nothing more. He was obeyed, yet he inspired neither love nor fear, nor even respect. He inspired uneasiness. That was it! Uneasiness. Not a definite mistrust—just uneasiness—nothing more. You have no idea how effective such a ... a.... faculty can be. He had no genius for organizing, for initiative, or for order even. That was evident in such things as the deplorable state of the station. He had no learning, and no intelligence. His position had come to him—why? Perhaps because he was never ill ... He had served three terms of three years out there ... Because triumphant health in the

---

1 all that is to no purpose: 一切都毫无成效
2 scrub and forest: 灌木丛林
3 flabby devil: 不负责任的混蛋
4 with great volubility and many digressions: 口若悬河, 拐弯抹角地
5 confounded nuisance: 令人捉摸不透的烦事
6 of ordinary build: 身材一般

general rout of constitutions[1] is a kind of power in itself. When he went home on leave he rioted on a large scale[2]—pompously. Jack ashore—with a difference—in externals only. This one could gather from[3] his casual talk. He originated nothing, he could keep the routine going[4]—that's all. But he was great. He was great by this little thing that it was impossible to tell what could control such a man. He never gave that secret away. Perhaps there was nothing within him. Such a suspicion made one pause—for out there there were no external checks. Once when various tropical diseases had laid low[5] almost every 'agent' in the station, he was heard to say, 'Men who come out here should have no entrails.' He sealed the utterance with that smile of his, as though it had been a door opening into a darkness he had in his keeping[6]. You fancied you had seen things—but the seal was on. When annoyed at meal-times by the constant quarrels of the white men about precedence, he ordered an immense round table to be made, for which a special house had to be built. This was the station's mess-room[7]. Where he sat was the first place—the rest were nowhere. One felt this to be his unalterable conviction. He was neither civil nor uncivil. He was quiet. He allowed his 'boy'—an overfed young negro from the coast—to treat the white men, under his very eyes, with provoking insolence.

"He began to speak as soon as he saw me. I had been very long on the road. He could not wait. Had to start without me. The up-river stations had to be relieved. There had been so many delays already that he did not know who was dead and who was alive, and how they got on—and so on, and so on. He paid no attention to my explanations, and, playing with a stick of sealing-wax[8], repeated several times that the situation was 'very grave, very grave.' There were rumours that a very important station was in jeopardy, and its chief, Mr. Kurtz, was ill. Hoped it was not true. Mr. Kurtz was . . . I felt weary and irritable. Hang Kurtz, I thought. I interrupted him by saying I had heard of Mr. Kurtz on the coast. 'Ah! So they talk of him down there,' he murmured to himself. Then he began again, assuring me Mr. Kurtz was the best agent he had, an exceptional man, of the greatest importance to the Company; therefore I could understand his anxiety. He was, he said, 'very, very uneasy.' Certainly he fidgeted on his chair a good deal[9], exclaimed, 'Ah, Mr. Kurtz!' broke the stick of sealing-wax and seemed dumfounded by the accident. Next thing he wanted to know 'how long it would take to'... I interrupted him again. Being hungry, you know, and kept on my feet[10] too. I was getting savage. 'How can I tell?' I said. 'I haven't even seen the wreck yet—some months, no doubt.' All this talk seemed to me so futile. 'Some months,' he said. 'Well, let us say three months before we can make a start. Yes. That ought to do the affair.' I flung out of his hut (he lived all alone in a clay hut with a sort of verandah) muttering to myself my opinion of him. He was a chattering idiot. Afterwards I took it back when it was borne in upon me[11]

---

1 in the general rout of constitutions：在健康情况普遍恶化的环境中
2 rioted on a large scale：闹得尽人皆知
3 gather from：从……推测，从……获悉
4 He originated nothing, he could keep the routine going：他没有任何创新，仅能维持日常事务。
5 laid low：使……倒下
6 in his keeping：在他的看管之下
7 mess-room：(军舰或海军基地的)食堂
8 a stick of sealing-wax：火漆棒
9 fidgeted on his chair a good deal：在椅子上动个不停，如坐针毡。
10 kept on my feet：老是站着
11 borne in upon me：我确信；我逐渐认识到

startlingly with what extreme nicety he had estimated the time requisite for the 'affair[1].'

"I went to work the next day, turning, so to speak, my back on that station. In that way only it seemed to me I could keep my hold on the redeeming facts of life. Still, one must look about sometimes; and then I saw this station, these men strolling aimlessly about in the sunshine of the yard. I asked myself sometimes what it all meant. They wandered here and there with their absurd long staves in their hands, like a lot of faithless pilgrims bewitched inside a rotten fence. The word 'ivory' rang in the air, was whispered, was sighed. You would think they were praying to it. A taint of imbecile rapacity blew through it all, like a whiff from some corpse[2]. By Jove[3]! I've never seen anything so unreal in my life. And outside, the silent wilderness surrounding this cleared speck on the earth struck me as something great and invincible, like evil or truth, waiting patiently for the passing away of this fantastic invasion.

"Oh, these months! Well, never mind. Various things happened. One evening a grass shed full of calico, cotton prints, beads, and I don't know what else, burst into a blaze so suddenly that you would have thought the earth had opened to let an avenging fire consume all that trash. I was smoking my pipe quietly by my dismantled steamer, and saw them all cutting capers in the light, with their arms lifted high, when the stout man with moustaches came tearing down to the river, a tin pail in his hand, assured me that everybody was 'behaving splendidly, splendidly,' dipped about a quart of water[4] and tore back again. I noticed there was a hole in the bottom of his pail.

"I strolled up. There was no hurry. You see the thing had gone off like a box of matches. It had been hopeless from the very first. The flame had leaped high, driven everybody back, lighted up everything—and collapsed. The shed was already a heap of embers[5] glowing fiercely. A nigger was being beaten near by. They said he had caused the fire in some way; be that as it may[6], he was screeching most horribly. I saw him, later, for several days, sitting in a bit of shade looking very sick and trying to recover himself; afterwards he arose and went out—and the wilderness without a sound took him into its bosom again. As I approached the glow from the dark I found myself at the back of two men, talking. I heard the name of Kurtz pronounced, then the words, 'take advantage of this unfortunate accident.' One of the men was the manager. I wished him a good evening. 'Did you ever see anything like it—eh? it is incredible,' he said, and walked off. The other man remained. He was a first-class agent, young, gentlemanly, a bit reserved, with a forked little beard and a hooked nose. He was stand-offish with[7] the other agents, and they on their side said he was the manager's spy upon them. As to me, I had hardly ever spoken to him before. We got into talk, and by and by we strolled away from the hissing ruins. Then he asked me to his room, which was in the main building of the station. He struck a match, and I perceived that this young aristocrat had not only a silver-mounted[8] dressing-case but also a whole candle

---

1 affair：指打捞沉入河底的汽船并进行修理

2 A taint of imbecile rapacity blew through it all, like a whiff from some corpse：从"象牙"这个字飘来一丝愚蠢、贪婪的气息，如同一具死尸散发出的臭味。

3 By Jove：天啊！

4 dipped about a quart of water：舀起了大约半桶水

5 a heap of embers：一堆灰烬

6 be that as it may：就算是这么回事吧

7 stand-offish with：与……相处得不大好

8 silver-mounted：镀银的

all to himself. Just at that time the manager was the only man supposed to have any right to candles. Native mats covered the clay walls; a collection of spears, assegais[1], shields, knives was hung up in trophies. The business intrusted to this fellow was the making of bricks—so I had been informed; but there wasn't a fragment of a brick anywhere in the station, and he had been there more than a year—waiting. It seems he could not make bricks without something, I don't know what—straw maybe. Anyway, it could not be found there and as it was not likely to be sent from Europe, it did not appear clear to me what he was waiting for. An act of special creation perhaps. However, they were all waiting—all the sixteen or twenty pilgrims of them—for something; and upon my word it did not seem an uncongenial occupation[2], from the way they took it, though the only thing that ever came to them was disease—as far as I could see. They beguiled the time by back-biting[3] and intriguing against each other in a foolish kind of way. There was an air of plotting about that station, but nothing came of it, of course. It was as unreal as everything else—as the philanthropic pretence of the whole concern, as their talk, as their government, as their show of work. The only real feeling was a desire to get appointed to[4] a trading-post where ivory was to be had, so that they could earn percentages. They intrigued and slandered and hated each other only on that account[5], but as to effectually lifting a little finger—oh, no. By heavens! There is something after all in the world allowing one man to steal a horse while another must not look at a halter. Steal a horse straight out. Very well. He has done it. Perhaps he can ride. But there is a way of looking at a halter that would provoke the most charitable of saints into a kick[6].

"I had no idea why he wanted to be sociable, but as we chatted in there it suddenly occurred to me the fellow was trying to get at something—in fact, pumping me. He alluded constantly to Europe, to the people I was supposed to know there—putting leading questions as to my acquaintances in the sepulchral city, and so on. His little eyes glittered like mica discs[7]—with curiosity—though he tried to keep up a bit of superciliousness[8]. At first I was astonished, but very soon I became awfully curious to see what he would find out from me. I couldn't possibly imagine what I had in me to make it worth his while. It was very pretty to see how he baffled himself, for in truth my body was full only of chills, and my head had nothing in it but that wretched steamboat business. It was evident he took me for a perfectly shameless prevaricator[9]. At last he got angry, and, to conceal a movement of furious annoyance, he yawned. I rose. Then I noticed a small sketch in oils, on a panel, representing a woman, draped and blindfolded, carrying a lighted torch. The background was sombre—almost black. The movement of the woman was stately, and the effect of the torchlight on the face was sinister.

"It arrested me, and he stood by civilly[10], holding an empty half-pint champagne bottle (medical comforts) with the candle stuck in it. To my question he said Mr. Kurtz had painted this—in this very

---

1 assegai: (南非土人所用的)长矛, 梭镖
2 an uncongenial occupation: 一件不符合志趣的差事
3 back-biting: 诽谤, 中伤
4 to get appointed to: 被委派去做
5 on that account: 由于那个缘故
6 provoke the most charitable of saints into a kick: 激怒世界上最仁慈的圣徒
7 like mica discs: 像两片云母似的
8 superciliousness: 傲慢
9 a perfectly shameless prevaricator: 一个厚颜无耻的撒谎者
10 stood by civilly: 彬彬有礼地站在一旁

station more than a year ago—while waiting for means to go to his trading post. 'Tell me, pray,' said I, 'who is this Mr. Kurtz?'

"'The chief of the Inner Station,' he answered in a short tone[1], looking away. 'Much obliged,' I said, laughing. 'And you are the brickmaker of the Central Station. Every one knows that.' He was silent for a while. 'He is a prodigy,' he said at last. 'He is an emissary of pity and science and progress, and devil knows what else. We want,' he began to declaim suddenly, 'for the guidance of the cause intrusted to us by Europe, so to speak, higher intelligence, wide sympathies, a singleness of purpose.' 'Who says that?' I asked. 'Lots of them,' he replied. 'Some even write that; and so he comes here, a special being[2], as you ought to know.' 'Why ought I to know?' I interrupted, really surprised. He paid no attention. 'Yes. Today he is chief of the best station, next year he will be assistant-manager, two years more and ... but I dare-say you know what he will be in two years' time. You are of the new gang—the gang of virtue[3]. The same people who sent him specially also recommended you. Oh, don't say no. I've my own eyes to trust.' Light dawned upon me[4]. My dear aunt's influential acquaintances were producing an unexpected effect upon that young man. I nearly burst into a laugh. 'Do you read the Company's confidential correspondence?' I asked. He hadn't a word to say. It was great fun. 'When Mr. Kurtz,' I continued, severely, 'is General Manager, you won't have the opportunity.'

"He blew the candle out suddenly, and we went outside. The moon had risen. Black figures strolled about listlessly, pouring water on the glow, whence proceeded a sound of hissing; steam ascended in the moonlight, the beaten nigger groaned somewhere. 'What a row the brute makes!' said the indefatigable man with the moustaches, appearing near us. 'Serve him right[5]. Transgression—punishment—bang! Pitiless, pitiless. That's the only way. This will prevent all conflagrations for the future. I was just telling the manager ...' He noticed my companion, and became crestfallen all at once. 'Not in bed yet,' he said, with a kind of servile heartiness[6]; 'it's so natural. Ha! Danger—agitation.' He vanished. I went on to the riverside, and the other followed me. I heard a scathing murmur at my ear, 'Heap of muffs—go to.' The pilgrims could be seen in knots gesticulating, discussing. Several had still their staves in their hands. I verily believe they took these sticks to bed with them. Beyond the fence the forest stood up spectrally in the moonlight, and through that dim stir, through the faint sounds of that lamentable courtyard, the silence of the land went home to one's very heart—its mystery, its greatness, the amazing reality of its concealed life. The hurt nigger moaned feebly somewhere near by, and then fetched a deep sigh that made me mend my pace[7] away from there. I felt a hand introducing itself under my arm. 'My dear sir,' said the fellow, 'I don't want to be misunderstood, and especially by you, who will see Mr. Kurtz long before I can have that pleasure. I wouldn't like him to get a false idea of my disposition...'

"I let him run on, this papier-mâché Mephistopheles[8], and it seemed to me that if I tried I could

---

1 answered in a short tone：简短地回答
2 a special being：一位特殊的人物
3 the gang of virtue：道德派
4 Light dawned upon me：我恍然大悟。
5 Serve him right：他真活该。
6 servile heartiness：奴态可掬
7 mend one's pace：加快步伐
8 papier-mâché Mephistopheles：纸糊的梅菲斯特。梅菲斯特是欧洲传说浮士德故事中的魔鬼。

Chapter Fourteen Cultural Studies

poke my forefinger through him, and would find nothing inside but a little loose dirt, maybe. He, don't you see, had been planning to be assistant-manager by and by under the present man, and I could see that the coming of that Kurtz had upset them both not a little. He talked precipitately, and I did not try to stop him. I had my shoulders against the wreck of my steamer, hauled up[1] on the slope like a carcass of some big river animal. The smell of mud, of primeval mud, by Jove! was in my nostrils, the high stillness of primeval forest was before my eyes; there were shiny patches on the black creek. The moon had spread over everything a thin layer of silver—over the rank grass, over the mud, upon the wall of matted vegetation standing higher than the wall of a temple, over the great river I could see through a sombre gap glittering, glittering, as it flowed broadly by without a murmur. All this was great, expectant, mute, while the man jabbered about himself[2]. I wondered whether the stillness on the face of the immensity looking at us two were meant as an appeal or as a menace. What were we who had strayed in here? Could we handle that dumb thing, or would it handle us? I felt how big, how confoundedly big, was that thing that couldn't talk, and perhaps was deaf as well. What was in there? I could see a little ivory coming out from there, and I had heard Mr. Kurtz was in there. I had heard enough about it, too—God knows! Yet somehow it didn't bring any image with it—no more than if I had been told an angel or a fiend was in there. I believed it in the same way one of you might believe there are inhabitants in the planet Mars. I knew once a Scotch sailmaker who was certain, dead sure[3], there were people in Mars. If you asked him for some idea how they looked and behaved, he would get shy and mutter something about 'walking on all-fours.' If you as much as smiled, he would—though a man of sixty—offer to fight you. I would not have gone so far as to fight for Kurtz, but I went for him near enough to a lie. You know I hate, detest, and can't bear a lie, not because I am straighter than the rest of us, but simply because it appalls me. There is a taint of death, a flavour of mortality in lies[4]—which is exactly what I hate and detest in the world—what I want to forget. It makes me miserable and sick, like biting something rotten would do. Temperament, I suppose. Well, I went near enough to it by letting the young fool there believe anything he liked to imagine as to my influence in Europe. I became in an instant as much of a pretence as the rest of the bewitched pilgrims[5]. This simply because I had a notion it somehow would be of help to that Kurtz whom at the time I did not see—you understand. He was just a word for me[6]. I did not see the man in the name any more than you do. Do you see him? Do you see the story? Do you see anything? It seems to me I am trying to tell you a dream—making a vain attempt, because no relation of a dream can convey the dream-sensation, that commingling of absurdity, surprise, and bewilderment in a tremor of struggling revolt[7], that notion of being captured by the incredible which is of the very essence of dreams..."

He was silent for a while.

"...No, it is impossible; it is impossible to convey the life-sensation of any given epoch of one's

---

1 haul up: 停止
2 the man jabbered about himself: 那个人在絮絮叨叨地谈论他自己。
3 dead sure: 非常确定
4 There is a taint of death, a flavour of mortality in lies: 谎言中包含有死亡的迹象，一种死亡的气味。
5 bewitched pilgrims: 鬼迷心窍的朝圣者
6 He was just a word for me: 那时我只是闻其名而已。
7 in a tremor of struggling revolt: 在挣扎和反抗的颤抖中

existence—that which makes its[1] truth, its meaning—its subtle and penetrating essence. It is impossible. We live, as we dream—alone..."

He paused again as if reflecting, then added:

"Of course in this you fellows see more than I could then. You see me, whom you know..."

It had become so pitch dark that we listeners could hardly see one another. For a long time already he, sitting apart, had been no more to us than a voice. There was not a word from anybody. The others might have been asleep, but I was awake. I listened; I listened on the watch for[2] the sentence, for the word, that would give me the clue to the faint uneasiness inspired by this narrative that seemed to shape itself without human lips in the heavy night-air of the river.

"... Yes—I let him run on," Marlow began again, "and think what he pleased about the powers that were behind me. I did! And there was nothing behind me! There was nothing but that wretched, old, mangled steamboat I was leaning against, while he talked fluently about 'the necessity for every man to get on[3].' 'And when one comes out here, you conceive, it is not to gaze at the moon.' Mr. Kurtz was a 'universal genius,' but even a genius would find it easier to work with 'adequate tools—intelligent men.' He did not make bricks—why, there was a physical impossibility in the way—as I was well aware; and if he did secretarial work for the manager, it was because 'no sensible man rejects wantonly the confidence of his superiors.' Did I see it? I saw it. What more did I want? What I really wanted was rivets, by heaven! Rivets. To get on with the work—to stop the hole. Rivets I wanted. There were cases of them down at the coast—cases—piled up—burst[4]—split! You kicked a loose rivet at every second step in that station-yard on the hillside. Rivets had rolled into the grove of death. You could fill your pockets with rivets for the trouble of stooping down—and there wasn't one rivet to be found where it was wanted. We had plates that would do, but nothing to fasten them with. And every week the messenger, a long negro, letter-bag on shoulder and staff in hand, left our station for the coast. And several times a week a coast caravan came in with trade goods—ghastly glazed calico that made you shudder only to look at it, glass beads value about a penny a quart, confounded spotted cotton handkerchiefs. And no rivets. Three carriers could have brought all that was wanted to set that steamboat afloat.

"He was becoming confidential now, but I fancy my unresponsive attitude[5] must have exasperated him at last, for he judged it necessary to inform me he feared neither God nor devil, let alone any mere man. I said I could see that very well, but what I wanted was a certain quantity of rivets—and rivets were what really Mr. Kurtz wanted, if he had only known it. Now letters went to the coast every week... 'My dear sir,' he cried, 'I write from dictation[6].' I demanded rivets. There was a way—for an intelligent man. He changed his manner; became very cold, and suddenly began to talk about a hippopotamus; wondered whether sleeping on board the steamer (I stuck to my salvage night and day) I wasn't disturbed. There was an old hippo that had the bad habit of getting out on the bank and roaming at night

---

1 its: 此处指 life's。
2 on the watch for: 密切注意着，监视着
3 the necessity for every man to get on: 人人都应往高处走
4 burst: 撑破，爆裂
5 unresponsive attitude: 不做回应的态度
6 I write from dictation: 我按照别人的口述来记录。

over the station grounds. The pilgrims used to turn out in a body and empty every rifle they could lay hands on at him. Some even had sat up o'[1] nights for him. All this energy was wasted, though. 'That animal has a charmed life[2],' he said; 'but you can say this only of brutes in this country. No man—you apprehend me?—no man here bears a charmed life.' He stood there for a moment in the moonlight with his delicate hooked nose[3] set a little askew, and his mica eyes glittering without a wink, then, with a curt Good-night, he strode off. I could see he was disturbed and considerably puzzled, which made me feel more hopeful than I had been for days. It was a great comfort to turn from that chap to my influential friend, the battered, twisted, ruined, tin-pot[4] steamboat. I clambered on board. She rang under my feet like an empty Huntley & Palmer[5] biscuit-tin kicked along a gutter; she was nothing so solid in make[6], and rather less pretty in shape, but I had expended enough hard work on her to make me love her. No influential friend would have served me better. She had given me a chance to come out a bit—to find out what I could do. No, I don't like work. I had rather laze about and think of all the fine things that can be done. I don't like work—no man does—but I like what is in the work—the chance to find yourself. Your own reality—for yourself, not for others—what no other man can ever know. They can only see the mere show, and never can tell what it really means.

"I was not surprised to see somebody sitting aft, on the deck, with his legs dangling over the mud. You see I rather chummed with the few mechanics there were in that station, whom the other pilgrims naturally despised—on account of their imperfect manners, I suppose. This was the foreman—a boiler-maker[7] by trade—a good worker. He was a lank, bony, yellow-faced man, with big intense eyes[8]. His aspect was worried, and his head was as bald as the palm of my hand; but his hair in falling seemed to have stuck to his chin, and had prospered in the new locality, for his beard hung down to his waist. He was a widower with six young children (he had left them in charge of a sister of his to come out there), and the passion of his life was pigeon-flying. He was an enthusiast and a connoisseur[9]. He would rave about pigeons.[10] After work hours he used sometimes to come over from his hut for a talk about his children and his pigeons; at work, when he had to crawl in the mud under the bottom of the steamboat, he would tie up that beard of his in a kind of white serviette he brought for the purpose. It had loops to go over his ears. In the evening he could be seen squatted on the bank rinsing that wrapper in the creek with great care, then spreading it solemnly on a bush to dry.

"I slapped him on the back and shouted, 'We shall have rivets!' He scrambled to his feet exclaiming, 'No! Rivets!' as though he couldn't believe his ears. Then in a low voice, 'You ... eh?' I don't know why we behaved like lunatics. I put my finger to the side of my nose and nodded mysteriously. 'Good

---

1 o': 此处是"of"的缩写。
2 a charmed life: 受符咒护佑的生命
3 hooked nose: 鹰钩鼻
4 tin-pot: 低劣的，微不足道的
5 Huntley & Palmer: 亨特利和帕尔默公司
6 she was nothing so solid in make: 她的身体一点也不结实。
7 boiler-maker: 制造锅炉的人
8 with big intense eyes: 眼睛炯炯有神
9 connoisseur: (艺术品的)鉴赏家，鉴定家
10 He would rave about pigeons: 一谈起鸽子，他便滔滔不绝，眉飞色舞。

for you!' he cried, snapped his fingers above his head, lifting one foot. I tried a jig. We capered on the iron deck. A frightful clatter came out of that hulk, and the virgin forest[1] on the other bank of the creek sent it back in a thundering roll upon the sleeping station. It must have made some of the pilgrims sit up in their hovels. A dark figure obscured the lighted doorway of the manager's hut, vanished, then, a second or so after, the doorway itself vanished, too. We stopped, and the silence driven away by the stamping of our feet flowed back again from the recesses of the land. The great wall of vegetation, an exuberant and entangled[2] mass of trunks, branches, leaves, boughs, festoons, motionless in the moonlight, was like a rioting invasion of soundless life, a rolling wave of plants, piled up, crested, ready to topple over the creek, to sweep every little man of us out of his little existence. And it moved not. A deadened burst of mighty splashes and snorts reached us from afar, as though an icthyosaurus[3] had been taking a bath of glitter in the great river. 'After all,' said the boiler-maker in a reasonable tone, 'why shouldn't we get the rivets?' Why not, indeed! I did not know of any reason why we shouldn't. 'They'll come in three weeks,' I said confidently.

"But they didn't. Instead of rivets there came an invasion, an infliction, a visitation. It came in sections during the next three weeks, each section headed by a donkey carrying a white man in new clothes and tan shoes, bowing from that elevation right and left to the impressed pilgrims. A quarrelsome band of footsore sulky niggers trod on the heels of the donkey; a lot of tents, camp-stools, tin boxes, white cases, brown bales would be shot down in the courtyard, and the air of mystery would deepen a little over the muddle of the station. Five such installments came, with their absurd air of disorderly flight with the loot of innumerable outfit shops and provision stores, that, one would think, they were lugging, after a raid, into the wilderness for equitable division. It was an inextricable mess of things decent in themselves but that human folly made look like the spoils of thieving.[4]

"This devoted band called itself the Eldorado Exploring Expedition[5], and I believe they were sworn to secrecy[6]. Their talk, however, was the talk of sordid buccaneers: it was reckless without hardihood, greedy without audacity, and cruel without courage; there was not an atom of foresight or of serious intention in the whole batch of them, and they did not seem aware these things are wanted for the work of the world. To tear treasure out of the bowels of the land was their desire, with no more moral purpose at the back of it than there is in burglars breaking into a safe. Who paid the expenses of the noble enterprise[7] I don't know; but the uncle of our manager was leader of that lot.

"In exterior he resembled a butcher in a poor neighbourhood, and his eyes had a look of sleepy cunning. He carried his fat paunch with ostentation on his short legs, and during the time his gang infested the station spoke to no one but his nephew. You could see these two roaming about all day long with their heads close together in an everlasting confab[8].

---

1 virgin forest：原始森林
2 exuberant and entangled：茂密而杂乱地纠缠在一起的
3 icthyosaurus：龙鱼
4 spoils of thieving：偷来的战利品
5 Eldorado Exploring Expedition：埃尔多拉多探险队。埃尔多拉多是西方理想中的的黄金之国。
6 sworn to secrecy：发誓保守秘密
7 noble enterprise：崇高的事业
8 in an everlasting confab：没完没了的交谈

"I had given up worrying myself about the rivets. One's capacity for that kind of folly is more limited than you would suppose. I said Hang[1]!—and let things slide[2]. I had plenty of time for meditation, and now and then I would give some thought to Kurtz. I wasn't very interested in him. No. Still, I was curious to see whether this man, who had come out equipped with moral ideas of some sort, would climb to the top after all and how he would set about his work when there."

II

"One evening as I was lying flat on the deck of my steamboat, I heard voices approaching—and there were the nephew and the uncle strolling along the bank. I laid my head on my arm again, and had nearly lost myself in a doze[3], when somebody said in my ear, as it were: 'I am as harmless as a little child, but I don't like to be dictated to. Am I the manager—or am I not? I was ordered to send him there. It's incredible.' ... I became aware that the two were standing on the shore alongside the forepart of the steamboat, just below my head. I did not move; it did not occur to me to move: I was sleepy. 'It is unpleasant,' grunted the uncle. 'He has asked the Administration to be sent there,' said the other, 'with the idea of showing what he could do; and I was instructed accordingly. Look at the influence that man must have. Is it not frightful?' They both agreed it was frightful, then made several bizarre remarks[4]: 'Make rain and fine weather[5]—one man—the Council—by the nose[6]'—bits of absurd sentences that got the better of my drowsiness, so that I had pretty near the whole of my wits about me when the uncle said, 'The climate may do away with this difficulty for you. Is he alone there?' 'Yes,' answered the manager; 'he sent his assistant down the river with a note to me in these terms: "Clear this poor devil out of the country, and don't bother sending more of that sort. I had rather be alone than have the kind of men you can dispose of with me." It was more than a year ago. Can you imagine such impudence!' 'Anything since then?' asked the other hoarsely. 'Ivory,' jerked the nephew; 'lots of it—prime sort[7]—lots—most annoying, from him.' 'And with that?' questioned the heavy rumble. 'Invoice[8],' was the reply fired out, so to speak. Then silence. They had been talking about Kurtz.

"I was broad awake[9] by this time, but, lying perfectly at ease, remained still, having no inducement to change my position. 'How did that ivory come all this way?' growled the elder man, who seemed very vexed. The other explained that it had come with a fleet of canoes in charge of an English half-caste clerk[10] Kurtz had with him; that Kurtz had apparently intended to return himself, the station being by that time bare of goods and stores, but after coming three hundred miles, had suddenly decided to go back,

---

1 Hang：〈俚语〉见鬼去吧
2 let things slide：一切顺其自然
3 had nearly lost myself in a doze：几乎是在睡得迷迷糊糊之中
4 several bizarre remarks：几句莫名其妙的怪话
5 make rain and fine weather：呼风唤雨
6 by the nose：来自于 lead... by the nose，意思是"牵着……的鼻子"。
7 prime sort：刚采下的那批
8 invoice：发票，(发货)费用清单
9 broad awake：完全清醒
10 an English half-caste clerk：一位英国籍欧亚混血的职员

which he started to do alone in a small dugout[1] with four paddlers, leaving the half-caste to continue down the river with the ivory. The two fellows there seemed astounded at anybody attempting such a thing. They were at a loss for an adequate motive. As to me, I seemed to see Kurtz for the first time. It was a distinct glimpse: the dugout, four paddling savages, and the lone white man turning his back suddenly on the headquarters, on relief, on thoughts of home—perhaps; setting his face towards the depths of the wilderness, towards his empty and desolate station. I did not know the motive. Perhaps he was just simply a fine fellow who stuck to his work for its own sake[2]. His name, you understand, had not been pronounced once. He was 'that man.' The half-caste, who, as far as I could see, had conducted a difficult trip with great prudence and pluck, was invariably alluded to as 'that scoundrel[3].' The 'scoundrel' had reported that the 'man' had been very ill—had recovered imperfectly... The two below me moved away then a few paces, and strolled back and forth at some little distance. I heard: 'Military post—doctor—two hundred miles—quite alone now—unavoidable delays—nine months—no news—strange rumors.' They approached again, just as the manager was saying, 'No one, as far as I know, unless a species of[4] wandering trader—a pestilential fellow[5], snapping ivory from the natives.' Who was it they were talking about now? I gathered in snatches[6] that this was some man supposed to be in Kurtz's district, and of whom the manager did not approve. 'We will not be free from unfair competition till one of these fellows is hanged for an example,' he said. 'Certainly,' grunted the other; 'get him hanged! Why not? Anything—anything can be done in this country. That's what I say; nobody here, you understand, here, can endanger your position. And why? You stand the climate[7]—you outlast them all. The danger is in Europe; but there before I left I took care to—They moved off and whispered, then their voices rose again. 'The extraordinary series of delays is not my fault. I did my best.' The fat man sighed. 'Very sad.' 'And the pestiferous absurdity of his talk[8],' continued the other; 'he bothered me enough when he was here. "Each station should be like a beacon on the road towards better things, a centre for trade of course, but also for humanizing, improving, instructing." Conceive you—that ass[9]! And he wants to be manager! No, it's—' Here he got choked by excessive indignation, and I lifted my head the least bit. I was surprised to see how near they were—right under me. I could have spat upon their hats. They were looking on the ground, absorbed in thought. The manager was switching his leg with a slender twig: his sagacious[10] relative lifted his head. 'You have been well since you came out this time?' he asked. The other gave a start. 'Who? I? Oh! Like a charm[11]—like a charm. But the rest—oh, my goodness! All sick. They die so quick, too, that I haven't the time to send them out of the country—it's incredible!' 'Hm'm. Just so,' grunted the uncle. 'Ah! my boy, trust to this—I say, trust to this.' I saw him extend his short

---

1 dugout: 独木舟
2 stuck to his work for its own sake: 全心全意为工作而工作
3 that scoundrel: 那个无赖、恶棍，文中指 Kurtz。
4 a species of: 一个……的人
5 a pestilential fellow: 一个不要命的家伙
6 snatches: 片段
7 stand the climate: 受得了这种气候
8 the pestiferous absurdity of his talk: 令人厌恶的愚蠢的闲话
9 that ass: 那个蠢驴
10 sagacious: 精明的，敏锐的
11 like a charm: 像是有神灵护佑，像是中了魔咒

flipper of an arm for a gesture that took in the forest, the creek, the mud, the river—seemed to beckon with a dishonoring flourish before the sunlit face of the land a treacherous appeal to the lurking death, to the hidden evil, to the profound darkness of its heart. It was so startling that I leaped to my feet[1] and looked back at the edge of the forest, as though I had expected an answer of some sort to that black display of confidence. You know the foolish notions that come to one sometimes. The high stillness confronted these two figures with its ominous patience, waiting for the passing away of a fantastic invasion.

"They swore aloud together—out of sheer fright[2], I believe—then pretending not to know anything of my existence, turned back to the station. The sun was low; and leaning forward side by side, they seemed to be tugging painfully uphill their two ridiculous shadows of unequal length, that trailed behind them slowly over the tall grass without bending a single blade.

"In a few days the Eldorado Expedition went into the patient wilderness, that closed upon it as the sea closes over a diver. Long afterwards the news came that all the donkeys were dead. I know nothing as to the fate of the less valuable animals. They, no doubt, like the rest of us, found what they deserved. I did not inquire. I was then rather excited at the prospect of meeting Kurtz very soon. When I say very soon I mean it comparatively. It was just two months from the day we left the creek when we came to the bank below Kurtz's station.

"Going up that river was like traveling back to the earliest beginnings of the world, when vegetation rioted on the earth and the big trees were kings. An empty stream, a great silence, an impenetrable forest. The air was warm, thick, heavy, sluggish[3]. There was no joy in the brilliance of sunshine. The long stretches of the waterway ran on, deserted, into the gloom of overshadowed distances. On silvery sand-banks hippos and alligators[4] sunned themselves side by side. The broadening waters flowed through a mob of wooded islands; you lost your way on that river as you would in a desert, and butted all day long against shoals, trying to find the channel, till you thought yourself bewitched and cut off for ever from everything you had known once—somewhere—far away—in another existence perhaps. There were moments when one's past came back to one, as it will sometimes when you have not a moment to spare for yourself; but it came in the shape of an unrestful and noisy dream, remembered with wonder amongst the overwhelming realities[5] of this strange world of plants, and water, and silence. And this stillness of life did not in the least resemble a peace. It was the stillness of an implacable force brooding over an inscrutable intention[6]. It looked at you with a vengeful aspect. I got used to it afterwards; I did not see it any more; I had no time. I had to keep guessing at the channel; I had to discern, mostly by inspiration, the signs of hidden banks; I watched for sunken stones; I was learning to clap my teeth[7] smartly before my heart flew out, when I shaved by a fluke some infernal sly old snag that would have ripped the life out of the tin-pot steamboat and drowned all the pilgrims; I had to keep a lookout for the signs of dead wood we could cut up in the night for next day's steaming. When you have to attend to things of that sort, to the mere

---

1 I leaped to my feet: 我立马站起身来。
2 out of sheer fright: 完全出于恐惧
3 sluggish: 行动迟缓的
4 alligator: 产于美洲的鳄鱼
5 the overwhelming realities: 压倒一切的现实
6 brooding over an inscrutable intention: 笼罩着一种捉摸不透的动机
7 to clap my teeth: 咬紧牙关

incidents of the surface, the reality—the reality, I tell you-fades. The inner truth is hidden—luckily, luckily. But I felt it all the same; I felt often its mysterious stillness watching me at my monkey tricks, just as it watches you fellows performing on your respective tight-ropes for—what is it? half-a-crown a tumble[1]—"

"Try to be civil[2], Marlow," growled a voice, and I knew there was at least one listener awake besides myself.

"I beg your pardon. I forgot the heartache which makes up the rest of the price. And indeed what does the price matter, if the trick be well done? You do your tricks very well. And I didn't do badly either, since I managed not to sink that steamboat on my first trip. It's a wonder to me yet. Imagine a blindfolded man set to drive a van over a bad road. I sweated and shivered over that business considerably, I can tell you. After all, for a seaman, to scrape the bottom of the thing that's supposed to float all the time under his care is the unpardonable sin. No one may know of it, but you never forget the thump—eh? A blow on the very heart. You remember it, you dream of it, you wake up at night and think of it—years after—and go hot and cold all over[3]. I don't pretend to say that steamboat floated all the time. More than once she had to wade for a bit, with twenty cannibals splashing around and pushing. We had enlisted some of these chaps on the way for a crew. Fine fellows—cannibals—in their place. They were men one could work with, and I am grateful to them. And, after all, they did not eat each other before my face: they had brought along a provision of hippo-meat which went rotten, and made the mystery of the wilderness stink in my nostrils[4]. Phoo! I can sniff it now. I had the manager on board and three or four pilgrims with their staves—all complete[5]. Sometimes we came upon a station close by the bank, clinging to the skirts of the unknown, and the white men rushing out of a tumble-down hovel, with great gestures of joy and surprise and welcome, seemed very strange—had the appearance of being held there captive by a spell[6]. The word ivory would ring in the air for a while—and on we went again into the silence, along empty reaches, round the still bends, between the high walls of our winding way, reverberating in hollow claps the ponderous beat of the stern-wheel[7]. Trees, trees, millions of trees, massive, immense, running up high; and at their foot, hugging the bank against the stream, crept the little begrimed steamboat, like a sluggish beetle crawling on the floor of a lofty portico[8]. It made you feel very small, very lost, and yet it was not altogether depressing, that feeling. After all, if you were small, the grimy beetle crawled on—which was just what you wanted it to do. Where the pilgrims imagined it crawled to I don't know. To some place where they expected to get something. I bet! For me it crawled towards Kurtz—exclusively; but when the steam-pipes started leaking we crawled very slow. The reaches[9] opened before us and closed behind, as if the forest had stepped leisurely across the water to bar the way for our return. We penetrated deeper and deeper into the heart of darkness. It was very quiet

---

1 half-a-crown a tumble: 半个克郎翻一个跟头。crown 为英国硬币，值 25 便士，昔时值 5 先令。
2 Try to be civil: 说话礼貌点。
3 go hot and cold all over: 全身忽冷忽热
4 stink in sb's nostrils: 使某人厌恶
5 all complete: 全都安然无恙
6 held there captive by a spell: 被符咒禁锢在那儿当了俘虏
7 stern-wheel: 螺旋桨
8 a lofty portico: 高大的门廊
9 reaches: 一段段河道

there. At night sometimes the roll of drums behind the curtain of trees would run up the river and remain sustained faintly, as if hovering in the air high over our heads, till the first break of day. Whether it meant war, peace, or prayer we could not tell. The dawns were heralded by the descent of a chill stillness; the wood-cutters slept, their fires burned low; the snapping of a twig would make you start[1]. Were wanderers on a prehistoric earth, on an earth that wore the aspect of an unknown planet. We could have fancied ourselves the first of men taking possession of an accursed inheritance, to be subdued at the cost of profound anguish and of excessive toil. But suddenly, as we struggled round a bend, there would be a glimpse of rush walls, of peaked grass-roofs, a burst of yells, a whirl of black limbs, a mass of hands clapping. of feet stamping, of bodies swaying, of eyes rolling, under the droop of heavy and motionless foliage[2]. The steamer toiled along slowly on the edge of a black and incomprehensible frenzy. The prehistoric man was cursing us, praying to us, welcoming us—who could tell? We were cut off from the comprehension of our surroundings; we glided past like phantoms, wondering and secretly appalled, as sane men would be before an enthusiastic outbreak in a madhouse. We could not understand because we were too far and could not remember because we were travelling in the night of first ages, of those ages that are gone, leaving hardly a sign—and no memories.

"The earth seemed unearthly. We are accustomed to look upon the shackled form of a conquered monster, but there—there you could look at a thing monstrous and free. It was unearthly, and the men were—No, they were not inhuman. Well, you know, that was the worst of it—this suspicion of their not being inhuman. It would come slowly to one. They howled and leaped, and spun, and made horrid faces; but what thrilled you was just the thought of their humanity—like yours—the thought of your remote kinship with this wild and passionate uproar. Ugly. Yes, it was ugly enough; but if you were man enough you would admit to yourself that there was in you just the faintest trace of a response to the terrible frankness of that noise, a dim suspicion of there being a meaning in it which you—you so remote from the night of first ages—could comprehend. And why not? The mind of man is capable of anything—because everything is in it, all the past as well as all the future. What was there after all? Joy, fear, sorrow, devotion, valor, rage—who can tell?—but truth—truth stripped of its cloak of time[3]. Let the fool gape and shudder—the man knows, and can look on without a wink. But he must at least be as much of a man as these on the shore. He must meet that truth with his own true stuff—with his own inborn strength. Principles won't do. Acquisitions, clothes, pretty rags—rags that would fly off at the first good shake[4]. No; you want a deliberate belief. An appeal to me in this fiendish row—is there? Very well; I hear; I admit, but I have a voice, too, and for good or evil mine is the speech that cannot be silenced. Of course, a fool, what with sheer fright and fine sentiments, is always safe. Who's that grunting? You wonder I didn't go ashore for a howl and a dance? Well, no—I didn't. Fine sentiments, you say? Fine sentiments, be hanged[5]! I had no time. I had to mess about with white-lead and strips of woolen blanket

---

1 make you start: 吓你一跳
2 under the droop of heavy and motionless foliage: 在纹丝不动的树叶遮蔽的浓荫之下
3 its cloak of time: 时间的外衣
4 at the first good shake: 第一次用力一摇
5 be hanged: 〈俚语〉去他妈的

helping to put bandages on those leaky steam-pipes—I tell you. I had to watch the steering, and circumvent those snags, and get the tin-pot along by hook or by crook. There was surface-truth enough in these things to save a wiser man. And between whiles[1] I had to look after the savage who was fireman. He was an improved specimen; he could fire up a vertical boiler. He was there below me, and, upon my word[2], to look at him was as edifying as seeing a dog in a parody of breeches and a feather hat, walking on his hind-legs[3]. A few months of training had done for that really fine chap. He squinted at the steam-gauge and at the water-gauge with an evident effort of intrepidity—and he had filed teeth[4], too, the poor devil, and the wool of his pate shaved into queer patterns, and three ornamental scars on each of his cheeks. He ought to have been clapping his hands and stamping his feet on the bank, instead of which he was hard at work, a thrall to strange witchcraft, full of improving knowledge. He was useful because he had been instructed; and what he knew was this—that should the water in that transparent thing disappear, the evil spirit inside the boiler would get angry through the greatness of his thirst, and take a terrible vengeance. So he sweated and fired up and watched the glass fearfully (with an impromptu charm[5], made of rags, tied to his arm, and a piece of polished bone, as big as a watch, stuck flatways through his lower lip), while the wooded banks slipped past us slowly, the short noise was left behind, the interminable miles of silence—and we crept on, towards Kurtz. But the snags were thick, the water was treacherous and shallow, the boiler seemed indeed to have a sulky devil in it, and thus neither that fireman nor I had any time to peer into our creepy thoughts[6].

"Some fifty miles below the Inner Station we came upon a hut of reeds, an inclined and melancholy pole, with the unrecognizable tatters of what had been a flag of some sort flying from it, and a neatly stacked wood-pile. This was unexpected. We came to the bank, and on the stack of firewood found a flat piece of board with some faded pencil-writing on it. When deciphered it said: 'Wood for you. Hurry up. Approach cautiously.' There was a signature, but it was illegible—not Kurtz—a much longer word. Hurry up. Where? Up the river? 'Approach cautiously.' We had not done so. But the warning could not have been meant for the place where it could be only found after approach. Something was wrong above. But what—and how much? That was the question. We commented adversely upon[7] the imbecility of that telegraphic style. The bush around said nothing, and would not let us look very far, either. A torn curtain of red twill[8] hung in the doorway of the hut, and flapped sadly in our faces. The dwelling was dismantled; but we could see a white man had lived there not very long ago. There remained a rude table—a plank on two posts; a heap of rubbish reposed in a dark corner, and by the door I picked up a book. It had lost its covers, and the pages had been thumbed into a state of extremely dirty softness; but the back had been lovingly stitched afresh[9] with white cotton thread, which looked clean yet. It was an

---

1 between whiles：时不时地
2 upon my word：的确
3 hind-legs：后腿
4 filed teeth：用锉子锉平的牙齿
5 an impromptu charm：临时符咒
6 creepy thoughts：烦乱的思绪
7 commented adversely upon：对……抱怨，发牢骚
8 red twill：红色斜纹
9 stitched afresh：重新装订的

extraordinary find. Its title was, *An Inquiry Into Some Points of Seamanship*[1], by a man Towser, Towson—some such name—Master in his Majesty's Navy[2]. The matter looked dreary reading enough, with illustrative diagrams and repulsive tables of figures, and the copy was sixty years old. I handled this amazing antiquity with the greatest possible tenderness, lest it should dissolve in my hands. Within, Towson or Towser was inquiring earnestly into the breaking strain of ships' chains and tackle, and other such matters. Not a very enthralling[3] book; but at the first glance you could see there a singleness of intention, an honest concern for the right way of going to work, which made these humble pages, thought out so many years ago, luminous with another than a professional light. The simple old sailor, with his talk of chains and purchases, made me forget the jungle and the pilgrims in a delicious sensation of having come upon something unmistakably real. Such a book being there was wonderful enough; but still more astounding were the notes penciled in the margin, and plainly referring to the text. I couldn't believe my eyes! They were in cipher[4]! Yes, it looked like cipher. Fancy a man lugging with him a book of that description into this nowhere and studying it—and making notes—in cipher at that! It was an extravagant mystery.

"I had been dimly aware for some time of a worrying noise, and when I lifted my eyes I saw the wood-pile was gone, and the manager, aided by all the pilgrims, was shouting at me from the riverside. I slipped the book into my pocket. I assure you to leave off reading was like tearing myself away from[5] the shelter of an old and solid friendship.

"I started the lame engine ahead. 'It must be this miserable trader—this intruder,' exclaimed the manager, looking back malevolently at the place we had left. 'He must be English,' I said. 'It will not save him from getting into trouble if he is not careful,' muttered the manager darkly. I observed with assumed innocence[6] that no man was safe from trouble in this world.

"The current was more rapid now, the steamer seemed at her last gasp[7], the stern-wheel flopped languidly, and I caught myself listening on tiptoe for the next beat of the boat, for in sober truth I expected the wretched thing to give up every moment. It was like watching the last flickers of a life[8]. But still we crawled. Sometimes I would pick out a tree a little way ahead to measure our progress towards Kurtz by, but I lost it invariably before we got abreast. To keep the eyes so long on one thing was too much for human patience. The manager displayed a beautiful resignation[9]. I fretted and fumed and took to arguing with myself whether or no I would talk openly with Kurtz; but before I could come to any conclusion it occurred to me that my speech or my silence, indeed any action of mine, would be a mere futility. What did it matter what any one knew or ignored? What did it matter who was manager? One gets sometimes such a flash of insight. The essentials of this affair lay deep under the surface, beyond my

---

1 *An Inquiry Into Some Points of Seamanship*:《航海术要领研究》
2 Master in his Majesty's Navy:皇家海军的一位船长
3 enthralling:吸引人的
4 in cipher:用密码
5 tearing myself away from:强拉我离开
6 assumed innocence:假装天真
7 at her last gasp:奄奄一息
8 the last flickers of a life:生命中最后闪动的光华
9 resignation:忍耐,顺从

reach, and beyond my power of meddling¹.

"Towards the evening of the second day we judged ourselves about eight miles from Kurtz's station. I wanted to push on; but the manager looked grave, and told me the navigation up there was so dangerous that it would be advisable, the sun being very low already, to wait where we were till next morning. Moreover, he pointed out that if the warning to approach cautiously were to be followed, we must approach in daylight—not at dusk or in the dark. This was sensible enough. Eight miles meant nearly three hours' steaming for us, and I could also see suspicious ripples at the upper end of the reach. Nevertheless, I was annoyed beyond expression at the delay, and most unreasonably, too, since one night more could not matter much after so many months. As we had plenty of wood, and caution was the word, I brought up in the middle of the stream. The reach was narrow, straight, with high sides like a railway cutting. The dusk came gliding into it long before the sun had set. The current ran smooth and swift, but a dumb immobility² sat on the banks. The living trees, lashed together by the creepers and every living bush of the undergrowth, might have been changed into stone, even to the slenderest twig, to the lightest leaf. It was not sleep—it seemed unnatural, like a state of trance³. Not the faintest sound of any kind could be heard. You looked on amazed, and began to suspect yourself of being deaf—then the night came suddenly, and struck you blind as well. About three in the morning some large fish leaped, and the loud splash made me jump as though a gun had been fired. When the sun rose there was a white fog, very warm and clammy, and more blinding than the night. It did not shift or drive; it was just there, standing all round you like something solid. At eight or nine, perhaps, it lifted as a shutter lifts⁴. We had a glimpse of the towering multitude of trees, of the immense matted jungle, with the blazing little ball of the sun hanging over it—all perfectly still—and then the white shutter came down again, smoothly, as if sliding in greased grooves⁵. I ordered the chain, which we had begun to heave in⁶, to be paid out again. Before it stopped running with a muffled rattle, a cry, a very loud cry, as of infinite desolation, soared slowly in the opaque air. It ceased. A complaining clamor, modulated in savage discords⁷, filled our ears. The sheer unexpectedness of it made my hair stir⁸ under my cap. I don't know how it struck the others: to me it seemed as though the mist itself had screamed, so suddenly, and apparently from all sides at once, did this tumultuous and mournful uproar arise. It culminated in a hurried outbreak of almost intolerably excessive shrieking, which stopped short, leaving us stiffened in a variety of silly attitudes, and obstinately listening to the nearly as appalling and excessive silence. 'Good God! What is the meaning—' stammered at my elbow one of the pilgrims—a little fat man, with sandy hair and red whiskers, who wore sidespring boots, and pink pyjamas tucked into his socks. Two others remained open-mouthed a while minute, then dashed into the little cabin, to rush out incontinently and stand darting scared glances, with Winchesters at 'ready' in their hands. What we could see was just the steamer we were on, her outlines blurred as

---

1 beyond my power of meddling：凭我的力量无法干预
2 a dumb immobility：鸦雀无声，没有动静
3 a state of trance：一种昏迷状态
4 it lifted as a shutter lifts：就像打开了一扇百叶窗
5 greased grooves：润滑过的凹槽
6 heave in：收回
7 modulated in savage discords：夹杂在野人疯狂的嘈杂声中
8 made my hair stir：使我的头发都竖起来了

though she had been on the point of dissolving, and a misty strip of water, perhaps two feet broad, around her—and that was all. The rest of the world was nowhere, as far as our eyes and ears were concerned. Just nowhere. Gone, disappeared; swept off without leaving a whisper or a shadow behind[1].

"I went forward, and ordered the chain to be hauled in short, so as to be ready to trip the anchor and move the steamboat at once if necessary. 'Will they attack?' whispered an awed voice. 'We will be all butchered in this fog,' murmured another. The faces twitched with the strain, the hands trembled slightly, the eyes forgot to wink. It was very curious to see the contrast of expressions of the white men and of the black fellows of our crew, who were as much strangers to that part of the river as we, though their homes were only eight hundred miles away. The whites, of course greatly discomposed[2], had besides a curious look of being painfully shocked by such an outrageous row. The others had an alert, naturally interested expression; but their faces were essentially quiet, even those of the one or two who grinned as they hauled at the chain. Several exchanged short, grunting phrases, which seemed to settle the matter to their satisfaction. Their headman, a young, broad-chested[3] black, severely draped in dark-blue fringed cloths[4], with fierce nostrils and his hair all done up artfully in oily ringlets[5], stood near me 'Aha!' I said, just for good fellowship's sake. 'Catch 'im,' he snapped, with a bloodshot widening of his eyes[6] and a flash of sharp teeth—'catch 'im. Give 'im to us.' 'To you, eh?' I asked; 'What would you do with them?' 'Eat 'im!' he said curtly, and, leaning his elbow on the rail, looked out into the fog in a dignified and profoundly pensive attitude. I would no doubt have been properly horrified, had it not occurred to me that he and his chaps must be very hungry: that they must have been growing increasingly hungry for at least this month past. They had been engaged for six months (I don't think a single one of them had any clear idea of time, as we at the end of countless ages have. They still belonged to the beginnings of time—had no inherited experience to teach them as it were), and of course, as long as there was a piece of paper written over in accordance with some farcical law or other made down the river, it didn't enter anybody's head to trouble how they would live. Certainly they had brought with them some rotten hippo-meat, which couldn't have lasted very long, anyway, even if the pilgrims hadn't, in the midst of a shocking hullabaloo[7], thrown a considerable quantity of it overboard. It looked like a high-handed proceeding[8]; but it was really a case of legitimate self-defence. You can't breathe dead hippo waking, sleeping, and eating, and at the same time keep your precarious grip on existence. Besides that, they had given them every week three pieces of brass wire, each about nine inches long; and the theory was they were to buy their provisions with that currency in riverside villages. You can see how that worked. There were either no villages, or the people were hostile, or the director, who like the rest of us fed out of tins, with an occasional old he-goat[9] thrown in, didn't want to stop the steamer for some more or less

---

1 without leaving a whisper or a shadow behind: 声影全无
2 discomposed: 心乱的, 不安的
3 broad-chested: 胸膛宽阔的
4 dark-blue fringed cloths: 深蓝色缀着边儿的衣服
5 in oily ringlets: 卷成一个个光亮的发环
6 with a bloodshot widening of his eyes: 瞪大了布满血丝的眼睛
7 a shocking hullabaloo: 令人震惊的喧嚣声
8 a high-handed proceeding: 专横的行为
9 he-goat: 公羊

recondite reason[1]. So, unless they swallowed the wire itself, or made loops of[2] it to snare the fishes with, I don't see what good their extravagant salary could be to them. I must say it was paid with a regularity worthy of a large and honorable trading company. For the rest, the only thing to eat—though it didn't look eatable in the least—I saw in their possession was a few lumps of some stuff like half-cooked dough, of a dirty lavender colour, they kept wrapped in leaves, and now and then swallowed a piece of, but so small that it seemed done more for the looks of the thing[3] than for any serious purpose of sustenance. Why in the name of all the gnawing devils of hunger they didn't go for us[4]—they were thirty to five—and have a good tuck-in for once[5], amazes me now when I think of it. They were big powerful men, with not much capacity to weigh the consequences, with courage, with strength, even yet, though their skins were no longer glossy and their muscles no longer hard. And I saw that something restraining, one of those human secrets that baffle probability, had come into play[6] there. I looked at them with a swift quickening of interest—not because it occurred to me I might be eaten by them before very long, though I own to you that just then I perceived—in a new light, as it were—how unwholesome[7] the pilgrims looked, and I hoped, yes, I positively hoped, that my aspect was not so—what shall I say?—so—unappetizing: a touch of fantastic vanity which fitted well with the dream-sensation that pervaded all my days at that time. Perhaps I had a little fever, too. One can't live with one's finger everlastingly on one's pulse. I had often 'a little fever,' or a little touch of other things—the playful paw-strokes of the wilderness, the preliminary trifling before the more serious onslaught which came in due course[8]. Yes; I looked at them as you would on any human being, with a curiosity of their impulses, motives, capacities, weaknesses, when brought to the test of an inexorable physical necessity. Restraint! What possible restraint? Was it superstition, disgust, patience, fear—or some kind of primitive honour? No fear can stand up to hunger, no patience can wear it out[9], disgust simply does not exist where hunger is; and as to superstition, beliefs, and what you may call principles, they are less than chaff in a breeze[10]. Don't you know the devilry of lingering starvation, its exasperating torment, its black thoughts, its sombre and brooding ferocity? Well, I do. It takes a man all his inborn strength to fight hunger properly. It's really easier to face bereavement, dishonour, and the perdition of one's soul—than this kind of prolonged hunger. Sad, but true. And these chaps, too, had no earthly reason for any kind of scruple. Restraint! I would just as soon have expected restraint from a hyena prowling amongst the corpses of a battlefield. But there was the fact facing me—the fact dazzling, to be seen, like the foam on the depths of the sea, like a ripple on an unfathomable enigma, a mystery greater—when I thought of it—than the curious, inexplicable note of desperate grief[11] in this savage clamor that had swept by us on the river-bank, behind

---

1 recondite reason: 不为人知的原因
2 made loops of: 用……做成圈套
3 for the looks of the thing: 做出吃东西的样子
4 go for: 去找，文中指进攻。
5 have a good tuck-in for once: 享受一顿美餐
6 come into play: 起作用
7 unwholesome: 不健康的
8 in due course: 及时的，在适当的时候
9 wear it out: 磨透，文中指使饥饿消失。
10 less than chaff in a breeze: 不足挂齿的
11 note of desperate grief: 无比凄婉的气氛

the blind whiteness of the fog.

"Two pilgrims were quarrelling in hurried whispers as to which bank. 'Left.' 'no, no; how can you? Right, right, of course.' 't is very serious,' said the manager's voice behind me; 'I would be desolated if anything should happen to Mr. Kurtz before we came up.' I looked at him, and had not the slightest doubt he was sincere. He was just the kind of man who would wish to preserve appearances[1]. That was his restraint. But when he muttered something about going on at once, I did not even take the trouble to answer him. I knew, and he knew, that it was impossible. Were we to let go our hold of the bottom, we would be absolutely in the air—in space. We wouldn't be able to tell where we were going to—whether up or down stream, or across—till we fetched against one bank or the other, and then we wouldn't know at first which it was. Of course I made no move. I had no mind for a smash-up[2]. You couldn't imagine a more deadly place for a shipwreck. Whether we drowned at once or not, we were sure to perish speedily in one way or another. 'I authorize you to take all the risks,' he said, after a short silence. 'I refuse to take any,' I said shortly; which was just the answer he expected, though its tone might have surprised him. 'Well, I must defer to[3] your judgment. You are captain,' he said with marked civility[4]. I turned my shoulder to him in sign of my appreciation, and looked into the fog. How long would it last? It was the most hopeless lookout. The approach to this Kurtz grubbing for ivory in the wretched bush was beset by[5] as many dangers as though he had been an enchanted princess sleeping in a fabulous castle. 'Will they attack, do you think?' asked the manager, in a confidential tone.

"I did not think they would attack, for several obvious reasons. The thick fog was one. If they left the bank in their canoes they would get lost in it, as we would be if we attempted to move. Still, I had also judged the jungle of both banks quite impenetrable—and yet eyes were in it, eyes that had seen us. The riverside bushes were certainly very thick; but the undergrowth behind was evidently penetrable. However, during the short lift[6] I had seen no canoes anywhere in the reach—certainly not abreast of[7] the steamer. But what made the idea of attack inconceivable to me was the nature of the noise—of the cries we had heard. They had not the fierce character boding immediate hostile intention. Unexpected, wild, and violent as they had been, they had given me an irresistible impression of sorrow. The glimpse of the steamboat had for some reason filled those savages with unrestrained grief. The danger, if any, I expounded, was from our proximity to a great human passion let loose[8]. Even extreme grief may ultimately vent itself in violence—but more generally takes the form of apathy...

"You should have seen the pilgrims stare! They had no heart to[9] grin, or even to revile me: but I believe they thought me gone mad—with fright, maybe. I delivered a regular lecture. My dear boys, it was no good bothering. Keep a lookout? Well, you may guess I watched the fog for the signs of lifting as

---

1 preserve appearances: 保全面子
2 smash-up: 崩溃, 瓦解
3 defer to: 服从
4 marked civility: 假装客气
5 be beset by: 被……包围, 为……困扰
6 short lift: 文中指浓雾散去的短暂时间
7 abreast of: 与……并进
8 let loose: 释放, 放出
9 had no heart to: 没有勇气做……

a cat watches a mouse; but for anything else our eyes were of no more use to us than if we had been buried miles deep in a heap of cotton-wool. It felt like it, too—choking, warm, stifling. Besides, all I said, though it sounded extravagant, was absolutely true to fact. What we afterwards alluded to[1] as an attack was really an attempt at repulse. The action was very far from being aggressive—it was not even defensive, in the usual sense: it was undertaken under the stress of desperation, and in its essence was purely protective.

"It developed itself, I should say, two hours after the fog lifted, and its commencement was at a spot, roughly speaking, about a mile and a half below Kurtz's station. We had just floundered and flopped round a bend, when I saw an islet, a mere grassy hummock[2] of bright green, in the middle of the stream. It was the only thing of the kind; but as we opened the reach more, I perceived it was the head of a long sand-bank, or rather of a chain of shallow patches stretching down the middle of the river. They were discoloured, just awash, and the whole lot was seen just under the water, exactly as a man's backbone is seen running down the middle of his back under the skin. Now, as far as I did see, I could go to the right or to the left of this. I didn't know either channel, of course. The banks looked pretty well alike, the depth appeared the same; but as I had been informed the station was on the west side, I naturally headed for the western passage.

"No sooner had we fairly entered it than I became aware it was much narrower than I had supposed. To the left of us there was the long uninterrupted shoal[3], and to the right a high, steep bank heavily overgrown with bushes. Above the bush the trees stood in serried ranks[4]. The twigs overhung the current thickly, and from distance to distance a large limb of some tree projected rigidly over the stream. It was then well on in the afternoon, the face of the forest was gloomy, and a broad strip of shadow had already fallen on the water. In this shadow we steamed up—very slowly, as you may imagine. I sheered her well inshore—the water being deepest near the bank, as the sounding-pole informed me.

"One of my hungry and forbearing friends was sounding in the bows just below me. This steamboat was exactly like a decked scow[5]. On the deck, there were two little teakwood houses, with doors and windows. The boiler was in the fore-end[6], and the machinery right astern. Over the whole there was a light roof, supported on stanchions[7]. The funnel projected through that roof, and in front of the funnel a small cabin built of light planks served for a pilot-house. It contained a couch, two camp-stools[8], a loaded Martini-Henry[9] leaning in one corner, a tiny table, and the steering-wheel. It had a wide door in front and a broad shutter at each side. All these were always thrown open, of course. I spent my days perched up there on the extreme fore-end of that roof, before the door. At night I slept, or tried to, on the couch. An athletic black belonging to some coast tribe and educated by my poor predecessor, was the

---

1 allude to：提到，暗指
2 a mere grassy hummock：野草丛生的小圆丘
3 uninterrupted shoal：连绵不断的沙洲
4 in serried ranks：密集地排成一排排
5 a decked scow：一只带甲板的驳船
6 in the fore-end：在船的前端
7 stanchion：支柱
8 camp-stool：折叠凳子
9 a loaded Martini-Henry：一把已装有子弹的马蒂尼—亨利式来福枪

helmsman. He sported a pair of brass earrings, wore a blue cloth wrapper from the waist to the ankles, and thought all the world of himself. He was the most unstable kind of fool I had ever seen. He steered with no end of a swagger[1] while you were by; but if he lost sight of you, he became instantly the prey of an abject funk[2], and would let that cripple of a steamboat get the upper hand of him in a minute.

"I was looking down at the sounding-pole, and feeling much annoyed to see at each try a little more of it stick out of that river, when I saw my poleman give up on the business suddenly, and stretch himself flat on the deck, without even taking the trouble to haul his pole in. He kept hold on it though, and it trailed in the water. At the same time the fireman, whom I could also see below me, sat down abruptly before his furnace and ducked his head. I was amazed. Then I had to look at the river mighty quick, because there was a snag in the fairway. Sticks, little sticks, were flying about—thick: they were whizzing before my nose, dropping below me, striking behind me against my pilot-house. All this time the river, the shore, the woods, were very quiet—perfectly quiet. I could only hear the heavy splashing thump of the stern-wheel and the patter of these things. We cleared the snag clumsily. Arrows, by Jove! We were being shot at! I stepped in quickly to close the shutter on the landside. That fool-helmsman, his hands on the spokes, was lifting his knees high, stamping his feet, champing his mouth, like a reined-in horse[3]. Confound him[4]! And we were staggering within ten feet of the bank. I had to lean right out to swing the heavy shutter, and I saw a face amongst the leaves on the level with my own, looking at me very fierce and steady; and then suddenly, as though a veil had been removed from my eyes, I made out, deep in the tangled gloom, naked breasts, arms, legs, glaring eyes—the bush was swarming with human limbs in movement, glistening, of bronze colour. The twigs shook, swayed, and rustled, the arrows flew out of them, and then the shutter came to. 'Steer her straight,' I said to the helmsman. He held his head rigid, face forward; but his eyes rolled, he kept on lifting and setting down his feet gently, his mouth foamed a little. 'Keep quiet,' I said in a fury[5]. I might just as well[6] have ordered a tree not to sway in the wind. I darted out[7]. Below me there was a great scuffle of feet on the iron deck; confused exclamations; a voice screamed, 'Can you turn back?' I caught sight of a V-shaped ripple on the water ahead. What? Another snag! A fusillade[8] burst out under my feet. The pilgrims had opened with their Winchesters, and were simply squirting lead into that bush. A deuce of a lot of smoke came up and drove slowly forward. I swore at it. Now I couldn't see the ripple or the snag either. I stood in the doorway, peering, and the arrows came in swarms. They might have been poisoned, but they looked as though they wouldn't kill a cat. The bush began to howl. Our wood-cutters raised a warlike whoop[9]; the report of a rifle just at my back deafened me. I glanced over my shoulder, and the pilot-house was yet full of noise and smoke when I made a dash at the wheel. The fool-nigger had dropped everything, to throw the shutter open and let

---

1 with no end of a swagger：摆出一副十足的架势
2 an abject funk：一个缩手缩脚（或卑躬屈膝）的家伙
3 a reined-in horse：一头被勒紧缰绳的马
4 Confound him：混蛋，该死的东西
5 in a fury：愤怒地
6 might just as well：不妨，还是……好
7 darted out：冲出
8 a fusillade：一大排箭
9 a warlike whoop：一阵战斗的呐喊声

off[1] that Martini-Henry. He stood before the wide opening, glaring, and I yelled at him to come back, while I straightened the sudden twist out of that steamboat. There was no room to turn even if I had wanted to, the snag was somewhere very near ahead in that confounded smoke, there was no time to lose, so I just crowded her into the bank—right into the bank, where I knew the water was deep.

"We tore slowly along the overhanging bushes in a whirl of broken twigs and flying leaves. The fusillade below stopped short, as I had foreseen it would when the squirts got empty. I threw my head back to a glinting whizz that traversed the pilot-house, in at one shutter-hole and out at the other. Looking past that mad helmsman, who was shaking the empty rifle and yelling at the shore, I saw vague forms of men running bent double, leaping, gliding, distinct, incomplete, evanescent[2]. Something big appeared in the air before the shutter, the rifle went overboard[3], and the man stepped back swiftly, looked at me over his shoulder in an extraordinary, profound, familiar manner, and fell upon my feet. The side of his head hit the wheel twice, and the end of what appeared a long cane clattered round and knocked over a little camp-stool. It looked as though after wrenching that thing from somebody ashore he had lost his balance in the effort. The thin smoke had blown away, we were clear of the snag, and looking ahead I could see that in another hundred yards or so I would be free to sheer off, away from the bank; but my feet felt so very warm and wet that I had to look down. The man had rolled on his back and stared straight up at me; both his hands clutched that cane. It was the shaft[4] of a spear that, either thrown or lunged through the opening, had caught him in the side, just below the ribs; the blade had gone in out of sight, after making a frightful gash; my shoes were full; a pool of blood lay very still[5], gleaming dark-red under the wheel; his eyes shone with an amazing luster[6]. The fusillade burst out again. He looked at me anxiously, gripping the spear like something precious, with an air of being afraid I would try to take it away from him. I had to make an effort to free my eyes from his gaze and attend to the steering. With one hand I felt above my head for the line of the steam whistle, and jerked out screech after screech[7] hurriedly. The tumult of angry and warlike yells was checked instantly, and then from the depths of the woods went out such a tremulous and prolonged wail of mournful fear and utter despair as may be imagined to follow the flight of the last hope from the earth. There was a great commotion[8] in the bush; the shower of arrows stopped, a few dropping shots rang out sharply—then silence, in which the languid beat[9] of the stern-wheel came plainly to my ears. I put the helm hard a-starboard[10] at the moment when the pilgrim in pink pyjamas, very hot and agitated, appeared in the doorway. 'The manager sends me—' he began in an official tone, and stopped short. 'Good God!' he said, glaring at the wounded man.

"We two whites stood over him, and his lustrous and inquiring glance enveloped[11] us both. I declare

---

1 let off：发射
2 evanescent：迅速消失的
3 went overboard：掉到河里
4 shaft：轴，杆状物
5 a pool of blood lay very still：那里积了一小摊血
6 an amazing luster：奇异的光彩
7 jerked out screech after screech：一声接一声猛拉汽笛
8 commotion：骚动，暴乱
9 languid beat：无精打采的击水声
10 a-starboard：向右弦
11 envelope：笼罩

it looked as though he would presently put to us some questions in an understandable language; but he died without uttering a sound, without moving a limb, without twitching a muscle. Only in the very last moment, as though in response to some sign we could not see, to some whisper we could not hear, he frowned heavily, and that frown gave to his black death-mask an inconceivably somber, brooding, and menacing expression. The luster of inquiring glance faded swiftly into vacant glassiness[1]. 'Can you steer?' I asked the agent eagerly. He looked very dubious; but I made a grab at his arm, and he understood at once I meant him to steer whether or no. To tell you the truth, I was morbidly anxious to change my shoes and socks. 'He is dead,' murmured the fellow, immensely impressed. 'No doubt about it,' said I, tugging like mad at the shoe-laces. 'And by the way, I suppose Mr. Kurtz is dead as well by this time.'

"For the moment that was the dominant thought. There was a sense of extreme disappointment, as though I had found out I had been striving after something altogether without a substance[2]. I couldn't have been more disgusted if I had traveled all this way for the sole purpose of talking with Mr. Kurtz. Talking with ... I flung one shoe overboard, and became aware that that was exactly what I had been looking forward to—a talk with Kurtz. I made the strange discovery that I had never imagined him as doing, you know, but as discoursing. I didn't say to myself, 'Now I will never see him,' or 'Now I will never shake him by the hand,' but, 'Now I will never hear him.' The man presented himself as a voice. Not of course that I did not connect him with some sort of action. Hadn't I been told in all the tones of jealousy and admiration that he had collected, bartered, swindled, or stolen more ivory than all the other agents together? That was not the point. The point was in his being a gifted creature, and that of all his gifts the one that stood out preeminently, that carried with it a sense of real presence[3], was his ability to talk, his words—the gift of expression, the bewildering, the illuminating, the most exalted and the most contemptible, the pulsating stream of light[4], or the deceitful flow from the heart of an impenetrable darkness.

"The other shoe went flying unto the devil-god[5] of that river. I thought, By Jove! it's all over. We are too late; he has vanished—the gift has vanished, by means of some spear, arrow, or club. I will never hear that chap speak after all, and my sorrow had a startling extravagance of emotion[6], even such as I had noticed in the howling sorrow of these savages in the bush. I couldn't have felt more of lonely desolation somehow, had I been robbed of a belief or had missed my destiny in life... Why do you sigh in this beastly way, somebody? Absurd? Well, absurd. Good Lord! Mustn't a man ever—Here, give me some tobacco."...

There was a pause of profound stillness, then a match flared, and Marlow's lean face[7] appeared, worn, hollow, with downward folds and dropped eyelids, with an aspect of concentrated attention; and as he took vigorous draws at his pipe[8], it seemed to retreat and advance out of the night in the regular

---

1 faded swiftly into vacant glassiness:迅速消逝变成空洞呆滞的眼神
2 altogether without a substance:完全不存在
3 a sense of real presence:真实存在感
4 the pulsating stream of light:搏动着的智慧之光
5 the devil-god:河神
6 a startling extravagance of emotion:强烈得令人惊诧的感情
7 lean face:瘦削的脸庞
8 took vigorous draws at his pipe:用力抽着他的烟斗

flicker of tiny flame. The match went out.

"Absurd!" he cried. "This is the worst of trying to tell... Here you all are, each moored with two good addresses, like a hulk with two anchors, a butcher round one corner, a policeman round another, excellent appetites, and temperature normal—you hear—normal from year's end to year's end[1]. And you say, Absurd! Absurd be—exploded! Absurd! My dear boys, what can you expect from a man who out of sheer nervousness had just flung overboard a pair of new shoes! Now I think of it, it is amazing I did not shed tears. I am, upon the whole[2], proud of my fortitude. I was cut to the quick[3] at the idea of having lost the inestimable privilege of listening to the gifted Kurtz. Of course I was wrong. The privilege was waiting for me. Oh, yes, I heard more than enough. And I was right, too. A voice. He was very little more than a voice. And I heard—him—it—this voice—other voices—all of them were so little more than voices—and the memory of that time itself lingers around me, impalpable, like a dying vibration of one immense jabber[4], silly, atrocious, sordid, savage, or simply mean[5], without any kind of sense. Voices, voices—even the girl herself—now—"

He was silent for a long time.

"I laid the ghost of his gifts at last with a lie," he began, suddenly. "Girl! What? Did I mention a girl? Oh, she is out of it[6]—completely. They—the women I mean—are out of it—should be out of it. We must help them to stay in that beautiful world of their own, lest ours gets worse. Oh, she had to be out of it. You should have heard the disinterred body of Mr. Kurtz saying, 'My Intended[7].' You would have perceived directly then how completely she was out of it. And the lofty frontal bone[8] of Mr. Kurtz! They say the hair goes on growing sometimes, but this—ah—specimen, was impressively bald. The wilderness had patted him on the head, and, behold, it was like a ball—an ivory ball; it had caressed him, and—lo!—he had withered; it had taken him, loved him, embraced him, got into his veins, consumed his flesh, and sealed his soul to its own by the inconceivable ceremonies of some devilish initiation. He was its spoiled and pampered favorite. Ivory? I should think so. Heaps of it, stacks of it. The old mud shanty[9] was bursting with it. You would think there was not a single tusk left either above or below the ground in the whole country. 'Mostly fossil,' the manager had remarked, disparagingly[10]. It was no more fossil than I am; but they call it fossil when it is dug up. It appears these niggers do bury the tusks sometimes—but evidently they couldn't bury this parcel deep enough to save the gifted Mr. Kurtz from his fate. We filled the steamboat with it, and had to pile a lot on the deck. Thus he could see and enjoy as long as he could see, because the appreciation of this favor had remained with him to the last. You should have heard him say, 'My ivory.' Oh, yes, I heard him. 'My Intended, my ivory, my station, my river, my—' everything belonged to him. It made me hold my breath in expectation of hearing the wilderness burst

---

1 from year's end to year's end: 从年初到年底；一年到头
2 upon the whole: 总的来说
3 cut to the quick: 非常难过。quick: (指甲下的)活肉
4 like a dying vibration of one immense jabber: 像一句漫无边际、毫无意义、渐渐消逝的余音
5 mean: 卑鄙下流
6 she is out of it: 她是个局外人
7 My Intended: 我的未婚妻
8 lofty frontal bone: 高高的前额骨
9 mud shanty: 用泥浆做的棚屋
10 disparagingly: 不以为然地

into a prodigious peal of laughter[1] that would shake the fixed stars[2] in their places. Everything belonged to him—but that was a trifle. The thing was to know what he belonged to, how many powers of darkness claimed him—for their own[3]. That was the reflection that made you creepy all over. It was impossible—it was not good for one either—trying to imagine. He had taken a high seat[4] amongst the devils of the land—I mean literally. You can't understand. How could you?—with solid pavement under your feet, surrounded by kind neighbors ready to cheer you or to fall on you, stepping delicately between the butcher and the policeman, in the holy terror of scandal and gallows and lunatic asylums[5]—how can you imagine what particular region of the first ages a man's untrammeled feet[6] may take him into by the way of solitude—utter solitude without a policeman—by the way of silence—utter silence, where no warning voice of a kind neighbor can be heard whispering of public opinion? These little things make all the great difference. When they are gone you must fall back upon your own innate strength, upon your own capacity for faithfulness. Of course you may be too much of a fool to go wrong—too dull even to know you are being assaulted by the powers of darkness. I take it[7], no fool ever made a bargain for his soul with the devil; the fool is too much of a fool, or the devil too much of a devil—I don't know which. Or you may be such a thunderingly exalted creature as to be altogether deaf and blind to anything but heavenly sights and sounds. Then the earth for you is only a standing place—and whether to be like this is your loss or your gain I won't pretend to say. But most of us are neither one nor the other. The earth for us is a place to live in, where we must put up with sights, with sounds, with smells, too, by Jove!—breathe dead hippo, so to speak, and not be contaminated. And there, don't you see? Your strength comes in, the faith in your ability for the digging of unostentatious holes to bury the stuff in—your power of devotion, not to yourself, but to an obscure, back-breaking business. And that's difficult enough. Mind, I am not trying to excuse or even explain—I am trying to account to myself for—for—Mr. Kurtz—for the shade[8] of Mr. Kurtz. This initiated wraith from the back of Nowhere honored me with its amazing confidence before it vanished altogether. This was because it could speak English to me. The original Kurtz had been educated partly in England, and—as he was good enough to say himself—his sympathies were in the right place. His mother was half-English, his father was half-French. All Europe contributed to the making of Kurtz; and by and by I learned that, most appropriately, the International Society for the Suppression of Savage Customs[9] had intrusted him with the making of a report, for its future guidance. And he had written it, too. I've seen it. I've read it. It was eloquent, vibrating with eloquence, but too high-strung[10], I think. Seventeen pages of close writing he had found time for! But this must have been before his—let us say—nerves, went wrong, and caused him to preside at[11] certain midnight dances ending with unspeakable

---

1 a prodigious peal of laughter：惊天动地的笑声
2 the fixed stars：恒星
3 claimed...for their own：宣称对……具有所有权
4 take a high seat：坐上头把交椅
5 lunatic asylum：疯人院，精神病院
6 untrammeled feet：自由的脚，不受约束的脚
7 I take it：依我看
8 shade：幽魂
9 the International Society for the Suppression of Savage Customs：禁止野蛮习俗国际协会
10 high-strung：高调的，情绪激动的
11 preside at：主持

rites, which—as far as I reluctantly gathered from what I heard at various times were offered up to him—do you understand? —to Mr. Kurtz himself. But it was a beautiful piece of writing. The opening paragraph, however, in the light of later information, strikes me now as ominous. He began with the argument that we whites, from the point of development we had arrived at, 'must necessarily appear to them [savages] in the nature of supernatural beings—we approach them with the might of a deity[1],' and so on, and so on. 'By the simple exercise of our will we can exert a power for good practically unbounded,' etc., etc. From that point he soared and took me with him[2]. The peroration was magnificent, though difficult to remember, you know. It gave me the notion of an exotic Immensity ruled by an august Benevolence. It made me tingle with enthusiasm. This was the unbounded power of eloquence—of words—of burning noble words. There were no practical hints to interrupt the magic current of phrases, unless a kind of note at the foot of the last page, scrawled evidently much later, in an unsteady hand, may be regarded as the exposition of a method. It was very simple, and at the end of that moving appeal to every altruistic sentiment[3] it blazed at you, luminous and terrifying, like a flash of lightning in a serene sky: 'Exterminate all the brutes!' The curious part was that he had apparently forgotten all about that valuable post scriptum, because, later on, when he in a sense came to himself, he repeatedly entreated me to take good care of 'my pamphlet' (he called it), as it was sure to have in the future a good influence upon his career. I had full information about all these things, and, besides, as it turned out, I was to have the care of his memory. I've done enough for it to give me the indisputable right[4] to lay it, if I choose, for an everlasting rest in the dust-bin of progress, amongst all the sweepings and, figuratively speaking, all the dead cats of civilization. But then, you see, I can't choose. He won't be forgotten. Whatever he was, he was not common. He had the power to charm or frighten rudimentary souls[5] into an aggravated witch-dance in his honor; he could also fill the small souls of the pilgrims with bitter misgivings: he had one devoted friend at least, and he had conquered one soul in the world that was neither rudimentary nor tainted with self-seeking. No; I can't forget him, though I am not prepared to affirm the fellow was exactly worth the life we lost in getting to him. I missed my late helmsman awfully—I missed him even while his body was still lying in the pilothouse. Perhaps you will think it passing strange this regret for a savage who was no more account than a grain of sand in a black Sahara[6]. Well, don't you see, he had done something, he had steered; for months I had him at my back—a help—an instrument. It was a kind of partnership. He steered for me—I had to look after him, I worried about his deficiencies, and thus a subtle bond had been created, of which I only became aware when it was suddenly broken. And the intimate profundity of that look[7] he gave me when he received his hurt remains to this day in my memory—like a claim of distant kinship affirmed in a supreme moment.

"Poor fool! If he had only left that shutter alone. He had no restraint, no restraint—just like Kurtz—

---

1 with the might of a deity: 带着神的力量
2 took me with him: 把我说服了
3 altruistic sentiment: 利他主义思想
4 indisputable right: 不容置辩的权利
5 rudimentary souls: 蒙昧的人，头脑简单的人
6 Sahara: 撒哈拉沙漠
7 the intimate profundity of that look: 饱含亲密、深情的眼神

a tree swayed by the wind. As soon as I had put on a dry pair of slippers, I dragged him out, after first jerking the spear out of his side, which operation I confess I performed with my eyes shut tight. His heels leaped together over the little doorstep; his shoulders were pressed to my breast; I hugged him from behind desperately. Oh! he was heavy, heavy; heavier than any man on earth, I should imagine. Then without more ado[1] I tipped him overboard. The current snatched him as though he had been a wisp of grass, and I saw the body roll over twice before I lost sight of it for ever. All the pilgrims and the manager were then congregated on the awning-deck about the pilot-house, chattering at each other like a flock of excited magpies, and there was a scandalized murmur at my heartless promptitude. What they wanted to keep that body hanging about for I can't guess. Embalm it[2], maybe. But I had also heard another, and a very ominous, murmur on the deck below. My friends the wood-cutters were likewise scandalized, and with a better show of reason though I admit that the reason itself was quite inadmissible. Oh, quite! I had made up my mind that if my late helmsman was to be eaten, the fishes alone should have him. He had been a very second-rate helmsman while alive, but now he was dead he might have become a first-class temptation[3], and possibly cause some startling trouble. Besides, I was anxious to take the wheel, the man in pink pyjamas showing himself a hopeless duffer[4] at the business[5].

"This I did directly the simple funeral was over. We were going half-speed, keeping right in the middle of the stream, and I listened to the talk about me. They had given up Kurtz, they had given up the station; Kurtz was dead, and the station had been burnt—and so on—and so on. The red-haired pilgrim was beside himself with the thought that at least this poor Kurtz had been properly avenged. 'Say! We must have made a glorious slaughter of them in the bush. Eh? What do you think? Say?' He positively danced, the bloodthirsty little gingery beggar. And he had nearly fainted when he saw the wounded man! I could not help saying, 'You made a glorious lot of smoke, anyhow.' I had seen, from the way the tops of the bushes rustled and flew, that almost all the shots had gone too high. You can't hit anything unless you take aim and fire from the shoulder; but these chaps fired from the hip with their eyes shut. The retreat, I maintained—and I was right—was caused by the screeching of the steam whistle. Upon this they forgot Kurtz, and began to howl at me with indignant protests.

"The manager stood by the wheel murmuring confidentially about the necessity of getting well away down the river before dark at all events[6], when I saw in the distance a clearing on the riverside and the outlines of some sort of building. 'What's this?' I asked. He clapped his hands in wonder. 'The station!' he cried. I edged in at once, still going half-speed.

"Through my glasses I saw the slope of a hill interspersed with[7] rare trees and perfectly free from undergrowth. A long decaying building on the summit was half buried in the high grass; the large holes in the peaked roof gaped black from afar; the jungle and the woods made a background. There was no

---

1 without more ado：非常干脆地，毫不费力地
2 embalm it：给它涂上香油
3 a first-class temptation：最大的诱惑
4 duffer：蠢货，笨蛋
5 at the business：在这一行业
6 at all events：无论如何，不管怎样
7 interspersed with：用……点缀

enclosure or fence of any kind; but there had been one apparently, for near the house half-a-dozen slim posts remained in a row, roughly trimmed, and with their upper ends ornamented with round carved balls. The rails, or whatever there had been between, had disappeared. Of course the forest surrounded all that. The river-bank was clear, and on the waterside I saw a white man under a hat like a cart-wheel beckoning persistently with his whole arm. Examining the edge of the forest above and below, I was almost certain I could see movements—human forms gliding here and there. I steamed past prudently, then stopped the engines and let her drift down. The man on the shore began to shout, urging us to land. 'We have been attacked,' screamed the manager. 'I know—I know. It's all right,' yelled back the other, as cheerful as you please. 'Come along. It's all right. I am glad.'

"His aspect reminded me of something I had seen—something funny I had seen somewhere. As I manoeuvred to get alongside, I was asking myself, 'What does this fellow look like?' Suddenly I got it. He looked like a harlequin[1]. His clothes had been made of some stuff that was brown holland[2] probably, but it was covered with patches[3] all over, with bright patches, blue, red, and yellow—patches on the back, patches on the front, patches on elbows, on knees; coloured binding around his jacket, scarlet edging at the bottom of his trousers; and the sunshine made him look extremely gay and wonderfully neat withal, because you could see how beautifully all this patching had been done. A beardless, boyish face, very fair, no features to speak of, nose peeling[4], little blue eyes, smiles and frowns chasing each other over that open countenance like sunshine and shadow on a wind-swept plain[5]. 'Look out, captain!' he cried; 'there's a snag lodged in here last night.' What! Another snag? I confess I swore shamefully. I had nearly holed my cripple[6], to finish off that charming trip. The harlequin on the bank turned his little pug-nose[7] up to me. 'You English?' he asked, all smiles. 'Are you?' I shouted from the wheel. The smiles vanished, and he shook his head as if sorry for my disappointment. Then he brightened up. 'Never mind!' he cried encouragingly. 'Are we in time?' I asked. 'He is up there,' he replied, with a toss of the head up the hill, and becoming gloomy all of a sudden. His face was like the autumn sky, overcast one moment and bright the next.

"When the manager, escorted by the pilgrims, all of them armed to the teeth[8], had gone to the house this chap came on board. 'I say, I don't like this. These natives are in the bush,' I said. He assured me earnestly it was all right. 'They are simple people,' he added; 'well, I am glad you came. It took me all my time to keep them off.' 'But you said it was all right,' I cried. 'Oh, they meant no harm,' he said; and as I stared he corrected himself, 'Not exactly.' Then vivaciously, 'My faith, your pilot-house wants a clean-up!' In the next breath he advised me to keep enough steam on the boiler to blow the whistle in case of any trouble. 'One good screech will do more for you than all your rifles. They are simple people,' he repeated. He rattled away at such a rate he quite overwhelmed me. He seemed to be trying to

---

1 harlequin：小丑
2 holland：荷兰亚麻布
3 patches：补丁
4 nose peeling：鼻子在脱皮
5 a wind-swept plain：大风吹过的平原
6 holed my cripple：戳破我这只破船
7 pug-nose：狮子鼻，扁平的鼻子
8 armed to the teeth：武装到牙齿，全副武装

make up for lots of silence, and actually hinted, laughing, that such was the case. 'Don't you talk with Mr. Kurtz?' I said. 'You don't talk with that man—you listen to him,' he exclaimed with severe exaltation. 'But now—'He waved his arm, and in the twinkling of an eye[1] was in the uttermost depths of despondency. In a moment he came up again with a jump, possessed himself of both my hands, shook them continuously, while he gabbled: 'Brother sailor ... honour ... pleasure ... delight ... introduce myself ... Russian ... son of an arch-priest ... Government of Tambov[2] ... What? Tobacco! English tobacco; the excellent English tobacco! Now, that's brotherly. Smoke? Where's a sailor that does not smoke?'

"The pipe soothed him, and gradually I made out he had run away from school, had gone to sea in a Russian ship; ran away again; served some time in English ships; was now reconciled with the arch-priest. He made a point of that. 'But when one is young one must see things, gather experience, ideas; enlarge the mind.' 'Here!' I interrupted. 'You can never tell! Here I met Mr. Kurtz,' he said, youthfully solemn and reproachful. I held my tongue after that. It appears he had persuaded a Dutch trading-house on the coast to fit him out with[3] stores and goods, and had started for the interior with a light heart and no more idea of what would happen to him than a baby. He had been wandering about that river for nearly two years alone, cut off from everybody and everything. 'I am not so young as I look. I am twenty-five,' he said. 'At first old Van Shuyten would tell me to go to the devil,' he narrated with keen enjoyment;'but I stuck to him, and talked and talked, till at last he got afraid I would talk the hind-leg off his favorite dog[4], so he gave me some cheap things and a few guns, and told me he hoped he would never see my face again. Good old Dutchman, Van Shuyten. I've sent him one small lot of ivory a year ago, so that he can't call me a little thief when I get back. I hope he got it. And for the rest I don't care. I had some wood stacked for you. That was my old house. Did you see?'

"I gave him Towson's book. He made as though he would kiss me, but restrained himself. 'The only book I had left, and I thought I had lost it,' he said, looking at it ecstatically. 'So many accidents happen to a man going about alone, you know. Canoes get upset[5] sometimes and—sometimes you've got to clear out so quick when the people get angry.' He thumbed the pages. 'You made notes in Russian?' I asked. He nodded. 'I thought they were written in cipher,' I said. He laughed, then became serious. 'I had lots of trouble to keep these people off,' he said. 'Did they want to kill you?' I asked. 'Oh, no!' he cried, and checked himself. 'Why did they attack us?' I pursued. He hesitated, then said shamefacedly, 'They don't want him to go.' 'Don't they?' I said curiously. He nodded a nod full of mystery and wisdom.'I tell you,' he cried, 'this man has enlarged my mind.' He opened his arms wide, staring at me with his little blue eyes that were perfectly round."

---

1 in the twinkling of an eye: 刹那间，转眼间
2 Government of Tambov: 坦波夫政府
3 fit him out with: 给他供应
4 the hind-leg off his favorite dog: 〈成语〉常指一个人爱唠叨。文中是开玩笑。
5 get upset: 翻掉

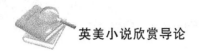

Understanding the Text

Heart of Darkness has been considered for most of the 20th-century as a literary classic, which sarcastically reveals the supposedly noble aims of European colonists and indicts the evils of colonialism and imperialism through Conrad's accurate recounting of the methods and effects of colonialism, thereby demonstrating Conrad's negative views of the moral superiority of white men and imperialism. Many critics note that Conrad presents colonialism through Marlow and the colonists. On his journey from the Outer Station to the Central Station and finally up the river to the Inner Station, Charles Marlow witnesses torture, cruelty, and near-slavery of colonial enterprise: natives cut off hands for noncooperation in Leopold's forced labor system, the chain gang and the "black shadows of disease and starvation" who are left to die in the "greenish gloom," the station described as an administrative nightmare and the machine as decaying. What Marlow sees is miserable enough. However, for Marlow, "the worst feature of imperialism may not have been its violence toward the 'miserable' and 'helpless,' but the lying propaganda used to cover its bloody tracks." (Brantlinger) The "faithless pilgrims" who work for the Company describe what they do as "trade," and what they do with the native Africans is just for their benevolent "civilization" of these natives. Actually, as Marlow says, "To tear treasure out of the bowels of the land was their desire, with no more moral purpose at the back of it than there is in burglars breaking into a safe." Different from the other men in the company, Kurtz, the embodiment of European imperialism, does not hide the fact that he does not trade but rather takes ivory by force, and rules through "suppression" and "extermination." He clearly states, "We whites...must necessarily appear to them/savages in the nature of supernatural beings... By the simple exercise of our will we can exert a power for good practically unbounded." The Central Station manager quotes Kurtz: "Each station should be like a beacon on the road towards better things, a centre for trade of course, but also for humanizing, improving, instructing." In "going native," Kurtz betrays the "civilizing" ideas with which he supposedly set out from Europe. All these descriptions in *Heart of Darkness* demonstrate the bitter irony that those who appear civilized are not actually civilized at all and those who look the most civilized are actually the most savage. Thus the true nature of European philanthropy in the Congo is revealed: hypocrisy inherent in their rhetoric to justify their exploitation and violence of the natives. " It thus makes perfect sense to interpret *Heart of Darkness* as an attack on imperialism." (Brantlinger)

However, in 1975, the essay of the Nigerian writer Chinua Achebe, "An Image of Africa: Racism in Conrad's 'Heart of Darkness'," prompted a lively debate over whether *Heart of Darkness* is a racist book. In this essay, Chinua Achebe, widely considered to be the first critic who made a post-colonial reading of this work, calls Conrad a "thoroughgoing racist." Achebe declares that Conrad (via Marlow) de-humanizes Africans and establishes them as others while reducing the native Africans to "limbs," "angles," "glistening white eyeballs," and stresses that "Clearly Conrad has a problem with niggers... his inordinate love of that word itself should be of interest to psychoanalysts." He further points out that Conrad "denied them language and culture, and reduced them to a metaphorical extension of the dark and dangerous jungle into which the Europeans venture." (Heart of Darkness, Wikipedia) And many scholars agree with Achebe that racism is present in the text and have argued that the story is actually a racist or colonialist parable in which Africans are depicted as innately irrational and violent and the land in which they live remain inscrutably alien, other. They argue that the title of this novella implies that Africa is the "heart of darkness," "where whites who 'go native' risk releasing the 'savage' within themselves." (Heart of Darkness, Wikipedia)

How is it possible for *Heart of Darkness* to provoke such a critical controversy? We may get some idea of this question if we make a careful analysis of the complicated, ambiguous style of this novella: "Its ambiguous language and narrative structure allow him to maintain contradictory values, or both." (Brantlinger)

In the first place, the narrative frame of this novella creates ambiguity. It "filters everything that is said not just through Marlow, but also through the anonymous primary narrator." (Brantlinger) Marlow is telling a story. His narrative is an examination of human spirit through his perspective with a hazy, dreamy and subjective quality. The reader cannot make certain how trustworthy his narrative is and at what point Conrad/Marlow expresses a single point of view, or in other words at what point Marlow speaks directly for Conrad, and he is not sure whether Marlow agrees with the values expressed by the primary narrator. Besides, the outside narrator only refers to what Marlow says and does and the reader understands the perspective of the other characters only through Marlow's account of what they say and do.

In the second place, Conrad portrays the atrocity and moral bankruptcy of imperialism by showing that European motives and actions are no better than African fetishism and savagery. He describes Kurtz and Africa in the same way. In his description, evil, embodied in Kurtz's Satanic behavior, is "going native." Europeans are as evil as Africans because some number of white men in the heart of darkness behave like Africans.

Conrad's stress on cannibalism, his identification of African customs with violence, lust, and madness, his metaphors of bestiality, death, and darkness, his suggestion that travelling in Africa is like travelling backward in time to primeval, infantile, but also hellish stages of existence—these features of the story are drawn from the repertoire of Victorian imperialism and racism that painted an entire continent dark. (Brantlinger)

"In the world of *Heart of Darkness*, there are no clear answers. Ambiguity, perhaps the main form of 'darkness' in the story, prevails." (Brantlinger) Achebe is therefore right to call Conrad's portrayal of Africa and Africans "racist" and some other critics call it "anti-racist."

Heart of Darkness remains a seminal work of the Western canon, and this debate is ongoing. After your reading of this novella, you are sure to have your distinctive view about this issue.

Further Reading

Cultural Studies

(美) 爱德华·萨义德著, 李琨译:《文化与帝国主义》,北京:三联书店,2003 年。

(美) 爱德华·萨义德著, 王宇根译:《东方学》,北京:三联书店,1999 年。

Bhabha, Homi K., ed. *Nation and Narration*. New York: Routledge & Kegan Paul, 1990.

———. *The Location of Culture*. London: Routledge, 1994.

Said, Edward W. *Joseph Conrad and the Fiction of Autobiography*. Cambridge: Harvard University Press, 1966.

Spivak, Gayatri Chakravorty. *In Other Worlds: Essays in Cultural Politics*. New York: Routledge, 1988.

Heart of Darkness

Achebe, Chinua. "An Image of Africa: Racism in Conrad's Heart of Darkness". *Massachusetts Review* 18 (1977): 782—94.

Brantlinger, Patrick. "'Heart of Darkness': Anti-Imperialism, Racism, or Impressionism?" *Criticism* 27.4 (Fall 1985): 363—85.

Brown, Tony C. "Cultural Psychosis on the Frontier: The Work of the Darkness in Joseph Conrad's Heart of Darkness". *Studies in the Novel* 32.1 (Spring 2000): 14—28.

Conrad, Joseph. *The Complete Short Fiction of Joseph Conrad*, ed. Samuel Hynes. London: William Pickering, 1992.

Parry, Benita. *Conrad and Imperialism*. London: Macmillan, 1983.

Saveson, John E. "Conrad's View of Primitive Peoples in Lord Jim and Heart of Darkness". Modern Fiction Studies 16.2 (Summer 1970): 163—83.

Stape, J. H., ed. *The Cambridge Companion to Joseph Conrad*. Cambridge: Cambridge University Press, 1996.

Works Cited

Achebe, Chinua. "An Image of Africa". *Research in African Literatures* 9(1978):1—15, reprinted from *Massachusetts Review* 18 (1977): 782—94.

Blythe, Hal. "O'Connor's 'A Good Man Is Hard to Find'". *Explicator* 55.1(Fall 1996):49—51.

Brantlinger, Patrick. "Heart of Darkness: Anti-Imperialism, Racism, or Impressionism?" *Criticism* 27.4 (Fall 1985): 363—85.

Brooks, Cleanth, and Robert Penn Warren. eds. *Understanding Fiction*. New York: Appleton-Century-Crofts, 1959.

Bylington, Juliet. *Introduction:Nineteenth Century Literature Criticism*. Michigan: Gale Group, 2001.

Carpenter-Houde, Renée. "Symbolism in 'Paul' Case'". *Hohonu* 2.2(2004). <http://www.uhh.hawaii.edu/academics/hohonu/writing.php?id=49>.

Cowlishaw, Brian T. "The Reader's Role in Ring Lardner's Rhetoric". *Studies in Short Fiction* 31.2(Spring 1994): 207—16.

Cracroft, Richard. *Washington Irving: The Western Works*. Boise: Boise State University, 1974.

Desmond, John. "Flannery O'Connor's Misfit and the Mystery of Evil". *Renascence* (2004): 129—38.

"D. H. Lawrence Criticism". <www.enotes.com/rocking-horse-winner>.

E. Pearlman. "David Copperfield Dreams of Drowning". *American Imago* 28(1971): 391—403.

Fiedler, Leslie. *Love and Death in the American Novel*. New York: Criterion Books, 1960.

Guerin, Wilfred L., et al. *A Handbook of Critical Approaches to Literature*. Oxford: Oxford University Press, 2005.

Gwynn, R. S. *Literature: A Pocket Anthology*. ed. New York: Longman Publishers, 2002.

"Heart of Darkness". <en.wikipedia.org/wiki/Heart_of_Darkness>.

Heiman, Marcel. "Rip Van Winkle: A Psychoanalytic Note on the Story and Its Author". *American Imago* 16.1 (Spring 1959):3—47.

Johnston, Kenneth G. "Hills like White Elephants". *Studies in American Fiction* 10.2 (Autumn 1982): 233—38.

Kennedy, X. J. *Literature: An Introduction to Fiction, Poetry, and Drama*. 2nd ed. Boston: Little, Brown and Company, 1979.

May, Charles E. "Lardner's 'Haircut'". *Explicator* 31.9 (1973): Item #69.

Meyer, Michael. ed. *The Bedford Introduction to Literature*. New York, Boston: Bedford/St. Martin's, 2008.

O'Brien, T. "Allusion, Wordplay, and the Central Conflict in Hemingway's 'Hills like White Elephants'". *Hemingway Review*12.1(Fall 1992): 19—25.

Snodgrass, W. D. "A Rocking Horse: The Symbol, the Pattern, the Way to Live". *The Hudson Review* 11.2 (Summer 1958): 191—200.

作者简介

师彦灵,1966年生,山西襄汾人。1988年毕业于兰州大学英语系,获学士学位;2001年毕业于兰州大学外国语学院,获英语语言文学硕士学位;2006年起在兰州大学文学院攻读现当代文学专业博士学位;2007年9月至2008年9月,在加利福尼亚大学圣巴巴拉分校英语系作访问学者。现为兰州大学外国语学院副教授,英语语言文学专业硕士研究生导师。主要从事美国少数族裔文学、文化诗学、英语教学等方面的研究,发表相关论文10余篇,合作出版著作1部,参与编写教材1部,主持校内教学与科研项目4项、横向项目多项,作为主要成员参与日本东京财团笹川良一青年奖学金基金资助项目3项。